W9-DED-037

A Theory of Employment Systems

A Theory of Employment Systems: micro-foundations of societal diversity

DAVID MARSDEN

OXFORD
UNIVERSITY PRESS

HF
5549.5
.J6
M375
1999

OXFORD
UNIVERSITY PRESS

Great Clarendon Street, Oxford OX2 6DP

Oxford University Press is a department of the University of Oxford.
It furthers the University's objective of excellence in research, scholarship,
and education by publishing worldwide in

Oxford New York

Athens Auckland Bangkok Bogotá Buenos Aires Calcutta
Cape Town Chennai Dar es Salaam Delhi Florence Hong Kong Istanbul
Karachi Kuala Lumpur Madrid Melbourne Mexico City Mumbai
Nairobi Paris São Paulo Singapore Taipei Tokyo Toronto Warsaw

and associated companies in Berlin Ibadan

Oxford is a registered trade mark of Oxford University Press
in the UK and certain other countries

Published in the United States
by Oxford University Press Inc., New York

© David W. Marsden

British Library Cataloguing in Publication Data
Data available

Library of Congress Cataloging in Publication Data
Marsden, David.
  A theory of employment systems: micro-foundations of diversity/David Marsden.
    p.   cm.
  Includes bibliographical references.
  1. Job analysis. 2. Occupations—Classification. 3. Diversity in the workplace.
  I. Title.
  HF5549.5.J6M375   1999   658.3′06—dc21   99–21237

ISBN 0–19–829423–9 (hbk.)
ISBN 0–19–829422–0 (pbk.)

1 3 5 7 9 10 8 6 4 2

Typeset by J&L Composition Ltd, Filey, North Yorkshire
Printed in Great Britain
on acid-free paper by
Bookcraft Ltd, Midsomer Norton, Somerset

To Cheung-Ling and Antony,
and
to my mother, and the memory of my father.

ACKNOWLEDGEMENTS

The origin of this book goes back to discussions with François Eyraud and Jean-Jacques Silvestre during my time at the Laboratoire d'Economie et de Sociologie du Travail in the late 1980s, and with François Eymard-Duvernay and Laurent Thévenot on the nature and significance of the job classifications used in firms and labour markets. Were they simply a way of organizing information about jobs, or did they fulfil a function more essential to the working of firms and labour markets?

The atmosphere at LSE has also been a great stimulus. Many friends and colleagues have given both criticism and encouragement, in seminars in the Industrial Relations Department and the Centre for Economic Performance and, especially, in the corridor. My students too have responded, often critically, to the ideas presented in lectures and seminar discussions. I should also like to thank the LSE Publications Committee for its support, and the publisher's referees.

In the course of writing this book I have benefited from advice and comments from many other friends and colleagues, through long conversations, in writing, and at seminars. I should like to thank the following for their comments on various parts of the argument: Robert Boyer, Ronald Dore, Carola Frege, Donatella Gatti, Howard Gospel, Annette Jobert, John Kelly, Christel Lane, Ned Lorenz, Alex Makaronidis, Marc Maurice, Mitsuharu Miyamoto, Sandro Momigliano, Michael Piore, Bénédicte Reynaud, Paul Ryan, François Sellier and Amitai Etzioni, who encouraged me to write a different book! Thanks are also due to David Musson of Oxford University Press for his patient encouragement.

Above all, I have benefited from long discussions with Alice Lam, my wife, whose sensitive ethnographic research in British and Japanese firms has been the source of the best ideas.

CONTENTS

LIST OF FIGURES

LIST OF TABLES

I

A THEORY OF EMPLOYMENT SYSTEMS

1

The Employment Relationship

1. EMPLOYMENT SYSTEMS

Two great innovations lie behind the rise of the modern business enterprise: limited liability and the employment relationship. The first revolutionized company finance, opening up a vast new supply of capital. The second has revolutionized the organization of labour services, providing firms and workers with a very flexible method of coordination and a platform for investing in skills. Today, nine-tenths of workers with jobs in advanced industrial countries are engaged as employees. Despite the sometimes rapid growth in contingent employment, there is no evidence that the open-ended employment relationship is about to lose its preeminence.

The key to the employment relationship is that it enables management to decide detailed work assignments after workers have been hired. Given the huge difficulty of anticipating the problems to be resolved in providing customers with the goods and services they desire, such flexibility is a formidable advantage. Much of the debate about productivity in recent years has focused on how to keep workers as fully occupied as possible, but it has neglected the other problem, of how to be sure that the necessary workers will be available when new customer orders arrive. This is addressed by the employment relationship which builds on workers' agreement to be available to undertake certain types of work as and when their employer directs.

There is one twist to the story, however: few workers would agree to giving their employers unlimited powers over work assignments. The tricky nature of work assignments is of more than academic interest. In their monumental study of workplace management in the US, Slichter and his colleagues (1960: 576) observed that 'a "job" is an arbitrary concept'. They warned that 'jobs must be defined to the mutual satisfaction of the parties to avoid continuous problems in employee classification, work assignment and transfer'. The rise of the employment relationship owes much to the development of job rules that square the apparent circle of providing employers with flexible job allocations and employees with limited liability to follow their employer's instructions.

The 'Theory of employment systems' explores the way managerial authority within employment is delimited. In common with the 'rational choice' models of Economics and Sociology, it sets out from the free choices of firms and workers, and assumes only that access to relevant information is difficult, both parties are subject to 'bounded rationality'[1] and know that they have partly convergent and partly divergent interests, and that finding alternative workers or jobs is costly. As a result, the conditions are ripe for opportunism. For the employment relationship to provide a stable framework for their collaboration, it must protect against these. Assessing how firms satisfy their needs for flexibility, and workers their needs for protection, and thus how the limits of managerial authority are agreed leads to some surprising conclusions.

First, there is not one but four types of solution delimiting management authority within an employment relationship. This property turns out to be one of the foundations of the international diversity of employment relations found in many comparative studies of recent years, and is the basis of the four broad models of employment system developed in this book.

Secondly, although, in formal terms, the employment contract is between individual employees and their employers, the solutions adopted by different firms and their workers are interdependent. As one type of employment relationship becomes more widespread, there are considerable advantages to other firms and groups of workers adopting the same model.

Thirdly, although employment models can diffuse in a decentralized fashion, and are to a degree self-enforcing, like evolutionarily stable games, their preeminence and their effectiveness are often increased by collective organization of employers and employees at the inter-firm level. The presence of such institutions is shown to increase the range of choice open to firms collectively over how the employment relationship is organized. Only one of the four models is compatible with weakly developed labour market institutions, and that is the least flexible of the four.

Fourthly, the model of employment relationship adopted shapes a whole array of human resource policies within the firm. Classification systems, shaped by the basic rules constituting the employment relationship, establish the basic categories of jobs and labour skills that firms may use. Performance management, which is the most 'intimate' area of management authority as it concerns the relationship between line managers and their staff, turns out to be shaped by the employment transaction rules, and is most problematic in the least-institutionalized environments. Choice of pay and incentive systems are also heavily influenced by the type of employment system in place, as are skill development and labour-deployment policies. The scope for developing functional and numerical flexibility[2] proves to be determined by the type of employment rule[3] in place and the quality of institutional support.

Fifthly, the interdependence between firms' choices and the support and stability provided by inter-firm institutions argues for treating the employment relationship as part of a more widely embracing 'employment system'. The latter may be defined as including both the basic rules limiting management authority and the supporting institutions that assist their enforcement.

The 'Theory of employment systems' offers an institutional theory of labour markets and human resource management, and in so doing stresses the interdependence between the decisions of different firms in these areas. 'Institutions' can be understood in the sense given by North (1990: 6) as mechanisms to 'reduce uncertainty by establishing a stable structure for human interaction'. They are 'rules of the game', and like all such rules, they constrain in order to enable. This element of constraint is manifest in two ways: when they enter an employment relationship, firms and workers exchange obligations which both sides want to be enforceable; and, the choices of individual firms and workers will influence those of others. As argued in Chapter 3, the more widely a particular type of employment relationship is adopted, the more effective it becomes both to constrain and to enable, and so the more likely it is to be chosen by others. It may not be the ideal form of contracting for a particular type of firm or service, but it is nevertheless adopted because everyone knows how it works, and is confident it will provide a stable framework for their collaboration. This sense of 'institutionalization' has been stressed by a number of writers seeking to explain the relative uniformity of organizations within particular societies (DiMaggio and Powell, 1983). A second level of institutionalization is provided by the integration of the employment relationship into employment systems which may themselves be strongly institutionalized, as in many EU countries, or weakly so, as in many of the non-union firms in the US economy. These patterns of institutionalization provide the key to understanding why there are such pronounced international differences in the way the employment relationship is organized, and the justification for referring to them as 'societal' rather than 'national'.

There are several ways in which the employment relationship and its international diversity could be tackled. In particular, it would have been possible to take an inductive approach, and try to build a theory from the available empirical evidence. For this book, it was decided instead to work deductively, and to see how far one can explain the role of institutions in labour markets and their known international diversity from a set of assumptions used by mainstream theories of Economics, and to a lesser degree, Sociology. The basic assumptions of 'rational choice' theory make no explicit reference either to institutions or to international diversity. It is therefore doubly interesting if one can show that even from such assumptions institutions play an essential part in labour markets and the internal organization of the firm, and that the firm is an integral part of its institutional context. As the evidence of Chapter 5 shows, one could reach a similar conclusion inductively, but this would always leave the question of how far the observed relationships are the result of particular circumstances as opposed to revealing fundamental characteristics of employment systems. This problem is especially severe in research using international comparisons because of the small number of available observations compared with the large number of possible variables.

Some sacrifices have been made in pursuing a deductive approach, one of the most important being the neglect of the state and its agencies. There have been two main reasons for this. The first is that one of the concerns of this book is to develop a theoretical model to explain the kind of institutions that would develop when firms and workers are left free to devise their own solutions in a decentralized way. The need for this kind of explanation has grown with the importance of the non-union sector, now over 80% of the US workforce, for whom non-union status means also lack of coverage by collective bargaining. Its coverage has also receded greatly in the UK private sector. So it becomes important to reflect on how the employment relationship would be regulated in the absence of strong unions, particularly when the decline of coverage in the two countries has been associated with a partial withdrawal of the state from regulating employment relations. Rather than build a theory of 'non-union industrial relations', it seemed more logical to rethink the whole question of the employment relationship, its purpose and the role of institutions within it. The second reason is that the state is not really an independent actor, and its influence is only partly 'exogenous'. As Sellier (1961: 16) remarked when commenting on the poor enforcement of French labour law despite an activist state: 'law is like currency: the state cannot make it circulate if society rejects it'.[4] Bringing in a theory of state action would complicate the model greatly, and as will be seen in the later chapters, a great deal can be done with the simple model proposed.

The book is organized into three parts. Part I, the first four chapters, develops the theory of employment systems. Part II, dealing with evidence and implications for personnel management, reviews the evidence for societal models of the employment relationship that match the typology of employment rules. It then traces the theory's outcomes in three major areas of human resource policy: performance management, pay and incentives, and skills and labour market structure. Part III concludes, returning to the themes raised by Coase and Simon to show the implications of the theory of employment systems for the theory of the firm, and for our understanding of labour institutions[5] and societal diversity more generally.

Chapter 1 introduces the problem of the employment relationship that was left unresolved by the ground-breaking work of Coase and Simon, and Chapter 2 introduces the typology of four fundamental rules that underpin the employment relationship. The chapter derives the four main types of rule from the conditions that must be satisfied for a viable employment relationship. This is a deductive and not an inductive typology. As a result, it is the basis for one of the book's key arguments: that firms and workers face a restricted menu of viable rules able to limit management authority to the satisfaction of both parties. This enables one to argue that the theory applies equally to union and non-union employment. Chapter 3 addresses the diffusion of employment systems across an economy, and shows that decentralized diffusion is possible without the intervention of the state or other collective bodies. However, their support can bring considerable benefits. Chapter 4 deals with one of the central mechanisms by which institutions shape employment relations, namely job and pay classification systems and conventions. These provide the categories in which labour services are bought and sold, but they are more than mere labels. They also play a key part in restraining potential opportunism by either party within the employment relationship

The second part of the book, on evidence and outcomes, begins with a review of empirical material on societal diversity in employment systems. This has been concentrated in Chapter 5 in order to keep a strong deductive focus in the early chapters, although inevitably some examples were needed to prevent the discussion from becoming too abstract. Chapter 6 explores the first of the personnel management outcomes: the effects of employment systems on performance management and the regulation of work quality. These prove to be strongly influenced by whichever of the four types of employment rule is present in the workplace. The chapter shows how the rules determine the nature of performance criteria used. A key reason is that the criteria have not only to regulate performance, but they must also be resistant to potential moral hazard by either party. Chapter 7 extends this analysis to pay, showing how the transaction rules shape pay structures both by their effect on job classifications and on performance criteria. The former can be thought of as regulating average, and the latter as regulating marginal, performance. The same chapter develops a theory of the price of labour as a set of rules regulating the exchange of obligations between employers and employees. Chapter 8 tackles the effect of the four employment rules on the structure of skills and labour markets, exploring the link between the transaction rules and patterns of internal and occupational labour markets. The way in which the enforceability of employment rules is handled leads to a classification of both internal and occupational markets according to the varying degrees of functional flexibility which they allow. The chapter concludes with an analysis of the boundary between employment and self-employment, and explores the implications of the theory for 'market-mediated' forms of employment.

Part III concludes the book, linking the theory of employment systems to current debates about the nature of the firm and corporate governance, and the societal diversity of economic institutions. The same institutional rules serve both to control opportunism and to provide a foundation for building the human skills and organizational capabilities of the firm. The theory of employment systems embeds the firm in its institutional and societal context, and thus helps explain the international diversity in its organization.

2. INCOMPLETENESS OF THE EMPLOYMENT CONTRACT

A useful way to think about the employment relationship is to contrast it with alternative ways of organizing economic relations, and to ask under what conditions freely choosing agents would opt for one form or another. The most common alternatives are the sales contract to provide a specified product or service, some kind of contingency contract in which terms may be adjusted, or even renegotiated, in certain specified circumstances, and the employment contract.[6] The latter is open-ended. Only a general indication of the range of tasks to be carried out is given in advance, their precise definition being left to the employer at a later date. This was the approach adopted by Coase (1937) in his famous article on the nature of the firm.

Each type of transaction involves different kinds of costs. Coase suggests that the sales contract involves costs of discovering the relevant market prices, for example, obtaining quotes from different suppliers, negotiating prices, and most important, the difficulty of knowing in advance exactly what services will be required and when. Compared with these, the employment relationship may appear attractive. A single contract is substituted for a series of contracts related to each operation. There is one initial negotiation, and the employer has the employee's agreement that the specification and timing of the tasks to be undertaken can be left until later. Thus Coase argues that entrepreneurs will assume the function of employer for those tasks where the transaction is more cheaply organized by the employment relationship than by a sales contract. Coase treads carefully, and points out that the employment contract gives the employer power to specify the employee's tasks only 'within certain limits'.[7] He asserts, but does not explain how, the contract sets these limits, although it is fair to assume that the employee may be indifferent between providing certain services.

Defining the limits within which management may determine the tasks to be assigned is problematic. One path, adopted by Simon (1951), is to treat the employer and employee as agreeing to a set of tasks from which the former may choose after the contract has been agreed. This might be contrasted with the sales contract in which the worker agrees in advance to provide a specified service (e.g. laying a concrete path to a particular specification).

Simon represents the employer's and worker's respective preferences by the following satisfaction functions which show the net gains to both parties from working together:

$S_b = F_b(x) - a_b w$ (for the employer, 'boss')

$S_w = F_w(x) + a_w w$ (for the 'worker')

There, $F_b(x)$ represents the value the employer gains from the execution of task x, and $F_w(x)$ the disutility to the worker of undertaking that task. w is the wage. For the two parties to agree to a contract, certain minimum conditions are necessary. For the employer, the value of the output for a given task should be at least equal to the wage, and its cost to the worker no greater than the wage. That is:

$F_b(x) \geq a_b w$, and $F_w(x) \leq a_w w$

Where this just holds, the net gains to each party are zero:

$S_b = 0$ and $S_w = 0$.

A simple graphical presentation captures the essence of his argument (Figure 1.1). Let us assume that the tasks in which the employer is interested can be arranged along the x-axis in terms of a single characteristic, for example, increasing complexity. The vertical axis measures the agreed wage and the employer's expected profit per worker. The employer's preferences can be mapped by a family of iso-satisfaction (or iso-profit) curves below line S_{b0}. This curve represents the contour of zero satisfaction (or zero profits), above which the employer has no interest in contracting. Contour S_{b1} and below represent increasing levels of employer satisfaction (or profits).[8] In the this example, one might explain the inverted 'u'-shaped employer's curve as follows. Given capital equipment, the more finely the employer divides tasks, the less complex and easier they become, but dividing them up is itself costly, and the more finely divided they are, the more rigid work organization becomes. On the other side, broad, complex jobs save a great deal of management time and are flexible, but, beyond a certain point, they become too difficult for workers to undertake. Hence, the employer gains initially from increasing task complexity, but after a while, the gains go into reverse.

For employees, the acceptable combinations of tasks and wage rates are shown by the region enclosed by the U-curve S_{w0} and above, which shows the lower limit of what is acceptable to them. For the present example, the

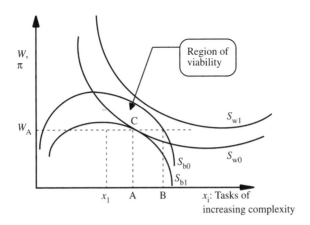

Fig. 1.1. Contracting over job tasks

shape of the curve might be explained as follows: tasks involving too low complexity may be very boring, incurring a high level of disutility, and so require a high wage in compensation. Likewise, those involving high complexity may be very taxing and also require a high wage.

The parties stand to gain by agreeing to contract for any of the combinations of tasks and wage rates where the two curves S_{bo} and S_{wo} overlap, the 'region of viability', zone C. Within this region, not all combinations of wages and tasks are equally preferred by either party, and, generally, employers will prefer task–wage combinations in the south-west direction (equivalent to higher profits), and workers, those in the north-east direction (equivalent to higher worker satisfaction).

Meaning can be given to the idea of an accepted set of tasks between which a worker would agree to an employer's authority if we consider those tasks available at wage rate W_A. To the right of point A, where S_{wo} and W_A intersect, the worker benefits, and will continue to do so until W_A and S_{wo} cross again. On the employer's side, there is no interest in tasks to the right of point B at wage W_A because these represent negative satisfaction. Thus, one could envisage a worker and employer agreeing to an employment relationship which gave the employer the right to choose tasks of any complexity between A and B in exchange for wage W_A.

This solution represents a cost for employers because they effectively pay for the full range of tasks at the wage required for those nearest A. Greater worker satisfaction for the tasks near to B means those could be obtained for a lower wage. Hence, the flexibility of the employment transaction comes at a price. In this model, by offering a higher or a lower wage, the employer can vary the range of tasks over which its authority may be applied.

However, at this stage of the argument, both employer and employee would still achieve their highest levels of satisfaction by selecting the single tasks at the tangencies between their two sets of preference curves, and so might still opt for a sales contract, for example, at A.

The deciding factor, in Simon's argument, like that of Coase, is uncertainty. It is advantageous for the entrepreneur to offer an employment contract if, at the time of agreement, it is not known precisely which tasks will be required. Figure 1.2 illustrates the problem of uncertainty concerning the likely demand for two tasks, x_a and x_b, the demand for each being a function of its likely value to the employer. The joint distribution of these values is shown by the oval contours near the origin.[*]

If the employer were to select tasks purely on the basis of their expected values, then it would opt for the one with the higher mean, x_a, and offer a sales contract. There would, however, be occasions on which the employer would have done better to wait, and choose x_b. This is illustrated in Figure 1.2 by the means of the joint distribution of values of the two tasks where the mean of x_a is zero and that of x_b negative at point B. To the left of the 45° line, $Fx_a = Fx_b$, the employer benefits by choosing x_b, and the area of the contours lying on that side shows the probability that it would be better to have

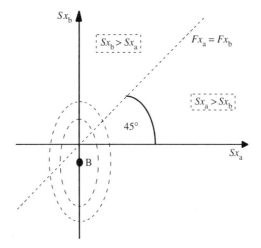

Fig. 1.2. Employer's choice between sales and employment contracts for tasks with uncertain demand
The firm's choice is between a sales contract for x_a or an employment contract with an option on either x_a or x_b. Adapted from Simon (1951).

chosen x_b. Thus, the greater the dispersion of outcomes associated with both tasks, that is, the greater the degree of uncertainty as to the future values of x_a and x_b, the more advantageous it is for the employer to seek an employment rather than a sales contract.

To summarize, the advantages of the employment over the sales transaction to employers and workers are threefold. Employers gain flexibility and the knowledge that labour will be available to them when they know more precisely what their work requirements will be. Workers gain by the continuity of activity, an important benefit when their principal source of income is the sale of their labour. Finally, both sides benefit, as Coase stressed, by substituting a single transaction for what otherwise might have been many.

2.1. Opportunism

Before going further, it is worth recalling the assumptions on which this approach to the employment relationship is built. They are that both parties are characterized by bounded rationality, and have only limited and uncertain information on which to base their decisions. Bounded rationality stresses that they make their decisions with a view to maximizing their own welfare, but that their ability to calculate and process information is rather limited. Such information as they have is also of variable quality, and there is considerable uncertainty about the future. These indeed are the reasons why, in Simon's view, the employment relationship is potentially so attractive to firms. It is a classic example of procedural rationality: it enables them to organize production and services without detailed information on future labour requirements, particularly when there is uncertainty about the precise tasks that they will need done.

Bounded rationality contains within it the assumption that agents are pursuing their own goals, and so it is but a small extra step to assume that when different agents collaborate, their goals will partly overlap and partly diverge. Likewise, the assumption of imperfect information brings the strong probability of asymmetry: that each agent will be better informed than the other about different aspects of their collaboration. Usually workers will have more detailed knowledge of the work tasks, and management will have better information about the production process as a whole and about the state of product markets.

All one needs is the additional assumption that for both firms and workers, respectively, it is costly to find alternative labour or jobs, and the conditions for opportunism are ripe. Thus, even on the assumptions on which his model is built, managerial authority is likely to be problematic both in its application by management and in its subsequent acceptance by workers. In a later article, Simon (1991) stresses other factors, such as loyalty and commitment, that will restrain opportunism, but these take us outside the range of simple assumptions deployed so far, and, more importantly, can be undermined by opportunistic behaviour and the fear of it.

The costs of finding another job or of recruiting other workers introduce a margin within which each party may seek to exploit the other. In many cases these costs can be quite high. For a worker whose skills are based on long experience in one organization, finding equivalent work can be very difficult. Likewise, for a firm to replace workers with skills that have been formed by long experience in its operations can take a long time. As result, individual workers or firms may have to tolerate quite wide margins in cooperation before quitting or firing becomes a viable option.

Returning to the analysis of work assignments, the employer might take advantage of the employee's difficulties in finding alternative employment to impose new or unpleasant tasks outside the area on which they have agreed. Simon considers the case in which both parties might agree a wage and then let the employer choose any tasks it pleases, but he rejects this as unlikely because there would be no guarantee that tasks would be chosen so as to maximize the joint satisfaction of both parties rather than just that of the employer. In terms of Figure 1.1, a worker might agree to wage W_A on the expectation of being assigned to tasks in the range between A and B. After hiring, however, the employer could obtain a higher level of satisfaction by assigning the worker to task x_1, which lies on a higher iso-profit curve.[9] The difficulties of changing job could well induce the employee to acquiesce. On the other side, the employee might insist on doing only those tasks that bring the highest satisfaction, and so restrict the employer's choice of tasks to those nearest to S_{bo}. Although this represents loss of flexibility and paying those tasks at a higher rate than necessary, again replacement costs may prevent the employer from ending the relationship.[10]

In both cases, the problems of opportunism are intensified by lack of clear definition of the range of tasks over which the employer's authority extends, and over the tasks on which the employee will agree to work. Such problems could easily undermine the advantages of the employment transaction. Faced with a restrictive attitude from employees, the employer would lose the supposed flexibility, and faced with demands for flexibility beyond the bounds of agreement, workers may prefer the additional bargaining power that they have when they can quit easily. More generally, the resulting conflict is likely to reduce the gains to either party from rolling everything up into a single transaction. Hence, unless a solution can be found to the problem of regulating the bounds of the employment transaction, it is much less likely to be preferred to the sales transaction.

3. DEFINING THE 'ACCEPTABLE SET' OF TASKS

It might be thought that careful definition of the set of tasks which employees may be required to perform would provide a straightforward solution. Thus, firms and their future employees would agree a detailed job description which would prescribe both the employee's duties and the limits of managerial authority. Indeed, could one not argue that in practice many employers tackle the problem in just this way? However, despite its apparent simplicity, such an approach cannot work in practice.

Important of the study → why clarification is a challenge?

3.1 Tacit knowledge and problems of codification

A first reason why work tasks cannot be exhaustively defined by means of highly detailed job descriptions is that they involve practical understanding of the ways of doing things, and the application of tacit knowledge. This applies especially to descriptions of the work processes that are to be undertaken, but it also applies to defining their outputs. Polanyi (1967) summarizes his intuition about the importance of tacit knowledge in our work by the aphorism 'we know more than we can say'. For example, clutch control in driving a car might appear a relatively simple operation to describe, and not so different from operating machines in a factory or office. Yet it is something one cannot convey to a trainee driver in words alone. One might describe the distance and rate of movement of the left and right feet, although this would need to be supplemented with information about how such distances vary with driving conditions and vehicle age. But this would

Importance of study [handwritten note]

be pointless, as no one could possibly drive and at the same time carry out the necessary calculations, and it is not what experienced drivers do. They rely on the 'feel' of when the position is right. Even though subsequently one might ask someone who has learned to drive to change gear and accelerate, the possibility of giving this instruction depends upon that person having already learned the operation by doing it.

It might be argued that if this were the only problem, then provided detailed job descriptions made sufficient allowance for tacit knowledge, a solution could be found: one might specify an operation such as 'operating a gear change smoothly'. However, with the considerable variability of tasks between work environments, their evolution over time, and the widespread importance of learning by doing, it is rare for there to be fully standardized ways of carrying them out, and an important part of work tasks lies in their adaptation. To specify this in detail would involve spelling out both the recognized kinds of difference in local conditions and the kind of adaptation required.[11]

Variations in work environments greatly affect job demands even within individual industries and for fairly narrowly defined tasks. A good illustration of the practical difficulties this causes is provided by the experience of training officials in the British construction industry seeking to identify a set of common job-related competencies that could be used as a basis for defining industry-wide training needs (Greenacre, 1990).[12] Job related know-how was found to be very dependent upon the context in which people worked: physical working conditions, size of construction site, size of firm and technology used. As a result, there was great disagreement among employers as to the know-how considered relevant even for fairly narrowly defined operations.[13]

Work tasks are not static, and evolve continuously over time. Piore (1968) provides some graphic examples of what he calls 'experimental job design', whereby managers assign workers provisionally to new equipment, and adjust tasks and jobs as they gradually learn how to operate it more efficiently. Although he was concerned with the staffing of new equipment, this process is in fact continuous. Many subsequent improvements are discovered by workers, who can use them either to raise productivity or to make their own jobs easier. This is what the pieceworkers studied by Roy (1952, 1955) did when they used their ability to find better 'angles' as a way of making it easier to achieve their piecework targets, 'making out'. As a result, the initial job description becomes increasingly irrelevant to the tasks actually undertaken. Such information may be withheld from management, and many observers from Slichter (1919) onwards have stressed the perverse incentives of piecework and similar payment by results systems whereby workers withheld such knowledge and refrained from achieving the high output levels within their grasp because they expected management to come back and re-time their jobs. A more relaxed pace of work was less likely to attract the attention of the work-study engineers than a high rate of piecework earnings.

evolvement of work

The tendency for work tasks to evolve from even very detailed job descriptions means that, when new employees are hired, the set of tasks comprising the job with which they become familiar will often diverge considerably from those detailed in the formal job description. It is in terms of their actual duties that they come to understand the limits of management's authority. Thus the actual agreement in the minds of individual workers is likely to differ from what has been formally set down. Likewise, Ribeill's (1984) account of French railway workers under a highly formalized and rationalistic system provides interesting examples of how the actual work content differed from the formal job descriptions. Even management would judge the time necessary for certain work tasks in terms of the actual practices, not in terms of the formal procedures.

3.2. Detailed job descriptions are not economic

A second reason is that, from an economic point of view, the advantages of precise definition of the tasks making up a job are quickly exhausted. Apart from being costly to devise, ever more precise job specifications can be self-defeating. Slichter and his colleagues remarked that codification in too fine detail would lead to focusing on 'the words in the manual', which then becomes a source of rigidity and litigation (Slichter *et al.*, 1960: 576). In his study of French railway workers, Ribeill (1984) describes how central management sought to regulate the enterprise by means of elaborate job descriptions and formalized work and safety procedures, but that efficient working was possible only because workers found short-cuts which effectively ignored large parts of the written code. Indeed, 'working to rule', sticking rigidly to one's job description, has been a common form of industrial action because it deprives management of all the short cuts needed for efficient working. Great detail in task definition is also likely to be uneconomic under conditions of uncertainty as these bring a higher probability of unanticipated demands. Such variation is more easily accomodated by broad job definitions than by narrow ones. Thus, the very detail would undermine one of the prime attractions of the employment contract to employers, namely that it provides them with flexibility.

There is also a problem of 'infinite regress' in seeking exhaustive job descriptions because there is no logical limit to how finely jobs can be described. It is always possible to go a step further. This is a rather philosophical problem in the present context because the diseconomies of ever more detailed job descriptions are felt quite rapidly. Nevertheless, a more important implication is that there is no bedrock of elementary tasks from which exhaustive job descriptions could be built up even in principle.

3.3 Work measurement, in practice, is negotiation

Thirdly, work measurement, as practised in firms, has generally not been about precise definition and measurement of work tasks, but rather about negotiation with work groups over rates of work and rates of pay. In his classic study of wage systems, Mottez (1966) summarized the North American and French experience of work study as follows:

> The work study engineer does not act simply as a technician, but as a negotiator. He is caught between management, which sees him as a technician, and the workers who seek, in their own interest, to deceive him. The work norm is the result of a compromise. Once it is fixed, the workers take care not to exceed it to such an extent that their good faith in the negotiation would be brought into question. (pp. 139–40)

In practice, management deal with limited codifiability of job contents by employing agents who are themselves familiar with the tacit elements in jobs rather than relying upon formal descriptions. Indeed, the formal descriptions often have a rather different role, enabling higher management to control first line management. The use of periodic 'crackdowns' by higher management, noted by both Roy (1952) and Burawoy (1979), stemmed from the recognition that higher management could not control work by means of detailed descriptions, and relied upon the access to tacit job knowledge of both supervisors and work-study engineers, but still needed some check on the concessions made by these in their negotiations with workers. Likewise, Ribeill argued that management did not in fact use its highly detailed job descriptions as a basis for organizing work, but rather as a means of attributing responsibility if something went wrong.

Thus, the idea that the open-ended nature of the employment transaction can be closed by means of detailed job descriptions is clearly mistaken. Detailed job descriptions cannot fulfil such a function because so much of the task content of jobs cannot be codified, and it would be very costly to try to achieve this and most likely counterproductive. And, in practice, detailed job descriptions when used by firms have a different function. If the Coase–Simon model is to help us understand the employment transaction then, we need to look at other ways of establishing limits to management's authority, for otherwise it is hard to imagine that sufficient numbers of workers would find an employment relationship attractive as compared with some other kind of transaction. The alternative approach, to be explored in this and the following chapter, is based on the idea that the assignment of tasks to jobs is regulated by some kind of classification criterion or rule.

4. USE OF CLASSIFICATION CRITERIA TO ASSIGN TASKS TO JOBS

Using a rule to identify the tasks that management may assign to particular workers provides a much simpler and more straightforward solution than trying to construct inventories of tasks. In the place of a complex list, there is a simple rule for allocating tasks; if the rules are sufficiently robust, they can be applied across a variety of workplaces; when they are known and understood by the parties, they give fairly predictable results and each knows what they are letting themselves in for; application of a rule also provides a key for settling disputes other than by naked power; and rules can be adapted logically to new situations.

A good illustration of a simple and robust task allocation rule is given by craft demarcation rules that have been common in British and North American industry. These allocate certain types of work, identified by the type of tools or materials used, to workers of a particular category or occupation. Thus, when an employer is organizing work on a new site, it is easy to know which tasks should be assigned to which categories of workers, and to know that normally these allocations will be accepted smoothly. As technology and tasks evolve, the same rules can also be of assistance and help reduce conflict, as is illustrated by the Webbs' analysis of demarcation rules in British shipbuilding at the turn of the century. As the sanitary appliances of contemporary ships became more sophisticated and more like those of houses, it was seen as natural that the plumbers should 'follow their work'. Yet, iron pipework on ships, whatever its purpose, had always been undertaken by engineers (Webb and Webb, 1902: 509). Since such rules obeyed a common logic of sharing work among different trades, they could often be resolved according to the same logic, namely, by allocating some kinds of sanitary work to one trade, and some to the other.

The Webbs' example also illustrates a number of other features desirable in such rules. They should be sufficiently robust to be easily applied in different work environments. Disputes of interpretation often interrupt work, so rules whose application demands a lot of analysis and needs to call on outside intervention have a high economic cost. In shipyards or on construction sites where short spells of employment have been common, workers and managers need rules that give quick answers because they may soon have to move on to other work and then any hope of redress would be lost. The rules should be easy to monitor by all parties concerned. This affects relations both between workers and management and among different groups of workers who may lay claim to certain kinds of work. This often has to be done in isolated and decentralized workplaces away from easy access to higher levels of management, work-study offices, and from union representatives who might have the expertise to apply complex rules.[14] The task allocation rules should lead to predictable outcomes, as the parties need to know what they are agreeing to and what will be the likely commitments. This can be achieved by using a rule which relates to the common experience of the parties. Again, the demarcation rule based on familiar work materials or on the tools related to a particular skill gives both employer and worker a clear idea of what tasks can be expected, and of the limits beyond which management may not go. Equally, management knows, in principle, that the workers concerned have agreed to undertake any tasks of a certain kind.

The inherent variability of economic life means that task allocations cannot be regarded as fixed for all time, and even where workers may have established a kind of 'job property' over certain types of task, adaptation to technical change and shifts in demand are never far removed. Unlike complex job descriptions which offer no guidance as to how task reallocations can be managed, reference to a system of task allocation rules offers a ready starting point. In the case of both disputes and adaptation to change, reference can be made to the overall purpose of the rules, as again is revealed in the brief example taken from the Webbs. The task allocation rules in the shipyards were part of a system for administering the division of labour in which all of the parties had a stake. In their example of new kinds of plumbing work, the dispute was resolved in a manner that was consistent with the basic principles of craft demarcations. They had evolved in order to afford a livelihood to workers in the different skill groups, and to provide firms with an adequate labour supply, so the solution lay in identifying which kind of pipework on ships should go to which category of workers.[15]

Other types of task allocation rule will be discussed in the next chapter, but what this example shows is how a simple rule enables employers and workers to allocate work without compiling inventories of tasks that may be required. The agreed limits of management's authority are established by identifying types of work rather than lists of tasks and complex statements about different contingencies. Thus, a more successful way to define jobs will be to identify a small number of simple rules for allocating tasks instead of trying to build up an inventory of possible tasks for each job. Discovering suitable transaction rules holds the key to the advantages of the employment relationship over the sales contract.

In recent decades, the task allocation rules just discussed have been widely criticized as a source of inefficiency, and there is no doubt that the way they have been applied can restrict labour utilization. Chapter 8 will deal with the general question of different kinds of task allocation rule and their effects upon functional flexibility, but for the moment, it is worth noting that the studies by both Zweig (1951) on restrictive practices in British industry, and Slichter et al. (1960) on the impact of agreed work rules on management in the US, were more circumspect. Such rules could indeed harm efficiency, but this was often a result of the spirit in which they were applied, and many employers saw compensating benefits of predictability and order.

5. THE FUNCTION OF JOB CLASSIFICATION SYSTEMS

The analysis so far has concentrated on the employment contract for a single job, and so has involved a single bargain. However, most workers are engaged in organizations with many employees engaged in different jobs, which raises a number of problems. First, to be sure of orderly production, employers need to distribute work in a way that meets the agreement of a large number of different employees. Secondly, controlling a large number of diverse jobs places great strain on management's ability to coordinate and keep track of who is responsible for which tasks. Thirdly, the more idiosyncratic individual jobs are, the harder it is for management to monitor and control substandard performance, and to resist opportunistic bargaining pressures from small groups of workers. Such factors lead management to organize work in such a way that more uniform sets of tasks can be assigned to different categories of jobs. These categories then establish contours of equivalence among families of jobs. The relationship could be a qualitative one but for the fact that employment involves an exchange of labour services against pay, thus imparting a strong quantitative dimension to any notions of equivalence. The difficulty of controlling work without dealing with whole categories of jobs can be illustrated by considering what would happen if an employer were to seek to reach individual agreements with each potential employee over pay and task allocations.

5.1. Use of job categories to simplify transactions

The problem of the number of agreements is illustrated in Figure 1.3 which shows the possible allocation of tasks between three jobs. For simplicity, the axes show two task dimensions, let us say skill level on the vertical axis and function on the horizontal one, and that each point represents a task. Assume the tasks may be distributed in any way among the three jobs, and that one worker will be allocated to each. Then the employer's problem

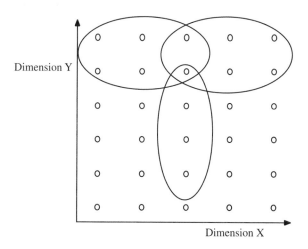

Fig. 1.3. Grouping of tasks into three overlapping jobs

is to devise a way of grouping the tasks so that they offer acceptable jobs to the three workers. The overlap between the three potential jobs represents the tasks to which each worker lays claim. These might be particularly attractive activities that each would like included in their job. As a result, for each additional worker hired, the employer needs to be sure of an increasing number of agreements among the workers over the boundaries between their respective jobs, if stable production is to be achieved. It is easy to see that, with individual bargains, the number increases at a much faster rate than does the number of employees, and very quickly gets out of hand. If we assume each job occupies one employee only, then, as the number of employees rises from one to five, the number of explicit and implicit two-way bargains increases from one to fifteen.[16] Indeed, if these were allowed to proliferate, then the supposed contractual advantages of the employment relationship would quickly be lost.

Grouping jobs into categories reduces the number of bargains by routinizing task allocations. Thus instead of each employee holding a unique job, they are assigned to job categories. In the place of individual negotiation over task allocations, potential employees are offered a fixed menu of job types. In the example above, grouping the three employees' tasks into two job categories reduces the number of two-way bargains from six to three (two between individuals and the employer, and one between the two sets of job-holders).

At first sight, this argument may appear a little academic. But a moment's thought should confirm that agreements on work allocation among workers can be just as problematic as those between workers and their employers. Slichter *et al.*'s (1960) study cited many examples of such conflict, particularly between skilled and semi-skilled workers, and among skilled groups themselves. A number of these, from the US and other countries, are considered in the next chapter. Reliance upon individual jobs and individual bargaining also raises serious problems of performance assessment and technical coordination within the firm. Management's ability to process the related information about who is responsible for what is limited in any organization so that, in the absence of simple organizing principles, the problems of allocating and coordinating work very quickly become intractable. It is much easier to work with a relatively small number of categories of jobs. By the same token, administrative costs are reduced.

Thus, simplifying the allocation of work by grouping jobs into different categories brings potential benefits in terms of simpler bargaining relationships, easier monitoring of performance and greater ease of coordination. Categories establish equivalence among similarly classified jobs, a relationship that helps workers judge the fairness of their job demands and the pay they receive.

5.2. Articulation into systems

The adoption of rules for allocating tasks to jobs implies a holistic approach to job design and classification as individual jobs are allocated to categories, and the latter articulated into systems (see Chapter 4). Rules for task allocation are only likely to help if they are mutually consistent. Those giving conflicting answers as to which tasks should form a part of certain jobs are likely to generate disputes as to which rule should prevail. Consistency requires a set of guiding principles, or an underlying logic, that can be applied in identifying and assigning tasks. It is not sufficient to develop a set of ad hoc categories because sooner or later fluctuating task demands and, in particular, the emergence of new or unexpected tasks are likely to generate conflicting claims. Thus beyond simply grouping tasks into jobs, the jobs themselves need to be organized into certain categories, along consistent lines.

6. TWO POTENTIAL OBJECTIONS TO THE ARGUMENT

Two potential objections to the argument need to be raised at this point. First, Williamson (1975) objects that Simon's treatment of the employment relationship is too narrow, and, secondly, some would object to the idea that the employment relationship is based on choice by workers as well as by firms.

Williamson objects to Simon's argument on the grounds that he sets up too simplistic a view of the alternatives. In particular, he objects to Simon's contrast of coordination by management authority with coordination by the market. Do not internal labour markets and 'sequential spot contracting', he asks, provide alternative procedures? Developing the first of these, Willman (1986: ch. 10) takes the point a step further, contrasting management in British retail banking under the 'authority' relationship in the 1950s and early 1960s with management by means of an internal labour market from the 1970s. Both authors are quite correct to argue that many of the grievance procedures and work rules of internal labour markets submit many employee management decisions to a degree of joint control, but the objection misses the fundamental insight of Simon's approach. The concept of management authority developed here concerns the agreement between firms and workers that management should be able to organize the work of their staff within certain limits. In neither author's account do internal labour markets remove this function from management, they simply regulate it in a different way. As will become clear in the next chapter, many of the governance procedures that Williamson and Willman associate with internal labour markets are in fact a special case of the rules governing the boundaries of management authority within the employment relationship. They are not a substitute for management authority, but different means of regulating it. Because Simon did not examine the limits of management's powers in assigning work, management authority appears like that of an absolute monarch. Within internal labour markets, it might be compared with that of a constitutional monarch, with the additional factor that people may choose under which monarch's jurisdiction they live, or even whether they live in a monarchy.

Under sequential spot contracting within the employment relationship, which boils down to a continuous process of negotiation over work assignments, adaptation to new demands is negotiated.[17] However, the danger, as Williamson shows, is that this raises the incentives to manipulate information, and increases the risk of opportunism by both sides. Willman analyses some examples of this in the British manufacturing and dock industries, and shows how this process deprived firms of the savings on transaction costs by employing people. As his case studies show, in the long-run such continuous negotiation was not economically viable. Opportunistic bargaining depressed productivity and slowed the introduction of technical change.

The second objection, that of lack of choice, can be refuted with two types of evidence. First, the OECD's (1992) study of employment and self-employment indicates that although self-employment grew in a number of countries from the 1980s, the amount of this made up by involuntary self-employment is quite small. Many of those entering self-employment were in professional and financial services, and few entered self-employment from unemployment, despite government schemes to encourage this. Such evidence accords with familiar problems faced by employers with their blue-collar-skilled workforces: the latter often sought the security of employee status when work was scarce, but liked the high earnings opportunities of self-employment when demand was buoyant (Leighton, 1983). Clearly, not all workers have suitable skills for self-employment, as the OECD study observed, but their number is too small to explain the nine-tenths of those in work engaged as employees.

The other type of evidence relates to the bargaining power even of non-union workers. Clegg (1972) built up his famous study of the British system of industrial relations from an analysis of the work group rather than trade unions. His reason was simple: there is ample evidence that even in non-union environments workers are able to exert collective power against management. In Clegg's view, the purpose of industrial relations institutions was to regulate such power relations. This is not a peculiarity of British industrial relations. One of the first systematic studies of 'output restriction' was among non-union workers in Germany (Weber, 1908), and one of the most famous was in the US of the 1930s (Roethlisberger and Dickson, 1939). Crozier's (1963) study, in France, of work group power in bureaucratic environments was also in a weakly unionized workforce. Evidence of such power means it is realistic to treat workers as actors rather than as passive victims in the development of employment relations.

7. INSIGHTS FROM THE HISTORICAL RISE OF THE EMPLOYMENT RELATIONSHIP

The relevance of the rather abstract model presented so far is greatly enhanced if it can be shown that it captures important elements of the historical emergence and generalization of the employment relationship. In all of today's advanced industrial countries, as recently as the late nineteenth and early twentieth centuries, other ways of organizing the sale of labour services predominated, the most common being some variant of the labour contract system. The aim of this section is to show that many of the key advantages of the employment relationship discussed earlier contributed to its gradual displacement of alternative forms of transaction. Although recent years have seen a resurgence of subcontracting and it has always continued to play a critical role in certain sectors, it will be shown that this does not fundamentally affect the argument.

One of the commonest forms of labour contracting to prevail in the industrial sector well into its development was that of the entrepreneur farming out tasks to a master craftsman or labour boss who contracted to undertake them at a specified price and by a certain date. This person would then hire and manage the labour carrying out the task. Mottez (1966) referred to this system as 'l'entreprise comme une affaire' where the firm exists primarily as a business rather than an organization. It was extremely widespread in nineteenth-century Europe and persisted in some activities into the early twentieth century. Writing about France, Mottez stressed the generality of subcontracting and out-working (marchandage) as the dominant form for the provision of labour services late into the nineteenth century. Likewise, in Germany, during early industrialization, severe skill shortages led even major firms to rely at first upon master craftsmen to whom they would subcontract work (Akkordmeister) who would themselves hire helpers to carry it out (Schmiede and Schudlich, 1976). In Britain too, Pollard (1965) describes the gradual emergence of employees on the one hand and professional managers on the other out of the complex system of subcontracting.

The system was not confined to Europe, and elements of it were to be found in both the US and Japan. According to Stone (1973), forms of the contract system were common in the US iron and steel industries until their transformation in the 1890s. Skilled workers were usually paid a price per ton that they produced according to a sliding scale based on product market prices, and hired their own helpers. The sliding scale shared commercial risks between the skilled contractors and the steel masters.

The [steel industry] employers had relatively little control over the skilled workers' income. Nor could the wage be used as an incentive to ensure them a desired level of output. Employers could only contract for a job. The price was determined by the market, and the division of labour and the pace of work were determined by the workers themselves. Thus, the sliding scale and the contract system defined the relationship between labour and capital in the nineteenth century. (Stone, 1973: 32)

In his study of the rise of 'employing bureaucracies' in the US, Jacoby (1985) shows the persistence of a number of forms of contracting in manufacturing industries into the early years of the twentieth century. At one extreme was the use of 'inside contracting' whereby the proprietor provided tools, materials and money, and the contractor dealt with labour and arranged to deliver the product at a specified time and cost (e.g. Buttrick, 1952). At the other extreme was a collective contract whereby the skilled workers contracted directly with the proprietor. However, by about 1900, the most common was the so-called 'drive system'. This was a diluted form of the labour contract system whereby the foremen retained many of the powers of the contractors, notably, hiring, firing, pay fixing and organization of specific areas of work. The main difference was that their income derived from a salary rather than the surplus of the contract price over the money paid to their helpers.

In his account of the rise of long-term employment in Japan, Taira (1970) also refers to the role of master craftsmen in the engineering industries that prevailed during the inter-war years:

In order to bring it [the seniority employment system] about, the firm had first to gain direct control over its work force in all the aspects of recruitment, training, assignment, promotion, dismissal, and retirement. But the formal job structure and informal worker groupings within the factory in the engineering industries were largely based on personal and personalised relations among master craftsmen and between each one of them and his underlings. The situation can be summed up as '*oyakata-kokata* relations'. (Taira, 1970: 158)

They commonly moved between their artisan workshops and the engineering firms as the latter's demand for labour varied, and in doing so, they would often take their apprentices and helpers with them (Taira 1970: 110).

Thus, in all five countries, versions of the labour subcontracting and drive systems prevailed before the rise to preeminence of the employment relationship. Although the labour contract system declined relative to the employment relation, in its context, it had been regarded by many as extremely efficient. Indeed, Mottez cites a number of nineteenth-century economists and other observers who were greatly impressed by the advantages of subcontracting, both material and moral. What struck them in particular were the system's flexibility and its efficiency in providing incentives for effective supervision. It was a system that enabled rapid labour force adjustments to cope with fluctuating markets. It was also a mechanism for sharing risks between the entrepreneur and the subcontractor, the one assuming most of the financial risks, and the other, those of production. In an age of rudimentary cost control, it also provided an element of certainty in cost-ings. Finally, it was regarded as a highly efficient form of supervision of work at each level 'as the eye of the master is thus subdivided and multiplied so that it is present always in every group' as the labour boss knew the secrets of the trade, and yet had the incentive to drive his workers.[18] Even such a strong critic of the drive system as Slichter (1919) conceded that it was most likely to be profitable in the short run.

The reasons for the decline of the contract system reflect a number of the advantages of the employment over the sales contract. These relate espe-cially to the problems of the predictability and quality of labour supply, which assumed increasing importance with the changing nature of indus-trialization in the twentieth century. First, neither the labour contract nor the drive systems proved able to ensure the availability of labour when employ-ers needed it. Problems of labour turnover, absenteeism and general instabil-ity were common, especially during periods of strong labour demand. These problems appear to have been especially pressing in Germany, the US and Japan. In German manufacturing, Schudlich (1994) attributes the growth of internal labour market policies in the early part of this century to employers' desire to combat the high levels of turnover that they associated with the contracting system. Taira's (1970) analysis of Japanese engineering draws a similar point. As in Germany, the dependence on master craftsmen for hiring labour and organizing production was seen as the source of lack of attach-ment, but in neither country could the employers make the transition until they had established an alternative supply of skilled labour. Large employers did this in Germany by reorganizing industrial apprenticeships in the late nineteenth century (Lutz, 1976). In the US, a large part of Slichter's (1919) study of factory labour turnover was devoted to an estimation of its costs to both firms and workers, and for him the prime cause of high turnover was the 'drive system', notably, its use of fear of dismissal as its principal moti-vator. Systematic use of firing by supervisors to instil fear tends to be indis-criminate with regard to worker quality. Indeed, to some extent it has to be because otherwise the more skilled workers would know that they were relatively safe. Thus, it bred instability as few workers would feel any attach-ment to their firm, or have any interest in developing skills useful to it. Job content and price were also unpredictable because of the reliance upon the fear of dismissal for labour discipline. As soon as the labour market tight-ened, as occurred in the US and Japan after the outbreak of the 1914–18 war, the disciplinary power of foremen and labour contractors began to break down. Although it could be reasserted when labour demand subsequently fell, it meant that labour availability was at its least dependable when firms needed it most.

A second major failing of the subcontracting system was the lack of incentive to develop skills in response to the needs of individual employers. Several accounts of the relationship between the firm and the subcontractor highlight the incentive for the latter to withhold information about production methods, and especially about possible improvements. Buttrick's (1952) study of the inside contract system at the Winchester Repeating Arms Company provides an excellent illustration. If the contractor revealed the extent of production improvements to the firm, then this would be used to bargain down the price agreed. Likewise, within the drive system, Slichter (1919: 203) stresses how the use of fear to bargain down piece rates removed any incentive workers might have had to develop their skills and raise output. Among the reasons for the decline of labour contracting in Britain, Pollard (1965: 52) also mentioned its inhibiting the development of high quality workmanship. Schudlich and Taira argue that by relying on master craftsmen to recruit and organize labour, German and Japanese firms were effectively depriving themselves of the means to adapt labour market skills to their own particular needs as these agents had no interest in doing so.

A third problem was the difficulty of controlling certain kinds of opportunism, notably among contractors both in relation to the firm and to workers, and as such, the system was not providing a reliable form of transaction. With regard to the proprietors, both Mottez and Pollard mention the frequent tendency to flog capital equipment, skimp on maintenance, and erode quality in an effort to maximize short-term output, which became more of a problem as the level of capital investment, and sensitivity to quality, increased. On the workers' side, Taira describes the breakdown of the training relationship between master craftsmen and young workers in the metal trades during the period up to the 1914–18 war.

Within the factory, the skilled workers were likely to neglect the training of the company-hired youngsters . . . the factory apprentices learned their trades not through training but through 'stealing', that is, they observed as best they could how the craftsmen worked while they were themselves doing insignificant tasks in the factory. When these youngsters felt they had seen enough, they would leave for the opportunity to practice the trades. (Taira, 1970: 110)

A fourth problem was that of social disorder. The avidity of the labour subcontractors was widely believed, and as Mottez points out, the incentives in place left them little alternative. Haphazard earnings differentials among workers, hard bargaining by contractors or supervisors in the drive system, and short-term employment meant that resentment and labour unrest were common. In the US, both Slichter *et al.* (1960) and Jacoby (1985) point out that once unions had become powerful, firms were exposed to unions' organizing drives which were a strong incentive to improve personnel management. In France, Mottez also stresses the importance of labour unrest associated with labour subcontracting as one of the reasons for its eventual demise.

For workers, labour subcontracting meant unstable short-term employment, and with it, frequent interruptions in earnings. Limited incentives to improve skills also deprived them of the opportunity to better their situation. Finally, the lack of attachment for all parties increased certain transaction costs, notably those of negotiating new agreements, acquiring information about the other party and the risk of shortfall either in labour availability or in income. Such arguments are of more than historical interest, as Felstead (1991) cites many of the same problems of opportunism besetting the use of franchising (as an alternative to employment) in Britain in the 1980s (v. Chapter 8).

8. CONCLUSION

This chapter set out from the analyses of Coase and Simon of the special nature of the employment relationship by comparing it with the commonest modern alternative, namely, some variant of the sales transaction. Why do businesses and workers most commonly enter employment rather than sales transactions? The answer lies in the great flexibility of the employment relationship, and the considerable benefits it provides to both parties. The historical decline of various forms of sales contract as manifest in the labour contract system arises from an increased need for the benefits provided by the employment relationship. The special flexibility stressed by both Coase and Simon is that it enables firms to contract for the future availability of labour when they know only roughly what kind of work will need to be done, being as yet unable to specify precisely what tasks should be undertaken. The other side of the coin is that workers contract to supply labour services of a certain kind in the future, and thereby gain continuity of employment. Both parties also save on related contracting costs.

As has been argued in this chapter, the fundamental problem left unanswered by Coase and Simon was that of specifying a viable form of transaction that would give sufficient protection to either party against possible opportunism by the other. Coase identified an essential feature of the employment relation that workers agreed to give management authority to specify their tasks within certain limits. But, how are these limits to be regulated? Virtually unbounded management authority has existed in slavery and bonded labour, but even when employment is 'at will', the costs of job changing and of finding new workers can be sufficient to expose either party to opportunistic behaviour by the other.

Jobs cannot be effectively defined by providing an exhaustive inventory of tasks that an employee might be called upon to undertake. The importance of tacit knowledge of how jobs are done, and the sheer rigidity and high economic cost of very detailed job descriptions in an uncertain world, make such an option impractical. An alternative is to agree upon a rule for identifying the tasks that workers may be called upon to undertake. To be effective, such rules need to be easily applicable in a variety of work environments, and it should be easy for the parties to distinguish correct or fair applications from incorrect or unfair ones, and one should be able to do so quickly and in the place of work. Unless they are fairly robust in this sense, they will raise the cost of using the employment contract compared with the alternative of some kind of sales contract. The next chapter takes the argument a stage further by developing a theoretical typology of transaction rules and considering four common types of rule. Their robustness is shown by their ability to deal with many common types of opportunism, and thus to provide some of the most important benefits associated with the employment relationship.

ENDNOTES

[1] That is to say, the actors are intentionally rational, but limited in their capacity to deal with all the necessary information.

[2] The term 'functional' flexibility refers to the ability of employers to deploy labour across job boundaries, and 'numerical' flexibility, to their ability to vary numbers employed (Atkinson and Meager, 1986).

[3] The term 'employment rule' is sometimes used instead of employment transaction rule because it is less cumbersome. It is, however, consistently used in this way.

[4] 'La législation est comme la monnaie. L'État ne peut la mettre efficacement en circulation si la société la refuse' (Sellier, 1961: 16).

[5] The term 'labour institutions' is used to embrace both the formal and informal insitutions set up by employers and employees, such as employer organizations, works councils and trade unions, and any joint bodies which they create.

[6] The terms employment 'relationship' and 'contract' are used interchangeably and varied for stylistic reasons.

[7] 'The contract is one whereby the factor, for a certain remuneration (which may be fixed or fluctuating), agrees to obey the directions of an entrepreneur *within certain limits*. The essence of the contract is that it should only state the limits to the powers of the entrepreneur. Within these limits, he can therefore direct the other factors of production'(Coase 1937: 391). Coase also considers the case in which there are no such limits, but remarks that this would be voluntary slavery, and cites Batt on the law of master and servant that such contracts would be void and unenforceable. By stressing the 'at will' nature of the employment contract, Commons (1924) makes a similar argument because the freedom to quit underlies the limits of what the employer can demand of the employee. 'The labor contract therefore is not a contract, it is a continuing implied renewal of contracts at every minute and hour, based on the continuance of what is deemed, on the employer's side, to be satisfactory service, and, on the laborer's side, what is deemed to be satisfactory conditions and compensation' (Commons, 1924: ch. 8 §1).

[8] In effect, Simon adapts the standard analysis of the employer and union preferences for wages and employment which is well described in graphical terms by Cartter (1959: ch. 8) and given a more modern treatment by Booth (1995). In this analysis, the employer's iso-profit, or average net revenue (per worker hired), curves take a similar form to the iso-satisfaction contours. In Cartter's analysis, the iso-profit curves follow an inverted 'u'-shape as a result of two tendencies: the rising and then declining marginal revenue product of labour given a fixed capital stock;

and the declining cost per worker of that capital as the number employed increases. Curve S_{bo} is analogous to the average net revenue curve and shows the combinations of tasks and wage rates that just exhaust the employer's revenue, leaving zero profits. Lower curves show higher levels of profit. The inverted 'u'-shape of curve S_{bo} can be explained in similar but not identical terms to the profit curve, using the example of task complexity.

[9] This is very similar to the problem of the optimal wage and employment bargain between a union and an employer whereby the optimal bargain is given by the tangency between their indifference curves, but it is off the demand curve so that, if the employer remains free to set employment, it can always raise profits by cutting employment and moving back onto its labour demand curve (see Cartter, 1959; Booth, 1995).

[10] We assume that employees can function at high levels of dissatisfaction, whereas employers cannot long continue in business at a loss.

[11] Wolf (1994) provides an excellent example of this problem in the context of establishing detailed standards for work competencies in Britain. In attempting to establish written definitions of standards of competence to be achieved by trainees in their workplaces, the authorities found it necessary to set out explicitly the range of tolerances that could be allowed under different local conditions, and then to define the types of local conditions. Thus, what were intended to be simple standards that employers could easily understand and relate to their own job demands turned into extremely complex sets of specifications that defeated the goal of simplicity, thus discouraging employers from using them.

[12] An official of the Construction Industry Training Board.

[13] Streeck's (1985) analysis of the reform of apprenticeship training in the German construction industry likewise revealed the difficulties in obtaining agreement on new skill norms that could support a common training system for the whole sector.

[14] In this regard, it is notable that job classifications in the construction industry are generally much simpler than in other sectors (Dunlop, 1958; Campinos-Dubernet (ed.), 1991). One interpretation might be that construction work is much simpler than work in other sectors, although it is hard to believe this of modern construction sites. A more plausible explanation is that the decentralization of activity across construction sites means that often the criteria for identifying which tasks form part of the job have to be applied by individual workers and supervisors without easy recourse to higher levels of management and union representatives who may adjudicate.

[15] Eldridge (1968: ch. 3) offers similar examples from British shipyards fifty years later of the resolution of demarcation disputes. The solution was a negotiated compromise, usually partitioning work in a manner consistent with the established principles of task allocation.

[16] In formal terms, this is equivalent to the number of ways of selecting r objects, in this case 2, irrespective of order, from a set of size N. That is:

number of two-way bargains $= N!/(r!(N-r)!)$,

where N is the number of employee-jobs, and r the number of parties involved in each agreement (see Hays, 1973: 176).

[17] Alchian and Demsetz (1972) have also stressed that managerial authority was merely a veil for continuous implicit negotiation over work assignments and

rewards on the ground that either party could end the relationship at will at any moment.

[18] 'Puisque l'œuil du maître s'est ainsi en quelque sorte subdivisé et multiplié au point d'être toujours présent dans chaque groupe.' Leroy-Beaulieu (1896: Vol. 2, 494).

2

The Limits of Managerial Authority

1. INTRODUCTION

The first chapter has established that limits must be set on management authority if the employment relationship is to have any appeal to workers: no one would sign up to unlimited obligations. Likewise, if management's access to task flexibility were to depend on continuous negotiation, as under implicit forms of sequential spot contracting, the employment relationship would have little appeal to firms. How are the limits of management authority to direct work established within the employment relationship, and what kinds of rules are able to achieve this? In this chapter, I argue that there are two fundamental constraints that any such rules must resolve: they must be enforceable and they must be productively efficient. To be enforceable, they must both limit employees' obligations and protect flexibility for the employer. To be efficient, they must enable both parties to be better off with an employment contract than under alternative forms so that both have a positive reason for choosing it. It is argued that satisfying these two contractual constraints is a necessary and sufficient condition for a viable employment relationship. As a result, they may be used to derive a typology of constitutive rules limiting employees' work obligations to their employers. In keeping with the argument of the previous chapter, this one builds on the ideas of bounded rationality and potential opportunism. Crossing the two contractual constraints gives rise to four types of transaction rules. These are shown to be sufficiently robust to withstand common forms of opportunism, which they must do if they are to provide a stable framework for exchange.

Unlike the many typologies of employment rules that are reached inductively from observation, the one presented here is deductive. It is derived from the basic theory of the employment relationship. With such a typology we know that the resulting categories are exhaustive, at least within the assumptions of the theory, and this has three important implications. First, it means we can argue that management and workers in fact face a restricted choice of alternative models of employment relationship, and secondly, it provides a basis for a theory of the diffusion of employment rules as evolutionarily stable games, explored in the next chapter. Finally, because it is deductive rather than inductive, we can use the findings of existing international comparative research as a partial test: does the theory predict the patterns observed, and what light does it shed on why there is such diversity?

The chapter begins by explaining the two contractual constraints which a viable employment relationship must satisfy, and establishes the exhaustiveness of a typology of rules derived from these constraints. It then examines some common examples of actual transaction rules belonging to each of the main types. These are the work post, the job territory/tools of the trade, the competence rank and the qualification rules. It then shows how these are able to restrain common forms of opportunism likely to occur within the employment relationship.

2. TRANSACTION RULES AND THE EMPLOYMENT RELATION

Two critical problems have to be resolved in constructing a stable framework for employment: those of providing a suitable means of aligning job demands and worker competencies; and of offering sufficiently robust criteria for assigning tasks to certain groups of workers that can be applied easily in a wide variety of work environments. These might be referred to as the 'efficiency' and 'enforceability' constraints, respectively.

The first of these constraints refers to the need for task assignments to be productively efficient. In a competitive product market, no firm can survive for long if it arranges jobs in a way that fails to match workers' tasks and their competencies. Either there will be waste, as it pays for competencies which it does not use, or there will be loss of quality if workers are not competent at the tasks which they are assigned. The enforceability constraint refers to the need for rules to be relatively unambiguous and applicable at a fairly low cost. The more ambiguous they are, the more open they will be to interpretation, and possibly deliberate misinterpretation, and the more likely they are to give rise to additional job-level bargaining. As a result they will provide less protection to either party against opportunistic action by the other, and the availability of labour will become more unpredictable. Equally, they will be less effective the more costly they are to enforce. Costs will rise quickly if the rules are so complex that supervisors must continually refer to experts in the personnel department. In both cases, the resulting unpredictability would make production harder to organize effectively, thus eliminating many of the gains of the employment transaction. Taken together, the two constraints provide allocative efficiency, which refers to the need for the employment relationship to maximize the benefits for both parties. With competitive labour markets, firms will find it hard to attract workers to sign up to contracts that are too one-sided or which underutilize their skills, and vice versa.

Each of these two constraints may be resolved in one of two ways. Combining them indicates four main types of rule governing the limits of jobs within the employment transaction, as shown in Table 2.1. Common examples of the rules to be discussed later are shown in the boxes.

2.1. Efficiency: competencies and jobs

There are two principle ways of organizing tasks into jobs, and matching them to worker competencies: one sets off from the production side, seeking complementarities between tasks in the production system (the 'production approach'), and the other seeks to group tasks according to complementarities in worker skills (the 'training approach').[1] These are shown in the columns of Table 2.1. Thus, in the production approach,[2] tasks are grouped so as to minimize time lost through worker displacements between work locations and to keep down the number of persons involved in carrying out a particular job. According to the training approach, competencies are grouped into families of related skills so as to economize on training costs, and tasks are organized to achieve high levels of skill utilization. Clearly, for efficient production, employers will wish to match job tasks and competencies, but the question is which should have priority in defining jobs.

Under the *production approach*, priority is given to technical complementarities arising out of the process of production or service provision, and training is adapted, most commonly by use of on-the-job learning. This approach corresponds closely to that identified by Piore (1968) in his early work on the effects of technology on labour skills, and his finding that, under the work systems he studied, the relationship ran in one direction only, namely, that employers chose their production techniques and then adapted their labour. He cites the aphorism of one engineer: 'mould men to jobs, not jobs to men' (619). Replicating a survey made twenty years earlier by Davis *et al.* (1955) of job design practice by engineers in the US, Taylor (1979) concluded:[3]

. . . both production engineers and system analysts select job design criteria remarkably similar to those of their predecessors in the 1950s. They still prefer to minimise the immediate costs of production rather than to emphasise a longer term approach

Table 2.1. *The contractual constraints and common employment rules*

The focus of enforcement criteria	Job demands identified by:	
	Production approach	Training approach
Task-centred	'Work post' rule	'Job territory'/'tools of trade' rule
Function- /procedure-centred	'Competence rank' rule	'Qualification' rule

to job design which recognises the economic costs of worker frustration and acknowledges employee satisfaction and motivation. (Taylor 1979: 61)

Littler (1985) reiterated this judgement in his review of work on job redesign in which he characterized 'the common managerial view' as being that meeting the requirements of technology alone would give the best performance. A notable outcome of the production approach is a good deal of task heterogeneity within jobs, leading to what Williamson (1975) characterized as 'job idiosyncrasy', and Doeringer and Piore (1971) as 'job specificity'. Maurice *et al.* (1986) also noted the effect of following the demands of the production system among French firms in the frequent lack of consistency among the tasks grouped into jobs, and characterized the resulting jobs as 'a collection of tasks sharing a certain technical content'.[4]

Under the *training approach*, firms group tasks according to complementarities in training needs rather than those of production. The essence of the 'training approach' is summarized by Sengenberger[5,6]:

... There has to be an approximate structural congruency between the division of skills (in the training market) and the division of labour or jobs in the firms participating in the occupational labour market. Each employer must design his jobs or job demands in such a way that they correspond to the range of skills offered by a particular occupation. (Sengenberger 1992: 248)

In their study of work organization and training in French and German manufacturing firms, Maurice *et al.* (1986) give another angle on the training approach, stressing the role of the supervisor in German firms allocating tasks according to worker skills, which is contrasted to the production approach taken in French firms:

Theoretically, a firm can organise its work system in one of two ways: it can define jobs according to its own criteria and require workers to adapt or train them to fit the job definition, or it can take account of the existing qualifications of the workforce and design jobs around the capabilities of the workers. (Maurice *et al.*, 1986: 67)

Apart from inter-country differences, there are also big differences between industrial sectors. Indeed, in many countries, the construction industry applies variants of the 'training approach', whereby tasks are allocated according to skill rather than production complementarities. Stinchcombe's (1959) contrast of 'bureaucratic' and 'craft' administration, the first of which applies the production, and the second, the training approach, was based on a comparison between manufacturing and construction sectors in the US. Looking respectively at the US and a wider range of industrial countries, both Slichter *et al.* (1960) and Dunlop (1958) observed that the geographical dispersion of construction sites, the diversity of skills needed and the short duration of work on many sites account for the primacy of a training-based pattern of work organization. Such conditions favour investment by workers in their own skills, and this requires a stable pattern of jobs across the industry.

The contrast between the production and training approaches is illustrated in Figure 2.1. The two curves show the cost per trainee for on-the-job and off-the-job training. Under the first, initially cost per trainee may be low, as experienced workers provide guidance and trainees learn by doing. However, as the ratio of trainees to experienced workers rises, the latter will suffer an increasing number of distractions from their own work. In contrast, with off-the-job training, there are high initial costs with the establishment of pro-grammes and training facilities, but cost per trainee falls as the number of trainees increases. As the number of trainees passes point 'A', the training approach becomes the more economical of the two.

Job design can play an important part by affecting the number of jobs with broadly similar training demands. The more jobs that are organized to have standard contents, the greater the potential economies of scale in off-the-job training. Thus, under the production approach, with jobs designed accord-ing to immediate production needs, the degree of heterogeneity will be large, and the scope for off-the-job training limited. Under the training approach, with jobs designed to take account of training needs, greater economies of scale are possible. Some large firms may be able to achieve sufficient stan-dardization of jobs to make their own private off-the-job training provisions economic. Indeed, Lutz (1976: 139 ff.) shows that the first significant steps toward setting up the new industrial training system in Germany in the late nineteenth and early twentieth centuries were taken by a small group of large industrial firms. They pioneered the adaptation of the traditional arti-san apprenticeship model to the new skill demands of large-scale industry. In doing so, they would have been designing jobs to fit the constraints of their new training systems. Thus, although the training approach may be more common when several firms design their jobs in similar ways, the training approach is not logically dependent upon the existence of an exter-nal market for a particular skill.

Why should there be only two dominant types rather than a continuum of varying mixes of the two approaches? The answer lies partly in the cost

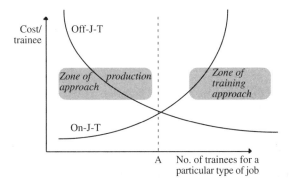

Fig. 2.1. **Training costs under the production and training approaches**

considerations just outlined, partly in the greater robustness of the two poles and partly in the mutual reinforcement between transaction rules and labour market structures discussed more fully in Chapter 8. Although the two cost curves in Figure 2.1 are only illustrative, they do reveal different logics. If one seeks to combine the approaches for the same set of basic skills and workers, then one is likely to lose some of the benefits of standardizing jobs and so raise the costs of off-the-job training. At the same time, shifting more of the burden back onto on-the-job training will raise the costs of that. In terms of Figure 2.1, one is moving leftwards up the off-the-job curve, and rightwards up the on•the-job curve. The cheapest solutions are either idiosyncratic jobs with a small number of on-the-job trainees on each job, or broader jobs with standardized contents that can be satisfied by off-the-job training.

The second factor, robustness of work allocation rules and their enforceability, discussed in the next section, is improved the more homogeneous the approach taken to a given set of jobs. Such clarity is lost if, within the same organization, the same basic jobs are organized along different lines, some following the training and others the production approach. Often, when employers seek to adopt different approaches, they will segment work on occupational or gender lines for example, although neither of these are entirely watertight against comparisons by employees.[7]

The third factor stems from mutual reinforcement between transaction rules and labour market structures, discussed more fully in Chapter 8, and is that the intermediate forms in internal and occupational markets are unstable. As shown in that chapter, internal labour markets help to reinforce the production approach, and occupational markets the training approach. Because the intermediate market forms are unstable, there is no equivalent reinforcement of intermediate positions in between the production and training approaches. Thus, for reasons stemming both from the internal dynamics of the production and training approaches, and from those of labour market structure, intermediate positions between the two approaches to job regulation will tend to be unstable, and over the longer run firms will opt for one or other pole.

2.2. Enforceability: transparency and the control of opportunism

The second constraint concerns enforceability. This requires that task allocation rules be transparent, otherwise it is hard to identify possible forms of opportunism and hence to enforce agreements. Transparency is also important for maintaining allocative efficiency against potential opportunism. In recent studies of work organization, it has been common to distinguish a focus on employee inputs into the work process, namely the execution of work tasks, from that on the outputs sought by employers, that is, the provision of certain functions or activities (Baraldi *et al.*, 1995). Whereas the task can be understood as relating to the physical and mental actions to be carried out by the employee, the function relates to the employee's output or contribution to the collective effort of production or service provision. Under a completely stable production system, fulfilling a given function would involve the same set of tasks over time. However, the more variable the production demands, the greater the variation in the required task content of jobs, and so the greater the divergence between the two.

One way of achieving transparency is to define the scope of jobs in terms of certain attributes of the tasks themselves, such as their technical complementarity as embodied in a work post's job description, or the tools required for their execution. This is shown in the top row of Table 2.1. Such rules have proved attractive on account of their simplicity and relative lack of ambiguity, which makes them easy to enforce. This logic may be taken a step further by organizing jobs so as to combine tasks whose performance criteria can be assessed in similar ways so that simpler monitoring and incentive schemes can be used (Holmstrom and Milgrom, 1991). By identifying particular task characteristics, and linking them to jobs, such rules create a one-to-one relationship that can become a source of rigidity in task allocations.

An alternative solution is to focus on the functions required by the organization, shown in the bottom row of Table 2.1. For the employer this has the distinct advantage of defining jobs more closely in relation to the final output required. However, it provides only an indirect link between individual tasks and jobs, and so leaves employees in considerable doubt as to the precise demands that employers may place upon them and the limits of management authority. Thus, on its own, the function is unlikely to be a suitable criterion for defining job contents, particularly if the reason for employers adopting it is to enable them to deal with variable demand. A solution, therefore, is to relate functions and tasks by means of some third factor, such as a special procedure for identifying which workers should undertake certain kinds of tasks. As will be seen below, this can provide a viable basis for employment transactions when incorporating a greater degree of flexibility than when jobs are defined in relation to specific tasks.

(a) Task-centred rules

Task-centred rules regulate the open-ended nature of the employment transaction by specifying the nature of the tasks which management may assign to individual workers. Two common methods, to be discussed later, include grouping complementary tasks into the job descriptions of work posts, which will be called the 'work post' rule; and using the kind of tools or materials applied in the execution of certain tasks to identify 'job territories', of which one example is the 'tools of the trade' rule. The first of these derives from the 'production approach' to task organization, and the second from the 'training approach'. In essence, both rules seek to give a clear and unambiguous answer to the question of which types of tasks management may legitimately assign to which groups of workers.

(b) Function-centred rules

Like the task-centred rules, those based on functions have to provide a satisfactory matching between the demands of different tasks and the competencies of workers, in addition to defining the bounds of management's authority. But they do so in different ways. Whereas task-centred rules identify individual tasks and assign them, function-centred rules identify a procedure to organize workers and tasks into different categories.

To be effective, a procedure must be closely related to the function so that it can be used to help define categories of workers and tasks. As with task-centred rules, the procedures have to be known and understood by both workers and management if they are to clarify the limits of managerial authority. Within the production approach, one solution is to adopt a ranking procedure of some kind. This might involve categorizing workers by the range and depth of their job-competencies, and allocating tasks according to their degree of complexity or the extent of problem-solving activities required. There is no one-to-one linking of workers to jobs and jobs to tasks, but rather a ranking of workers coupled with an appropriate method for identifying tasks. The ranking procedure gives workers and management a guide as to what tasks may be allocated to whom. Under the training approach, workers may be identified by certain types of training they have undergone, such as apprenticeship or professional training, and tasks grouped broadly according to the type of skills they require.

The problems of robustness limit the range of possible procedures that may work effectively. Under the production approach, worker seniority commonly plays a very important role in ranking workers because it is easy to observe and, once its frame of reference has been fixed, it can be applied with a minimum of ambiguity. Under the training approach, having undergone some kind of workplace traineeship is also very common and for similar reasons. One might ask why educational diplomas should, in practice, play a rather small part by comparison. The answer lies in the importance of learning how to apply the rule in practice when faced with a great variety of workplaces. Traineeships provide, in addition to formal knowledge, a great deal of tacit knowledge about type of work and the practical functioning of work groups. Thus equipped, former trainees are much more familiar with task allocation norms, and, as a result, are better able to identify and enforce limits to managerial authority.

The two approaches are polar types, as with the training and production approaches, because they represent different enforcement equilibria. The task-centred approach provides one such equilibrium, as enforcement focuses directly upon identification of individual tasks: by the job description or the tools used for example. The function-centred approach is more

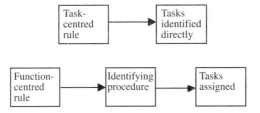

Fig. 2.2. Task assignment with task- and function-centred rules

indirect, and the focus on some publicly observable procedure holds the key to enforcement. This provides a firm point of reference so that disagreements do not become just a worker's word against that of her supervisor. Another factor distinguishing the two approaches is the degree to which workers are held individually responsible for tasks. This is direct with the task-centred rules, but indirect with the function-centred ones (Figure 2.2).

2.3. The exhaustiveness of the classification

There may be many possible ways of classifying the rules regulating the employment relationship. Ideally, a classification should be exhaustive so that one can be sure that all important cases are dealt with, and it should comprise the smallest number of categories needed to classify observations. In order to demonstrate this, one needs to show that a particular classification captures elements that are both necessary and sufficient for the occurrence of certain events, in this case, the occurrence of an employment relationship. Because the two contractual constraints have been used to develop the typology of transaction rules in this book, we need to show that fulfilling the conditions they impose represents both a necessary and sufficient condition for the actors to choose the employment relationship over the alternatives.

It should already be clear from the previous discussion that satisfying the enforceability constraint is a necessary condition. If employees find that the limits on their obligations cannot be enforced, they will eschew this form of contract and seek alternative arrangements. Similarly, if employers find that they cannot obtain the expected flexibility because agreements cannot be enforced, they will eventually seek other forms of coordination. However, it is only a necessary condition because some rules can be enforceable but wholly inefficient, for example, assigning tasks according to the colour of an employee's eyes.

What is more difficult is to show that fulfilling the contractual constraints represents a sufficient condition for adoption of an employment relationship: that the parties find it more beneficial than alternative arrangements.

Sufficiency cannot be established in the absolute, but only in relation to other known forms of contracting. As one can never rule out human ingenuity developing new forms of contracting, the simplest way to proceed is to take the most probable alternative, namely some form of open-market contracting, or sales contract. Earlier, it was shown that internal labour markets are simply a form of employment relationship, and not, as Williamson argued, a third alternative in between employment and sales contracts (Chapter 1 §6). Thus the sales contract captures the main rival to the employment relationship both at the time of its emergence, and, more recently, in relation to the various forms of subcontracting, self-employment, and other market-mediated relationships that have been growing in recent years.

In fact, Simon's (1951) analysis of the employment relationship takes just this approach, as the alternative he considers is that of hiring self-employed labour to undertake specific tasks. Given conditions of uncertain demand, he shows that both firms and workers are better off if they opt for employment over self-employment. The firm secures the availability of labour services as and when needed, and the worker, greater continuity of employment. Both economize on the negotiating and search costs associated with open-market contracting. The main conditions under which self-employment is more attractive are when the timing of demand is known with great certainty, the tasks can be easily specified in advance and when an employer lacks sufficient work to occupy a whole person continuously. Thus, laying a single concrete path can be dealt with easily by self-employment, whereas secretarial work is much more tricky.

However, Simon's argument takes us only part of the way. Sufficiency requires that the relationship be mutually beneficial, and this may not occur if one side can recoup all the gains, potentially leaving the other one worse off. Remember that the employer has to pay a wage sufficient to cover the tasks that are least attractive to the employee within the zone of acceptance, and that the employee faces the possibility of being forced to undertake work outside that zone because of the cost of moving to another job (see Chapter 1 §2).

Employment rules that satisfy the two contractual constraints contribute to sufficiency in two ways. First, the enforceability constraint restricts the scope for such opportunism, and so ensures the employment relationship is mutually advantageous. Secondly, given that there must be rules, the efficiency constraint plays a special role in promoting the gains from the relationship. As shown earlier in this chapter, the production and training approaches maximize the gains from the employment relationship by minimizing the mismatch between workers' competencies and employer's job demands. This depends partly on the cost structures of on-the-job and off-the-job training, and partly on the instability of positions in between the two polar types. As these two approaches maximize the gains from the employment relationship, they are instrumental in ensuring its advantages over the sales contract. As will be seen later, the efficiency constraint plays a special part in the shaping of job classification systems (Chapter 4 §2) and determining the content of job performance criteria (Chapter 6 §5), and so contributes to the 'added value' arising from the employment relationship.

Combining the two contractual constraints leads to employment rules which are both enforceable and productively efficient. Indeed, productive efficiency becomes allocative efficiency once the enforceability constraint is satisfied. This ensures that the relationship is mutually satisfactory, or at least, as far as is permitted by the initial negotiation before hiring and before either party has incurred significant sunk costs. Thus rules which satisfy the two contractual constraints are both necessary for a viable employment relationship because they ensure continued mutual satisfaction of both parties, and they are sufficient because they ensure the relative gains to be had compared with other forms of contracting.

Since meeting the two contractual constraints represents both a necessary and a sufficient condition for the occurrence of the employment relationship, any other set of constraints would also have to satisfy them, and so can be subsumed within them.[8] Hence, we may conclude that the two sets of conditions are exhaustive, given the initial assumptions about the parties being free to choose the form of transaction, seeking to maximize their respective benefits under limited and uncertain information, and facing a choice between employment and sales contracts.

3. EXAMPLES OF EACH TYPE OF TASK ALLOCATION RULE

Having sketched out the main categories of transaction rule for the employment transaction (Table 2.1), and argued that they are exhaustive, we may now look at common examples of the type of rule to be found in each category to see how they deal with the problems of task identification and assignment.

3.1. Work post

The 'work post' rule comprises two essential elements: the identification of a set of complementary tasks, and their assignment to an individual job holder who is held responsible for their execution. Taken together, they imply that work is divided up into a set of discrete, non-overlapping areas for which workers are held individually responsible.

Of the four types of rule, the 'work post' comes closest to the idea of defining the tasks assigned to a job by means of an inventory. Several of the authors cited earlier have referred to it as a bundle of tasks related by common technical demands and cost minimization. Nevertheless, it stops a long way short of the inventory approach to job definition that was rejected earlier (v. Chapter 1 §3). In practice, the rule operates at a far higher level of abstraction, and, as will be argued later (§4.1 below), more often provides a point of reference for periodic enforcement than a list of tasks to be undertaken on a day-to-day basis. Indeed, over-detailed job descriptions are likely to destroy the very flexibility that the employment relationship is intended to secure. Writing about workplace management in the US, Slichter *et al.* (1960) warned that over-detailed job descriptions would cause people to focus on 'the words in the manual'.[9] Likewise, Crozier's (1963) analysis of the 'vicious circle' of bureaucracy in French organizations showed how detailed job instructions were too rigid to deal with unexpected changes in work post demands and likely to prove counter-productive.

Using a system of work posts resolves a number of the problems raised by the Coase–Simon model. First, the tasks required are divided up clearly among the jobs which the employer wishes to fill so that, on being hired, employees know fairly precisely what kinds of tasks they will be asked to undertake. Although they may have only a vague idea of the job requirements beforehand, they will know that there is a system of work posts each with fairly precise job descriptions. In particular, workers know that under such a rule, management's authority over one worker stops where another worker's job begins. Tasks can be assigned within work posts, but workers know that they will not normally be expected to undertake work belonging to other work posts. Likewise, management knows that there is an understanding as to who is responsible for carrying out which tasks, these being identified with individual job holders, so that non-performance can be quickly determined. Cole described the work post system as found in many US firms as follows:

Specifically jobs tend to be organised . . . [in US business firms] . . . with a standard performance level established for each job. There tends to be a one-to-one relationship between the individual and the job, with the goal being to ensure accountability. (Cole, 1979: 233)

Thus the work post system gives, in the first instance, a relatively clear answer as to the limits within which management may exercise its authority over work assignments. Employees may be directed between those tasks in the job description attached to the post for which they are responsible.

3.2. Job territory/tools of the trade

The second type of task-centred rule defines the bounds of management's authority by establishing a criterion for identifying the tasks associated with a particular job territory. A common example, of great historical importance in blue collar work, has been to identify the tasks by the kind of tools used or materials handled. In British trade union circles these have commonly been known as the 'tools of the trade'. Workers of one trade would accept management's right to direct them to undertake tasks within their area, as defined by use of the tools of their trade, but no further. It has the added advantage that the tools required will also be closely related to the kind of competence to be applied, such as the electrician's screwdriver. Thus, task and competence can be identified simultaneously by application of the same rule. In white-collar and professional work, where less use is made of distinctive tools, the 'job territory' rule may take a different form, for example, focusing on particular types of administrative transaction or technical operation. Usually these are selected on the basis of their relationship with an occupation's core skills, and thus follow a similar logic to identifying certain key tools for blue-collar skills. In recent years, the definition of different levels of programming work has played an important part in regulating the boundary between skilled blue collar and technicians' work in relation to new technology.

Although the term 'job territory' avoids the blue-collar connotations of 'tools of the trade', it has some disadvantages because of an apparent similarity with the notion of the work post as a grouping of tasks. Under the training approach, a job territory's key operations are determined in relation to training and skill needs rather than complementarities in production, and so usually, but not necessarily, it relates to an occupational job territory. While 'occupational job territory' avoids this confusion, its initials are shared with another key concept, 'on-the-job training' (OJT), which has squatters' rights. Another reason is to avoid the impression that the notion of job territory is dependent upon the prior existence of occupational labour markets. The term 'job territory' itself has a long pedigree in job regulation under the training approach (e.g. Perlman, 1928), and is applicable to both blue- and white-collar professional work.[10] The 'tools of the trade' rule is therefore a particularly famous example of the 'job territory' rule, and illustrates its application to blue-collar work. Because 'job territory' also has wider connotations, it is often coupled with 'tools of the trade' in this and later chapters, although this may sometimes appear a little cumbersome.

The 'work post' and 'job territory' rules have attracted a great deal of criticism in recent years as obstacles to greater efficiency, largely because of the difficulties of adapting them to the more variable work demands associated with new technology and team-working. Otherwise, both models have provided very effective frameworks for workplace cooperation. Slichter *et al.* (1960) and Jacoby (1985) for the US, and Mottez (1966) for France, identified the gains of greater workplace order and cooperation resulting from the introduction of work post systems, replacing the 'drive system', which contained many elements of spot negotiations over short-term work assignments. Likewise, the 'tools of the trade' criterion can promote orderly task allocations in the workplace, as is well-illustrated by the Webbs' study of their workings in late-nineteenth-century British industry (Webb and Webb, 1902), and more recently by Eldridge (1968). Similarly, Zweig (1951), in his survey of 'restrictive work practices' in British industry, found that very often employers believed there were valuable compensating advantages of greater workplace order:

... but even if rules involve a certain sacrifice of production by restricting freedom of enterprise, they offer valuable compensation which finds expression in stability and continuity of production without disturbances. (Zweig, 1951: 25)

Indeed, Prais (1981: 57), a well-known student of British productivity problems, has cautioned against too rapid condemnation of skill demarcations as a cause of low productivity. In the presence of skill shortages, they help to ensure that skilled labour is used mostly on the tasks for which it has been trained.

3.3. Competence rank

The attraction of the task-centred rules is that they establish clear and direct limits to employees' obligations. In contrast, function-centred rules provide only an indirect guide to work allocation, and, at first sight, look very like the solution considered but rejected as untenable by Simon (1951): that the parties should agree a wage and then let the employer select tasks according to its needs. The reason, as discussed in the previous chapter, was that there appeared to be no means of preventing the employer from then selecting tasks that maximized its own utility rather than the joint utility of both parties. If that were so, workers would have little or no incentive to accept an employment relationship. A closer examination of systems with more flexible job boundaries reveals other more subtle means of limiting employees' work obligations by relying on procedures that regulate the distribution of work within groups. The competence ranking procedure is one such rule within the production approach to work organization.

Given the production approach, vocational qualifications will be a poor guide to work assignments. There is a need for a principle that is internal to the workplace and internal to the functions provided. A common solution within the production approach has been some kind of status seniority system to rank workers. This can reduce competition between members of a work group which might otherwise get in the way of cooperation. Although pure seniority may work well with clearly prescribed work roles for which management has assumed the job of coordinator, it is less effective when cooperation within the group depends upon positive action by its members. Under a competence ranking system, status depends upon the range and depth of competencies mastered by individual workers. Workers are guided as to expected task assignments by the rule that more difficult and demanding tasks will go to higher-ranking workers. Rank also serves as a guide to the expected flow of training, with higher-ranking workers helping train more junior ones, and the latter accepting their position in the expectation that they will some day rise to a higher rank. Two outwardly visible indicators can assist workers in judging the fairness of work assignments: seniority, which is correlated with average competence levels; and rank, which reflects the recognized competencies against which actual task assignments can be judged. Together, these give structure and predictability to work roles while at the same time allowing a greater degree of flexibility in task assignments than does the work post rule.

Koike (1997) has argued that the 'competence rank' rule may be further reinforced by the additional flexibility it gives employers and the greater autonomy it gives workers as compared with the work post rule. He argues that it can provide enough structure to enable workers to function in semi-autonomous groups, which enhances their ability to tackle unusual tasks and work-related problem-solving activities, and so increases the depth and breadth of skills that they acquire through OJT. Both workers and employers may benefit from this, provided they can maintain a cooperative relationship.

Such positive gains come with a risk. The work post system offers employers a safety net should cooperation break down: they have a clearly defined minimum level of cooperation that is prescribed. With the diffuse job boundaries of the competence rank system there is no such safety net. If cooperation breaks down, it is hard for management to identify any particular individual who is responsible, and there is no clear specification of duties that can be used to draw the line collectively. Thus, if management were to assign tasks in a way that maximized its own gains at the expense of worker preferences, and in doing so undermined workplace cooperation, the consequences would be far more serious than when it has easily enforceable job descriptions. In this way, the ranking system enables workers to accept greater flexibility in management's right to assign tasks while at the same time feeling sufficiently protected against possible abuse. As with riding a bicycle, stability depends on continued forward movement.

3.4. Qualification rule

The 'qualification' rule exemplifies a function-centred rule within the training approach. It sets task assignments by identifying the competencies required for certain kinds of work and then assigning them to workers on the basis of recognized qualifications. Such recognition may be conferred by formal agreement or convention, or it may rest on peer group custom.

The training approach means that work has been organized according to skill requirements. These will often shape the definition of functions, for example, determining whether some maintenance operations are treated as belonging to a separate maintenance function or to be integrated into production. Organizing work around functions rather than individual tasks gives management more freedom over work assignments, especially for incidental tasks that do not belong to a skill's core competence, but which cannot easily

be assigned to other workers without loss of efficiency. If tackling a maintenance job means doing a bit of minor carpentry and a bit of simple fitting in
order to carry out a key electrical repair, then taking the function-centred
approach means assigning these tasks to the same skilled worker rather than
insisting that all those whose tools are used should be present. Of course, there
is always a point beyond which 'simple' skilled tasks require skilled judgement,
but if the key priority is that the function should be carried out efficiently, then
this can often be assessed by skilled workers and their supervisors.

The key to this more flexible rule lies in the process of skill recognition,
and the identification of appropriate work in different workplace functions.
On the whole, the link is better assured by skills involving some form of
workplace traineeship than by vocational qualifications obtained away from
the workplace. The traineeships thus provide the procedures by which different kinds of workers can be identified and work distributed.

There are two reasons for this. First, the traineeship brings an important
element of practical experience which is costly to acquire and is missing
from school-based qualifications. For reasons discussed in Chapter 8, outside the public sector it has always been hard for workers, as indeed for
state-educational institutions, to get formal qualifications accepted in the
workplace. This therefore usually rules out formal educational qualifications
as providing a suitable basis for regulating work assignments. Qualifications
based on workplace traineeships overcome the problem of work experience,
and they also bring a very important element of socialization to workplace
norms. Because both workers and managers have learned how they work in
practice, such norms are much more robust and are more easily enforced
should the need arise.

4. HOW EACH RULE DEALS WITH DIFFERENT KINDS OF OPPORTUNISM

Both firms and workers often invest a great deal in the employment relationship, and finding alternative workers with the right skills or finding alternative jobs in which one can use one's skills may be difficult. As a result,
there is plenty of scope for one or other party to try to better its position by
pressurizing the other into making concessions: the so-called 'hijack problem'. Such opportunistic behaviour is made all the more possible because of
the large tacit element in the definition of jobs and the considerable variation in their content over time, precise information on which is often hard to
obtain. The robustness of these task allocation rules can be assessed in
relation to how well they cope with different types of opportunistic behaviour and so provide sufficient stability to the employment relationship.
Generally, it will be apparent that the two task-centred rules are more robust
than those based on procedures, but at the price of being less flexible.

There are four major areas in which workers and firms derive benefits from the employment relationship, and which could be jeopardized by the unilateral action of the other party. These concern:

- job boundaries and work allocation;
- continuity of employment;
- task variability and 'unusual tasks'; and
- recognition and transmission of skills.

How the four rules deal with opportunism arising in these four areas is the subject of the coming section. In each case, we start by examining the nature of opportunistic behaviour and then look at how each rule helps to contain it.

4.1. Job boundaries and work allocation

The first question concerns the control of work assignments. Pressures for unilateral addition or subtraction of tasks may come from either party. Employers may seek to impose additional tasks, thus increasing employee workloads: [11] one form of work intensification. Alternatively, workers might seek to improve their job prospects by encroaching on the tasks of other groups. They might also be tempted to do so if that were to bring access to more pleasant or more lucrative tasks. Such tensions can lead to an inefficient pattern of work organization or generate conflict between different groups of workers. In the other direction, unilateral reassignment of tasks can threaten employees' job prospects and their future continuity of employment. By the same token, unilateral refusal to continue to undertake certain tasks by workers can deprive employers of the availability of labour when it is most needed. The problem was well summarized by Slichter *et al.*:

. . . The preoccupation with work assignment among skilled workers is understandable. The introduction of work elements alien to the basic skill threatens the dignity and worth of the job in their opinion, and in the long run this could jeopardise the high rate for the job. By the same token, subtraction of work elements inherent in the job skill could lead to the same results . . . In this connection it should be emphasised that the so-called incidental tasks are the principal cause of work assignment difficulties in large companies. The question of who is entitled to perform or who is obligated to do the fringe tasks not easily identifiable with any given craft continues to be a source of discontent among maintenance crew members. (Slichter *et al.*, 1960: 250–1)

Where work is organized on the basis of work posts, the clear and unambiguous assignment of each task to a different post reduces the scope for such opportunism. The work post establishes clear, individual responsibilities for the execution of certain tasks, and so checks potential moves by employees both to cut tasks from their jobs and to encroach on the tasks of other workers. The clarity of task assignments to work posts enables both management and workers to identify those who are, and those who are not, responsible for certain tasks. The other function of work posts is to establish lines of accountability so that employees' task obligations can be better enforced. It is notable that under many work post systems management have opposed workers assisting each other in the fulfilment of their tasks because this blurs the lines of accountability.[12] The clarity of work assignments protects both parties from unilateral job enlargement and reduction because the demarcation lines have been clearly set out.

In practice, the job descriptions associated with work posts often diverge considerably from the work actually undertaken. There are many reasons for this, ranging from management's desire to adapt swiftly to changing production conditions without rewriting job descriptions at every twist and turn, through to 'drift' in work standards associated with work group bargaining. Often management are aware that a degree of vagueness or generality in job descriptions can be advantageous, and clauses that refer to 'other such duties as may be required from time to time' are common even though it is often not easy to enforce them.[13] However, formal rules, such as job descriptions, do provide a basis for periodic management 'crackdowns' to reign back the drift in the administration of work rules, as observed by Roy (1955) and Burawoy (1979). Likewise, Ribeill (1984) noted that the primary use of formal job descriptions in the French railways was to allocate responsibility.[14] They are less concerned with dictating the content of actual jobs and worker behaviour than preventing the drift from becoming too great, and too unfavourable for either party. In such cases, the formal rules provided a necessary point of reference. Lest it be thought that these operate to protect only management, it should be remembered that the studies of office work by Crozier (1963) and Sainsaulieu (1988) showed how bureaucratic rules could also be used by workers to protect themselves against arbitrary management. More recently, Clark's (1994) study of new work organization patterns with new technology showed that many workers were leery of flexible working because it blurred the lines of accountability, and it was no longer clear where their responsibilities ended.[15]

The 'job territory' rule also gives clear answers. Management knows that if a particular task requires the use of certain tools, then it can be assigned without further negotiation to a particular category of employees, and it knows who is responsible if certain tasks are not performed. As with the 'work post' rule, unilateral reassignment of tasks by either party would upset the equilibrium with other groups. For the employee, the same clarity of the rule makes it difficult for management to reassign and to add tasks unilaterally, thus both parties gain protection against opportunism.

For the two functional rules, the indirect link with work tasks makes monitoring more difficult, and increases the scope for opportunism, but there are compensating mechanisms to hold it in check. Taking first the production approach, assignment of tasks by work function depends upon the internal equilibrium of the work group. The indirect reference to individual work tasks creates scope for jobs with diffuse and overlapping boundaries. This enables great flexibility in allocating tasks to different workers, but at the same time deprives them of any clear reference point limiting their contractual obligations to their employer. There is no longer any unique relationship between individual tasks and individual jobs as under the work post system. How then can the scope of management authority be limited? It is important to remember that the production approach leads to a heavy emphasis on on-the-job training so that the progression of work group members between work assignments within the group enriches their skills. Such a process is facilitated if senior workers teach their junior colleagues the tricks they need to know in order to undertake their work effectively. Thus an exchange can develop between the two groups of workers whereby the former pass their skills and know-how to the latter, provided they respect the established rules of progression through work assignments and thus avoid threatening the position of the 'seniors'. The employer benefits from more flexible working practices and a greater quality of skills so long as it respects the internal norms of the work group over task allocation. In this case, opportunism is controlled by monitoring certain key indicators. For example, the employer's continued commitment to the rule can be signalled by maintaining long-term employment, essential for OJT and job rotation, and by respecting the pay and other norms which sustain the competence rank model. If these are violated, the work group can retaliate by withdrawing cooperation, so that flexible work assignments, which are such a benefit for management, are turned against it, as diffuse job boundaries make it much harder for management to pin down non-performance than under the work post system.

The last of the four rules, combining the training and the functional approaches, also involves an indirect link between tasks and jobs, and so also supports a more flexible system of work allocation than the 'job territory' rule. In contrast to the 'competence rank' rule, this one centres most commonly on occupational skills which guide the allocation of work. The clear identification of such skills has a double function. It facilitates investment in such skills by workers because the skill's identity shapes its labour market, and most important in the present context, it serves as a well-recognized guide to the allocation of work. A job can be constituted as management thinks best, but if it involves core skilled tasks then it should go to someone of the appropriate skill (v. Meil, 1994).

The price mechanism helps to ensure the system's solidity by discouraging employers from regularly assigning unskilled tasks to skilled workers. The clear labelling of skills by qualifications and their associated training procedures, which is absent under the production approach, enables skilled workers to identify easily who should receive the skilled rate of pay, whatever the tasks on which they may be currently engaged. Thus, they are able to control task assignments effectively by making it more expensive for the employer to assign them to a whole range of lower-valued tasks.

4.2. Continuity of employment

Continuity of employment is of great benefit to both parties in the employment relationship. Workers gain from the continuity of activity and income it affords, whereas employers benefit from the availability of labour when needed. Two main sources of opportunism and conflict are common in this area, notably, use of task reallocation to cut jobs, and use of the tacit element in job definitions to restrict the availability of labour to undertake certain tasks. Generally, the two concerns vary inversely over the business cycle, as does their value to either party. Continuous employment is of greatest value to workers during recession (Leighton, 1983), and availability of labour is of most value to employers during a boom.

The two task-centred rules protect short-run employment levels by making it harder for employers to redistribute work unilaterally. Faced with a fall in demand, the employer may well wish to enlarge some individual work posts in order to dispense with others completely. Slichter *et al.* (1960: 251–2) stressed that 'concern with work jurisdiction will be greatest and certainly most widespread when job opportunities are low'. Likewise, 'tools of the trade' rules have often been seen as 'make work' rules in times of job cuts (Eldridge, 1968). The effect of such measures is to oblige firms to 'hoard' labour in times of recession (Bowers *et al.*, 1982). The same concerns explain why workers have been leery of 'polyvalence', or the ability to undertake a number of different work posts, in environments with work post systems (Maurice *et al.*, 1986: 67). Polyvalence, often introduced to help cope with absenteeism, makes it easier for employers to cover unfilled vacancies, and so makes the demand for labour more variable. By limiting employers' ability to redistribute work, they also limit their ability to use the threat of dismissal to impose changes in terms of employment. For employers, the main benefit from the two task-centred rules concerns the continued availability of labour. The very clarity of work post job descriptions provides them with a minimum set of tasks on which there already exists clear agreement, even though there may still be disputes of interpretation.

The two procedure-centred rules, in theory, give employers a freer hand in task allocation that they could use to cut jobs more severely in a recession. However, under both the 'competence rank' and the 'qualification' rules, several factors are likely to restrain them. First, it may damage the environment of flexible working, and given the absence of the safety net provided by precise job descriptions, employers may feel that the stakes are too high. In addition, the competence rank system relies on progression between ranks over time, and depends on long-term employment. With the 'qualification' rule, the possession of an occupational skill means workers can quit if their employer looks like offering employment less stable than that elsewhere, so a degree of reciprocity is possible: if workers believe their employer will keep them on during a recession, they are more likely to stay during a boom.

4.3. Unusual tasks and task variability

'Unusual' tasks generally arise as unexpected production problems or consumer demands emerge, and they give rise to problem-solving activities (Koike and Inoki, 1990). Their quantitative importance is hard to gauge, but a number of job analysts have long argued that they are becoming more important as routine tasks become embodied in technology (e.g. Davis, 1971; Lawler, 1994), and workers have increasingly to respond to the remaining unanticipated problems. Their significance is now widely recognized. On the positive side, they are a source of problem-solving activities, and hence of incremental improvements in workers' skills, productivity and quality (Koike and Inoki, 1990). On the negative side for management, they can be a source of information asymmetry, and so threaten management control even in environments where workplace unionism is weak. Of the four types of rules, the two task-centred ones generally provide less satisfactory solutions than the two function-centred ones.

The 'work post' rule offers three broad strategies for dealing with unusual tasks: new rules may be set; polyvalence may be encouraged, both of which may deal with how the work should be allocated; and management may intervene directly in the problem-solving activities itself, thus limiting potential information asymmetries. Setting new rules and clarifying existing ones is not wholly satisfactory. This often leads to even more unwieldy sets of work rules.[16] Establishing special polyvalent posts for workers able to cover a variety of different work stations enables adaptation to unanticipated demands without disrupting the established work posts, which can thus retain their close identification with precise job descriptions. Potential disruption to the established task allocations is confined to a special category of polyvalents whose workload can be monitored by all parties. However, the status of polyvalent workers and their posts is often problematic (Maurice *et al.*, 1986). It is in the interest of other workers that their number should remain limited to protect the integrity of the work post system, and this puts a potential brake on the amount of flexibility that may be obtained. It also restricts the ability to deal with unusual tasks whose content and demands cannot be anticipated.

The third solution is direct and extensive management intervention in problem-solving activities. This helps management to keep tighter control over the work system and limits potential information asymmetries, but at the cost of depriving workers of much incentive to tackle unusual tasks. Thus, although the work post system limits many of the informational problems associated with task variability and unusual tasks, it does so at the cost of heavy management intervention, and a strong division between tasks of conception and those of execution.

The 'competence rank' rule offers a different approach to unusual tasks. Because it avoids close identification of individual workers for task assignments, and encourages job rotation, unusual tasks do not disturb work allocations so much as offer scope for their enrichment and for new learning opportunities (Koike and Inoki, 1990). The risk management takes is that much useful knowledge will reside with the work group and could potentially be used against it. Hence, the importance of work group organization, and the ranking system. Management can gain a measure of control through staff appraisals by line managers, and can use this to govern the rate of progression between ranks. However, if the progression were to slow too much it would lose its incentive effect, which would be particularly dangerous because this rule lacks the safety net provided by the explicit job descriptions of the work post system.

The 'job territory' rule deals with unusual tasks and potential information asymmetries in a different way. By focusing on attributes of tasks rather than on the tasks themselves, unusual tasks can be allocated according to the tools and materials used. Where ambiguous answers are given because the unusual or new tasks involve several sets of tools, or where new tools do not fit neatly into existing categories, then the rule still indicates the skill groups between which a solution has to be found. A good historical example was given in the previous chapter with the question of allocating new work in ship-fitting between plumbers and engineers. In more recent times, similar issues have arisen over the allocation of simple programming work on machine tools. The main drawback of the 'job territory' rule in dealing with unusual tasks lies in the number of specialist trades that may be involved if the rule is applied strictly, and the effect on productivity. Although workers are often quite flexible (e.g. Jürgens *et al.*, 1993: ch. 6), this always runs the risk of undermining the rule's integrity, and one's ability to enforce it at a later date.

Under the 'qualification rule', the anchoring of worker competencies in their previous basic training means that unusual tasks will have less effect upon the subsequent development of their skills. As a result, these should remain more transparent to management and workers alike, affording fewer occasions for opportunistic behaviour. Because tasks are assigned by skill and not made dependent on the use of certain tools, there can be greater variety in problem-solving, and more flexible use of labour. In particular, there is correspondingly less threat to the integrity of the allocation rule by workers behaving flexibly.

Whereas the 'job territory' rule gives a rather static definition of skill, and so provides little incentive to develop OJT by tackling unusual tasks, the situation with the 'qualification' rule is rather different. There, the skill categories signal previously acquired training rather than competencies with certain tools and materials, so that there is less of a problem if unusual tasks lead to the development of new competencies that lie outside the core skills and involve new tools or materials. Thus the workers concerned have a stronger incentive to tackle unusual tasks in a constructive way than under either of the task-centred rules, so enriching the gains to the employer from the employment relationship. As with the 'competence rank' rule, the greatest protection against opportunism stems from the desire to maintain the gains from controlled flexibility, rather than from the defensive protections of the task-centred rules.

4.4. The recognition and transmission of skills

Two major concerns of workers and management are the recognition of skills applied on the job and establishing conditions under which experienced workers will agree to transmit their skills to new workers. Both of these need to be resolved if workers' competencies and employers' job demands are to evolve together over time.

Earlier, it was noted that the priority given to complementarities in production means that job contents under the production approach tend to be heterogeneous, with the result that OJT plays a central role in skill formation. Because so much of OJT is tacit and uncodified, the recognition of skills it creates can be very problematic. The basis on which workers may claim higher status or pay, and on which they can seek skill development and progression by OJT, is less certain than it is with the training approach, where skills are more amenable to certification. It might be argued that this is unimportant if the employer has assumed all the costs of investment in such OJT, but the arguments for employers to link the accumulation of OJT to rising pay profiles are strong: at the very least, to offer workers an incentive to stay with the firm usually implies their sharing of some investment costs. But if the nature of the skills developed is hard to define, and the employer refuses to recognize them subsequently, workers may find it hard to defend their claim to pay and skill progression.

The 'work post' rule provides a solution to skill recognition in two ways: through stability of task allocations associated with each post and by providing a common language for describing competencies. Rather than define their competencies in relation to diplomas or formal training, they may do so by reference to the job they normally undertake and its position in the firm's job classification. This establishes contours of equivalence between jobs, and it bears the stamp of management recognition (see Chapter 4).

The effect of these conventions can be seen when management tries to move away from the work post to more skills-based classifications (Dugué, 1994). In her study, employees were very concerned about the lack of objective reference for their skills which management defined in terms of such traits as 'adaptability' and 'polyvalence' instead of the technical demands of their jobs. The latter gave workers a clear understanding of the competencies valued by management. However, the task variability required by the new work system deprived jobs of a stable set of technical demands with which OJT skills could be identified. Although management promised 'careers' based on changing functional demands, the workers feared the loss of an objective criterion for their skill and were suspicious of management's control over the recognition and measurement of skills. They also feared that other employers would be even less likely to recognize their skills than they would be under the work post system.

For skill transmission, OJT relies heavily on the willingness of experienced workers to share their knowledge. As the workers in Burawoy's (1979) Illinois workshop insisted: 'one does not have to "show everything" to a new employee'. Withholding such information enabled experienced workers to ensure that they retained access to the best jobs, but it also provided protection against others passing on such information to management. Fear that other employees might learn by observation meant that 'operators on lathes often changed their set-ups before the end of the shift so that the following operator could not exploit their ingenuity' (105). Significantly, senior workers only shared some of their knowledge with Burawoy himself when they felt they could trust him, and that he would not compete for their work.[17] The work post system provides a partial solution to these problems by providing a framework for organizing job progression, and within which seniority can protect experienced workers from competition from new recruits.

Under the 'competence rank' rule, jobs lack the distinct identity given by the precise job descriptions of the 'work post' rule, and so it might seem bereft of any way of dealing with skill recognition. Senior workers lack the protection of clearly defined posts and junior workers lack the visible sign of progression between tasks that might encourage them to learn. Without a clear job structure, seniority has nothing on which to bind.

One of the most important protections of the competence rank model is the ranking process itself. This is the outward visible sign of management's recognition of worker competencies. As it is linked to appraisal, workers can compare their own rank with that of colleagues engaged in tasks of similar complexity, and with a similar position in their work group. In some firms, according to Koike (1997), this may be formalized into a 'job grade matrix' which makes public the range and difficulty of tasks management credits that individual workers are able to achieve. This gives them a further check on the rank they have reached. The 'competence rank' rule also protects senior workers who share knowledge with junior ones, as the status difference makes the category of worker assigned to particular kinds of work visible for all to see. It also provides an incentive to junior workers to accept training and not to compete with senior workers because the ranking system establishes a queue. If they spend too long in a junior position, they have a standard by which this can be judged. Finally, management obtains some guarantee of reasonable effort by linking pay to rank, and progression between ranks to appraisal. The practice of job rotation gives employees knowledge of each other's jobs and enables them to judge how far their own job abilities match those of their colleagues in a similar rank. A final incentive in the system is the employer's commitment to long-term employment. The 'competence-ranking' rule is a dynamic one resting on accumulation and development of competencies over time. Because pay and rank depend on service, such incentives could not function without an implied promise of long-term employment.

Turning to the two training approach rules, training for 'whole role' skills is considerably more transparent than piecemeal OJT, and the skills acquired under the training approach are potentially far more marketable. Workers gain by virtue of having more widely recognized skills, and employers no longer depend on their own senior workers to transmit skills because they can always recruit externally. The wider recognition and external market do however open up other problems dealt with in more detail in Chapter 8. These concern the viability of training for transferable skills, and the problems of poaching if training costs are shared between employers and trainees. For workers to invest, there needs to be some assurance that there will be appropriate job vacancies at the end. Both of the training approach rules provide an important guarantee, identifying which tasks appropriately trained workers may expect to undertake.[18] They also protect them against some forms of employer opportunism. For example, some employers may wish to use cheaper, partially trained, labour for some skilled tasks, and so erode the demand for skilled labour. However, if such tasks involve use of certain tools of the trade, then skilled workers can easily monitor any attempts at this kind of substitution. The 'qualification' rule provides similar, albeit less precise, guarantees. However, there is a grey area in which some skilled tasks are routine and can be learned by experience rather than formal training. There, the scope for substitution can be considerable.

Some form of regulation is also needed to protect skilled workers from competition from the trainees to whom they pass their knowledge. An interesting example of the breakdown of such relations is provided in Taira's account of craft training in Japan in the inter-war period, which is cited in the previous chapter. At that time craftsmen took little interest in the welfare of their apprentices, and the latter sought to 'steal' their skill, and set up in competition (Taira, 1970: 110). Both rules provide some protection. The clearly defined status of skills and trainees helps to prevent employers from assigning the latter to unrelated unskilled work, as this would not involve use of the critical tools. For skilled tasks, the problem is more tricky, but some check is given by the dependence of such training on the willingness of experienced workers, and supervisors drawn from the same trade, to provide instruction. Thus, both of the training approach rules provide employees with important and robust task identification rules that can be applied across a wide variety of workplaces. They also provide a number of protections to employers, in particular those funding training for occupational skills; this is discussed in Chapter 8.

To bring together the main strands of this rather complex analysis, the ways in which each type of allocation rule deals with the main forms of opportunistic behaviour are summarized in Table 2.2. What it shows is that the transaction rules are able to provide a relatively stable framework within

Table 2.2. *Summary of how the rules cope with different types of opportunism*

Area of possible opportunism	Work post (WP)	Job territory (JT)/tools of trade (TT)	Competence rank	Qualification rule
Work assignments & job boundaries	Regulated by task description of job	Tasks allocated by tools, materials, or types of operation	Ranking system stabilizes task allocations	Skill categories used to allocate work
Employment continuity:				
Task reallocation to cut jobs	Jobs protected by difficulty of redistributing tasks unilaterally		Ranking system implies long-term employment	Skill categories limit reallocation, but less than TT
Task availability	Clarity of rules gives employers greater certainty			Guidance from level in rank
Given by skill categories				
Unusual tasks:				
Allocation of tasks and related OJT	Restricted by WP rule, but a threat to stability and codification	Controlled by JT rule. Enables limited response, cost in productivity	Acceptance given by incentives for OJT in ranking system	Primacy of training in categories → incentives to develop OJT within skill categories
Information asymmetry	Limited by clarity of post and management control	Scope limited by task identification rule	Potential great, but rank guides to location of competencies and gives incentive for information sharing	Reduced by transparency of skill categories
Skill formation:				
Skill recognition	Focus provided by WPs	Tied to JT	Occurs within ranking system	Given by skill category
Transmission of skills	Local monopolies over job knowledge eased by progression	TT identify work and so limit substitution by trainees and SSK. Tension on cost sharing	Senior workers protected by ranking system	Clear trainee status limits substitution

Key: WP, work post; JT, job territory; TT, tools of the trade; SSK, semi-skilled; OJT, on-the-job training.

which workers and firms may organize the employment relationship, and in which each has sufficient guarantees against opportunistic behaviour by the other parties to consider it a worthwhile arrangement.

5. CONCLUSION

This chapter has established that there are four main types of transaction rule capable of limiting management's authority over work assignments sufficiently to make employment attractive to workers. It was argued that these four types form an exhaustive typology of such rules because they satisfy the necessary and sufficient conditions for a viable employment relationship. They represent efficient and enforceable solutions to providing flexible but limited scope for management to specify the full content of an employee's contractual obligations *ex post*. A large part of this chapter was devoted to showing how the four types of rules control common kinds of opportunism surrounding the supply of labour services and therefore are sufficiently robust to provide the necessary guarantees to firms and workers for them to adopt the employment contract.

We can say that firms and workers confront a fixed menu of viable options for organizing the employment relationship. This is a first step towards to understanding societal diversity in employment relations, but we need still to understand how such rules may spread across an economy, and why the same sectors should often be governed by different rules in different countries. To do this, we need to explore the forces for diffusion as a result of decentralized choices made by firms and workers, and how these are reinforced by the action of labour market institutions, which is done in the next two chapters.

ENDNOTES

[1] A interesting example of complementarities within the 'production approach' is that of cherry pickers and cherry selectors (Lazear, 1995). The grower wishes to maximize the net value of the crop of cherries, whereas the cherry pickers may wish to maximize the weight of cherries picked per day. There is then a potential divergence of interest as the pickers maximize their income by picking only the easiest cherries. But this reduces the yield per tree for the grower. Because the grower does not know the state of the crop of each tree, it might be thought advantageous to employ specialist fruit 'spotters'. However, Lazear argues that the gains from the complementarities are probably such as to outweigh the potential losses from this kind of divergence of interest, hence the rarity of specialist cherry spotters.

[2] Lazear (1995, pp. 86 ff.) has an interesting discussion of the job as a set of tasks.

What he calls the 'production approach' is to define the job as a collection of tasks, based on a partitioning of the firm's production technology. Complementarity of tasks, he argues, explains why professors do both teaching and research, and why the tasks of fruit spotting and fruit picking are done by the same individuals, even though different problems of output monitoring apply between the two tasks. An interesting constraint on this has been posed by Holmstrom and Milgrom (1991), who argue that, under certain kinds of incentive scheme, jobs should not contain tasks that differ greatly in the degree to which their performance can be monitored. Otherwise, employees have an incentive to neglect those tasks whose performance is hardest to monitor.

[3] The detail of some of the replies to Taylor's questionnaire is of some interest. Engineers and systems analysts were asked to rank seven considerations in dividing up work among employees so that they could achieve the greatest quality at lowest cost. Maximizing throughput per unit of time was ranked first, and efficient use of machinery second. Third was making machines perform as simple tasks as possible (fourth for systems engineers), and fourth was reducing manpower. Job satisfaction came sixth. In combining tasks into jobs, first came 'assign each employee one particular set of tasks as a full-time job', and second, 'assign each one particular task'. Lower down the ranking came ideas of job rotation and holistic jobs.

[4] One consequence of stressing production complementarities is likely to be great heterogeneity of task contents between jobs. This was noted in French firms using the production approach to the design of work posts by Maurice *et al.* (1982: 164): 'On several occasions, we have stressed the importance assumed, in the French firms, by the heterogeneity of work posts and of the tasks actually undertaken.' They also characterized the work post as 'an aggregation of tasks sharing a certain level of technical demands' ('un aggrégat de tâches ayant une certaine technicité') (p. 124).

[5] McKersie and Hunter (1973: 345–6) signal the relevance of this distinction in their study of productivity bargaining in Britain compared with the US. Inspired by Stinchcombe's (1959) contrast between administrative and craft systems, they wrote: 'If, from a theoretical point of view, work can be organised either according to management principles of engineering economy or according to established occupational lines, then the craft system represents the most notable example of the latter approach. The essential feature of a craft-type occupational system is that each single craft maintains a considerable degree of autonomy in regulating the standards and conditions for the performance of particular tasks. The base of this autonomy is the skill and specific knowledge required to perform the tasks. Since it usually takes considerable time and effort to become proficient in performing such tasks, it is more economical to grant monopoly over the service to a certain group which, in return, guarantees certain standards of performance by apprenticeship, certification and self-supervision. The administrative system . . . rather than allowing job design to be determined by occupational definitions existing in the local labour market, management packages job duties based on technology, scale of operations, and other economic considerations internal to the firm.'

[6] 'The job structures and the skill demands in each firm on a particular labour market correspond to occupational qualifications. In the ideal case, the firm's division of labour and occupational boundaries should match completely. Changes in the job contents of an occupation must be coordinated: among employers as among workers in each occupational market, and in each of the individual firms involved in that particular market.' (Translated by the author from Sengenberger, 1987: 126.)

[7] A telling example of this is given in Lam's (1992) study of work relations in a large Japanese department store. When the annual bonus was announced, there were different rates for the regular and non-regular employees, and this was commonly a cause of tension.

[8] If P is a necessary and sufficient condition for Q, then so too is Q for P. Therefore, if a second condition, R, is also a necessary and sufficient condition for Q then P is also a necessary and sufficient condition for R, and so R can be subsumed in P (Lemmon, 1965).

[9] The concern that if duties are minutely specified employees may refuse to undertake those that are not specified has a long history. In determining the job specifications of clerks in the US State Department in 1835/36, the Secretary of State added the qualification: 'Notwithstanding the foregoing partial distribution of duties, each clerk will from time to time perform such other duties as the public service may render necessary and as shall be directed by the Secretary.' Congress 1, session H, doc. 247, cited in Betters (1931: 5).

[10] The term 'job territory' was popularized by Perlman's (1928) account of craft union principles in the US. Job territories were identified by certain kinds of work that belonged to certain occupations. The 'tools of the trade' has been a common rule to identify such work.

[11] Recent work on functional flexibility in banking in Britain and France has illustrated how increased functional flexibility may often be a form of work intensification rather than enrichment, especially if the additional tasks that workers are expected to undertake are of limited skill content (O'Reilly, 1992).

[12] Several writers have commented on the frequent and long-established ban on production workers helping each other with their work: Cole (1979: 233) mentions this, as do Roethlisberger and Dickson (1939: 505).

[13] Slichter et al. (1960: 252) mention this.

[14] Some very interesting examples of such localized cooperation to ease the rigidities of centralized formal rules can be found in Ribeill's (1984) study of French railway workers. 'Safety regulations, in particular, represent a tangle of overlapping rules, to be followed sometimes as alternatives sometimes in sequence, intended to deal with all possible circumstances, and thought out a priori on the basis of an abstract technical rationality. . . One may wonder at the usefulness of a system of rules that is customarily infringed . . . The rules serve less to define norms and actual practices than to allocate responsibility when things go wrong or there is an incident or an accident.' (pp. 25–6 and 36–8, translated by the author). D'Iribarne's (1989) workplace study notes similar application of responsibilities and management intervention in breakdown. Roy (1955) cites examples of foremen ignoring management's rules 'to keep the boys on production' and 'to get the work out'.

[15] Formal job descriptions may also provide workers with some protection against arbitrary management action in the event of crackdowns. In a study of British workers in plants using 'full flexibility', Clark (1994) found that many workers (and managers) in fact wanted 'ownership' of tasks so that workers knew for what they were to be held responsible.

[16] An interesting example in a closely related area arises from the current debate in France stimulated by Alain Supiot's critique of the attempts to make French employment law more flexible. He argues this has been sought by increasing the number of exceptions to the general legal principles of the employment contract, for example, special employment and training contracts for young workers, special

contracts for other categories and so on. Far from making the law more flexible, the additional distinctions have in fact made it more complex and harder to enforce, and they have not achieved the desired goal of increasing employment (Le Monde, 26.6.96, 'Le niveau de protection juridique n'aurait pas de corrélation avec l'état de l'emploi').

[17] Burawoy (1979) gives some very good examples of this from the Illinois company in which he and Roy before him had worked. By Burawoy's time, workers had become more leery of sharing knowledge in case they should lose overtime opportunities. Without that help it was hard for them to make out. In addition, workers took care with whom they shared knowledge, as his experience with relations between shifts illustrates. Apart from competition between workers, an additional fear was that one could not trust other workers to exercise discretion and keep such ingenuity secret from management, which would then adjust work times.

[18] Some of the employers interviewed by Zweig (1951) replied that they saw the associated demarcation rules as a natural extension of apprenticeship training, and that the training system and the work areas were mutually reinforcing.

3

Diffusion and Predominance of Employment Rules

1. INTRODUCTION

The argument so far has established that the four types of transaction rule are fundamental to the employment relationship. They are constitutive rules in the sense that without them there would be no lasting agreement between firms and workers to cooperate in this way: as employers and employees. However, the argument so far has been essentially static, and gives no clue as to their genesis and to the forces sustaining their diffusion. This chapter looks at how such rules can emerge out of a system of uncoordinated, decentralized decision-making by the actors. First, it looks at how the four transaction rules can emerge and prevail over two alternative modes of contracting as a kind of middle way between very detailed and very diffuse specification of employees' duties. Then it looks at how one type of rule can come to prevail over the three others in a given context. There is a partial analogy with the notion of 'evolutionarily stable strategy' that Maynard Smith (1982) developed to explain the emergence and prevalence of territorial rules among many species of animals. Such patterns of behaviour are neither dictated by central authority nor enforced by collective institutions. They emerge out of repeated interaction among animals of the same species as a rule that maximizes their collective survival chances. A very important element in human behaviour, which may or may not be present among animals, is that we learn interaction rules, both in how to behave ourselves and in how to interpret and respond to the behaviour of others. Thus a key aspect of any evolutionarily stable strategy in the employment arena is that once a particular rule has become widespread, it is easier to predict how others will behave. A widely diffused and well-tested rule is one we can trust, and as a result, whatever its intrinsic merits for a particular business, our choice of rule will be influenced by the choices of others. In this way, one can explain why the four types of rule are so widespread within and between countries even in the absence of collective coordination.

At the same time, the rules' effectiveness can be greatly enhanced by the support of collective institutions, such as employer and labour organizations. In brief, such institutions can make the rules more robust, enable greater flexibility of application and provide a framework for renegotiation when necessary. Finally, as the book is about the micro foundations of societal diversity, we need to examine the scope of these collective institutions, and how they mesh in with other social institutions. How do employment systems grow up from the four types of employment transaction rules? This question is introduced at the end of this chapter and then is taken further in the next with the discussion of job and pay classification systems, which, it will be argued, are one of the key mechanisms through which the rules are extended across labour markets.

2. TASK ALLOCATION RULES AS PARTIAL 'EVOLUTIONARILY STABLE STRATEGIES'

In order to show the transaction rules as partial 'evolutionarily stable strategies', we need to see how they can develop as a more stable and effective framework for cooperation than their main rivals: highly detailed contract specification and heavy reliance upon diffuse cooperation. In his classic study of trust in workplace relations, Fox (1974) identified these as the 'low-trust' and 'high-trust' strategies.

The first of these, the 'low-trust–low-discretion' strategy, is an extension of a common response to perceived opportunism in contractual relations: to tighten up the specification of services to be provided so that the agent has less discretion and hence less scope for cheating. Fox characterizes the work roles when this strategy is pursued as consisting of five related elements, of which the first is the key:

- workers perceive management as behaving as if it believes that they cannot be trusted, of their own volition, to deliver desired work performance, and hence;
- there is specific definition of job activities and close supervision;
- coordination of activities among workers is constrained by standardized rules and routines;
- failures draw punishment because they are presumed to stem from careless indifference to job rules and organizational goals; and
- conflict with superiors is handled by bargaining of an adversarial nature.

Fox saw this as developing into a spiral of low trust relations, or 'syndrome' as he preferred to call it. The same elements are present in Williamson's (1975) account of sequential spot contracting and contingent claims contracts. With the first, work is organized as a series of discrete contracts for specified services, each of which has to be negotiated afresh, and with the second, all the contingencies have to be recognized and specified *ex ante*. The complexities and arm's length nature of both make them ripe for opportunistic behaviour.

Heavy reliance on diffuse contracts is the other pole, and is analogous to both Fox's 'high-trust' strategy and Simon's (1951) account of the authority relation in employment: the extent of the employee's obligations is left unclear, and the employer is trusted to maximize joint welfare and not just its own.

The emergence of the employment transaction rules in relation to the other two strategies is illustrated in Figures 3.1–3.3. If we consider the low-trust path, greater specification of employment obligations, for example in the form of more-detailed job descriptions, will initially lead to gains from closer definition of performance and reduced scope for opportunism. Beyond a certain point these will begin to level off as the easiest moves by the other party are closed off, as shown in the upper curve of Figure 3.1. Against these, we have to set the costs of greater specification, initially low, but later rising sharply as detailed job descriptions inhibit the flexible deployment of labour. A major cause of the rising cost is the difficulty of adapting increasingly rigid jobs to unanticipated events: markets vary, technology breaks down, people fall sick and so on. Ironically, the more complex the rules governing work allocation become, the more prone they are to manipulation, as Sainsaulieu (1988) found. In addition, beyond a certain point, increased codification will distort job performance towards those elements that are most easily defined. Milgrom and Roberts (1992) prove what was intuitively known by many practitioners, that tying incentives to measurable aspects of work will bias employee performance towards those and away from more qualitative ones.[1] Thus we see the net benefits to greater specification rising then levelling off, and its costs rising slowly at first, and then steeply giving rise to net benefits from specification that follow an inverted U-curve, as shown in Figure 3.2.

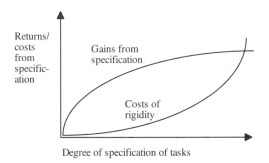

Fig. 3.1. Gains and costs of increasing specification of tasks

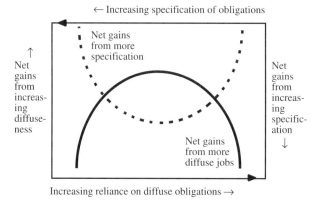

Fig. 3.2. **Net gains from increasing specification or diffuseness of employment obligations**

Likewise, taking the high-trust path, initially, diffuse job boundaries, combined with trust relations, bring about growing functional flexibility. However, beyond a certain point this exceeds the employer's need for flexibility as the finite breadth of employee skills limits how far they may be assigned to different work. On the cost side, the further diffuse job boundaries are taken, the more vulnerable cooperation is to breakdown under pressure of unanticipated shocks.[2] In a capitalist market economy, employers and employees know that their interests partly converge and partly diverge. As markets are subject to unanticipated variations, it is often not possible to guarantee reciprocity. A firm may promise not to lay people off after agreeing to a programme of work organization reforms, but then find market conditions prevent it from honouring its word. Of course, all are aware of such risks, but the problem is how to convince the other party of one's good faith given that the same information may be used strategically. As the number of shocks increases over time, it becomes increasingly hard to convince the other party that there has been genuine force of circumstances, so that trust becomes increasingly fragile, and with it, the possibility of operating with very diffuse employment obligations. Thus, the gains from relying increasingly on diffuse jobs and cooperation follow a similar path to those of relying on increasing specification of duties.

The net gains from increasing specification and from increasingly diffuse jobs both follow an inverted U-curve, and are superimposed in Figure 3.2. The area of overlap in the middle shows where a balance between specification and diffuseness may be struck, providing a basis for a stable employment relationship.

If we follow Fox's analysis of trust dynamics, a striking feature is their instability. In particular, once the low-trust cycle sets in, there is little to stop it deepening. Typical causes he cites are external shocks that force manage-

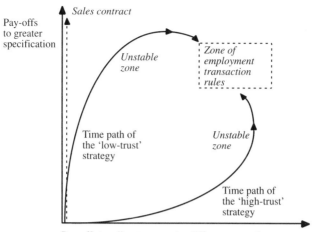

Fig. 3.3. Employment transaction rules as an ESS
Convergence over time of the low- and high-trust strategies towards reliance on transaction rules.

ment to alter its policies in the face of falling market share or technical change. Once the reaction to the shock is perceived by the other party as revealing a lack of goodwill, then a low-trust dynamic is likely to follow as 'tit for tat' cooperation switches into reverse.

Figure 3.3 traces out the working of the two strategies over time as the 'game' of increasing specification or increasing diffuseness is played over successive rounds. The two curves might be thought of as showing the gains to following the low-trust/high-specification, and high-trust/high-diffuseness strategies over time. At first the gains to either rise steeply, as was shown in Figure 3.2, but subsequent gains depend on increasing reliance on elements of the other strategy. As either strategy is pursued over time, in its pure form, it becomes increasing vulnerable to unanticipated shocks. As specification and diffuseness vary inversely, combining them is not stable unless they are brought together within a framework of rules. This is a key factor driving the convergence towards an employment relation regulated by one of the four types of transaction rule.

Taking the first strategy, if one were to seek fuller specification, the most likely outcomes are either a sales contract, and hence no employment relation, or entry into the unstable zone of the employment transaction. Increasingly detailed specification does not solve the problem of giving greater stability to the employment relationship. Instead, it leaves it more vulnerable to unanticipated shocks as there is less built-in flexibility with which to respond.

The problem of unforeseen circumstances can be dealt with by shortening the time horizon of contracting: the shorter the time period, the less difficult it is to anticipate events that will alter job requirements or will affect performance. This pushes one towards ever-shorter contracts, and ultimately to sequential spot contracts in which the parties contract only for the current period's demands. This is very flexible in one respect—adaptability to an employer's changing job demands—but it is also unstable, as Williamson showed, because continuous negotiation increases the incentives to use information strategically and to keep one's options open rather than to commit oneself to a particular employer or group of employees. In effect, the parties are sliding away from an employment contract and towards a sales contract.

The more 'arm's length' the relationship becomes under sequential spot contracting, the smaller the remaining advantages of employment over a sales contract. The increasing rigidity of content reduces the flexibility of the employment relationship, and the sequential negotiations and lack of mutual commitment from one contract to the next deprive employers of the predictability over labour supply that it would normally offer. The employees may well not be available at the time when the employer most needs them.

Thus within the employment relationship, one can see diminishing returns to increasingly detailed specification of an employee's duties. Beyond a certain point, the employment relationship loses its advantages over the sales contract. However, if a way can be found of sustaining sufficient flexibility while at the same time protecting both parties from opportunism by the other, then these problems can be avoided. Hence the curved path of the left-hand arrow.

The practical significance of these problems can be seen in Willman's (1986) study of contracting within the British automobile, dock and printing industries in the 1960s and 1970s. He argues that the employment relationship had, under extensive shop floor bargaining, slid into what was effectively a series of sequential spot contracts. Changes in job assignments of individual employees all had to be negotiated and pay rates agreed, and, given the adversarial nature of labour relations at the time, the temptations of opportunistic bargaining were strong, and the chances of getting away with it, high. As a result, Willman argues, costs rose, productivity trailed and the introduction of new technology was severely delayed in these industries.

The second strategy, of high trust, relies heavily upon diffuse exchange. Under this, precise task allocations are left open, giving the employer great flexibility in labour utilization. What is given in exchange may also be open-ended, possibly some package of pay, upgrading prospects and employment security. Diffuse exchange of this nature depends upon the parties' confidence in the good faith and ability to deliver of the others. However, the variability of market conditions itself means that parties often cannot keep commitments because of external pressures, and the divergence of interests mean that assurances of good faith will not always be believed.

Thus, neither very detailed specification of terms, nor heavy reliance on diffuse exchange provide a stable basis for the employment relationship. In both cases, they may work well for a period, and provide attractive gains, but as the number of external shocks accumulates over time, both are likely to prove unstable and in need of elements of the other. Detailed specification is likely to require an element of flexibility and diffuse exchange, and some firm points of reference for defining task and performance expectations against which non-performance can be judged. Hence the 'zones of instability' in Figure 3.3, which show both strategies breaking down and converging towards an employment transaction that is underpinned by a set of rules defining jobs.

The transaction rules considered in the previous chapter are likely to be considerably easier and less costly to enforce than either of the two options just discussed. Unlike the strategy of full specification, even the work post rule appears flexible when one remembers that the primary purpose of the job descriptions is to provide a point of reference for crackdowns should tasks drift too far from the employer's original intention, and to allocate individual responsibility should there be substandard performance. Unlike the strategy of fully diffuse exchange, even the competence rank model provides a structure within which workers may assess the degree of employer reciprocity and employers know which workers can be expected to provide the widest range of tasks and to train the inexperienced.

The previous chapter showed that in all four cases the rules provide both means of evaluating whether the other side is responding in the way it should and some important protections against opportunism. As a result, they provide a viable basis on which employment relationships may develop, with both parties able to ensure that they obtain some of the key benefits that they are seeking: on the employer's side, flexibility in labour utilization; and on the employee's side, protection against unlimited demands by management and some protection against employment instability. The next step of the argument is to show why individual transaction rules tend to predominate over the others in different contexts.

3. PREDOMINANCE OF INDIVIDUAL TRANSACTION RULES

One of the striking features of labour markets and work organization is that despite a good deal of variety, there is also a great deal of uniformity, as firms and workers across whole economic sectors and occupations adopt the same kinds of solutions to similar problems. To capture this idea, some scholars have argued that individual actors make the choices and decisions within an 'iron cage' which constrains them to uniformity or 'isomorphism' (DiMaggio and Powell, 1983). The authors see the progressive adoption of a particular set of rules across large parts of a society as a form of 'institutionalization', even when adoption is voluntary. As the rules spread from early innovators, they come to be seen as the best or most appropriate way of doing things. A similar process is at work with the decentralized diffusion of employment rules, and by tracing out the logic of the transaction rules, it is possible to predict that one type of rule will come to predominate a given context. Such dominance can be achieved by any of the individual rules, and it will be argued that often the same type of environment could potentially be dominated by any of the four types of rules. Predominance feeds on itself. Thus, the more dominant a particular rule becomes, the greater the advantages to others of adopting the same rule. Three main arguments are developed: any one rule will become more robust as larger numbers of actors use it and become familiar with it; once a rule begins to predominate in a particular environment, those seeking to innovate and adopt other rules will be faced with additional costs; and finally, the logical incompatibilities between the four types of rules will favour adoption of a single rule for a particular group of workers.

3.1 Greater robustness

Employment rules are robust when they are easy to apply across a variety of workplaces and give rise to outcomes that are readily understood by workers and their line managers. Two important factors shape the robustness of rules: their innate complexity and difficulties of interpreting the context in which they are applied. Generally, the more complex rules are, and the harder it is to interpret their context, the less predictable their outcomes, the greater the scope for manipulation and consequently the greater the need for outside intervention to assist with interpretation.

There is a parallel with rules in sports matches. The rules of the game need to be easily understood by those playing, and there must be a clear decision on whether or not they have been breached. The referee's decision must be treated as final because delay could allow a defending team to regroup, and so change the course of the match. If the rules are too complex, the referee's judgement is more easily contested, and in any case is more likely to be felt unjust.

An important ingredient of swift and clear application is that all the players and the referee should know the rules well and have experience of how they are applied, and in particular, where the boundary line between legitimate play and infringement of the rules is usually drawn. At what point does a hard tackle become a foul? Such judgement, and the confidence of the players in the referee's judgement comes from repeated experience of applying the same rules. It is not just the rules that are learned by constant practice, but, more important, experience in their application is developed by applying the same rules to slightly different, and sometimes new, cases. Experienced referees and players develop a sense of how the rules are to be applied, and of what is fair and unfair play. Of course, cheating always remains possible, but it requires new levels of sophistication, as with the so-called 'professional foul': deliberate, but unseen by the referee.

A key to learning the rules of the game is that all individual matches should be played by a common set of rules. The same applies to the transaction rules of the employment relationship. The more widely diffused they are, the greater is familiarity with them, and hence, the greater the sureness with which they are applied. There are, therefore, considerable advantages to having everyone apply the same kind of rule, and once a particular rule has gained a foothold in a particular environment, it becomes easier for those establishing new workplaces to adopt the best-established rule. They can recruit workers and line managers who already have experience of them. When firms have to replace those who leave by the normal process of labour turnover, it is considerably easier to integrate new workers if they are already familiar with the type of work rules in force.

The advantages to smooth working are not confined to those between workers and their line managers, but extend also to relations between colleagues. In Chapter 4, it is shown that employment rules also shape the division of labour between colleagues doing different jobs. How are the lines of demarcation between one worker's responsibilities and those of another to be established? For example, are people responsible solely for the tasks of their own work post, or are they part of a team with joint responsibility for a particular function? Understanding how their jobs relate to each other is a critical ingredient of workplace cooperation between colleagues as well as between workers and management.

A third advantage of using a widely adopted rule is that the rule itself will have been tested in different environments and so will incorporate the learning experiences which they generate. The rule's progressive adjustment in the face of new circumstances represents a learning process albeit a tacit and collective one. Nelson and Winter (1982) argue that a similar process underlies the development of many organizational routines: standard ways organizations develop for doing things which evolve more often by practice and experimentation than by management design.

If the rules are practised in many different workplaces, then the range of tests to which they are subjected will be considerably wider than if they develop within a single enterprise. The bigger the range of tests, the less likely a particular rule is to encounter completely new challenges, and therefore the less likely it is to break down due to conditions with which the actors are unfamiliar or to which the rule has yet to be applied.

One reason why many individual states within the US borrowed large chunks of labour legislation from their neighbours when designing their own labour laws was to benefit from the learning process associated with the inevitable teething problems that confront any new piece of legislation (Piore, 1994). The greater the number of states that have tested a particular type of legislation, the more law makers will know about the conditions for successful implementation, and the more confident they can be about how it will work in their own states. Currently, in western Europe, one can see a great deal of experimentation by governments in the design of the basic rules of the employment contract as they try to strike a balance between having one clear, universal standard that all can see, and needs of particular groups of workers whose lack of skills limits their access to jobs (Supiot, 1995). Discovering what kinds of rule will work in practice across a range of environments is a difficult and costly process.[3] Thus, other things being equal, the more people in a particular sector are familiar with the operation of one of the types of transaction rule, the greater the advantages of adopting it.

3.2 First-mover difficulties for innovators

The dominance of any given rule in a particular environment is enhanced by the corresponding difficulties for firms that try to develop different rules. The main costs faced are that the firm will need to invest more in training its staff in the new work rules, in convincing them that it will stick to them and getting its employees to read its own behaviour in terms of the new rules.

The first problem, training staff and new recruits in the firm's new methods of working, is arguably the least serious of the three. Firms regularly introduce new payment and staff evaluation systems, quality circles, team working and so on, all of which require a major investment which is presumably justified by the expected, or at least hoped for, return. Introducing a new transaction rule is not qualitatively different, although being more fundamental, it could be more expensive.

Convincing staff that the firm will continue to play by the new rules is often harder, especially when its management has a reputation for changing personnel policies with each new personnel director. This was cited by Appelbaum and Batt (1994) as one of the obstacles to US firms' developing employee participation in a decentralized fashion, and the same problem applies here. For employees to shift to a new set of work rules involves a number of risks, notably, giving up the guideposts that gave them a degree of predictability in their work relationships. How can they be sure that a new management will not take advantage of this to drive a harder effort bargain? The best way to demonstrate one's commitment to a policy is to show that one will stick to it over time even when it would be advantageous in the short-run to drop it. For example, convincing employees that one will stick to a policy of employment security is best done by demonstrated by actually doing so during a recession. Sufficient time is needed for critical events in order to demonstrate one's commitment. A person's honesty is tested when it would be easier for them to lie, not by whether they routinely give true information.

Such events do not occur at predictable intervals, and they often do not occur at the beginning of a programme of reform. Indeed, cynics might not be convinced by positive action at the start of a new policy because they suspect it is intended to deceive. So in a sector where other firms apply one employment rule and a lone firm wishes to apply a different one, the latter will face severe problems of credibility over and above any additional training needs. On the whole, its staff will expect them to behave like other firms, and they will read its actions in that way. A very good practical illustration was provided in the previous chapter by the attempts of some French firms to move away from the work post rule towards something more like the functional rule. Many employees saw this as removing the protections against possible management opportunism they had worked out under the previous system and leaving them exposed to a new system of evaluation over which they had little control. So they resisted it, and sought ways to protect themselves under the new system which threatened its viability (Dugué, 1994; Baraldi *et al.*, 1995).

3.3 Incompatibilities between the rules

A final factor in the dominance of one or other system lies in the incompatibility between their basic logics. This makes it hard for firms to 'pick and mix'. In effect, the production and the training approaches are mutually inconsistent, and so cannot be applied to the same categories of workers. The same is true of the task- and function-oriented rules. Attaching accountability to individual tasks is incompatible with methods of flexible working and diffuse job boundaries.

There are cases where different rules may coexist within the same enterprise, but this usually requires a sharp demarcation between the status of the groups concerned. For example, in the British coal mining industry, there has long been a sharp divide between the internal labour market, with promotion runs for the highly skilled coal face workers, and the occupational market for all those with maintenance skills such as electricians and mechanics (Marsden, 1982). A similar divide can be found in many process industries such as chemicals. It has also been common to divide white- and blue-collar workers into two rigid status categories, and as Osterman (1988) shows, in the US, this led to two contrasted types of internal labour markets: 'industrial' and 'salaried'. Eyraud and Rozenblatt's (1994) evidence discussed in the next chapter shows a similar distinction continues to apply in many advanced industrial countries. However, there is a price to pay in terms of restrictions on the deployment of labour, and there is the long-term probability that employees in the two groups will compare their conditions and demand similar advantages.

4. THE NEED FOR INTER-FIRM INSTITUTIONS

The argument so far has focused very much on the micro-level, dealing with relations between workers and individual firms. However, although the four transaction rules have many qualities of evolutionarily stable systems, they are not completely so. In theory, they are capable of diffusing across a whole economy on the basis of their merits, but their robustness and general effectiveness can be greatly reinforced with the help of inter-firm institutions. These may be formal organizations such as unions and employer organizations, or they may be less palpable social customs and conventions which can none the less be just as powerful.

Inter-firm institutions can reinforce the employment transaction in a number of ways:

- Rules are more robust when widely used. Inter-firm institutions help to 'normalize' transaction rules, and the job classifications associated with them, by bringing both greater uniformity in their logics and increasing the number of people familiar with their operation. This makes them more robust and the parties can use them with greater confidence.
- Enforcement of transaction rules is easier, and opportunism less likely, when the parties can call upon outside support for their interpretation of how the rules should be applied. This enhances their stability, and especially that of the more 'high-trust' rules.
- The rules can be applied with greater flexibility when there is a clear fall-back position, and less danger that flexibility will create precedents that dilute them.
- Finally, renegotiation of transaction rules and how they are to be applied is easier with the support of institutions outside the enterprise.

4.1 Improving the robustness of transaction rules

Labour institutions play an important part in boosting the robustness of the employment relationship. They do this by speeding up the diffusion of particular rules, making their coverage more complete, and by establishing a more stable power balance so that it is easier to punish opportunistic action by the other party. The first increases robustness by ensuring that greater numbers of workers and managers are familiar with the rules in question, and the second makes their operation more predictable.

Regulation of labour conditions by collective agreements is one of the most obvious channels through which employers and workers can establish the basic transaction rules of the employment relation. A necessary precondition for any kind of wage agreement is agreement on the categories to which wages rates will be attached. Thus, without some kind of job or skill classification system it is impossible to have collective agreements on pay unless one were to agree a single rate of pay for all workers whatever the nature of their work, or one were to agree individual rates for every worker. Neither alternative makes much sense. The extreme egalitarianism of the first has not been practised anywhere on a lasting basis, and the second would be self-defeating for a bargaining group of any size. It is therefore necessary to have some method of setting rates of pay for categories of workers, and therefore to have some kind of classification system.

People contribute economically to the organizations they work for through the jobs they do, so it makes sense to relate their pay to the kind of work they do and therefore to organize pay and job classifications according to the same principles used to delimit workers' job obligations. Thus, pay and job classification systems become at one and the same time an important piece of the architecture of collective agreements and a channel for extending employment transaction rules across the organizations covered by the agreement. In this way, collective agreements play a critical part in the diffusion and generalization of particular transaction rules in the sectors which they cover. As generalization was a key factor in making them more robust, collective agreements thus contribute to making the rules which they support more useful to employers and employees.

Collective agreements are not the only collective channels capable of extending the influence of particular transaction rules, although they are one of the most visible. Some others are discussed when looking at diffusion at the end of the next chapter. Another mechanism has been government action, for example, through the US government's establishment of the highly influential Dictionary of Occupational Titles during the Second World War. Transaction rules may also be supported by informal, unwritten conventions recognized by firms and workers in a particular industry. Indeed, Rowe (1928) argues that collective bargaining took over the 'common rule' from a much older system of customary pay regulation that tended to fix labour prices in particular localities.

Under the training approach, a powerful external normative influence is provided by the presence of occupational labour markets, discussed in detail in Chapter 8. These maintain common standards of skill formation and job design, and the labour mobility they permit itself helps to transmit norms from one enterprise to another and to sustain their homogeneity between organizations. Thus, inter-firm institutions contribute to the functioning of employment transaction rules by imparting greater uniformity to the ways in which they emerge and are applied within individual firms. This increases their predictability, and hence the confidence that individual employers and employees can place in them.

4.2 Power balance and policing members' actions

Collective institutions can also reinforce the robustness of transaction rules by giving more structure to the power relations between the parties. Under a wholly decentralized system, the ability of either party to punish opportunism depends on whether they can find alternative employment or dismiss the workers concerned. Such power relations fluctuate with the state of labour markets, and with the personal circumstances of individual workers. Thus, although the transaction rules may provide greater stability than the sales contract, the ebb and flow of individual bargaining power will still leave long periods when either party is vulnerable to opportunism by the other. The highly conflictual shop floor industrial relations of many British industries during the 1960s and 1970s illustrate the effects on the general manageability of firms, as does the collapse of shop floor militancy in the late 1970s and early 1980s.

Collective organizations that span several firms play an especially important part in this respect. They enable shop floor groups, and sometimes also individual firms, to retaliate against opportunism by drawing on the collective strength of their peer group organizations. 'Tit for tat' is a powerful mechanism for developing cooperation, as Axelrod (1984) has demonstrated, but it does depend upon the ability of either party to punish as well as to reward the other. Indeed, if one party is seen to reward cooperative action out of weakness, it may encourage the other to 'exploit' in the next round of the game.

In order to maintain their ability to escalate support for individual groups, collective organizations must keep their powder dry, and avoid dissipating their strength by intervening too often. They have therefore to select which groups to support, and on what occasions, and this gives them considerable influence over their members. They can thus police the actions of their own members to discourage frivolous disputes. This is critical to their maintaining their overall bargaining relationship with the other party.

The reality of such powers is illustrated in Mottez's observations about effort bargaining under incentive pay schemes cited earlier: the workers would exercise collective self-restraint in operating the systems to ensure that they did not destroy the overall credibility of their position. In Britain, despite their public reputation for militancy, shop steward committees often restrained the actions of individual work groups from pressing claims which they considered unreasonable, even though they had a good argument in terms of precedent and they were probably attainable (Brown, 1973). The stewards wished to maintain their overall bargaining relationship with management, which was the key to effective representation of all work groups. Eyraud (1981) provides similar illustrations of French unions refusing to back what they considered unreasonable claims by particular groups of members.

The importance of the 'policing powers' of peer group organizations can be seen in another example concerning cooperation around work-organization issues, and the strengthening of 'tit-for-tat' strategies to avoid prisoner's dilemma problems. Although Axelrod (1984) presents some powerful examples to boost the plausibility of his case, such as the experience of cooperation between rival armies discussed shortly, his theoretical defence depends upon the length of the game. By the argument of 'reverse induction', Dasgupta (1988) shows that, in finite games, because defection in the final round cannot be punished (there being no further possibility of reciprocity or retaliation), cooperation in each preceding round becomes less certain. As a result, the whole process unravels. Boyer and Orléan (1995) show that 'tit for tat' only works if the game is very long and the probability that it will end at the next round is very small.

A practical echo of this problem can be found in the obstacles to diffusion of 'high performance' human resource models in the US (Appelbaum and Batt, 1994). One of the factors that the authors highlight is management turnover and the frequent short tenure in the personnel function. As managers often do not feel bound to follow the policies of their predecessors, and may improve their own careers if they can 'make their mark' by doing something different, the cooperation game with the workforce may often be rather short. Even more important, many employees may believe that management's interest will be only short-lived, and so the probability of defection is high. A great many of the quality circle programmes in Western firms, one popular vehicle for worker–management cooperation, have shown just that: a short life span which was often due to lack of long-term commitment by top management (Hill, 1991).

The involvement of inter-firm institutions in such measures, and their underpinning by collective action, can help reduce the ease with which one party can withdraw unilaterally. Cole (1989) gives one such example in his account of the spread of quality circles in Japan. The key factor in this process lay in the collective momentum built up by employers which encouraged individual firms to persevere with rather than drop such schemes when they encountered difficulties or when new managers took over. Employers took the lead in promoting quality circles nationally through JUSE (Japanese Union of Scientists and Engineers). An important part of Cole's account describes the means by which Japanese employers transformed quality circles from a personnel technique into a 'mass movement' for quality control upheld by 'decentralized coordinated activity'. JUSE was powerfully backed by the main employer organizations, but it also managed to trigger employer activism at the local level, establishing strong local networks of firms which built commitment, for example by the annually rotating company leadership of JUSE's local chapters. A great many of their individual employees took part, for example, by making presentations about their QC successes and failures, thus deepening the companies' involvement beyond their key managers. In contrast, he argues that the weakness of the central organization, its lack of support from powerful employer organizations, and the conflict of interest between private consultants selling QCs and the public interest organizations seeking to propagate them, left QCs in US firms heavily dependent on the commitment of individual managers. What the Japanese collective mobilization achieved was a guarantee to employees sharing information through QCs that management commitment would be long-lasting and hence that the cooperative game itself would be long rather than short, thus increasing the effectiveness of 'tit-for-tat' cooperation.

More generally, therefore, the contribution of labour institutions can be to increase the predictability with which transaction rules function in the workplace, making their outcomes less dependent on short-term fluctuations in the bargaining power of the groups concerned. It might be argued that the same problems of cooperative action would recur at the higher level. However, there are a number of limiting factors. The greater cost of conflict at this level increases the incentive to seek other ways of resolving difficulties. Also, there is a greater number of channels of communication and of sources of information, so opportunities for communication are considerably greater than is presupposed by the prisoner's dilemma.

4.3 Greater flexibility of application

Collective institutions can also increase the flexibility with which transaction rules are applied in the workplace. They do this in three ways: they can provide an anchor for key indicators of work rules, and thus a benchmark against which the degree of cooperation can be assessed; they can help prevent 'tit-for-tat' cooperation from becoming a source of rigidity; and they can assist by validating the information provided by the other party.

(a) The provision of anchor points

Working flexibly poses employees a difficult dilemma. On the one hand, it involves a relaxation of the transaction rules in the interests of greater productivity, which may benefit both parties. On the other, it exposes employees, in particular, to possible dilution of the very rules that are meant to protect them against employer opportunism.

This dilemma is particularly difficult in many work environments because of the role played by workplace custom. A large part of any job's definition is in practice tacit and not codified. As a result, a job's content is as much defined by how other incumbents of the same job do it. The importance of such customary definitions is widely recognized in employment law. Under British law, for example, even home workers can be deemed to be employees with employment rights if in practice they work on a regular basis for one employer (Leighton, 1983). In the US, under the presumption of employment 'at will', if a person continues to turn up for work after their employer has announced a change in the conditions of employment, they are deemed to have accepted them even though no written consent has been given (Malcomson, 1997). Custom is therefore far more pervasive than the shop floor studies of 'custom and practice' would lead one to believe.

This means that the effective rules in operation are more often those observed in practice rather than those set down in formal agreements. As practice evolves, so do customary rules. This puts cooperation by flexible interpretation of transaction rules in a very tricky position. Flexibility in the observance of job boundaries can be to the benefit of all parties, but how much of it can be provided and for how long before workers find that the old rule has been lost, and a new more-flexible norm emerged? If employers can claim that the new more-flexible set of assignments has now replaced the old one, what protections can workers derive from the transaction rules and their job classifications?

Without clear guideposts that can be called upon when disputes arise, workers are in a weak position. It may sometimes even be hard to define clearly the point from which a cooperative interpretation of the transaction rule came into operation. Hence, the safer strategy is to stick closely to the original understanding of the rule and to forego some of the potential benefits of flexibility. On the employers' side too such guideposts are important. In the operation of incentive schemes in Burawoy's examples, management had a similar perspective: it tolerated a certain amount of slack in the application of work rules because it knew it could reinstate them in periodic crackdowns. It is here that an external point of reference can be extremely important. If undertaken locally in an environment in which tacit knowledge and custom are important, it is hard to distinguish exceptions made in goodwill for greater flexibility from a gradual transformation of the rule itself.

An external standard or point of reference enables the parties to apply the rule more flexibly in the confidence that the other party will not use this as a precedent to argue that the rule has now changed its scope or content. A good example can be found in the observation of Jürgens et al. (1993) that although job grades were highly differentiated and clearly defined in the German car plants which they studied, there were none of the demarcation restrictions on task allocation that they found in British and US plants. This was because, in the German plants, the widespread recognition of skills, strongly sanctioned in collective agreements, enabled the parties to be more flexible over job demarcations than in the British or US plants. Recognition of these skills provided strong external criteria against which goodwill could be identified and distinguished from minimum required performance. This limits the degree to which either party can manipulate and dilute job rules unilaterally. Thus, having a strong external anchor for the rule made it easier for people in their workplace to be flexible about its application.

(b) Spontaneous 'tit-for-tat' relations as a source of rigidity

A further limitation of decentralized cooperation, and the benefit that can be derived from a wider institutional support can be seen from the way in which spontaneous 'tit-for-tat' cooperation can become a source of rigidity. Ironically, the most persuasive example Axelrod (1984) cites for the power of 'tit for tat' to lead to cooperation in fact highlights some of its weaknesses and resulting rigidities.

In presenting 'tit for tat' as a solution to the prisoner's dilemma, Axelrod has a very powerful example in the development of the 'live and let live' system that developed between the soldiers in opposing armies during the 1914–18 war. There, the trench fighters in the British and German armies developed an elaborate code of ritualized aggression designed to cause the minimum damage to the ordinary soldiers in the enemy lines while appearing aggressive to their own high command, which became known as 'live and let live' (Ashworth, 1980).

In formal terms, the soldiers on either side surely faced a classic prisoner's dilemma. Visible communication with the enemy was punishable by execution, and each army's high command was strongly opposed to any loss of aggressiveness by their troops. Cooperation could only emerge in a decentralized fashion because any open attempts at coordination would have soon been noticed and punished by high command. Yet, in large sections of the front, ordinary soldiers on both sides deliberately refrained from harming each other, and maintained the situation by a system of 'tit for tat', their only means of communication. Thus, if the trench fighters of the opposing army fired high, the others would reciprocate, and if a new contingent that fired accurately arrived, the soldiers on the other side would again reciprocate until the message was understood. If cooperation could evolve under such circumstances, then surely the limitations of 'tit for tat' are more theoretical than real.

There is, however, a major difference between the underlying structure of the game in the trench warfare example compared with the employment relationship. Maintaining the status quo was the preferred outcome for the ordinary soldiers on both sides because that involved least risk to life and limb. In contrast, in the workplace, maintaining the status quo is often the least good outcome as this inhibits response to swiftly changing markets. There, 'live and let live' cooperation could develop between line management and workers as management abstained from tackling obvious sources of inefficiency because it was afraid of losing cooperation on other issues. The reason why a form of 'sequential spot contracting' prevailed for so long within parts of the British printing and car industries analysed by Willman (1986) was that management and workers had evolved a 'live and let live' understanding by which both sides refrained from fundamental challenges to existing work arrangements despite the declining competitiveness of the firms involved. Neither side was willing to tackle the modernization of industrial relations procedures and working practices until the crises of the late 1970s and early 1980s. Katz (1985) describes a comparable situation in the US automobile industry, in the years leading up to crisis of the late 1970s, in which management and worker representatives cooperated in what was described as an 'armed truce'.

The limitations of 'live and let live' cooperation are that it lacks any external support so that cooperation has to develop without threatening, or appearing to alter, any of the basic rules governing relations between the two sides. In this respect, it increases the rigidity of employment rules. It is easier to cooperate by camping on one's own position and allowing the other party to do the same than by doing anything that might alter each other's position and so shift the equilibrium between them. External institutional support eases this restriction because the parties in the workplace are able to consider more radical changes in the knowledge that they have some external backing if their partner fails to reciprocate. In Katz's 'armed truce', both sides will cooperate in so far as that does not threaten either's fundamental position, but any major changes or adaptation of work rules that bring that into question are off the agenda. In the US automobile industry, it took the major crisis of the late 1970s and the near bankruptcy of the major firms to break this deadlock and to launch the programmes of new working practices and Quality of Working Life. In contrast, comparing the US and German automobile industries, Turner (1991) shows how the strong institutions outside the enterprise, unions and employer organizations, facilitated a longer-term adjustment and a more flexible application of basic work rules.

(c) Information validation

A final area in which inter-firm institutions can increase the flexibility and adaptability of employment transaction rules concerns the difficulties of maintaining localized cooperation when reciprocity is made difficult by an uncertain environment. Firms find that they cannot meet their commitments to stable employment or they need to reorganize jobs to deal with a surge in demand. Employees may find that the demands of their jobs exceed their capabilities. Most cooperative economic relationships therefore include some kind of understanding about 'force majeure'.[4] In employment, no one expects their firm to provide absolute employment security, and most employers make allowances for personal sickness or 'human error' in the performance of their employees.

However, because information may be used strategically, it is often difficult to determine whether such 'force majeure' is genuine. Has reciprocity failed because the other party could not deliver, or has it changed its intentions and expectations about the relationship? Were the offending party's claims of 'force majeure' genuine or hypocritical? If it had changed its intentions, it might well wish to conceal this, in the short run at least, so any information that it provided itself could be part of a wider deception. For example, when firms introduce organizational or technical change, it is common to promise that there will be no compulsory lay-offs as a direct result. But suppose market conditions unexpectedly decline afterwards, and the employer seeks lay-offs, how far can the workers trust their employer's word? Might the downturn be used as a pretext for getting rid of those the firm had expensively promised to find alternative jobs? Alternatively, when employees complain that new work methods are far more demanding than the previous ones and that is why previously promised productivity gains have not materialized, how far can an employer believe them?

It is hard to get verifiable information on people's intentions. However, concealing one's intentions usually involves manipulating information, and one can verify whether factual information is being used in a way that is likely to deceive. How serious is the decline in the demand for the firm's product, and have other firms been able to find ways of redeploying labour to avoid redundancies? What has been the experience of other employers with staffing similar new equipment? Unions and employer organizations can, and often do, provide valuable information to their members at enterprise level. It is not uncommon for employer organizations to synthesize the experience of their members in different personnel issues and then provide advice on what outcomes might be realistically expected. Likewise, on the employee side, unions, through their contacts in different firms, can piece together a picture of what other firms are able to do. All of this can serve as a valuable check on the quality of information exchanged and claims made within an individual firm. Such additional information resources make it easier for the parties in a local dispute to judge whether the other party is behaving opportunistically or facing a genuine problem of 'force majeure'. The more easily opportunistic action can be detected 'in the bud', the less the incentive to follow this path. In doing so, they facilitate more flexible application of employment rules.

4.4 Renegotiation of transaction rules

A feature of incomplete contracts like the employment relationship is that they have to allow for periodic renegotiation. The transaction rules enable firms to manage task assignments without the need for continuous negotiation, but the way they are applied, and sometimes the rules themselves, need to be adapted. Technology and organizational methods change, and job classifications become out of date. Jobs are frequently of long duration, commonly lasting fifteen years and more even in the US, so some procedure for revision is necessary. For procedural rules especially, such updating is not straightforward.

Commons identified a fundamental consequence of the idea that employment is always subject to its continuing acceptability to the parties involved:

that it is not a contract as such, but rather a 'continuing implied renewal of contracts at every minute and hour' (Commons, 1924, ch. 8 §1). Both parties remain free to terminate the relationship with due notice, even in western Europe, so there is an ever-present element of negotiation. The transaction rules hold this at bay under normal circumstances, but renegotiation may be compared to repairing a dam wall while it is still holding the water back. How can the terms of the employment relationship be updated in a controlled way without releasing the implicit negotiation that is ever present?

One apparent solution might be to try to identify certain specific elements that need to be renegotiated and for the parties to agree to restrict themselves to that. This might be possible for substantive rules, such as pay and benefits, but is much harder for basic procedures such as regulating task assignments. The customary nature of the employment relationship, which stems in part from the element of implicit negotiation noted by Commons, makes it difficult to 'ring-fence' negotiations over particular procedures of the relationship without simultaneously calling other aspects into question.

Another mechanism for change might be to allow employers to alter work rules unilaterally and to see whether their employees accept them by continuing to work for them without protest. Something like this is recognized under American labour law whereby employees are deemed to have accepted changes in their employment conditions if they carry on working without protest under the new rules (Malcomson, 1997: 1920). However, as a regular employment practice, this is a dangerous path to take because it risks undermining the integrity of the transaction rules. If they can be altered unilaterally by one party then they will provide little if any protection against opportunism by either side. One of the rules' most important functions is that they enable employees to agree to management flexibility in assigning work without fearing that they will be pushed too far. To accept powers of unilateral revision routinely would be self-defeating. As a result, some kind of negotiated procedure must be used, and the question is whether this is better handled at the individual or the collective level.

(a) The limitations of individual renegotiation

The method of individual renegotiation, or change by mutual consent, offers adaptation to individual circumstances, but it has a number of drawbacks. The large investments that employees have often made in their jobs, and the difficulty of finding alternative jobs in other firms, place them in a vulnerable position *vis-à-vis* their employers. Management also has a very considerable advantage over workers because it has a view of the whole process of change, whereas workers have knowledge mostly of their individual jobs only. Without the view of the whole, it is hard to judge how change will affect their individual job prospects within the firm. Faced with such uncertainty, employees often protect themselves by demanding more structured jobs with clearer specification of duties. A large tacit element is fine when one can rely on reciprocity by one's employer, but if the employer cannot be trusted, then a higher degree of specification provides more protection.

Evidence to support this argument can be found in the contrast between job ladders in union and non-union workplaces in the US. In their Chicago study, Bridges and Villemez (1991, 1994) found that employees in non-union firms, where due process arrangements tended to be weaker than in unionized ones, demanded more highly structured internal mobility systems. These took the form of more highly structured careers and promotion opportunities. Baron *et al.* (1986a), like Pfeffer and Cohen (1984) before them, also found that non-union plants tended to have more structured job ladders than unionized ones. The effect of union presence seems to have been to encourage due process procedures that underpinned more open internal mobility opportunities and extended them across a wider range of employees. This is manifest in union support for open bidding for internal vacancies.

Thus, the more restricted, but also more structured, career ladders of non-union plants can be seen as reflecting the need employees feel for greater substantive guarantees when the procedural ones are weak or employer-dependent. As employee collective power will be less in non-union that in unionized internal labour markets,[5] one may presume that the more structured job ladders reflect what non-union employers have to offer in order to attract and retain skilled staff. This American evidence is useful because of the institutional diversity to be found there. The contrast between union and non-union workplaces suggests that procedural regulation of the employment relation can be substituted for agreement on its substantive content.

(b) The advantages of collective negotiation

Collective negotiation of basic employment rules addresses a number of these problems of individual negotiation. It can help reverse the information imbalance; it can reduce the individual bargaining weakness by reducing the employee's dependence on the threat to quit; and it offers a form of risk spreading to even out imbalances of power over time and between individual workers. Several of these arguments have already been presented, and so do not need repeating, but the special difficulty of revising basic employment rules deserves mention. Whereas a poor bargain over substantive issues such as pay and benefits can often be reversed in a later bargaining round, changes in basic procedures are less frequent and harder to change. Thus, if employees strike a bad bargain when renegotiating basic procedural issues, they may have to live with the consequences for a long time. If individual employees face risks that are too high, they will be likely to resist change. Collective negotiation may be effective at the level of the firm, but the support of inter-firm organizations can be especially important when the changes affect many workers in the same plant, as often occurs at times of crisis for the firm when fear of job losses in the short-term could destabilize normal bargaining relationships. The workers in a plant may give away too much compared with their long-term position, or they may just seek to block change in the belief that they have nothing to lose either way. Then, an inter-firm union and employers' organization can help average out temporary power imbalances and facilitate a more steady approach to change.

5. CONCLUSION: EVOLUTIONARILY STABLE STRATEGIES AND LABOUR INSTITUTIONS

This chapter has shown how the basic rules governing the employment relation can evolve out of a decentralized process of repeated interaction between workers and firms. This is because the alternative methods of running an employment relationship either by specifying duties in ever greater detail, or by relying on total flexibility, were shown to be unstable. Under the first, there comes a point at which specifying duties in ever greater detail becomes more costly than direct contracting for specified goods and services on the open market. Too great a specification destroys the very flexibility that makes the employment relationship attractive. Likewise, ever greater reliance on diffuse jobs places an increasing burden on trust relations, and there comes a point at which the uncertainties of economic life and the known divergence of interests cause reciprocity to fail and set 'tit for tat' into reverse. An intermediate position, in which jobs were regulated by a mixture of specification and diffuseness, would avoid these two problems, but it would need a framework of rules to give it stability.

Firms and workers may arrive at such rules on their own, by a process of decentralized experimentation, but they may also be assisted by labour market institutions. We know that, historically, subcontracting gradually gave way to employment as the dominant norm over many decades, and in the process many different forms were tried. We shall see also in the next chapter that in several countries there have been periods of intense institutional activity which greatly assisted the spread of one or other kind of transaction rule. In France, the Popular Front was one such period. In the US, the decade between the Wagner Act and end of the Second World War was another period in which new norms became generalized and embedded in the personnel practice and collective agreements of a great number of firms. Nevertheless, although labour institutions and governments may assist the diffusion and rise to preeminence of a particular type of rule, it would be a mistake to conclude that these can just be imposed as if by an act of political will. There have been numerous occasions on which legislation has failed because of opposition to its application. French industrial relations law has offered many examples of state activism that could not be enforced at plant level (see Sellier, 1961; Reynaud, 1975). And in Britain, the rise to preeminence of 'job territory' rules was much more gradual, and much more occupationally specific than in other countries.

In contrast, this chapter has focused more on the support that institutional frameworks give to transaction rules, because they help them become the norm with which most people are familiar, and make them more likely to function predictably and reliably. Such support can greatly enhance the robustness of individual employment rules. In this way, institutions also make particular transaction rules more useful to employers and employees. Although all rules constrain to some extent, the transaction rules are essentially enabling rules: they make it possible to have a stable employment relationship, and so provide a framework for what can be a mutually beneficial economic relationship.

This chapter has looked at a number of the ways in which inter-firm institutions can support the diffusion and operation of employment transaction rules, but it has not provided much on which they bite directly. The next chapter looks at job and pay classification systems, which play a central role in linking the action of inter-firm institutions to the workplace regulation of jobs and job boundaries.

ENDNOTES

[1] This is referred to as the 'equal compensation principle': that unless two tasks within a job are equally rewarded, the employee will allocate time to the one that is best rewarded (Milgrom and Roberts, 1992: 228).

[2] Applying Figure 3.1 to the high-trust path, the horizontal axis would show the increasing degree of diffuseness, and the vertical one, costs and returns. The upper curve would show the diminishing gains from increasing functional flexibility, and the lower one, the rising costs associated with the increasing risk of breakdown.

[3] There is an interesting parallel with software development: the greater the number of users involved in its development, the wider the range of problems to which it is exposed, the more likely 'bugs' are to be exposed and the less likely it is that it will crash in unforeseen circumstances. This was the gamble taken by Netscape in its competition with Microsoft for Internet navigation software. By making its new programme available on the internet before its final release, Netscape planned to make use of the large numbers of potential users who would try out the software for them and come up with suggestions for improvements and adaptations (*Le Monde* 13 April 1998, 'Netscape dévoile ses recettes', by Denis Delbecq).

[4] In a very interesting study of inter-firm relations, Deakin and Wilkinson (1998) show that such provision is also built into some legal systems. Under German law, for

example, if a firm has difficulties meeting an order, there is provision for discussion and renegotiation, and commercial contracts are often long-term and include hardship clauses. In Italy, on the other hand, the cost of using the legal system was very high, so contracts tended to be short, and the usual procedure in the event of difficulty was for the client firm to terminate the contract.

[5] Kalleberg *et al.* (1996) confirm also that the presence of internal labour markets in firms is unrelated to union status.

4

Classification Rules and the Consolidation of Employment Systems

1. INTRODUCTION

So far, exploring the limits within which management may direct work assignments has led to a focus on regulating employees' obligations at the margin. Job and pay classification systems focus primarily on job contents rather than job boundaries. It is on the former that job evaluation focuses, and for which employees are rewarded. This chapter explores the relationship between the two, arguing that the way job boundaries are resolved also shapes the basic rules governing their contents. It argues that job definition and classification is a 'holistic' process, and that there is a strong logical link with the transaction rules as they are incorporated into the guiding principles of classification systems. The latter provide one of the most important channels through which inter-firm institutions help to consolidate the job level transaction rules.

After setting up a theory of job classification systems, the chapter begins to map the incidence of dominant classification models in different economies. A first step is to look at the occupational classifications used in national earnings statistics, treating these as social facts. This can be done because statistical conventions are strongly influenced by the social reality that they are designed to measure. The second step is to look at the predominant classification systems in different countries. This is done using the results of a major International Labour Office (ILO) study of job classification systems in advanced industrial countries, but reinterpreting their main findings. This analysis gives a first mapping of the diffusion of transaction rules as incorporated in classification systems. It is then possible, in Chapter 5, to compare this mapping with more detailed indicators showing the presence of job rules following the production and training, and the task and function-oriented approaches. The focus then turns to the role of institutions at the critical stages in the diffusion of different classification systems as a guide to the spread of the transaction rules. Finally, the chapter draws together the main elements developed so far on the nature of employment systems.

2. A THEORY OF JOB CLASSIFICATION

One of the most important functions of job classification systems is to reduce job idiosyncrasy and make job contents more transparent to management and staff alike. However, increased transparency comes at a price: selecting certain attributes, such as the level or type of skill, means downplaying or ignoring others. In part, this is for reasons of economy: job classifications are part of information management, and collecting and storing information is costly. In part, it is because organizing information, and jobs, according to one set of principles limits further analysis to principles that are mutually consistent. For example, classifying jobs according to vocational qualifications precludes classifying them according to the amount of OJT they require.

2.1 A simple model

The best way to understand job classification is to take a 'holistic' approach, and to start by considering the totality of work that a firm needs to have done, rather than starting from the individual job. This emphasizes how firms use job classification systems to divide up work between different types of jobs and allocate it to different categories of workers. Because employment is an economic transaction—the supply of labour services in exchange for reward—pay relations are also intimately affected by the contours of similarity established between jobs. These processes are illustrated in Figure 4.1.

The figure starts from the totality of work needed by the firm. This is analysed and distributed between jobs with the aid of a system of job categories—the job classification system. Work of different kinds is parcelled out to the various categories of jobs, and thus, to the appropriate job holders. With each category there will be a job description which may range from a detailed written document to a customary understanding. Job classification is therefore an activity distinct from pay classification, which assigns the various categories of jobs (or workers) to different points on a system of pay scales, usually by some kind of job evaluation. In practice, as shown by the double-headed arrow between job and pay classifications, there is a reciprocal relationship between the two. Job design is undertaken subject to a cost constraint so that the values attached to different kinds of jobs are likely to have a direct effect on the distribution of work, and, in the long-run, they

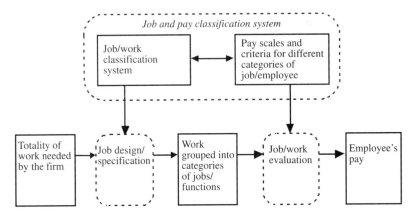

Fig. 4.1. A model of job and pay classification

may affect the design of the job classification system itself. For example, in recent years, to reduce the cost of redeploying staff between different kinds of work many employers have sought to rearrange jobs into broader categories.

Job classifications operate with two main kinds of job information: substantive and relational. On the substantive side, job descriptions establish the general contents of particular types of job. For example, a Senior Grade Secretary job may involve certain kinds of duties and require certain levels of qualification and responsibility. These will be more demanding than those of a Junior Secretary's job. When 'staffing up' a new office, management will normally estimate the expected workload, and organize it across a number of job categories from their organization's classification system. A degree of experimentation may follow as work assignments are adjusted to fit the office's actual workload when it is up and running. A small building firm would go through a similar process in evaluating a new project. Before hiring its employees, it would need to decompose the total job into components that can be parcelled out to the various building trades (bricklayers, carpenters, plasterers etc.).[1] In this example the classification is provided by the familiar skill categories of the industry. In both cases, the firm breaks down the new operation into the different kinds of work that can be assigned to the various categories of job holders or skills.

Job classifications also compare and relate jobs to each other. By applying the same system of job descriptions across an organization, or across a labour market in the case of the construction skills just mentioned, jobs are not just being carved out on a one-off basis—they are being organized into different categories. Thus, a Junior Secretary anywhere in the organization is likely to be able to undertake similar kinds of work, and to be subject to similar limitations of skills or experience. This knowledge enables colleagues to coordinate their activities more effectively. Detailed understanding of each other's jobs is unnecessary so long as they know how far one can rely on their colleagues in other jobs to provide the services they depend on to do their own. Line managers also need to know what kinds of work different members of their staff can undertake, and their job descriptions assist work organization, knowing who can do what, and where responsibility lies when something has not been done. Provided the categories are fairly stable over time and fairly uniform across the organization, people have a chance to learn what is the normal type of performance that can be expected from the holders of different jobs.[2] The shared job descriptions enable staff and line managers alike to compare the services they get from those in certain jobs, and this helps to establish a normal standard of job performance. Although there remains a margin of idiosyncrasy, the jobs of different colleagues are made much more transparent.

An important driving force behind the comparability of jobs that are classified in the same categories is pay. Job evaluation is the second point at which classifications enter into the employment relationship: translating the employees' contribution into their rewards. Although the question of pay is examined in greater detail in Chapter 7, it is clear that if pay is to be related to employees' contribution, then the contours of similarity in the classification system will prove very influential. The criteria used in job evaluation will generally follow closely those used in job classification, if only because the reward is related to performance in the jobs within the classification. Thus, if vocational skills or job demands are at the centre of the job classification, then the job evaluation system will focus respectively on measures of qualification or of job demands.

Although it is theoretically possible to construct a job classification scheme that has nothing to do with pay, for example, if everyone in the organization were paid the same irrespective of their work, in practice this is unlikely. The reason is that the job classification defines certain dimensions of performance that the organization seeks from its employees, and to base job evaluation on different principles would risk sending contradictory messages to employees as to the importance of different aspects of their work. This would reduce the transparency of jobs and encourage renewed bargaining over work roles.

2.2 'Atomistic' and 'holistic' views of job classification

As mentioned earlier, there are two views of the nature of job classification: 'atomistic' and 'holistic'. Under the first, the relationship between the transaction rules and job classifications is contingent, whereas under the second it is logical. It will be argued that the atomistic view is fallacious. The holistic one is then explored to bring out the nature of the relationship between the transaction and classification rules.[3]

According to the atomistic view, jobs are made up of a number of tasks, and although the way tasks are grouped varies between firms, there is a level at which they are the elementary building blocks out of which jobs are constructed. This conception has no doubt been reinforced by the Taylorist programme of 'de-skilling': breaking down complex jobs into their constituent parts or building blocks that could be reassembled into simpler jobs that can be learned more quickly. When applied to job classification, the atomistic view projects job design and classification as a process of combining the same elementary building blocks in different ways to compose different jobs. The resulting jobs are then classified according to the demands they place upon their incumbents. Thus basic maintenance tasks may be assigned to specialist maintenance jobs or to semi-skilled production jobs. The atomistic view has gained plausibility from wide familiarity with Adam Smith's account of pin manufacture. Were not the resulting operations so elementary that one might find them in any pin-making establishment either as separate tasks assigned to specialist jobs, or grouped into broader jobs?

For all its apparent simplicity, the atomistic approach rests on a fallacy. Just as describing jobs exhaustively was shown in Chapter 1 to lead to a problem of infinite regress, one can always provide a more detailed description, so with tasks, it is always possible to imagine a finer division. For example, cleaning an office floor might be considered a single task assigned to one cleaner, or it might be subdivided into several, each one assigned to a different person. If one adopts the atomistic approach to definition, then it follows that each cleaner in the latter case would be undertaking a separate task. We should therefore have to treat the cleaner who cleaned the whole office as undertaking, at least implicitly, all the tasks undertaken by the others rather than simply doing a single task called cleaning the office floor. Although there is an obvious economic limit as more and more cleaners will end up by getting in each other's way, there is no logical limit within the atomistic approach. Tasks can always be more finely subdivided, so to think of a classification system as building upwards from a set of elementary tasks does not work because there is no such set.

The atomistic approach also falls down on the treatment of relational tasks and those connected with problem-solving. Relational tasks involve co-operation with the holders of other work roles in the organization, such as one's line managers and colleagues. Even if it is supposed that jobs are combinations of universal elementary tasks, relational tasks still are shaped by current work roles, and it therefore makes little sense to abstract from these. Likewise, with problem-solving tasks, as the bounds of these are by definition uncertain, there is no obvious way in which they can be broken down into a set of elementary operations that would be constant for all contexts. Thus, on three separate counts the atomistic approach to job definition and classification falls. There is a wider philosophical debate as to whether it is workable under any circumstances, but this is more than is required in the current context. Attempts to patch up the logical inconsistencies in the atomistic approach, such as setting an arbitrary limit on the subdivision of tasks, will simply undermine the effectiveness of resulting classifications in dealing with idiosyncrasy.

The alternative view is that job definition and classification are holistic, that is to say, firms start off from a mass of work that needs to be done, and apply certain organizing principles to define jobs and their relationships with each other (as shown in Figure 4.1). A strong implication of this approach is that the same principles governing job boundaries also shape their contents. This is because the process of dividing up the totality of work and establishing separate categories simultaneously fixes the content of jobs and the boundaries between them. For example, if we were to divide maintenance work into that assigned to 'craftsmen' and that assigned to 'mates' (their helpers) then we simultaneously identify two separate categories of tasks (those requiring skill and those not) and draw a boundary between them in terms of skill demands. After a while, people may become so familiar with this particular division of tasks that it appears natural, and this may well reinforce the belief that there are elementary tasks that are simply grouped in different ways. But this should not obscure the nature of the categories into which they are divided.

Defining the content of jobs and the boundaries between them establishes their identity, and their difference from other categories. A classification implies that a large number of jobs are assigned to a much smaller number of categories, and therefore establishes contours of similarity among jobs. The nature of this similarity, and of the corresponding differences, between categories brings a third essential element of classification systems. They 'map' jobs onto a space that is structured according to a set of organizing principles. If this were not so, classifications would do nothing to reduce job idiosyncrasy. Jobs are not just grouped into arbitrary categories: the categories themselves are defined in relation to a certain whole or totality. The nature or meaning of this totality is the third element. In some cases it might be skill, so that categories of jobs are differentiated by their skill demands, or it might be a view of the organization as an administrative unit, in which case they would be differentiated into a set of work posts. Alternatively, the whole might be the enterprise as a community of work groups so that work is differentiated by status or rank within the organization.[4]

2.3 Incompleteness of job descriptions

The last important aspect of job classifications is that the job descriptions with which they operate are incomplete, and deliberately so. Job descriptions are primarily illustrative rather than prescriptive. Recalling the words of the manager quoted by Slichter *et al.* (1960: 576), too much detail can lead to jobs being done according to 'the words in the manual'. Fearing exactly the same processes more than a century earlier, the then US Secretary of State insisted on adding the words 'and other such duties . . .' to the job descriptions of federal civil servants (Betters, 1931: 5).[5] They do not therefore eliminate job idiosyncrasy entirely. Rather, in conjunction with the transaction rules, as argued in Chapter 2, they contain it.

Job classifications are confronted by the same problem as that discussed earlier: how can a sufficient degree of flexibility be maintained without opening the door to opportunistic behaviour? What limits the Secretary's authority to direct employees to 'other such duties'? Thus, the transaction rules introduced earlier come to play a central part not just in regulating individual jobs, but also in the working of job classification systems, and they do so for the same reason as that concerning individual jobs. The transaction rules and the job classification system need to follow the same logic. In effect, the transaction rules will regulate tasks at the job's margin, whereas the main job description will give an account of its core. If the core and the margin are defined in different terms, a coherent outcome is unlikely. For example, if the transaction rule follows the training approach and the core activities of the job follow the production approach there will be frequent tensions in work allocation. Dugué's study (1994) provides an illustration of the attempt to graft a skill-based approach onto the work post system, but the employees remained deeply suspicious because the skills were being defined in the same way that management defined work posts: top-down. As a result, they had little confidence in the resulting competencies, and felt that they were manipulated by management.

3. SOME LESSONS FROM OCCUPATIONAL CLASSIFICATIONS USED IN EARNINGS STATISTICS

A brief look at the occupational classifications used by national statistical institutes (NSIs) for their earnings statistics brings out two points, one methodological and the other empirical. On the method side, they illustrate the holistic nature of job classification, showing how differently skills employed in similar industries may be classified. On the empirical side, such classifications are also social facts, for reasons to be explained shortly, and therefore give a first view of the dominant classification principles used by firms in different countries.

In the absence of a detailed international study of the classification systems used by firms that can be related to the different types of transaction rule, the approaches imposed on national statisticians by their environments provide a remarkably good first approximation.

The impact of the different approaches to occupational classification on the actual categorization of workers is shown in Figure 4.2. For simplicity, the picture is confined to blue-collar and middle-management employees. To enable comparison, the figure shows the approximate location of workers of

	Work posts on job ladders	Ranks	ISCO-88	Qualification group
Middle management	Middle managers	Section manager	Managerial occupations	Managers within CB
	Supervisors as classified by firm	Chief		Certified senior supervisors
		Foreman		Junior supervisors
Skilled	Work posts in skilled classifications	Blue-collar workers and their team leaders	Supervisors in skilled occupations	
	↑ ∣ ↑ ∣ ↑	Blue-collar workers	Skilled occupations	Certified skilled workers
Semi-skilled	Work posts in semi-skilled classifications	↑	Supervisors in SSK occupations	
	↑ ∣ ↑ ∣ ↑		SSK occupations	OJT-experienced workers
Unskilled	Work posts in unskilled classifications	↑	Supervisors in USK occupations	
		USK occupations	Uncertified and inexperienced workers
	↑ ∣ ↑ ∣ ↑			

Fig. 4.2. The impact of different classificatory principles on pay classifications
Key: ISCO, International Standard Classification of Occupations; CB, collective bargaining; SK, skilled; SSK, semi-skilled; USK, unskilled. Shaded areas denote supervisory and line management functions.

different skill levels, and of those exercising some degree of management responsibility.

Looking at the national surveys of earnings by occupation, it is immediately apparent that there are quite radical differences in the definition of skilled occupations. Four broad concepts of skill can be identified within the classifications:

- position of jobs on job ladders and within job grades in the firm;
- levels of workers in a status hierarchy within the enterprise;
- occupations that are discrete labour market categories; and
- levels of skill based on the recognized inter-firm training and qualifications.

The first approach is used for the Employment Cost Index (ECI) in the US (see the work post/job ladder column). The novelty of this conception arose from the need to measure increases in the price of labour independently of any movements up job ladders with increasing seniority. The presence of these is illustrated by the parallel vertical columns within the work post column, and the shaded areas spanning several skill levels, thus denoting their vertical spread, which of course makes it difficult to assign them to a single skill grade. In the presence of extensive job ladders, standard measures of labour cost will normally underestimate labour price changes in an upswing because increasing recruitment tends to be at the bottom of job ladders, and will overestimate them at the start of a recession. Thus, the Bureau of Labor Statistics devised a survey which sends field economists to firms to select the grades within occupations or on certain job ladders for which employers would then supply earnings and other labour cost data (Bureau of Labor Statistics (BLS), 1992). A fundamental assumption of this approach is that the job is the central focus of the exchange between workers and their employers, and the central unit of work organization, and that skill is primarily a function of job demands. A skilled worker is one who has acquired the necessary aptitudes to respond to the demands of a skilled job.

A striking feature of the second approach shows up in the dominant position of rank and the ambiguous position assigned to skill level and occupation in Japanese earnings structure statistics.[6] By rank, greater detail is shown for managerial and white-collar staff than in many other countries, although blue-collar workers are assigned to a single category. The survey does in fact publish data separately for about 100 occupations under a classification scheme dating from the 1950s, and which distinguishes women's from men's occupations. Many of these are either licensed or typical of small firms that have to rely more on external recruitment (Ohkusha et al., 1997). However, one searches in vain for many of the industrial professional and skilled blue-collar occupations such as engineers, fitters and electricians. This reflects the difficulty of defining skill levels for statistical purposes when there is a good deal of job rotation and workers are not assigned individually to well-defined jobs, and the lack of interest on the part of Japanese employers and unions in data on pay by occupation. Koike (1997) observes that it is common under Japanese job classifications for there to be a form of egalitarian task rotation so that particular tasks are unlikely to be uniformly assigned to workers possessing a particular skill level. It would therefore be very difficult for Japanese firms to provide earnings data by job type as used in the US ECI. Nor could they do so by level of occupational skill, as this concept is not reflected in Japanese firms' patterns of work organization and classification. In contrast, unlike in the other countries, the Japanese survey provides a wealth of data by rank, age, length of service, employment status and firm size, all variables of great interest to Japanese unions and employers.

The third approach is illustrated by ISCO-88. Although an international classification, its logic is close to that long used for British earnings statistics, where a version of ISCO is in fact now used. Here, the skill levels shown are not levels of qualification at all, but groupings of different three- and four-digit occupations into one-digit skill levels. As each of these individual occupations contains its own supervisors engaged in the same occupation, the ISCO-88 approach therefore includes supervisory staff in each level of skill. It will also include unqualified workers who are engaged in the same type activity and not obviously labourers.

To bring out the significance of this compared with the other three types of classification, the approximate locations of staff with managerial responsibilities are shaded, although they are not separately identified in the classification. This is not an arbitrary choice and reflects the underlying reality for occupations with strong identities. There, it is common for supervisors to be selected from within the occupation, and there may be also some intermediate levels of supervision, such as team leaders, in which the supervisors are not full-time and have only very limited decision powers. As the rules for identifying these vary between occupations, any simple definition of a category of supervisors is likely to be rather arbitrary, and thus would give poor quality information.

The classification that looks most like a hierarchy of skill is that used in German earnings statistics. The German qualification groups ('*Leistungsgruppe*') follow the lines established by externally certified skills and supervisory qualifications. As a result, skill is more consistently defined between firms, and the distinction between ordinary workers and supervisors is sharper, as supervision itself often requires certification. Employers returning the information receive guidance as to how to assign their employees to different occupational categories, and this makes reference to qualifications and job classifications with which they are familiar. Indeed, it would make little sense to do anything else.

What emerges from these four cases is that behind the apparent similarity of levels of skill lie fundamental differences in the notion of skill and in the principles according to which jobs and workers are organized and classified. These differences go deeper than saying there are different ways of assigning universally occurring tasks between jobs, and concern the way in which tasks themselves are conceived within the enterprise.

Although created for statistical rather than management purposes, the occupational classifications used for earnings statistics can tell us something about dominant classification practices because they are strongly influenced by the practice in firms and in collective agreements in any one country. There are two reasons: one methodological, and the other related to user demand. The first is quite simply that the quality of earnings data provided by firms is better the closer the statistical categories are to those used in company records. If the latter use the categories of collective agreements, for example, then it is relatively easy for firms to extract the relevant earnings data by occupation and to do so with a minimum of ambiguity. The smaller response burden will also improve the response rate, and hence the quality of the data. Alternatively, one might ask firms to write down job titles followed by a brief description of the work undertaken. Where the categories are widely used, coding is easy and accurate. Where they are unfamiliar or idiosyncratic, it is hard and the error rate is high. Normally, in the preparation of such surveys, the institutes consult widely with practitioners.

The second pressure aligning statistical classifications with those used in firms and in bargaining is that the users want earnings information according to their own everyday categories. Thus, firms want to know how much skilled electricians are paid in competitor firms, and unions want to know how the average earnings of the groups they represent compare with those of others and with price changes. Nobody wants earnings data shown according to categories which they do not use.[7]

In practice, collecting earnings data involves a good degree of aggregation, so no one will get quite the categories they want, but it is common in the questionnaires sent to firms to specify how the statistical categories compare with those used in collective agreements or some form of occupational licensing or to widely used diplomas. Thus, without being an exact picture of the classifications used in firms, those used in established national earnings surveys based on employers are strongly shaped by the systems used by the majority of respondents. We can therefore use information from national earnings surveys to learn about the dominant forms of firm-level job classification in the five countries.

It might be objected that the above cases prove only that national statistical institutes are good citizens and seek the most economical way of gathering data. If this means keeping close to the classifications used in firms, then that is what they will do. With greater resources, they could, in theory, adopt the BLS approach and send out teams of field economists to seek identical tasks and try to measure the earnings attached to these.[8] However, the different approaches to classification in the earnings statistics reveal different logics in the underlying classification systems used in firms. In the US, it is based on the occupants of the particular jobs or work posts selected, as these provide the most reliable focus for data collection from employers. In the Japanese case, the employee's rank provides the most reliable focus for collecting data by occupation, or as near an approximation to that concept as is possible there. In the British case, occupational categories prevail, and in Germany, certified skill and supervisory categories.

Overall, it is still just possible to achieve a rough alignment of workers by skill level, but it is a very rough one, and the cause of variation lies largely in the way in which job classification principles shape the definition of skill and other categories used within the firm. Thus the radical implication of the holistic approach to job classification is to see that jobs are not built up from universal types of tasks that can be found in all environments given a certain production technology. Instead, the choice of classification system shapes the way in which the tasks themselves are identified in different work processes and managed. To put it another way, if we had the chance to study Adam Smith's pin manufacture in different organizational contexts, we should expect to find the basic operations constructed differently, and modelled in the light of the prevailing principles of job classification. In the work post system, quality inspection would be identified as a separate task, as would most of the constituent operations that Smith identifies. Under the competence rank model, tasks would be weakly differentiated with varying boundaries and, depending on how they arose on a particular occasion, they might be done by one or another worker, and included as a part of one or another operation. Preventive action and responding to unusual tasks do not lend themselves to sharply defined tasks. Under the tools of the trade rule, maintenance tasks, being allied to particular skills, would be sharply differentiated from production work, whereas under the qualification rule, skilled work may include whatever operations are necessary that fall within a worker's competence, so again, many operations would not be separately identified.

4. LABOUR MARKET CONVENTIONS AND JOB CLASSIFICATIONS

Although inter-firm institutions have an important part to play in supporting workplace cooperation, the argument of the last chapter does not give them much to bite on. It is hard to judge whether or not one party's claim about work assignments and attached rates of pay or new technology is legitimate without a general language in terms of which they may be expressed. Herein lies the importance of job and pay classifications. The most explicit ones are the multi-employer job classifications associated with industry agreements, but the categories established by labour market custom and conventions can also be very influential.

4.1 Multi-employer job classification agreements

A very important channel through which task allocation rules can be strengthened is by means of job classification agreements. They establish a framework for categorizing jobs within firms, and set up principles for relating them to each other. In many instances, they are a critical supplement to industry bargaining over pay, and play a major role in countries with industry bargaining systems such as France and Germany, but in other countries, equivalent functions can be filled by other processes. In Britain, for example, customary boundaries of skilled work are often backed up by the apprenticeship system, and this has been widely recognized in company agreements, and so has provided a backbone around which company-level job classifications are constructed for blue-collar workers. In the US, Jacoby (1985) shows the role played by the Dictionary of Occupational Titles in establishing standard job definitions. As recently as 1994, Lawler (1994) cited it as reinforcing the prevailing 'job-based' pattern of work organization in American firms.

It has long been known that markets need ways of categorizing goods and services in order to function properly (Thévenot, 1985). Indeed, it is hard to imagine how the process of competition can function without employers being able to compare the asking wages of different workers offering the same skill, and vice versa. Yet, job classification systems existed in the twilight zone of research until the recent work on France of Eyraud *et al.* (1989), and an international ILO study reported by Eyraud and Rozenblatt (1994). What we learn from these is how the transaction rules regulating the employment relation are supported by the inter-firm rules embodied in the classification agreements.

The French case provides a particularly interesting illustration, showing both why such agreements have been neglected in the past, and why their role needs to be re-evaluated in the light of the theory of the employment relationship. It is also an important example for my argument because it is generally assumed that employers have considerable discretion over the organization of their internal labour markets. As French firms rely heavily upon this type of labour market, and have generally been reluctant to recognize state vocational qualifications as either a prerequisite for holding jobs of certain levels or as entitling the holders to a certain minimum job grade, one's immediate presumption is that firm-level autonomy would be the rule.

The industry classification agreements in France set up a means of classifying jobs and linking basic rates of pay to them. Although they have evolved considerably over the last five decades, a number of basic principles have remained fairly constant. Job categories are assigned to a number of job grades and ranked on a hierarchical scale to which pay indices are attached. In the firm, individual work posts are then assigned to job grades such as highly skilled manual, technician or supervisor, and so on. Within the grades, there may be a number of levels between which incumbents progress, or into which certain work posts may be slotted. Individual firms may also have their own classification systems on condition that the workers concerned can be shown to be no worse off than under the provisions of their industry agreement.

At first sight, the evidence of a large wage gap between the pay scales set in industry agreements and the gross earnings of workers on the equivalent grades appears to suggest the agreements have only a marginal role. For example, in the chemical industry in the early 1980s, Jobert and Rozenblatt (1985) estimated the wage gap to be about 20%, up slightly on the 1970s' figure. The later work of Eyraud *et al.* (1989) also showed that company-level agreements could also either raise or reduce the wage differentials set in industry agreements. On this evidence, therefore, it would seem that firms have a good deal of freedom and that the industry classification agreements do not impose much in the way of constraints. How then could they reinforce job level transaction rules and restrain opportunism?

Closer analysis reveals a much greater degree of influence. First, when the earnings gap is analysed at the level of individual workers, it proves to be largely explained by length of service, age and diploma, all criteria that are fundamental to the industry classification agreements. Secondly, the compression and expansion of intra-plant wage differentials as compared with the pay scales of the industry agreements is explained by the same variables: accounting for about 50% of the variance overall, and considerably more among blue-collar workers, supervisors and technicians (Eyraud *et al.*, 1989: 206 ff.). More recently, the 1992 structure of earnings survey shows that for six out of ten employees the job classifications used are those of their industry agreements (Barrat *et al.*, 1996). A further one in eight were covered by classifications based on company agreements, more common in large firms, but often these are quite close to the norms of industry agreements. Thus, the agreements prove to reinforce a number of key rules that are related to the work post system, notably the hierarchical ordering of jobs, the role of length of service in progression and the recognition of external qualifications at entry points, thus segregating internal and external training.

An impression of the qualitative influence of the industry classification rules is given by the methods adopted by French sectoral level employers and unions to deal with new technology, and the growing demand for skills in between those of skilled blue-collar and technician. The old metal industry classification agreement offered no easy solution to integrating this emerging category. The solution adopted was to establish a new job category of workshop technician ('technicien d'atelier'), inserted in between the blue-collar and technician categories (Carrière-Ramanoelina and Zarifian, 1985). Other solutions might have been possible, for example, a complete re-organization of blue-collar and technician skills, bringing more technicians into the workshop or by aiming at a more flexible pattern of work organization based on the increased competencies of individual workers. Both strategies would have blurred existing work post boundaries and called into question the principle of determinate categories of jobs and individual responsibility for a set of tasks. Instead, the logic of the classification system was maintained by the insertion of the new grade of work post. The authors also showed how the interests of the incumbent parties were reflected in the solution adopted. Employers insisted that only those competencies required by the post should be rewarded, whereas flexible jobs require workers to hold some 'excess' qualifications that can be called on when needed. The white-collar unions, and notably the middle management Confédération Générale des Cadres (CGC), wanted the new grade confined to blue-collar work to prevent an erosion of their own work posts, and the blue-collar unions were happy to have an extra grade to which their most skilled members could accede. At the company level, in their study of new technology in French firms, Eyraud *et al.* (1988) also found that the new jobs were mostly assimilated into the existing job classification categories. Thus, if one thinks of the sectoral classification agreements as dictating precise patterns of remuneration or detailed task assignments, then their influence on day-to-day work relations is bound to be small, and the latter would almost certainly be intended so. However, their true importance lies in the principles they enshrine. They have been shown to exert a powerful influence on the principles of work organization and the related pay incentives despite the 'wage gap' in earnings.

Another production approach example is given by the competence rank system as widely practised in Japan. There too, the importance of enterprise internal labour markets would suggest a great deal of autonomy, and the pattern of diffuse jobs militates against any parallel to the French and German sectoral classification agreements. Is there then a functional equivalent to these, that underpins employee confidence in the principles regulating work organization? Although there is no formal equivalent of western-European sectoral bargaining, the annual spring offensive is the occasion of intensive information exchange, discussion and negotiation among firms and enterprise unions and their federations (Sako, 1997). In these, certain signals play an extremely important part and bear strongly on the norms governing the employment transaction. The concept of the 'standard worker' (who is also 'regular') serves as the inter-firm standard for gauging demands for improvements in pay and conditions, and serves as the 'orbit of comparison' between firms and for changes over time. Focus on the regular worker highlights the second principle, that of long-term or life-time employment, the second orbit of comparison.[9] The power of these rules is well-illustrated by the reactions of large Japanese firms to the very deep recession of the early 1990s. Lincoln and Nakata (1997) show that despite wide media coverage of albeit small lay-offs by western-European and US standards, firms have gone to great, and expensive, lengths to avoid eroding the principle of long-term employment for their regular workers.

There are two reasons for this. First, as argued earlier, it is the key signal employers can give to their employees of their intention to maintain the competence rank system, and any serious departure from it would risk undermining the patterns of cooperation associated with it. But, secondly, its very clarity is greatly enhanced because it is a rule followed collectively by large Japanese firms for their domestic regular workforces. Any serious dilution of this commitment by one firm would erode the collective reputation of all large Japanese firms. Whereas cartels are notoriously prone to break down because of the rewards to the first partner to move independently, the intensive contacts among Japanese employers and between them and their unions create powerful informal channels through which moral pressures can be exercised to restrain potential defaulters. Strong links among enterprise unions, especially those grouped in the same federation, likewise help to reinforce pressure to maintain certain key standards, and especially valued among these is long-term employment. Indeed, Shirai and Shimada (1978) argued that union pressure was one of the prime causes behind the emergence of the lifetime employment system as union members were so dependent upon firm-specific skills. Thus, even among firms widely using internal labour markets, and in the absence of formal sectoral classification agreements, it is possible for an inter-firm functional equivalent to develop and to underpin confidence in job-level transaction rules.

4.2 Familiarity and convention

Customs and widely accepted labour market conventions may play a similar role to that of formal classification systems. Much has been made of their importance within workplaces, and in most countries where there is a tradition of empirical workplace research, one can find references to workplace custom. Brown (1973) highlighted the importance of workplace custom in shop steward bargaining in Britain, and Doeringer and Piore (1971) its importance in job regulation in North-American internal labour markets. But in Germany too, Bosch and Lichte (1982) provide examples of customary seniority rules in some workplaces, and Morel (1979) provides examples of such practices in France. When work rules are customary, the workers and managers concerned know how they will be applied, and know what outcomes to expect. It is relatively easy then to detect a change of behaviour by one or other side. Seniority in task allocations is a good example, as is allocation of work according to the tools required or materials used. There is usually a simple and unambiguous answer, and so rapid acceptance of a management decision that conforms to them. Morel provides a different kind of example from colder rural areas of France: the practice of employees being allowed to arrive late on the first day of heavy snow without prior agreement of management. The employees know this will not be penalized as absenteeism, but by the end of the first day they should have made their own arrangements to cope with getting to work in adverse weather conditions, or come to some agreement with management.

What is often less appreciated is the importance of particular practices being widespread in a particular sector or region. Although one can imagine repeated games in which such rules might emerge in a firm taken in isolation, they take time to become established. Typically, they would require the actors to go through several rounds, which in practical terms means encountering the same kinds of problem many times over. In some cases, such problems may recur frequently, but in Morel's example of the first heavy snowfall, this would happen perhaps only once a year or even less frequently. In the meantime, supervisors and their staff would be in considerable uncertainty as to how such events should be treated, with all the attendant dangers of suspected opportunism. For example, supervisors might be suspected of using lateness as a way of penalizing union activists, or they might fear that employees would use the heavy snow as the thin end of the wedge to gain acceptance for lateness under all kinds of weather conditions. In another example, that of wet weather compensation, Dunlop (1958) showed that special treatment of such conditions was common in the construction industries of all the countries that his study surveyed. In some cases it was formalized into collective agreements, while in others, it was of a more customary nature. The point is that once the rule is widely recognized within a sector, it is easy to apply because everyone understands its meaning, and the scope for opportunistic manipulation by either side is limited.

The 'tools of the trade' rule provides another example. Although commonly seen as a restrictive practice, the Webbs' (1902) study shows how useful familiarity with it could be across a host of independent workplaces which all used a large variety of different skills engaged on quite complex work. When management was faced with the complex task of assigning work to people of many different skills on sites in which the stability of factory work was absent, the tools of the trade generally gave clear and unambiguous answers. Plumbers had their work, and other trades theirs. As work on shipyards was unstable, and people were often hired for the construction of a particular ship, familiarity with such a rule in the local communities enabled orderly work organization to develop.

Similar conventions can also assist operation of formal classification agreements in the workplace. Although the 'work post' rule has been more commonly identified with Taylorist management, there too one can find evidence of such wider understandings. In theory, work posts could be organized in a number of different ways while still respecting task complementarity, as Lazear's discussion of why cherry picking and cherry spotting tend to be combined into a single role illustrates (Lazear, 1995)[10]. Nevertheless, Touraine (1955) observed that it was common, under this system, for each skilled worker to have 'his machine', a common custom inherited from the craft tradition of people being responsible for their own tools.

In the previous chapter (§4), it was argued that inter-firm rules and conventions support workplace transaction rules by making it easier to detect opportunistic action, by dispute-settling procedures, by policing the actions of one's own side and as a last resort, enabling the workplace actors to escalate their action. The argument would, however, be incomplete unless one could show there is also congruence between the type of rules shaping work roles at the job level and those of industry level classifications and conventions. The next section seeks to show that there is indeed a high degree of congruence.

5. SOME COMPARATIVE EVIDENCE ON CLASSIFICATIONS AND THEIR DIFFUSION

In a recent international comparative study of job classification systems at industry and company level, Eyraud and Rozenblatt (1994) proposed a typology that is quite close to that derived in Chapter 2 from the constraints on the employment relation. They argue that job classifications which they observed could be situated between two poles: classification according to the attributes of either the work post or of the individual worker. They identified also a third pole, namely, that of qualification which they sometimes present in an intermediate position in between the other two, and sometimes as a separate pole. Classification of jobs by work post attributes, they argue, is common in France and the US, and that by worker attributes, in Japan. The use of qualification or trade, which they present as a form of individual attribute, is widespread in Germany, and has been common in many other countries, such as Britain and Australia, but there it is in decline in the face of increased use of work post attributes, notably in job evaluation.

Eyraud and Rozenblatt start from wage determination rather than work role definition, and so concentrate on the link between classification systems and wage rules. Here they identify two types of wage relation under the work post system depending on whether job evaluation alone is used or whether it is supplemented by the recognition of certain status groups, such as, in France, those of 'blue-collar', 'white-collar and supervisory' and 'managerial employees' (cadres). These systems establish pay classifications according to the demands of categories of work posts, and workers are graded according to the work post which they occupy. Under such systems, skill is treated as an attribute of the work post and not of the individual job-holder.

The second broad category, which they identify primarily in Japan, is associated with the individual characteristics pole, namely a classification and remuneration system that is internal to the firm, in which employees are graded according to educational qualifications that are recognized at entry, and service and performance that are recognized thereafter. As the authors point out, there is no direct link between the work post and pay, nor does the personnel department have any information enabling them to establish one.

Two other types of classification system which they identify belong to the qualification pole: the British and Australian models in which craft or trade communities receive special recognition and gain the dominant position in company classification systems; and the German model, in which vocational qualifications play the key role. In the British classification systems they studied, the craft skills tended to occupy a prestigious but discrete position, as if the craft-skilled category was of a different nature to lower level skills. In the German ones, there was more of a continuous gradation of skill. For example, in many German agreements, length of service may be recognized as a partial equivalent, although not being allowed to displace formally acquired vocational skills.

5.1 Reinterpreting the ILO evidence

At first sight, their typology seems to provide partial support for the argument of this book, but only partial because of their emphasis on the qualification pole as an intermediate case in between the other two. However, I hope to show that if one resolves some of the tensions within their typology, then their model coincides very closely with the typology of transaction rules derived from the constraints on the employment relation (see Figure 4.3).

The basic difficulty of their typology lies in the problematic position of the 'qualification' pole. If one takes the contrast between classification by job or by individual characteristics, then publicly recognized vocational qualifications do not fit. Hence the fluctuation in the authors' treatment of that pole. There are two basic problems: first, skill based on vocational qualifications clearly is not an attribute of individual jobs. If the two coincide, it is because the training approach to job design has been adopted. Nor is such qualification really an individual attribute. Its effectiveness depends upon its widespread use by many firms; otherwise, for reasons explained in Chapter 8, the size of the market for the skill concerned is too small to warrant workers investing in it. Nor can it be seen as an intermediate case, as it clearly is not a mix of two different logics but follows a distinct one of its own.

The second problem in their classification is that length of service and performance are not strictly individual attributes as practised in the large

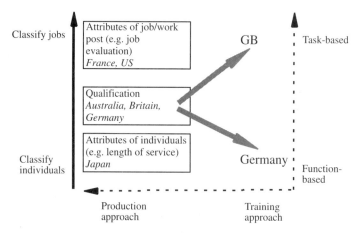

Fig. 4.3. Eyraud–Rozenblatt model of classification agreements
Key: The hatched lines show the categories of transaction rules; the solid lines show those of Eyraud and Rozenblatt. The thick shaded arrows show the amended version of the authors' treatment of qualification-based classification systems.

Japanese firms on which we have most evidence (see for example Koike and Inoki, 1990). Length of service signals the duration of a person's membership of a particular enterprise community, and performance is carefully assessed by management based on such criteria as contribution to the work group's effort. In this respect, length of service and performance have a rather different meaning compared with that which they often have under work post systems where the same criteria often apply.

In fact, one can resolve these problems by locating Eyraud and Rozenblatt's examples within the typology of transaction rules. The German and British classifications based on qualification and craft rules clearly belong to a different logic to that of the US, French and Japanese systems, which are based on variants of the 'production approach'. The French and US classification systems clearly belong together because they classify work posts, even though there may be differences of emphasis in the precise way in which they are divided up. In the Japanese case, the classification systems are not assessing individual characteristics in relation to specific jobs but in relation to contribution to team output, and the teams are primarily engaged in fulfilling certain functions in production. It is true that, as in the US and France, where employee performance appraisal is also used increasingly, appraisal in the large Japanese firms is by supervisors, but more often these are 'player managers' rather than specialist supervisors, hence the large number of supervisors noted by Jürgens and Strömel (1987) in their comparison of two Japanese and German car plants. The work team, including the supervisors, has been likened by Koike and Inoki (1990) to a semi-autonomous work group. Thus, what is being evaluated is the contribution to a team, and as the job boundaries are diffuse and flexible, it is not a contribution readily identifiable with certain tasks, but rather with the quality of cooperation or interaction with other team members.

The results of the Eyraud and Rozenblatt study show, therefore, a marked convergence between the micro-level transaction rules needed to establish job level cooperation and the company and industry-wide classification systems. This conclusion is especially important for the ways in which inter-firm conventions sustain workplace transaction rules. The convergence between the substance of workplace rules and classification principles illustrates how the latter provide the external point of reference for workplace rules.

5.2 Coverage of classification systems

One limitation of Eyraud and Rozenblatt's study is that it relies heavily on evidence from collective agreements and their effects, and so it does not necessarily establish a picture of job classification principles in other sectors of the economy. This matters more in some countries than in others, as can be seen from the estimates of union density and bargaining coverage (Table 4.1). In both France and Germany, nine out of ten workers in those countries are covered by collective agreements, and an important part of their structure is established in industry level pay and job classifications. In Britain too, up to the early 1980s, collective agreements were also a powerful vehicle helping to generalize models of pay and job classifications. In all of these countries, and especially France and Germany, collective agreements have been the vehicle by which employers and unions have established common principles of job classification.

The position in the US and Japan is harder to evaluate, as bargaining coverage has never been as high, and it is necessary to turn to other data sources to assess how far common principles apply across these economies. Nevertheless, the evidence reviewed in the next chapter (especially in §4) based on surveys of personnel practices in individual plants shows a good deal of conformity to the national classification models that Eyraud and Rozenblatt describe. In the US, several studies attest to the continued influence of the 'bureaucratic' employment systems that prevailed under the Wagner industrial relations system, and a great resilience of the internal labour market practices associated with them. Change there has been, but from an international perspective, the basic employment norms have continued to shape practices in most workplaces. Likewise, in Japan, plant level survey evidence shows a high degree of diffusion across plants of the key employment practices associated with the dominant employment system. Thus, in both the US and Japan it is clear that the diffusion of the job classification and job regulation principles examined in the ILO study extend well beyond firms covered by collective agreements, and that the picture painted by Eyraud and Rozenblatt, suitably reinterpreted, can be taken as fairly representative of the countries included. The classification rules exert a powerful influence extending across the majority of employment in the different countries.

Table 4.1. *Union density and collective bargaining coverage rates 1970–90*[a]

Country	Union density 1970[b]	Union density 1990	Bargaining coverage 1980	Bargaining coverage 1990[c]
France	22	10	85	92
Germany	33	33	91	90
Great Britain	45	39	70	47
Japan	35	25	28	23
United States	23	16	26	18

[a] % of wage and salary earners; [b] US, 1977; [c] France, 1985; Germany, 1992; Japan, 1989. *Source*: OECD (1994: 184, 185).

6. THE ROLE OF INSTITUTIONS IN DIFFUSING CLASSIFICATION RULES

Although the previous chapter showed that the transaction rules are capable of diffusion on their own merits, a brief historical look across the five countries shows that labour institutions and the state have played an important part at various stages in their development. One reason for this lies in the holistic nature of classification systems, that is they classify by the application of key principles rather than by doing so inductively. Like a language, both employers and employees use the classification systems as a way of reading the information they have about jobs in an organization, and one cannot change the meaning people attach to such things unilaterally. The Queen in Alice in Wonderland could say words meant what she wanted them to mean, but she could not make other people understand them in this way. Because change has to come from both sides, the emergence of a new set of classification principles will more often occur with a 'big bang' rather than by a slow process of incremental change. This quality also enhances the ability of classification systems to resist pressures to move towards another system.

In France, one such period occurred after the 1936 Popular Front. Peak-level unions and employers came together with the active encouragement of the then government to re-found the system of industry bargaining which had fallen into abeyance after the early 1920s. In doing so, they had to develop a system of job classifications for each industry. The state played a major part in setting up and guiding the tripartite job classification commissions (Sellier, 1984). Surveying the bargaining landscape at the outbreak of the war, two eminent labour lawyers observed that the close association between the activities of unions and employer organizations and those of the state had become the normal method for regulating industry level employment relations (Rivero and Savatier, 1970: 270).[11] The wage and price controls of the Liberation period used these classifications under the 'Parodi system' as part of the apparatus of labour market administration, and so helped establish familiarity with their norms across all economic sectors. The 'Parodi classifications' continued into the 1970s when they were re-negotiated, but as Eyraud (1978) showed, even that involved a good deal of continuity with the preceding system.

In the US, the period between 1935 and 1945 was also a watershed, with the spread of union agreements and wartime state labour market administration. These were critical to the establishment of the set of principles surrounding the work post system there and of the 'bureaucratic' model of employment. Union influence was visible in the action of the Congress of Industrial Organizations (CIO) to spread work post rules rather than defend the older craft orientation of the American Federation of Labor (AFL) (Baron *et al.*, 1986b). The influence of the state on classification was felt through the

War Manpower Commission (WMC) and the War Labor Board (WLB), which respectively sought to coordinate manpower planning and administer wage controls (Jacoby, 1985). The WMC used the newly established Dictionary of Occupational Titles to manage training and labour transfers, and this obliged firms to conduct extensive job analyses using the titles of the dictionary. The WLB would only allow pay increases for genuine promotion, and to prove this, firms had to be able to show that they had orderly promotion procedures such as job ladders or job classification charts.[12]

Unions have also been very influential in Britain in the spread of employment norms. As was clear from the Webbs' account of 'industrial democracy' at the turn of the century, the job territory principle was already deeply rooted, but union action has also been important at certain critical junctures. Rowe (1928) describes the 'standardization' movement of the late nineteenth and early twentieth centuries that reduced local variation in jobs and pay rates.[13] Another interesting case can be found in the reaction of the skilled engineering unions to the rise of semi-skilled work, especially during the 1914–18 war. This was one of the important historical junctures, when events could have gone either way. Skilled workers could adopt the AFL strategy of holding themselves aloof from the growing organizations of the semi-skilled, or they could do a deal with them. In the British engineering industry they did a deal, and Turner (1952) shows how they made concessions on skilled wage differentials in order to bring the new categories of semi-skilled workers into their unions. In doing so, they built an alliance that enabled them to maintain the key principles of craft organization in the face of a rising tide of Taylorism. Studying job classifications and bargaining practices in Britain and France in engineering fifty years later, Eyraud (1981) observed a continuing willingness by the skilled unions in Britain to forego pay in order to maintain principles of job regulation.

In Germany, employer mobilization to sustain the system of occupational skills can be seen in a number of individual industries. Streeck's study (1985) illustrates the role of employer mobilization in defending the construction industry apprentice system against state intervention, and their success in gaining support for provisions that were more stringent than those proposed by the state. Drexel's study (1980) of the extension of apprenticeship training to the chemical and iron and steel industries, respectively, in 1949 and 1966 provides another example. There the firms made use of existing employer organizations to adopt an inter-firm solution to the need to modernize the skills developed previously by OJT within firm internal labour markets.

Another example occurred in Japan with the employer-led industry-wide mobilization to raise quality in Japan, mentioned in the previous chapter. Like training for occupational skills, improving quality also faces externality problems because no firm is an island, and it cannot raise the quality of its own products unless that of its suppliers also improves. The quality control circle (QCC) movement in Japan promoted a method of workplace problem-solving that raised workers' skills because they were directly involved, and sought to embody the solutions discovered into new organizational routines, thus promoting organizational learning. In fact, the diffusion of QCCs is of double interest. First, it helped establish common incentives across firms (combined with long-term employment, job rotation and high initial education) for the development of broad skills and the competence ranking system (Koike, 1997). Secondly, it illustrates the role of employer organization in its development. Such organization can be seen as a functional equivalent to the formal job classification systems to be found in France and Germany. The Japanese Union of Scientists and Engineers (JUSE)'s success can be measured by the rapid spread of QCCs compared with the other countries of Cole's (1989) study (the US and Sweden), and in the high degree of participation: by 1987 JUSE had 1,800 company members and involved 140,000 employees in its grass roots activities, which included such things as comparing notes on QCC activities. The only other movement of comparable scale is probably the REFA[14] association in Germany, which has about 50,000 members, mostly company and union experts in a system of job design and evaluation that is used by both sides.

In all these examples, an important aspect of the consolidation of particular classification systems and related employment practices has been the intense mobilization of the key actors for a relatively short time. In relatively few years, such action established new methods for organizing work and classifying jobs, or led to the adaptation of existing models. There does not seem to be a general rule concerning the precise form of the institutions mobilized, except that they generate a sufficient level of focused activity to enable many firms and workers to move to a new set of employment principles in a relatively concentrated time period, and overcome some of the disadvantages of innovating in isolation from other employers.

7. EMPLOYMENT SYSTEMS: INTEGRATING TRANSACTION RULES AND INTER-FIRM INSTITUTIONS

The employment transaction rules are able to spread across an economy as a result of decentralized decisions by firms and workers. Because their choice is limited to the four basic types of rule, and because the more highly diffused a rule is the more attractive it becomes to others, the model predicts that employment relationships across large areas of any economy will tend to be governed by a single type of rule. Thus, even without the support of inter-firm institutions, one would expect a measure of societal diversity in the organization of employment relations.

The last two chapters have also shown that inter-firm institutions can boost the diffusion and effectiveness of individual transaction rules. They can do so in four main ways:

- improving the ability of individual workers and firms to enforce their side of the bargain;
- facilitating the renegotiation of employment terms;
- establishing a common language and set of norms for classifying and regulating jobs; and
- supporting activities such as training to common standards when there are important externalities.

Improving the enforceability of employment rules helps to reinforce the effectiveness of 'tit-for-tat' solutions to the prisoner's dilemma. The support of union and employer organizations means that workers and management at the firm level can take the risk of cooperating more easily without fearing that it will weaken their individual long-term bargaining position. If the other party defects and this leads to a dispute, either side has the opportunity to escalate the action if its peers consider it justified. The latter condition also gives inter-firm bodies the power to police the actions of their own members, as they can decide to withhold support from frivolous or opportunistic actions. Perhaps even more important, unions and employer organizations often have the resources to help vet information provided locally by the other party, and to check whether it is provided in good faith or is being manipulated.

Renegotiation of employment terms, and especially those concerning the limits of managerial authority, is very difficult for individual workers because of the large asymmetries involved. Management can see the whole picture, but employees can usually see only their own and closely related jobs. If the purpose of the basic employment rules is to provide a framework in which flexible working is protected from opportunism, then trying to change them puts the framework itself at risk. Individual employees are then very exposed and the natural response is to resist change. In such conditions, unions especially can provide a protective shield, and it was in this sense that Appelbaum and Batt (1994) argued that unions can be a great organizational asset when management wants to introduce fundamental changes in work organization.

Job classifications enable employees and management to address flexibility issues with a common language and reduce the problems of job idiosyncrasy that figure so large in Williamson's treatment of the employment relationship. They are an essential component of enforceability, making the employment rules more robust, and without them unions and employer organizations have little to bite on in their role of sustaining workplace order. If jobs are too idiosyncratic, it is difficult to assist dispute resolution procedures and difficult to vet information. Indeed, if such idiosyncrasy is too strong it is hard for even the basic transaction rules to function, and hard to resist the pressures of continuous spot bargaining.

Finally, many activities, such as training to common standards across firms and promoting long-term workplace reform, raise important externalities and so create scope for opportunism, for example, poaching skilled labour trained by other firms. If allowed to develop, this discourages individual firms from actions which could, if pursued by all, lead to common benefits. Collective organizations can therefore provide an important support in such cases (see Chapter 8).

In all four cases, although the functions served by inter-firm institutions may be clearly defined, their organizational form appears to leave a good deal of variation. There is variation according to the type of transaction rule in force, and even for the same kind of rule. One might say, therefore, that the mutual support that transaction rules and inter-firm institutions provide to each other requires only that they be, as Cole put it, 'loosely coupled'. If we look across the five countries covered in this book, we see that there is a great deal of institutional diversity, and even where the formal institutions are rather similar, as between France and Germany, which both have works councils and industrial unions, the way in which they operate in practice is quite different. German unions and works councils have been able to provide powerful support to workplace cooperation over job-related issues, whereas those in France have been more notable for their weakness at this level. Although job and pay classifications in France and Germany are supported by industry agreements, which help ensure the wide diffusion of common principles, in Japan, as Koike (1997) has explained, inter-firm influence has been almost accidental. As he argues, the wide diffusion of broad skills and broad jobs was an unanticipated consequence of other practices widely diffused among firms (see §5 above). A third example of such 'loose coupling' can be found in the discussion in Chapter 8 of the way in which occupational markets have been upheld more by union action in Britain and more by the action of employer organizations in Germany.

Hence, the concept of an employment system leaves a degree of freedom as to how the function of support to the employment relationship is to be achieved. There are however some limits, which will be more fully discussed in the concluding chapter, although they may be mentioned now. First, the function-centred rules are more dependent upon cooperative relations between workers and management than are the task-centred rules, and this suggests that the former will be favoured by more cooperative and less adversarial styles of employee relations. Secondly, the training approach is more heavily dependent upon strong inter-firm institutions to sustain high rates of employer-provided training for occupational skills, and to maintain the integrity of the training approach to job design. Finally, of the four types of rules, the work post is the one that is least dependent on inter-firm institutions. It is the most robust in environments of adversarial relations, but it is also the most rigid in terms of work assignments. As will be argued in the final chapter, it places least demands on inter-firm institutions, but this very strength can be a weakness when firms wish to make the transition to more flexible patterns of work organization.

ENDNOTES

[1] Stinchcombe (1959) provides an interesting example from the US construction industry in which the customer commissions an architect to organize some building work which is put out to a general contractor, who then parcels it out further to members of the different building trades.

[2] The link with performance management has long been recognized. For example, the US Civil Service Commission 1903 Annual Report stressed that promotion on merit depends upon the ability to compare employees' performance, and this depends upon their doing comparable jobs. Thus, the report argued that standardized job classifications were an essential tool of performance management (Betters, 1931).

[3] The basic idea behind the contrast between the atomistic and holistic approaches can be captured by analogy. In the first case, one might obtain bricks by dismantling an old wall and using them to build something different, say a brick path. The same basic elements are used, but they are arranged differently to achieve different ends. The second case is more like moulding bricks from clay. The dimensions and shape of the bricks are variable until they have been cast into moulds. In this case rectangular bricks may be cast for a wall, and rounded ones for building a round chimney. The shape of the basic units is determined according to the use to which they will be put. Shaping them for one use precludes assigning them to a range of other uses.

[4] In his study of the way workers categorized themselves, Touraine (1966) set out three key principles: of identity, difference and totality. A similar logic applies within the holistic definition of categories within job classifications.

[5] Indeed, as early as 1835, the then US Secretary of the State cautioned against using over-detailed job specifications in the reform of the federal civil service, and to avoid staff refusing to undertake work not included in their specifications, insisted on including the catch-all phrase of 'other such duties' as directed by Secretary (Betters, 1931: 5).

[6] I am grateful to H. Nohara for explaining this to me.

[7] The author was consultant to the Statistical Office of the European Communities during the preparation of the 1995 European Structure of Earnings Survey and its European Employment Cost Index, and was party to the discussions about the occupational classification to be used. ISCO-88 was the clear favourite because it had already been adopted for censuses and the Labour Force Survey, but there was considerable opposition from employers' organizations in several countries because ISCO categories did not mean anything to their members who would have been using the statistics.

[8] In France, the wide coverage of collective agreements means that statisticians can use the categories of collective agreements instead of having to go to the expense of the US method, although this does involve an approximation.

[9] I am grateful to Mitsuharu Miyamoto for explaining how this functions.

[10] In the example discussed in Chapter 2, Lazear suggests that it might be more efficient on incentive grounds to separate the spotting of cherries to be picked and the actual picking. The picker has an incentive to gather the most accessible fruit and to leave the rest, whereas the grower may wish to maximize the return on each tree. By hiring a specialist fruit spotter the grower could ensure that more

cherries were picked. However, the gains from the technical complementarity of the two roles means that it may still prove more economical to combine the roles in a single worker.

[11] Job classification was taken further during the Occupation by the Vichy government, which substituted a system of labour market administration which likewise required detailed job classifications (Jobert, 1990). Thus, as Sellier (1961) observed, for the decade 1939–50, France had administratively set wages, with maxima and minima set for each category in the classification.

[12] Seniority pay rises were also allowed by the WLB, and this encouraged firms to adopt that norm.

[13] Rowe's main interest was in wage rates, but it is clear that these cannot be standardized without a similar move to establish the common categories of labour to receive the same pay rates.

[14] Reichsausschuß für Arbeitszeitermittlung. The organization was set up in the early 1920s, and played a major part in the reform of payment by results systems and the introduction of Taylorism (Lutz, 1975: 115).

II

EVIDENCE AND PERSONNEL
MANAGEMENT IMPLICATIONS

Societal Diversity of Employment Systems: Comparative Evidence

1. SOME EVIDENCE OF INTER-COUNTRY DIFFERENCES IN EMPLOYMENT SYSTEMS

The aim of this chapter is to present the evidence that each of the four models of the employment relationship set out in the preceding chapters holds sway over large sectors of different national economies. This provides an empirical test of whether the same sectors in different countries are characterized by major differences in the organization of employment relations, and whether these correspond to the patterns predicted by the theory developed here. It does so by assembling indicators for the presence of the four types of transaction rule. Owing to the reliance on secondary data, the analysis focuses largely on the sector that has been studied most, namely, production industries. Ideally, the net should be cast more widely to include services, but the number of international comparative studies for this sector is even more limited.

In an ideal world, one would organize a research project to study differences in the organization of employment systematically across countries, combining a mixture of carefully matched establishment case studies with more aggregated data from statistically representative surveys. This was what Maurice *et al.* (1986) did for France and Germany when they showed that not only were there systematic differences in pay, skills and work organization between matched pairs of French and German manufacturing plants, but also that the French plants uniformly employed a higher percentage of the relatively better-paid categories of workers. In order to explain this, they collected data on sectoral patterns of vocational training, industrial relations and management control systems in each country. However, such detailed plant level studies are few and far between. The evidence actually available is more like a jigsaw puzzle from which many pieces are missing. This chapter presents a partial survey of evidence relevant to the

Table 5.1. *Dominant employment rules by country*

	Production approach	Training approach
Task-centred rules	France, US	Britain
Function-centred rules	Japan	Germany

organization of the employment relationship in the five countries covered in this book.

The evidence reviewed is divided into two parts: first a summary of the studies which show the incidence of the production and the training approaches to job regulation and work assignments; and second, a similar analysis of the incidence of the task- and function-centred approaches to control systems and work coordination. Taken together, these two analyses summarize the indicators of the dominant employment rules in the five countries' industrial sectors as shown in Table 5.1. They mirror the results on job and pay classifications of the previous chapter.

The last part of the chapter takes a special look at evidence on diffusion in the US and Japan, where collective bargaining coverage is weaker and the patterns of coordination between firms could be thought to give rise to a greater variety of employment systems than in the other countries, and possibly even to the absence of a dominant model.

The evidence is drawn from a variety of different sources. First, there are comparative studies of plant-level employment relations, such as that by Maurice *et al.* (1986), which was extended from the initial Franco-German comparison by Sorge and Warner (1986) to include plants in Britain. Other examples include the plant level comparisons of Britain and Japan by Dore (1973), Lam (1994, 1997) and Whittaker (1993), and of Japanese, South-east Asian and US plants by Koike and Inoki (1990), and of plants in the US, Japan and western Europe by Jürgens *et al.* (1993). At this level, one has to work with several two- or three-way comparisons within different sectors. But there is no representative study of plants in all five countries capable of providing the kind of qualitative observations required.

To broaden the range of variables and sectors covered, a small number of national studies have been added which have adopted similar methods of data collection and analysis. These help to locate the countries with respect to certain indicators. Examples include the classic local labour market studies of Rees and Shultz (1970) in the Chicago area, and of MacKay *et al.* (1971) in Britain. Such studies may also be complemented by the judgements of researchers who have carried out establishment-level fieldwork in different countries, albeit not as part of systematic comparative projects, for instance Sengenberger (1987).

A second type of evidence comes from the small but increasing number of comparative surveys of firms' employment practices in different countries.

As yet there is no international equivalent of the British Workplace Industrial Relations Survey or the US National Organizations Study. But there is now a useful number of smaller-scale comparative surveys, especially comparing the US and Japan, such as those of Cole (1979) and Lincoln and Kalleberg (1990).

A third source of evidence comes from the growing international comparability of official earnings and employment surveys, encouraged by the work of the ILO and Eurostat. Such material has proved very useful for testing the representativeness of some of the establishment case studies (e.g. Eyraud *et al.*, 1990; Marsden, 1990) as well as to test institutional models of labour market behaviour (e.g. Hashimoto and Raisian, 1985; DeFreitas *et al.*, 1991), as well as more recent comparative studies of pay structures by Freeman and Katz (1995) and Tachibanaki (1998).

2. PRODUCTION VERSUS TRAINING APPROACH: KEY INDICATORS

Five key indicators have been selected to judge whether or not firms use primarily the production or the training approach to job design and task assignment. Based on the argument in Chapter 2, these are:

- job design: priority given to technology or to workers' skills, and assignment of tasks associated with new technology;
- skill transferability;
- reward for seniority;
- treatment of occupational skills in job classifications; and
- wage contours of occupational and internal labour markets.

The full range of studies is summarized in two special tables (5.11 and 5.12) at the end of the chapter.

2.1 Job design

The most direct test of the prevalence of the production or training approach lies in the priority which management gives in job design to the demands of production technology or to those of skills and training. Broadly speaking, the evidence on the diffusion of job design principles follows the pattern as shown in Table 5.1 above, with the production approach dominant in industrial firms in the US, France and Japan, and the training approach holding sway in Germany and Britain.

Direct survey evidence on approaches to job design can be found only in one case: that of production engineers' views in the US surveyed by Davis *et al.* (1955) and repeated fifteen years later by Taylor (1979). For further evidence of the dominance of the production approach in job design in US industry, we have to turn to the plant level interviews with production engineers by Piore (1968), and the study of work reorganization and productivity bargaining by McKersie and Hunter (1973), and more recently, in the automobile industry, by Jürgens *et al.* (1993). The latter highlighted the narrow job structures and narrow base of team working in US plants compared with those in European countries.

French firms similarly make heavy use of the production approach. This was analysed in detail in the establishment case-study comparisons with German plants by Maurice *et al.* (1986) as well as in the work of Eyraud *et al.* (1988), which showed the production approach applied to job design for new technology. The influence of the production approach can also be seen in the active management role in job design in Gallie's (1978) comparison of maintenance work in French and British oil refineries. As a consequence, the French maintenance workers were much more closely supervised than their British counterparts.

Japanese industrial firms also follow the production approach, albeit with a function-centred rather than the task-centred approach widely used in France and the US. In a number of his field and statistical studies of work and skill organization, Koike (1997) has stressed the use of job rotation for developing broad-based skills according to task structures that are unconstrained by external skill requirements. The work by Jürgens *et al.* (1993) on the automobile industry also stresses the organization of work for task rotation within homogeneous work teams in Japan. They also highlight one of the key features of rotation within the production approach: the tasks between which workers move tend to be rather narrow, particularly when compared with models of team-working developed in Germany. The same observation was made by Turner and Auer (1994).

In Britain, the dominant position of craft skills has served as a model for other less-skilled occupations, and has shaped principles of job design to give priority to established skills. Sengenberger (1987) notes this in his review of approaches to work organization and internal labour markets in Britain, Germany and the US, and it was also apparent to McKersie and Hunter in their work on productivity bargaining, as it was to Jürgens *et al.* in their automobile industry study. The persistence of the craft influence is confirmed by Whittaker's study (1993), which provides another comparative illustration of the role of craft skills in determining the design of jobs for new technology. In comparison with the Japanese firms of his study, the British ones practised a marked segmentation between craft and programming skills with CNC equipment in Britain. Although apprenticeship, the traditional basis of craft skills, has been in decline in Britain for two decades, Elger's (1991) review of studies of skill flexibility in Britain during the 1980s showed that firms had achieved mostly only modest changes, despite the publicity given to some radical changes.

In Germany, the continued dominance of job design by the system of occupational skills has been more secure than in Britain, and several studies highlight their strong position in new forms of work organization as well in the more traditional ones. Sengenberger (1987) presents the training approach as deeply rooted in Germany through much of the post-war period for skilled work, and the studies of new production concepts by Kern and Schumann (1984) and by Jürgens *et al.* (1993) show that their position has if anything been reinforced. As in Britain, semi-skilled occupations have generally been less clearly structured on occupational lines, but full development of the production approach for them is limited by two factors: very restricted upgrading to skilled work for the semi-skilled effectively truncates any kind of job ladders; and the skill model serves as a standard for other less-structured occupations.

2.2 Skill transferability and occupational markets

Skill transferability and the rewards for seniority are shaped by the adoption of either the training or the production approach. Chapter 8 argues that skill transferability depends heavily on the adoption of the training approach by a large number of firms so that transferability is incompatible with the production approach. Likewise, the reward for seniority, either in the form of internal job mobility or of pay increments, is strongly associated with use of the production approach. In the same chapter, it is argued that the training approach entails costly restrictions on firms' freedom to design jobs so that they would be unlikely to adopt it unless suitable occupational skills were available. Therefore, one can expect skill transferability to be greatest in contexts in which the training approach is used, and for seniority to be most valued in those in which the production approach prevails. Thus, skill transferability would be a feature of German and British occupational labour markets, and seniority-based practices would be more deeply rooted in France, the US and Japan. Two types of evidence are relevant: the nature and diffusion of training systems for occupational skills, and the maintenance of skill status on changing employer.

The dominant position of occupational skills at the intermediate level in industry in Germany, and to a lesser extent in Britain, and their relative weakness or absence in the other three countries is confirmed by a number of recent reviews of the evidence. Büchtemann *et al.* (1993) compare Germany and the US, Crouch (1995) compares Britain and Germany, Dore and Sako (1989) compare Japan implicitly with Britain, and Marsden and Ryan (1990b) France, Germany and Britain. Apprenticeship training in Britain underwent a long decline from the late 1960s, but the stock of skilled workers who have been through this form of training remains large. Moreover, in the face of failure of other forms of vocational training to fill the gap

(Steedman, 1998), since the early 1990s there have been major attempts to renovate and revive apprenticeship (Gospel, 1998).

Such occupational skills are transferable in practice, as is shown by the ability of workers to maintain their skill levels while changing employer in Britain and Germany. Eyraud *et al.* (1990) noted this in Labour Force Survey data for Britain compared with France, and German cohort studies document how apprentice-trained young workers change firms while remaining in skilled positions (Hofbauer and Nagel, 1987). A number of other surveys also highlight the way in which British employers can generally recruit skilled labour directly from outside. MacKay *et al.*'s local labour market study (1971) in Britain, which mirrors that in the Chicago area of Rees and Shultz, found their firms recruiting from outside at all skill levels, and that seniority promotion, common in the US, was much less so in Britain. The continued ability of British employers to recruit skilled labour externally was confirmed in employer responses to the Warwick employer survey (Brown, 1981). In contrast, the probability of losing one's skill status on changing employer is considerably higher in France, reflecting the lesser transferability of skills (Eyraud *et al.*, 1990). In the US, Lynch's (1992) of young job-changers also showed a lack of transferability of their newly acquired job skills, which suggests occupational downgrading on changing jobs.

2.3 Internal promotion and internal labour markets

Several studies have attested to the importance of internal promotion and seniority in many US firms. In Rees and Shultz's (1970) study of firms in the Chicago labour market, seniority was the most consistent source of earnings growth within occupations within plants across the twelve occupations studied.[1] Although there has been considerable debate as to whether this reflects rising productivity from OJT (as Brown's evidence (1989) suggested), or the application of incentive schemes to encourage commitment and stability (e.g. Medoff and Abraham, 1980), both interpretations are consistent with the presence of the production approach and the resulting value of job tenure to employers.

In France too, limited skill transferability combined with upgrading and seniority mechanisms indicate prevalence of the production approach. Comparing France and Britain, Eyraud *et al.* (1990) found that internal upgrading continues to be a force in French firms, as was observed in the France–Germany comparison by Maurice *et al.* (1986). Compared with Britain, one notable feature was the tendency of skill to rise with seniority. This relationship is confirmed by cohort studies of qualified new entrants (e.g. Podevin and Viney, 1991), which showed that the effect of vocational qualifications was to improve access to better OJT and subsequent promotion, rather than qualifying someone for a skilled position. Likewise in Japan, Dore and Koike show that skills are not transferable between firms unless organized in the form of personnel transfers by the employers themselves. The latter is usually in one direction only, from large to smaller firms, and then often to avoid lay-offs. Comparing the US and Japan, Koike (1988), for earlier years, and Lincoln and Kalleberg (1990), more recently, highlight the importance of seniority mechanisms in plants in both countries.

2.4 Treatment of skills in job and pay classifications

As shown in the previous chapter, the job classification systems widely practised in the five countries mirror the logic of the employment transaction rules (Eyraud and Rozenblatt, 1994). In France and the US, classifications focus on the work post, and in Japan, on workers' ability to contribute to the productive effort of a flexible work group. The continued vitality of the work post system in France is illustrated by the failure by both unions and governments to encourage greater recognition of vocational training in job and pay classification systems. Their position remains problematic because firms maintain that job demands, not worker skills, are the focus. In both Britain and Germany, occupational skills are powerfully recognized in enterprise job and pay-classification systems, and seniority generally has only a small role, if at all. Occupational skills dominate the position of skills based on OJT, as they set a strict ceiling on upward mobility by semi-skilled workers. German collective agreements set strict limits on how far semi-skilled employees without an apprenticeship may progress up the pay scales.

2.5 Wage contours and occupational and internal labour markets

In labour markets where the training approach and occupational skills predominate, one would expect such skills to establish pay contours across the labour market. In contrast, where the production approach and internal labour markets predominate, pay contours are more likely to be internal to the firm and more strongly influenced by seniority.

(a) Contours based on occupational skills

With occupational markets, pay contours between firms will be strong as firms compete to hire the same recognized skills. This creates an orbit of comparison which may be based both on feelings of equity, that the same work merits the same pay, and competition among employers. With ILMs, even though firms may, as they do in France, use the same industry classification systems, these leave individual firms with more freedom over pay

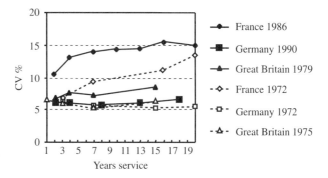

Fig. 5.1. Impact of pay contours between firms on industry wage levels
Dispersion of earnings (CV%) between industries by length of service (years).
Sources: 1972, Saunders and Marsden (1981); updated with data from the 1986 French structure of earnings survey (Rotbart, 1991); the 1990 German survey (Statistisches Bundesamt, 1993/4) and the 1979 British New Earnings Survey.

and job design, and the more limited scope for inter-firm mobility means that competitive pressures on the pay for individual jobs will be weaker.

The stronger inter-firm pay linkages created by occupational skills can be seen in two indicators: a smaller effect of worker length of service on the variation of pay levels between firms and industries; and a stronger effect of skill levels. Figure 5.1 shows the effect of increasing length of service on the increasing heterogeneity of worker skills in France (shown by the increasing inter-industry variation of pay with service) compared with the virtual absence of such effects in Britain and Germany.

Table 5.2 shows the variation of earnings between industries for different skill levels. The CV within skill groups rises with skill in France, but falls in Germany and Britain, again showing the tendency for skill heterogeneity to be greater in France, where ILMs prevail, than in the other two countries, where OLMs are more influential.

(b) ILM contours based on seniority

Another angle on the same question, and for the same European countries, is given by the effect of length of service on pay generally (Table 5.3). Among firms in these countries, those in France stand out consistently as valuing length of service the most.

For later years, the continued influence of length of service was confirmed by the French wage-structure surveys of 1986 and 1992. In 1992, length of service was especially important for blue-collar and junior white-collar workers. After controlling for other variables, 20 years' service added 20% to average blue-collar pay and 33% to junior white-collar pay among males and a bit less among females (Bayet, 1996).[2] In recent years there has been

Table 5.2. *Impact of skill contours between firms on industry wage levels: CV% of male hourly earnings by industry within skill grades*

	France		Germany		Great Britain
	1972	1978	1972	1978	1978
Skilled	10.2	11.8	5.1	8.0	10.2
Semi-skilled	9.6	10.3	5.1	8.7	10.9
Unskilled	8.3	10.3	6.5	9.8	11.5
All	9.9	13.6	5.6	9.2	10.9

Figures based on 42 two- and three-digit NACE headings in industry and construction. *Source*: Eurostat, ESES (1972 and 1978); data from the latest 1995 survey were not available at the time of writing.

some debate about the effects of seniority on pay in French firms, which appear to have declined since the 1970s (e.g. Béret, 1992; Nohara, 1995; and Mitani, 1998). The authors who observe this argue that French employers have not abandoned their internal labour market practices so much as changed their emphasis. As a result of the success of the government's Continuous Training Scheme, and the increasing numbers remaining at school until 18, employers have switched to formal, but firm-specific, continuous training, for which they can get government grants. This has replaced the more informal OJT and seniority that were dominant when Maurice *et al.* (1986) carried out their study (Géhin and Méhaut, 1993). Thus Béret and Dupray (1992) argue that the focus of French internal labour markets has shifted from a logic of accumulating OJT-based skills to one of selection for higher paid jobs by successive rounds of further training, and the best returns for further training are associated with the firm-specific kind. It also appears that the French practice of combining promotion and training noted by Maurice *et al.* has been maintained: further evidence that OJT has been formalized enabling firms to tie pay more precisely to OJT than under the seniority system. However, the scale of the shift may be exaggerated. Although the rewards for seniority have fallen sharply at the aggregate level, they remain strong among blue- and junior white-collar workers who get less continuous training. The measured effects of tenure may also be affected by the combination of widespread use of ILMs with the steep rise in youth unemployment in France in the 1980s. The sharp decline of workers in short tenure positions is likely to depress standard estimates of the returns to seniority because the strongest rewards for tenure come early on. Likewise, its continued lack of influence in Germany was confirmed by the 1990 wage structure survey. A striking feature, not shown in the table, is the generally greater importance of length of service for women workers: for manual women, its effect exceeds that of skill in all three countries. This shows the

Table 5.3. *Length of service and earnings in France, Germany and the UK*

	France (%)	Germany (%)	UK (%)
1978:			
Manual:			
Skill	40 (19)	40 (13)	n/a
Length of service	30 (9)	10 (2)	n/a
Non-manual:			
Occupation	74 (58)	75 (54)	n/a
Length of service	14 (6)	14 (2)	n/a
1972:			
All workers (M + NM):			
Occupation	41	23	25
Length of service (All)	17	8	12
Male manual only	9	3	5

Note: Industrial sector. Percentage of variance in monthly earnings explained by occupation or length of service. The adjusted figure in parentheses takes account of skill, sex, length of service, industry, firm size and region.
Source: 1978, CERC (1988); 1972, Saunders and Marsden (1981).

exclusion of women from the blue-collar skill systems, which are predominantly filled by men.

The effects of seniority on pay appear stronger in the US, and especially Japan, compared with the three European countries, according to an international study based on micro data coordinated by Tachibanaki (1998). Earnings functions which took account of the effects of experience, education, occupation, industry, plant size and gender showed earnings growing at about 3% for each year of seniority in Japan, about 2% in the US, about 1% in France and about 0.5% in Germany. In all countries, the earnings grew more slowly as seniority increased.[3] Although every effort was made to standardize the regressions, the figures are best seen as relative orders of magnitude, owing to data limitations. These findings echo the comparisons based on earlier data by Koike (1988) who found that for white-collar workers, the steep age and length of service profiles in Japan were more like those in France than in Germany. The big difference, he argued, concerned blue-collar workers, who, in Japan, benefit from similar age and service-based pay systems to those of intermediate white-collar workers, unlike those, especially, in Britain and Germany

There is some evidence that the reward for seniority declined in Japan during the 1980s (Clark and Ogawa, 1992; Genda, 1998), due in part to shortages of young workers in the early 1980s forcing up entry-level pay (Hashimoto and Raisian, 1992). However, on an international scale, the effect of seniority remains strong. Tachibanaki mentions the controversy over whether seniority effects in the US are a statistical artefact, discussed shortly, but it seems unlikely that this should be so in Japan, given the strong company-level evidence of seniority mechanisms in company pay systems (e.g. Brown *et al.*, 1997). Best's (1984: ch. 3) detailed study of the pay system at Sumitomo Metal Industries, which is similar to that in many large companies, still provides a very good illustration of how length of service shapes blue-collar workers' pay systems. Basic pay and 'efficiency' pay, which accounted for about two-thirds of total pay, were based solely on length of service and age. Pay for job ability comprised two elements: pay related to job demands, which took account of knowledge, proficiency, tension and environment; and pay related to the employee's rank and post. Progression through ranks, although based on merit assessment, is also related to service, as the latter depends upon the accumulation over time of performance points which are not usually taken away if performance dips in a particular year.

In the US, length of service has long been recognized as a major force in pay systems, one of the most persuasive pieces of evidence being the plant-level studies of Rees and Shultz (1970), who found it to be the key factor explaining the variance of earnings within occupations, especially when fringe benefits were included.[4] More recently, Hashimoto and Raisian (1985, 1992) underlined the importance of seniority pay in both the US and Japan, although its effect was considerably stronger in Japan. Ohtake (1998) replicated their analysis using 1991/2 micro data, confirming the earlier results, and showing a strengthening of tenure effects in the US (Table 5.4). He also found that these effects, in both countries, were largely independent of occupational level. Instead, inclusion of occupational level caused the explanatory power of education variables to decline, suggesting that education determined the job level at which one entered firm internal labour markets.

In the US, there has been considerable controversy over how to interpret

Table 5.4. *Growth in earnings attributable to tenure by firm size*

		Small %	Peak year	Medium %	Peak year	Large %	Peak year
Japan	1980	75	30	51	25	91	30
US	1979	35	25	35	35	53	35
Japan	1992	64	30	109	35	104	35
US	1991	39	25	43	30	50	30

Note: Tenure is measured from entering the current firm to peak year of tenure for firm-specific tenure-related earnings. Estimated from earnings functions including experience (age), tenure and education for full-time male non-agricultural employees. In 1980, in small Japanese firms, the tenure-earnings profile peaked at 30 years tenure, at which point firm-specific tenure had raised starting pay by 75%.
Source: Ohtake (1998: 132).

the relationship between earnings and firm tenure, whether it is due to firm-specific human capital (e.g. Brown, 1989) or incentives based on deferred pay (Medoff and Abraham, 1980). Both of these interpretations are consistent with the presence of internal labour markets and the production approach.

More troubling are the findings of Abraham and Farber (1987), whose panel data appear to show that the seniority effects visible in cross-sectional data of the kind reviewed above overestimate the true effects of tenure because matching good workers to good jobs will lead to both lower turnover and higher pay.[5] However, using the same data source, Topel (1991) showed that their method of calculating completed job tenures leads to underestimates of the returns to tenure. His own results showed that firm-specific tenure for a typical male worker with 10 years' seniority would raise pay by at least 25%.

Given that all five economies have substantial numbers of long-term jobs which employers presumably seek to fill with equal care, it would be hard to explain why job-matching processes should generate strong cross-sectional seniority effects in some countries but not in others.[6] A crude test of whether the relationship between tenure and pay is real is to see whether it applies across occupations, on the assumption that 'bad' jobs are concentrated in lower-paid and less-qualified occupations. Tachibanaki's study is of some help here, as it shows the influence of tenure is also present within major occupations for those countries with suitable data, and notably, France, Japan and the US. For Germany, tenure effects were weak both overall and within occupations, and for Britain there were no suitable tenure data. This would suggest that the effect is a real one and not a statistical artefact.

3. TASK-ORIENTED VERSUS FUNCTION-ORIENTED APPROACH: KEY INDICATORS

The second axis is that of the task-oriented versus the function-oriented approach to task assignment and accountability. The limited evidence available can be arranged on five main dimensions:

- control systems: assignment of responsibility for work;
- work-flow rigidity;
- functional specialization/segmentation of work roles;
- hierarchical segmentation; and
- patterns of functional flexibility.

3.1 Control systems

The most direct indicator of the way in which tasks are identified and assigned to jobs can be found in the operation of control systems, as these are concerned with sanctioning performance and non-performance of tasks. There has been rather little comparative empirical work in this area. Maurice *et al.* (1986) provide good information for their matched sample of French and German firms. In the former case, the work post is clearly identified as the focus of task organization and employee accountability, and it is essentially based on the idea that each worker is accountable for one post. This they show creates serious problems for French firms in the handling of absences and variations in workloads. Cole (1979, 1994) refers to similar practices as being the dominant pattern in the United States in comparison with Japan. Lawler (1994) describes the 'job' and individual responsibility for its performance as key features of US organizations.

Extending the Franco-German comparison to Britain, Sorge and Warner (1986) also refer to the exclusive responsibility individual workers have for their jobs, and the property-like relations exercised by skilled workers over their areas of work. In her study of engineers' work organization in Britain and Japan, Lam (1994) found a tendency in the British firms to assign definite responsibilities to particular individuals, which stood in marked contrast to the experience of the Japanese engineers in her sample.

Turning to Japan, several authors observe the diffuse job boundaries of individual workers and that workers are held accountable not for the duties associated with a particular job, but rather for their contribution to a team effort in which each person has a broad-based job. While there is some disagreement as to the relative importance of team working as opposed to broad-based skills (e.g. Koike, 1997), there is considerable overlap between the two concepts, and both entail, as a logical consequence, the absence of any one-to-one responsibility for a particular set of tasks. As will be argued in Chapter 6, work performance is sustained by a pattern of peer group interaction rather than individualized responsibility.

For Germany, Maurice *et al.* (1986) stress the scope for job rotation in the German firms they studied. Quite different from the approach in Japanese firms, that in German firms stressed the responsibility for functions associated with a particular skill. Both these authors and Jürgens *et al.* (1993) observed that although the German firms had a large number of job categories, in practice these did not constrain work allocation, and that skilled workers did not see restrictions of this kind as appropriate. Moreover, job rotation within certain functions was seen as a part of the process of skill enhancement, which again militates against a strict one-to-one assignment of workers and task responsibilities. As both studies point out, regulation of disputes with management is handled through the works council, thereby avoiding many of the problems associated with job-level bargaining.

3.2 Work-flow rigidity

A second, but more indirect, indicator of the task or function related focus can be found in measures of work-flow rigidity. The underlying idea is that strict individual accountability for work tasks comprising one's job may enable blame or praise to be applied quickly and easily, but it makes work-flow very rigid. It becomes hard to vary the distribution of work in response to unexpected fluctuations. In contrast, less direct assignment of responsibility enables more flexibility. As job rotation is also facilitated by less direct assignment of responsibility for job performance, one may use that as an additional indicator.

Work-flow rigidity, based on the Aston score, was measured directly by Lincoln *et al.*'s (1986) comparison of production organization in Japanese and US plants. They found it to be markedly higher in the US than in Japan. The alternative indicator, that of job rotation, is hard to compare directly between countries because its measurement depends on how narrowly or broadly jobs are defined. Maurice *et al.* (1986) showed it to be considerably higher in Germany than in France, and recent studies of flexible working and teamwork and suggest that it is generally lower in the US and Britain than in Germany (e.g. Jacobs *et al.*, 1978; Sorge and Warner, 1986; Turner and Auer, 1994). The difficult comparison is between the two countries in which job rotation has been practised for much longer: whether it is higher in Japan than in Germany. Direct measurement is probably impossible because of differences in the design of tasks and jobs, but it seems fair to argue that in both Japan and Germany job rotation is greater, and indicates a lesser degree of work-flow rigidity than in the other three countries.

3.3 Functional specialization of work roles

A third indicator of the presence of the task- or the function-centred approach can be found in the segmentation of work roles and functional specialization. The task-centred approach will generally lead to a finer and stricter segmentation of work-roles and to greater functional specialization in the sense of the Aston measure. The US emerges as a country with a high degree of work-role segmentation in a number of comparative studies. Cole (1979) and Lincoln *et al.* (1986) compare US and Japanese plants in this respect. Comparing the US and German automobile industries, Berg (1994) observes narrow job-based skills predominating in the US compared with broad-based occupational skills in Germany, implying narrower role specialization in the US plants.

Comparing French and Japanese engineers, Maurice *et al.* (1988) reach a similar conclusion, placing France close to the US position. Comparing

British and Japanese engineers, Lam (1994) observed a strong emphasis on the employee's own specific area of expertise in Britain as opposed to the systematic sharing, and diffusion, of expertise by rotating engineers through different functions in Japan. Comparing France and Germany for blue-collar and technician skills, Maurice *et al.* (1986) also find greater work-role segmentation in France than in Germany, echoing the earlier remarks about work posts and job rotation, or its absence.

Thus, on work-role segmentation, the US, France and Britain appear to share the task-oriented approach as a general rule, and Japan and Germany the more function-centred approach, with less-structured work roles and less-exclusive areas of action.

3.4 Hierarchical segmentation

Hierarchical segmentation, or the degree to which managerial and skilled tasks diverge, provides another view of the same kind of issue. If task-oriented work rules segment work roles horizontally, then they will probably also divide them vertically. The reason is that within each specialist activity on the horizontal plane, workers will have a less-complete view of the totality of operations, and will be more dependent on coordination by management. In contrast, if they have a better degree of understanding of each other's work, then they are better placed to understand coordination problems and better able to settle problems directly. The first situation implies a greater hierarchical segmentation between management's coordinating activities and the skilled and technical personnel's areas of work.

Comparing Britain with Japan and Germany, the limited evidence available suggests that in the first country, management is a specialist coordinating activity, whereas in the other two countries, 'player manager' roles are much more common. Lam (1994) found that Japanese line managers were much more likely to maintain a strong involvement in their area of technical expertise than did their British counterparts, who saw a move into management as a promotion out of technical work. Stewart *et al.* (1994) reached similar conclusions when comparing middle managers in Britain and Germany, with the British as specialist coordinators and the Germans as 'player managers'. Maurice *et al.* (1986) drew similar conclusions in their Franco-German comparison: German managers were more heavily involved in solving day-to-day technical problems than their French counterparts. The three country comparison by Sorge and Warner (1986) suggested that management segmentation was less pronounced in Britain than in France and that Britain lay in between France and Germany, but nearer the French than the German pole. Finally, Lincoln *et al.* (1986) found that, in terms of formal authority relationships, Japanese managers were more distant than their US counterparts, but when it came to what they

Table 5.5. *Variations in the nature of OJT*

	Enterprise-specific skills	Occupational skills
(a) models of organizational problem-solving activities		
Management-led	France, US (technicians and engineers solve)	Britain (technicians and engineers solve)
High employee involvement	Japan (QCs, 'Ringi')	Germany (led by player-manager foremen)
b) common organizational routines for coping with uncertainty: flexible working and job-rotation		
'Specialist' flexible staff	France: 'polyvalents', US: 'utility men'	Britain: 'over-manning', and élite 'multi-skilled' craftsmen
Job rotation	Japan: built into training and work organization	Germany: built into training of broad-based skills

actually did in practice, the position was reversed, reflecting Lam's observation of the Japanese being 'player managers'.

3.5 Patterns of functional flexibility

It is possible to take a more synthetic view of these variables by looking at functional flexibility, which will be strongly affected by whether the task- or function-centred rules predominate in a given workplace. As argued earlier, even when interpreted flexibly, the task-centred rules can give only limited functional flexibility compared with the function-centred rules. The scope for functional flexibility is reflected in the treatment of problem-solving activities and organizational routines for dealing with uncertainty (Table 5.5).

Problem-solving activities in British, and particularly in French, manufacturing plants tend to be management-led, bringing in technicians and engineers to find solutions. Maurice *et al.* (1986) and Sorge and Warner (1986) show that in France there is a sharp division of labour between the blue- and white-collar functions. In Britain, the divide is not identical, but Sorge and Warner, and more recently Stewart *et al.* (1994) find a high degree of role segmentation. In contrast, in German and Japanese plants, there is commonly scope for greater involvement of skilled workers in such activities, and closer interaction between management and skilled workers. Comparing the US and Japan, Cole (1994) arrived at similar conclusions, this time with Japanese middle management being more actively involved with workers in job-level problem-solving activities, and US management operating with a clearer division of labour between problem-solving and execution.

As Koike argues, job rotation developed initially as an organizational routine to deal with uncertainty caused by absenteeism. There is in fact a number of alternatives, reflecting variation in the scope allowed by each of the four transaction rules. French and US manufacturing firms have tended to assign such work to specialists. Maurice *et al.* (1986) show how a special category of 'polyvalent' workers was created to deal with absences and other unforeseen problems. In Britain, a common solution has been for firms to 'hoard labour' so that they keep sufficient slack to cope with variable demand because they lack the ability to redeploy workers easily between jobs (Bowers *et al.*, 1982). More recently, considerable effort has gone into developing multi-skilled workers, although case-study evidence suggests that progress has been relatively slow apart from a few dramatic and much reported cases (Elger, 1991). In contrast, Japanese and German firms have tended to rely upon task rotation as a means of developing workers with a sufficiently wide range of competencies which enables them to tackle variations in work demands due to both absence and unusual tasks.

From the pieces of the jigsaw assembled so far, there emerges thus a picture in which industrial firms in France, the US and Japan tend to adopt the production approach, and those in Britain and Germany the training approach. Turning to the second contractual constraint, enforceability, firms in France, the United States and Britain tend to govern work assignments with task-centred rules, whereas those in Japan and Germany tend to adopt the more diffuse function-centred rules.

4. DIFFUSION OF MAIN EMPLOYMENT SYSTEMS

At the end of the last chapter, it was shown that classification systems borne by collective bargaining were widespread in France, Germany and, to a lesser degree, Great Britain, but that lower levels of union density left the picture more uncertain in the US and Japan. This section looks at additional evidence on the diffusion of the dominant type of employment system in these two countries in an effort to assess how far common principles apply across these economies.

4.1 The United States

For the US, Eyraud and Rozenblatt's (1994) evidence drew mainly on the unionized sector, where internal labour markets have generally followed the 'industrial model' with strictly defined jobs, a clear linkage of pay rates to jobs and strong notions of seniority, all closely related to the work post

Table 5.6. *Prevalence of bureaucratic personnel procedures in the US, 1935–46, in all industries and services, in firms with >250 employees*

Personnel practice	1935	1946
Personnel department	46	75
Centralized employment decisions	53	75
Job analysis	24	45
Job evaluation	18	61
Employment/promotion testing	8	22
Rating system	16	35
Time/motion study	35	51
Promotion/transfer system	17	n/a
Service emblems	17	40
Seniority provision[a]	58	83

[a]1939 and 1946.
Source: Baron *et al.* (1986b: table 1).

rule. However, a significant proportion of non-union firms has followed the 'salaried model', which affords a greater degree of functional flexibility and employment security, and it has also been more common among white-collar than among blue-collar workers (Osterman, 1988). Indeed, Piore and Sabel (1984) argue that under the American Plan in the 1920s, it was a serious rival to the then emerging industrial model. In view of the small fraction of the workforce now covered by unions, it is important to see how far key features of the work post system can be said to apply across both the industrial and the salaried models.

We know from a number of historical studies that the establishment of the job or the work post as the basic building block in job and pay classification systems was consolidated during the bureaucratization of employment relations during the 1930s and 1940s (Table 5.6). Slichter *et al.* (1960) show how the job or the work post lay at the centre of the bureaucratic personnel management system built up between the 1930s and the 1950s, and Jacoby (1985) traced out its emergence. In a later study, comparing the spread of the 'salaried model' in Japan and the US, he argued that the diffusion of the radical version in the US was limited by the reluctance of US managers to forego the pay/job link, and by their scepticism that productivity could be maintained without the threat of job loss (Jacoby, 1993). Baron *et al.* (1986b) provide quantitative confirmation on the diffusion of bureaucratic personnel practices, comparing Conference Board surveys of the 1930s and 1940s. Although one cannot measure directly the centrality of the job as a key factor in personnel organization and in job and pay classification, clear signs of its presence can be seen in the spread of job analysis, job evaluation, rating systems, time and motion study, and, according to some interpretations, in the spread of seniority provision.

Table 5.7. *Extent of formal work control systems in US organizations, 1991*

'Formalization items'	% of employees covered
Rules and procedures manual	80
Documents on fringe benefits	78
Written job descriptions	74
Documents on safety and hygiene	74
Written performance records	70
Documents on hiring/firing procedures	67
Documents on personnel evaluation	67

Source: Kalleberg *et al.* (1996: 75).

The enduring influence of the work post in job classifications can be inferred from more recent US data. One of the most striking points to emerge from the 1991 National Organizations Study (NOS) was the broad similarity of personnel policies between what the authors describe as unionized and non-union bureaucracies (Kalleberg *et al.*, 1996). Together, these account for over 40% of the establishments and 90% of the employment in their sample.[7] Compared on eight organizational control profiles, they differed in only one: the use of detailed written employment contracts (Table 5.7). The others included measures of administrative intensity, departmentalization, vertical levels, formalization, use of firm internal labour markets and formal dispute resolution procedures. The authors compare their union and non-union bureaucracies to the Aston organization study's 'work-flow bureaucracy', characterized by highly structured work activities. The overall results for their sample show a high use of explicit, formalized control systems, and a high-degree of continuity with the results for the 1940s. Particularly important are the high percentages of employees with written job descriptions and performance records.

A number of other studies also highlight both the continued prevalence of bureaucratic control systems for work and the rather limited differences between union and non-union plants. In their survey of Chicago firms, Bridges and Villemez (1994: 61) reported that about three quarters of employees had written job descriptions and performance evaluation, and about half had written job instructions, all of which are consistent with clearly specified job responsibilities. Ichniowski (1990), like Osterman (1994), found that flexible job structures were confined to a rather small group of firms, and that the majority of both union and non-union firms had rather rigid job structures.[8] The main distinguishing feature of non-union firms lay in the greater influence of merit as opposed to seniority in upgrading decisions, and in lesser use of grievance and arbitration procedures, but on work organization principles, union and non-union firms were very similar (Ichniowski, 1990).

If we turn to 'transformed' human resource practices, although non-union

Table 5.8. *Internal labour market items in FILM scale, US 1991*

	% of employees
Vacancies filled with current employees:[a]	
Core occupations	57.5
Managerial and admin. occupations	72.3
Multiple grades/levels within occupation:	
Core occupations	51.6
Managerial and admin.	66.1
Promotion often or very often occurs from:	
Core occupations	30.8

[a]'Sometimes'.
Source: Kalleberg *et al.* (1996: 94).

firms are more likely to have been 'transformed', the great majority have so far remained with more traditional methods. In Ichniowski's (1990) sample, only 13% of firms combined flexible job design, training and communication policies, although that increased to 40% if one takes combinations of two such policies. Osterman (1994) recognized that his estimate of 37% of establishments as 'transformed' (using two new work practices for more than 50% of the workforce) as being high compared with other studies, but under 10% of his firms had adopted all four of the policies that he used to measure 'transformation'.[9] Lawler *et al.* (1992) also recognized that only a small minority of firms had made a decisive break with traditional HR policies by adopting a large number of new HR practices. Overall, a great many union and non-union firms have remained with traditional methods or only adopted new practices piecemeal, and only a minority of firms, either union or non-union, have 'transformed'.

A second feature echoed across the surveys is the widespread use of firm internal labour markets (FILMs) and in particular of internal promotion, which would tend to anchor US firms in the production approach. Again, the NOS highlights the continued prevalence of internal recruitment by US firms to fill many vacancies (Table 5.8).

Osterman (1994) echoed these results for firms' 'core' occupations, finding seniority hiring in 70%, and seniority promotion in 30%, of organizations in his sample. Ichniowski (1990) reports widespread use of internal promotion across all but one of the human resource management systems he identifies. In the Chicago study, around 30% of employees were in jobs with high internal promotion prospects, and about 50% in jobs reported by their employers as being on job ladders (Bridges and Villemez, 1994: 61). Again, a notable feature of these studies is that internal promotion is not especially a result of union presence. Indeed, several of the studies suggest that internal promotion is more likely in non-union environments (e.g. Bridges and Villemez, 1991).

A final piece of evidence that 'the job' remains the basic building block of most US firms concerns the influence of job-related factors on the structure of their internal labour markets. Baron *et al.* (1986a) found that job-related characteristics, such as the need for firm-specific training, played a much bigger part in determining job ladders than did the type of establishment. Establishment characteristics were important in determining whether or not there were job ladders, but they had little influence on their structure. Likewise, Lincoln *et al.* (1986) found that the effect of operations technology on the structure of firm internal labour markets was stronger in US plants than in those in Japan.[10] Taking all these studies together shows that the dominant employment model in American industry continues to be shaped by the work post, combining the production approach and task-centred forms of accountability, and that it extends well beyond the unionized sector. The studies also show that even though the 'salaried model' has wide currency in the US, in most cases, it represents a more flexible application of the work post system as compared with the 'industrial model', but the differences are not such as to carry it over from task- to function-centred rules.

4.2 Japan

As with the US, the relatively low levels of bargaining coverage mean that other sources are needed in order to check how far the Eyraud–Rozenblatt typology of classification systems is accurate for Japan beyond the unionized sector. As with the US, the type of classification system cannot be directly observed on a representative basis from collective agreements, and we have to turn to more indirect measures from large-scale surveys. The first concerns the diffusion of different types of ranking systems in Japanese firms. According to Yamanouchi and Okazaki-Ward (1997), the job ranking system was introduced during the period of 'Americanization' of Japanese management, and was a work-post-oriented system with strict job demarcations between job ranks. This never really worked in Japanese firms,[11] and its declining usage is clear in Table 5.9. The competence ranking system, analysed in the previous chapter, has spread rapidly during the 1960s and 1970s, and, according to more recent evidence cited by Yamanouchi and Okazaki-Ward, had spread to 84% of firms by 1990.[12]

These observations are supported by a second source, underpinning the broad nature of skills, and, by implication, the actual jobs that people do. Koike (1984, 1997) assembled extensive evidence on the wide diffusion of key personnel practices across Japanese firms, relating particularly to the use of seniority, long careers and job rotation. These are preconditions for the development of broad skills. As the competence ranking system is one of the key incentives for employees to develop these, Koike's evidence on internal job mobility is indirect but revealing. By the late 1970s, not only was job mobility within and between workshops common in Japanese firms,

Table 5.9. *Relative diffusion of the competence ranking system in Japan 1958–74*

% of firms	1958	1963	1968	1974
Job ranking system	27.9	18.9	16.7	17.0
Ranking system of workers	47.0	–	–	–
Competence ranking system	n/a	30.0	45.1	64.0
Seniority-based ranking system	n/a	38.8	33.1	35.5
Ranking based on white-/blue-collar distinction	34.2	21.8	13.5	5.5

Source: Nihon Keieisha Dantai Renmei (1975), cited in Yamanouchi and Okazaki-Ward (1997: 205).

Table 5.10. *Diffusion of internal job mobility and broad-based skills: Japan 1979*

% of firms replying (by employment size)	<100	100–999	>1,000
Common for 5–10 years' service workers to have experienced most jobs in workshop	44	35	45
Job mobility is common between:			
Jobs in the same workshop	48	61	68
Jobs in related workshops	49	62	61
Mobility used to promote broad skills:			
Within workshop mobility	25	30	45
Between workshop mobility	25	33	37
n	222	541	212

Source: Koyo Shokugyo Kenkyusho (1982), cited in Koike (1997: 31).

but a key reason that firms reported was to promote broad-based skills (Table 5.10). Although many smaller firms are not covered by collective bargaining, it is significant that many of them also seek to use these personnel practices. Koike (1997) also cites more recent surveys to show that job rotation is spreading, and concludes that a key reason behind this is to develop broad skills.

Thus, in both the US and Japan it is clear that the diffusion of the job classification and job regulation principles examined in the ILO study extend well beyond firms covered by collective agreements, and that the picture painted by Eyraud and Rozenblatt (1994), as reinterpreted in the previous chapter, can be taken as fairly representative of the countries included.

5. CONCLUSION

The previous chapter concluded with the evidence of the ILO study of job and pay classification systems that fits the typology of transaction rules derived in Chapter 2, and suggested that each predominated in the industrial sectors of certain countries but not others. This chapter has shown that the distribution of the four transaction rules across countries mirrors that of the classification systems. It showed this first using indicators of the presence of the production and training approaches, and then with indicators of task-centred and function-centred rules. It showed also that the prevalence of occupational skills by country matched that of the training approach, with the production approach holding in the absence of occupational skills.

This enables two conclusions to be drawn. The first concerns the concordance of three levels of evidence, and the second, the distribution of employment rules across countries. On the first point, there is a consistent patterning of job and pay classifications, the prevalence of occupational or ILM skills, and the indicators of job rules that fit with the theory. This gives a considerable boost to the idea that employment transaction rules, and the inter-firm institutions that support occupational skills and job and pay classification systems, are constituted into employment systems in which the inter-firm and job-level factors are mutually supporting. Turning to the inter-country differences, these show that each of the rules that firms and workers develop in response to the two contractual constraints has its own area in which it is the dominant rule, and these areas cover large sectors within each of the five countries studied. This was predicted by the chapter on diffusion, which showed the advantages accruing to any one rule once it achieved a position of strength within a given sector.

Taken together, the evidence shows that the employment transaction rules hold the key to understanding the nature of 'societal' differences in the employment relationship, their claim to a societal nature resting at once on the way they interact with other institutions within employment systems, and on the capacity each has to dominate a particular area of employment.

Table 5.11. *Incidence of the production and training approaches*

Production/training approach indicators	Production approach		Training approach	
	Task-centred	Function-centred	Task-centred	Function-centred
Job design: priority to technology or to skills:	US: Davis *et al.* (1955), Taylor (1979), Piore (1968) US production engineers prioritize technology	Japan: Koike (1997) job design for broad OJT skills	GB: Sengenberger (1987): firms prioritize occupational skills	G: Sengenberger (1987): firms prioritize occupational skills
Maurice *et al.* (1986) comparison of matched F & G plants	France: production engineers prioritize technology			G: production engineers prioritize occupational skills
McKersie & Hunter (1973) work reorganization in productivity bargaining	US: firms prioritize technology		GB: prioritize skills but less so over time	G: prioritize skills
Jürgens *et al.* (1993) auto industry teamwork strategies	US: narrow, job-based teams	Japan: homogenous teams based on OJT	GB: teams built around existing skills	G: mixed teams based on existing skills & unskilled
Work patterns with CNC operation	France: new tasks integrated into work post system, Eyraud *et al.* (1988)	Japan: 'technical approach' integrates setting & programming into broad jobs, Whittaker (1993)	GB: 'craft approach' segments setting & programming around existing skills, Whittaker (1993)	G: new tech. built into existing skill élite, Kern & Schumann (1984); Jürgens *et al.* (1993)

	France/US	Japan	GB	Germany
Management control of maintenance skills, Gallie (1978)	France: mgt direct control		GB: mgt devolve autonomy	
OLM/ILM, Skill transferability indicators:				
Pattern of intermediate-level vocational training	US, F: specialist training institutions and OJT, Büchtemann et al. (1993); Marsden & Ryan (1990)	Japan: specialist training institutions and OJT, Dore & Sako (1989)	GB: apprenticeship for occupational skills, Marsden (1995); Gospel (1998)	Germany: apprenticeship for occupational skills, Büchtemann et al. (1993); Streeck (1985)
Skill loss/retention on change of firm	France: skill loss, Eyraud et al. (1990) US: skill loss on job change, Lynch (1992)		GB: skill retention, Eyraud et al. (1990)	Germany: skill retention, Hofbauer & Nagel (1987)
Firm-specific OJT widespread for skilled labour	France: Maurice et al. (1986); still yes, but evolving, Géhin & Méhaut (1993) US: Hashimoto & Raisian (1985, 1992) US: Ohtake (1998) US: Brown (1989), esp. in early career US: Baron et al. (1986a) key to job ladders	Japan: Sako (1991) and Dore & Sako (1989)	GB: for semi-skilled mainly, Steedman & Wagner (1987, 1989)	Germany: Drexel (1993) apprenticeship still the key to skill, & use of OJT restricted

Table 5.11. *Incidence of the production and training approaches (Continued)*

Production/training approach indicators	Production approach		Training approach	
	Task-centred	Function-centred	Task-centred	Function-centred
Extensive job ladders offered by firms	US: Kalleberg *et al.* (1996) (job ladders offered) seniority (re-hiring) Koike (1988), Osterman (1994), Lincoln and Kalleberg (1990) France: Maurice *et al.* (1988)	Japan: yes, Shirai & Shimada (1978) Japan: yes, Lincoln & Kalleberg (1990) Maurice *et al.* (1988)		
Pay rises with job tenure	France: high, Maurice *et al.* (1986), Saunders & Marsden (1981); Marsden (1990); CERC (1988) US: high, esp. non-wage benefits: Rees & Shultz (1970) US: Hashimoto & Raisian (1985), Ohtake (1998) high but <Japan	Japan: high, Lincoln & Kalleberg (1988) US: Hashimoto & Raisian (1985) strong effect >US	GB: low, Saunders & Marsden (1981); Marsden (1990); GB: MacKay *et al.* (1971) very limited internal upgrading & little reward for seniority GB: Manning (1998) weak effect of job tenure	Germany: low, Saunders & Marsden (1981); Maurice *et al.* (1986); CERC (1988); Marsden (1990)

De facto recognition of external skills:	France: weak, Podevin & Viney (1991) US: weak, Lynch (1992); Büchtemann et al. (1993)	Japan: weak	GB: strong for craft & prof. skills, Eyraud et al. (1990)	Germany: strong for craft & prof. skills, Sengenberger (1987)
Classification principles: Seniority recognized	France: yes, Maurice et al. (1986)	Japan: yes, Koike (1988); Dore (1973)	GB: no, Eyraud et al. (1990)	Germany: no, Maurice et al. (1986)

Table 5.12. *Incidence of the task- and function-centred rules*

	Production approach		Training approach	
	Task-centred	Function-centred	Task-centred	Function-centred
Task-/function-centred indicators				
Control systems:				
Cole (1994): task responsibility	US: individual, focused on job; also Lawler (1994), Slichter et al. (1960)	Japan: focused on work group		
Maurice et al. (1986): task responsibility	France: focused on job, work post			Germany: focused on skilled group
Lam (1994)		Japan: diffuse accountability & overlapping jobs	GB: task assignments are responsibility of individual engineers	
Turner and Auer (1994)	US: narrowly defined teams & close monitoring by mgt			Germany: broadly based teams with much autonomy
Buttler et al. (1995)	US: narrowly defined job-worker links			Germany: loosely defined job-worker links
Work-flow rigidity:				
Lincoln et al. (1986)	US: high work-flow rigidity	Japan: low		
Maurice et al. (1986), Sorge & Warner (1986)	France: high		GB: high	Germany: low

	France / US	Japan	GB	Germany
Job rotation	France: low, Maurice *et al.* (1986)	Japan: high, Koike & Inoki (1990)	GB: low, Sorge and Warner (1986)	Germany: moderate, Maurice *et al.* (1986)
Segmentation of work roles/functional specialization: Lam (1994), young electronics engineers		Japan: low work role segmentation—gradual rotation between functions	GB: high—stress own area of expertise	
Maurice *et al.* (1986): skilled blue collar	France: high	Japan: low		Germany: low
Cole (1979, 1994): mgt/blue collar	US: high	Japan: low		
Lincoln *et al.* (1986) 'Aston score' of functional specialization	US: high	Japan: low		
Dore (1973) skilled blue collar		Japan: low	GB: high	
Berg (1994) auto firms, broad versus narrow skills	US: narrow job-based skills			Germany: broad occupational skills

Table 5.12. *Incidence of the task- and function-centred rules (continued)*

	Production approach		Training approach	
	Task-centred	Function-centred	Task-centred	Function-centred
Treatment of job rotation	France: interferes with responsibility of own job, Maurice *et al.* (1986) US: interferes with responsibility of own job, Cole (1979, 1994)	Japan: built into OJT for broad skills, Koike	GB: interferes with occupational segmentation, Elger (1991)	Germany: built into skill enhancement & progression, Maurice *et al.* (1986)
Hierarchical segmentation: Lam (1994) electronics engineers		Japan: low hierarchical segmentation (player managers)	GB: high (specialist managers)	
Stewart *et al.* (1994) middle managers (industry & services)			GB: high (specialist managers)	Germany: low (player managers)
Maurice *et al.*(1986), Sorge & Warner (1986)	France: high (specialist managers)		GB: moderate (specialist managers)	Germany: moderate (player managers)
Lincoln *et al.* (1986)	US: in practice high	Japan: in practice low		

ENDNOTES

[1] An important feature of their earnings variable was that it included some fringe benefits, notably, paid vacations, which are strongly related to seniority. However, seniority remained an important influence on straight hourly pay, albeit less powerful. This may go some way to explaining why Abraham and Farber (1987) found that the effect of seniority virtually disappeared when the expected duration of jobs was taken into account. Their panel data took no account of fringe benefits.

[2] This was based on an analysis of variance including the effects of occupation, diploma, age, service, working time regime, industry, plant size and region.

[3] The authors regressed the variables on the log of earnings using the standard approach developed by Mincer. The coefficients on seniority were for Japan, 0.0304, for the US, 0.0205, for France, 0.0081 and for Germany, 0.005. The declining impact of higher levels of seniority was captured by using the square of seniority, which, in all cases, had a negative coefficient. For Japan, see Genda (1998), the US, Ohtake (1998), France, Mitani (1998), and Germany, Tomita (1998).

[4] The other variables included in their regressions were education, whether their previous job had been in the same occupation (experience), work performance tests, age, industry, plant size, ethnicity, gender and distance to work.

[5] It should also be remembered that their measure of pay excluded fringe benefits, such as paid vacations, which had contributed so much to intra-occupational pay variations by seniority in Rees and Shultz's data.

[6] Not all panel data sources show this effect. For example, work on the German socio-economic panel confirms that Germany's internationally low seniority effects on pay are indeed due to seniority and not to job matching (Schasse and Vatthauer, 1990). It would indeed be interesting to apply a panel analysis to the Japanese data, but according to Ohta and Tachibanaki (1998: 56) no suitable data set yet exists.

[7] These figures were calculated from the data given in Kalleberg et al. (1996), shown here in Table 5.4. The table shows data for 582 of the 724 organizations in the sample. Given the sampling method, based on the employers of a random sample of employees, a very rough estimate of employees covered by each type can be gained from the numbers of organizations reported and their average full-time employment.

[8] Ichniowski's sample showed flexible job design in only 22% of the firms that could be classified.

[9] His measures of 'transformation' were the use of self-directed teams, job rotation, TQM and employee problem-solving groups or quality circles. These were surveyed for 'core' employees, that is the largest group directly involved in making production or providing a service on the sampled firm's location.

[10] Among the measures of ILM structure that Lincoln et al. used were the rigidity of work-flow processes, and the degree to which employees were assigned functions as their sole responsibility.

[11] I am grateful to Professor H. Hazama for drawing my attention to this point. See, H. Hazama, 'Nihon Romu Kanrishi Kenkyu', translated by M. Sako as 'History of Labour Management', Macmillan, Basingstoke, forthcoming.

[12] Rômugyôsei Kenkyûgo (1994: 59), cited in Yamanouchi and Okazaki-Ward (1997: 206).

Performance Management

1. INTRODUCTION

This and the next two chapters apply the theory of employment systems to three key areas of human resource management, and in doing so give further substance to the idea that firms are embedded in their institutional and societal contexts. Maintaining the earlier assumptions of information asymmetry, bounded rationality and potential opportunism on either side, the chapters show how the employment rules limiting managerial authority shape the policy options available, as they did for work assignments. This chapter deals with performance management, the next with pay and incentives, and the third with skills and labour market structures.

In recent years, the growing attention to the quality of products and services has generated a corresponding interest in the quality of employees' job performance. Performance management has become a major preoccupation of private and public organizations. This chapter applies the theory developed so far to look at the regulation of job performance. There are several reasons for doing this. The first is that performance management goes right to the heart of the employment relationship. It is the most intimate area of management prerogative: the relationship between line managers and the staff they supervise. It is also the level at which one would expect job demands to be most closely determined by firms' business objectives. Thus, if one can show that societal factors play an important part even at this level, then there is a strong argument that no major area of employment relations eludes the pervasive effects of the transaction rules and societal context on employee management.

The simplicity of the performance criteria applied in practice is one of the paradoxes of performance management. The work employees undertake is often complex and varied, and many employers have developed quite sophisticated measures of organizational performance reflecting a wide variety of characteristics that are relevant to customer satisfaction. There is also widespread evidence that workers vary greatly in their productivity at the same jobs. For example, Cook (1993) opens his advocacy of improved personnel selection by stressing 'the best is twice as good as the worst'. Even treating this as an exaggeration, there is a puzzle as to why the criteria applied in performance assessment are mostly simple.

The argument develops in four steps:

- inherent difficulties of performance measurement;
- how these are exacerbated by mutual suspicion and distrust;
- how the two contractual constraints impose a small number of robust and efficient criteria; and
- why the influence of societal factors should be so pervasive.

The reason for the simplicity of performance measures lies partly in the inherent difficulties of the process and partly in the background of mutual suspicion between employers and employees. Evidence for the first point is fairly well known and is briefly reviewed before new evidence is brought in of the degree of mutual suspicion that pervades many performance management systems. These two factors are interdependent: suspicion might be less if measurement were less ambiguous, and suspicion makes the whole process of measurement more controversial. Hence, the parties need some protection against potential moral hazard by their opposite number. It is then argued that performance criteria face the same contractual constraints as do work assignments within the employment relationship: they must be robust and lead to efficient matchings of employees' job performance and employers' job demands. A close correspondence is brought out between the rules defining job performance and those regulating work assignments, generating a balance between the flexibility needed within the employment relationship and protection against opportunism.

Finally, institutional and societal factors exert a strong influence over the criteria by which performance is gauged and assessed because of the way they make performance norms more or less robust in a particular environment. Generally, it will be shown that performance norms are more robust when they are widely used, and the fixed menu of transaction rules open to employers and employees limits the range of alternatives in any given context. It will be shown that it is still possible for individual firms to 'buck the trend', but that the cost of doing so and the risks involved are high. The remarkable thing is not that firms such as IBM and Hewlett Packard could for so long run their own personnel policies independently of their societal context. If they could not, the scope for experimentation and change would be limited indeed. What is striking is that they should remain exceptions.

2. THE INHERENT DIFFICULTIES OF PERFORMANCE MEASUREMENT

2.1. Objective/non-judgemental criteria

Although output measures of performance have been widely used in certain kinds of incentive schemes, and notably in piecework and payment-by-results for blue-collar manufacturing jobs, they have been on the wane in recent decades. Landy and Farr (1983: 41) described them as the unattainable 'Holy Grail' of performance measurement when reviewing the many difficulties involved. These fell into two categories: the complexity and interdependence of work in most organizations that makes it difficult to link individual input to objective measures of individual output; and the practical impossibility of avoiding subjective judgement by management.

There is a well-known danger with objective measures that if they do not measure all aspects of work equally well, then they will tend to direct employee effort towards those aspects that can be most easily monitored (Holmstrom and Milgrom, 1991). Most commonly, there is a danger of biasing performance away from qualitative and toward quantifiable aspects of work. This Landy and Farr illustrate with the attempts to use the number of arrests by police officers as a performance indicator. There, the difference between a 'good' and a 'bad' arrest can be critical. Likewise, sales staff commonly have their rewards tied to the value of sales, and there too the difference between a 'good' and a 'bad' sale can be very costly. As a result of Britain's pensions scandal uncovered in December 1993, major insurance companies suffered a publicity disaster and had to pay out hefty compensation to the many customers sold unsuitable personal pensions over the previous few years by sales reps paid on commission. More generally, the usefulness of output measures diminishes when jobs involve many different activities. Unless these can all be monitored equally well by management, there is a danger that employees will concentrate their effort on those that are most easily monitored and rewarded.[1] In the above examples, concentrating monitoring on quantity of arrests or sales encourages employees to neglect quality. Dependence of workers' performance on that of other colleagues and management also poses serious difficulties for objective performance criteria, although they can sometimes be attenuated by job design and the choice of criteria used. In addition, many studies have shown that output-based measures are mostly ineffective, from those of the 1950s on the 'crisis of incentive pay' such as in the German steel industry by Lutz (1975) and in British manufacturing by Wilfred Brown (1962), through to Jürgens *et al.*'s (1993) account of the retreat from industrial engineering techniques in the automobile industry in the 1980s. In the latter case, quality problems were one of the key considerations behind management's decision to move to different patterns of work organization and performance management. To deal with such problems, Landy and Farr argue that 'judgemental' performance measures, have become the most widely used performance measurement techniques (p. 57). These may be supplemented by non-judgemental, object-ive measures, but the element of management judgement is critical.

The argument could be taken a step further to show that judgement is a necessary component of all performance management systems for reasons similar to those advanced in Chapter 1, explaining why exhaustive job descriptions are self-defeating. To show this, one could imagine the prob-lems of trying to define performance purely in objective terms. For blue-collar workers, this might involve setting some ideal 'widget' as the standard which they should seek to reproduce, or in the case of white-collar work, it might be applying specified administrative procedures. One of the criteria for 'bad' arrests cited by Landy and Farr was when failure to follow the correct procedures led to an acquittal. Could one not, therefore, supplement the arrest data by additional data on whether the appropriate procedures for the context were followed? Thus, rule 'x' is applied for arrests in such and such a context, and rule 'y' for others, and so on. To make 'following the procedure' a definition of good performance one has also to deal with the inevitable variability in the contexts and types of arrests. Likewise, taking the ideal widget as an objective standard would require one to specify what margins of variability are tolerable, and under what circumstances.[2] Yet the advantage of the employment relationship lies in enabling management to deal with work allocation as demands vary. Trying to cope with the variability by defining ever more complex contingencies is perverse because it increases rigidity and creates opportunities for manipulating the rules, as Sainsaulieu's (1988) study well illustrates.[3]

Thus, judgemental criteria are not only an essential element of perfor-mance management—they also go to the heart of the employment relation-ship. One might say that management appraisal of performance is the counterpart in performance management to management's right to decide on task assignments.

2.2 Judgemental criteria

The popularity of judgemental criteria for assessing employees' performance might lead one to think that they are supremely adapted to the intricacies of evaluating complex work. Surely, one might ask, line managers have often been promoted from among the groups they supervise, share much of the tacit job knowledge they possess, and so are able to avoid some biases of output-based measures; they also understand the interdependency between the performance of different workers. In addition, they know the objectives that higher management are seeking, and as a result of this focal position within organizations, they should be uniquely able to assess the contribution of the individual employees whom they supervise. No other group in the organization has such a vantage point. Higher management are too distant from the day-to-day work of most staff, and rank-and-file staff themselves usually lack the overall perspective to enable them to coordinate between different work groups. If this is so, then surely, performance criteria applied by line managers could be made to follow the contours of the performance required in individual jobs.

There are, however, some well-known limitations on supervisory performance assessments. Much of the Personnel Management literature is directed at how to avoid the worst excesses, but they cannot be eliminated. The main problems include:

- halo effects in criteria and appraisals;
- rater inconsistencies; and
- lack of effective management support to supervisors.

In their review of mainly US evidence, Milkovitch and Wigdor (1991) showed that, even though many firms may seek to incorporate a wide range of criteria into their performance appraisal schemes, 'halo effects' are very common: that is rating on one key dimension colours all the others. As a result, the fineness of detail of appraisal criteria has relatively little effect on appraisal outcomes. Landy and Farr (1983: 243 ff.) come to a similar conclusion from their own review. They reject the 'traditional view' of raters as 'rational processors of information', arguing that there is no such thing as an ideal rating instrument, nor do raters generally work on accurately remembered specific behaviours of each employee. Instead, they use what they call 'simplifying strategies' to enable them to cope with the information they have. These include person categories, recalling traits rather than behaviours, and use of inappropriate judgement rules or 'heuristics', all of which make assessments unreliable, and militate against the use of complex performance appraisal criteria. Landy and Farr also comment on the widespread evidence of 'halo effects' based on misplaced theories among raters about the relationships between the different rating criteria.

Inconsistency in the ratings given by different appraisers of the same employees is also widely acknowledged. Based on the meta-survey evidence of Hunter (1983) and King *et al.* (1980), Bishop (1987) argued that such imperfections in supervisory ratings explained the small percentage set aside for performance pay increases in his sample of US firms. His survey supported the psychological evidence by showing large productivity differences between workers doing the same jobs that were only weakly correlated with pay. Knowing the rating process to be unreliable, risk-averse employees, he argues, would wish to minimize their exposure to unfair ratings by keeping performance pay a small percentage of total pay.

In addition, firms do little to help the line managers resist the pressures that lead to simplified, conventional performance judgements. A first step in this direction would be for firms to carry out serious evaluation of the effects of their performance appraisal schemes. Yet, despite the widespread practice of linking pay to supervisor-assessed performance, in the US, the Wyatt (1989) survey showed that very few US firms carried out any rigorous evaluation of their appraisal systems for their accuracy or their effects on performance, and many provided very little training on their conduct and did not regularly update the criteria used. For Britain, similarly, an IPM/NEDO survey of about 350 organizations using performance pay found that very few of them carried out any systematic evaluation of their schemes (Cannell and Wood, 1992).[4]

Finally, the task flexibility of the employment relationship itself often makes it hard to measure how far performance obligations have been realized, and this is a further constraint on how complex performance criteria can be in practice.

3. MUTUAL DISTRUST AND PERFORMANCE MANAGEMENT

Much of the literature on performance management and the quality of job performance has focused on how to get workers to perform, and how to design appropriate incentives. Yet, just as much attention needs to be devoted to potential opportunism by management, and even more important, employee perceptions and suspicion of potential management duplicity. Recent research on public sector performance management illustrates how serious a problem this is. The results are all the more telling owing to the absence of shareholders who might 'cream off' the fruits of improved performance, the greater employment stability in public services and the widespread existence of independent grievance procedures to protect employees. In the US federal service, which played a pioneering role in the development of performance management (Milkovitch and Wigdor, 1991), systems for linking pay to appraised performance have been in place for many staff groups since the 1960s, yet the studies by the Merit Systems Protection Board showed widespread suspicion among staff of management duplicity in its operation. They believed that line managers exercised favouritism in promotions and the award of performance pay, and that higher management operated quota systems on good appraisals to save money (MSPB, 1988). More recently, Marsden and French (1998), in the first large-scale study across the British public services as a whole, reached similar conclusions. Despite the sophistication of the schemes,[5] suspicion that management operated their performance pay schemes unfairly was widespread, to the extent that measures designed to ensure 'procedural justice' in the system were widely seen as further proof of management's duplicity.[6] Review of the distribution of awards, which one has to do in order to monitor equal opportunities by gender and ethnic origin, was seen as an opportunity for higher management to overrule favourable awards made by line managers. Quotas negotiated with the unions which should ensure that management commits money to performance pay were seen as arbitrary limitations on the recognition of good performance, and as in the US, there was a widespread belief that line managers indulged their favourites. Even the process of agreeing annual performance objectives seemed tainted by this perception. In the civil service departments, many staff felt that performance awards went to those 'cleverest at negotiating their performance agreements'. There was also a widespread suspicion that despite the performance management scheme's explicit emphasis on individually agreed targets and on quality, in reality most staff were given the same targets: increased output. A similar study by Carroll (1993) revealed comparable suspicions in a private-sector bank. Lest it be thought that such attitudes are simply a product of British 'them and us' social attitudes brought into the workplace, Marsden and French (1998) found that in the one civil service department for which comparisons could be made over time, they had greatly intensified over a five-year period. Moreover, recent case studies on performance pay and performance management in French firms confirm that substantial numbers of employees there too are deeply suspicious of their management (Eustache, 1996).[7]

What these public service studies show is the depth of employee suspicion of management's good faith in its appraisal of performance for pay purposes. Of special note is that measures to ensure procedural justice are often not sufficient to free management from suspicion over distributional questions. If these fail to work in the public sector, where distributional questions are attenuated by the absence of shareholders and a high value is attached to the intrinsic rewards of work, then there is even less reason to believe that they will be sufficient in the private sector. It will be seen shortly that this proves to be a major constraint on the operation of performance measurement. The studies also show a great deal of continuity in the problems of performance management with regard to the earlier studies of incentives for blue-collar factory work.

On their own, measurement problems might be tricky but soluble. Fear of moral hazard might be less if the scope for it were limited. Together, however, these factors are an explosive mix. The measurement problems create lots of scope for opportunism by either party, and especially by management, as it generally leads the performance appraisal process. The perceived unfairness of operation makes the definition and improvement of performance measures very difficult because of fears that one side will manipulate them to its advantage.

4. SOME CONVENTIONALLY USED PERFORMANCE CRITERIA

To make the discussion more concrete, it may be helpful to look at some practical examples of commonly used performance criteria. Employee performance appraisal has become one the most important channels through which management communicates work objectives and their quality to employees and monitors their achievement. A closer look at appraisal can therefore tell us a good deal about the nature and enforcement of performance obligations in practice. Practitioner guides, such as the handbooks produced by the British government's Advisory, Conciliation and Arbitration Service (ACAS, 1990), stress two main approaches to assessing job performance standards. The first is to look at performance in the job as a whole, and the second, to agree a set of targets or objectives for the jobholder.

The first approach, taking the job as a whole, is very common and widely used, especially for non-managerial staff.[8] Here ACAS gives some common, 'good practice' examples where the employee's job performance is assessed according to a number of criteria (see Appendix 2). Although the number and detail of criteria vary greatly, they can be summarized under four main headings:

- diligence;
- cooperation;
- initiative; and
- skills and job knowledge.

Diligence concerns partly how hard people work and the care they take on their jobs, but also their time-keeping, attendance and general reliability. Cooperation often refers to willingness to cooperate with management, especially in adapting to changing job demands, but it also often refers to cooperation with colleagues. Initiative relates to readiness to act independently within their jobs, to solve problems and take decisions without waiting for management to tell them what to do. Finally, appraisal of skills relates to whether employees have, and apply, the competencies needed for particular tasks and to achieve an appropriate level of quality, and their readiness to develop them.

The second approach, setting specific targets from within the employee's job area, is necessarily selective, establishing priorities among an employee's set of tasks, and basing performance measurement on achievement of these. As an example, ACAS considers the case of an office supervisor who might be assigned half a dozen objectives for the coming period such as reducing the error rate on customer records to under one per cent; producing a report on how best to reorganize the recording procedure; ensuring that customer enquiries to the office are dealt with within 48 hours; and to hold regular team briefings. Setting such detailed objectives is expensive with regard to managerial time and monitoring results, and so is more common for managerial jobs where staff have a good deal of discretion.

Although conceptually distinct, in practice, the two approaches often boil down to rather similar outcomes and operate on a small number of similar types of criteria. This is due to the measurement and opportunism problems already discussed. In the British tax service, for example, when staff were appraised on their whole job according to certain standard criteria, most of them believed that one criterion dominated all the others, namely, the quantity of work done (Marsden and Richardson, 1994). Carroll (1993) found that many staff held the same view in her study of a private sector retail bank. Five years later, in the same government department, when individual performance targets were used, despite the policy of individual performance agreements, two-thirds of the staff believed everyone was, in reality, given the same targets, and that staff were pressured into accepting performance objectives set by management. There was a widespread belief too that the staff gaining high appraisal ratings were those cleverest at negotiating their objectives, and most staff confessed to being more concerned to avoid a bad rating than to obtain a good one (Marsden and French, 1998).

Like the more general evidence on the limitations of judgemental criteria discussed earlier, this suggests that the more sophisticated one makes performance criteria the less robust they become. Given the large margin of error introduced by the difficulty of the process itself, anything other than rather conventional performance criteria will be hard to make stick. Thus, it is not surprising that the same simple performance criteria should recur in many different schemes, and that despite the apparent sophistication of agreeing individual performance objectives, in the end, the appraisal boils down to the same kind of broad criteria whether one is assessing performance against targets or that against the demands of the whole job.

A final point to note about the four types of performance criterion illustrated above is that each makes reference to different assumptions about performance even though they are often all applied simultaneously. Skill clearly presupposes some identifiable standard of training, and initiative makes little sense unless managers believe that staff have enough skill to enable them to exercise their initiative usefully. Diligence and skill can often feed directly into individual performance, whereas cooperation and initiative, especially when the latter involves stepping beyond one's immediate job, require a number of relational capabilities.

5. HOW THE CONTRACTUAL CONSTRAINTS SHAPE PERFORMANCE CRITERIA

The reason why job performance criteria tend to be rather simple and conventional lies in the need for performance quality to be defined in a way that is enforceable and efficient for both parties. The range of options open to management is limited by the very factors of bounded rationality, information asymmetries and potential opportunism that constrain the choice of rules governing task allocations. The same factors place supervisors in a central position because they often share some of the tacit job knowledge of those they supervise, and they are in touch with the goals of higher levels of management. This section (§5) looks at the influence of the two contractual constraints on performance criteria. It shows the critical role played by patterns of accountability and occupational standards in shaping performance criteria. Section 6 takes this further and argues that different kinds of performance criteria will be emphasized according to the prevailing transaction rules. This is largely because each transaction rule leaves critical areas of performance subject to employees' discretion, and so is exposed to a different kind of moral hazard problem. To control these, employers will rank certain performance criteria more highly than others. Finally, as performance criteria need to be mutually acceptable in order to be effective, it is important to show that there are also adequate protections for workers against manipulation of standards by their employers.

5.1 The enforceability constraint

To be enforceable, performance standards need to identify who is responsible or accountable for performance, and to be defined in a way which can be easily applied by supervisors and those whose work they are directing. Unless defined in a way that enables both managers and employees to identify who is responsible, particularly in cases of substandard work, performance norms cannot be enforced. Accountability might be defined directly, holding particular individuals responsible for the quality of performance of their tasks, or indirectly, by focusing on groups of employees.

Whether performance obligations and their accountability are defined in individual or group terms has profound implications for the nature of performance criteria. Focusing on individual accountability necessarily reduces the scope for recognizing interdependence between the performance of individual workers. Under many work systems, responsibility is individualized, as for example, in the account of classic Taylorist systems of quality control given by Cole (1994). Each worker is held directly accountable for her or his own job.

On the other hand, stressing group performance requires an emphasis on the quality of interaction within the group and hence on relational skills in addition to any outcome-related measures. When responsibility is assigned to groups, each individual is only indirectly accountable, through the group of which she or he is a member, and performance obligations become diffuse rather than specific. *Relational skills* are of particular importance, as individual employees' contributions to the group depend as much on execution of their own tasks as on how they cooperate with other group members. Such group working is not confined to team working. It also arises when workers need to know how to respond when equipment starts to malfunction or when established procedures prove inadequate. Touraine (1955) referred to this in his study of the then emerging automated work systems as 'le sens des incidents', that is, a sense of how to respond when things start to go wrong, and who to call upon. In such unpredictable situations, a group response is essential. Similar observations about relational and response skills were made by Davis (1971) *à propos* new work systems in the US, and by Kern and Schumann (1984) on new production concepts in Germany.

Although they might appear like two extremes on a scale, in fact, attributing responsibility for performance directly or indirectly represents two contrasting logics, each with its own incentives. A heavy emphasis on direct, individual accountability, for example, militates against valuing relational activities, even if they are not explicitly forbidden.[9] Indeed, rather than helping one's colleagues, there is every temptation to pass the buck and pass on difficult cases that might harm one's own performance. As one of office workers under a system of individualized responsibility in Sainsaulieu's study put it:

When you are given a difficult job, for example, you can't do it, you are afraid it will take too long, or you are afraid you can't understand it, you try to pass it on to a colleague. Well, in the end, you can always find someone you can pass it on to, but without forcing them, you see, because they can get their own back. (Sainsaulieu, 1988: 134)[10]

In order to foster relational skills, management needs to play down individual accountability, and to find some way of promoting greater co-operation within the work group. Helping one's colleagues perform well has to become part of performing well oneself. On the other hand, the risk management takes in promoting relational skills is that the work group will use its increased independence to pursue other goals, possibly opposed to management. In his comparison of the 'traditional', Taylorist approach to quality control with the 'modern' work-group-learning approach, Cole (1994) argues that they are distinct paradigms, each with its own special, and mutually incompatible, logic. Thus, the contrast between these two methods implies a fundamental difference of approach to establishing performance quality standards. In particular, it will determine the weight attached to aspects of individual task performance as compared with relational skills, such as cooperation and initiative.

A second feature of performance standards is the need for some external point of reference or some objective indicators to back up subjective judgements by line managers, as Landy and Farr have stressed. These are needed in case of disputes. If the judgement is purely subjective, there is no independent check that managers can fall back on if called upon to justify their assessment, and there is no guarantee to the employee. Good performance becomes simply what management judges to be good, and vice versa. There are two common types of external reference: reliance on critical indicators, such as absences or hours worked; and comparison against professional standards.

The choice of key events or indicators is necessarily selective, and often they only approximate the desired quality of performance. As this is difficult to measure, it is common to work indirectly by assessing behaviour in certain 'critical incidents' that can be more easily identified. For example, rather than monitor diligence itself, firms may record absenteeism or discipline cases, or take note of additional hours after the normal working day, even though the underlying relationship with productivity is weak. If managers' appraisals of staff are challenged, they can point to a poor record for absence or time-keeping. Although this may not have been essential for good performance, it is used as an indicator of a disposition likely to lead to poor performance. Employees may also challenge this. For example, was a particular person's absence rate worse than average, or were there relevant mitigating circumstances?

The ambiguities of such critical indicators of performance are illustrated by the Landers *et al.* (1996) study of the 'long hours trap' in professions. The very long hours worked were widely recognized to be inefficient, yet they continued to be used to identify good performers. In the professions they studied, which used an income-sharing rule, there was an incentive for partners to work shorter hours than their colleagues, so when assessing associates' bids to become partners, existing partners looked for a sign that the candidate was a 'hard-worker'. The critical aspect of their behaviour that reveals this is their willingness to work very long hours while associates. Although everyone may prefer shorter working hours, hard-workers will find long hours less onerous than will others, and so find the entry cost to the profession somewhat lower. In this way, the authors argue, long hours serve as a critical signal of diligence, even though the long hours themselves may not be very productive in practice.[11] Dore (1973: 189–90) makes a similar observation in relation to the long hours of Japanese factory workers: they signal willingness to perform, which firms do value. The problem is that such indicators are relatively few and inevitably somewhat crude.[12] As the two examples show, often they may not be very closely correlated with the kinds of performance that management values most, but they are the best of a bad lot.

Standards of performance that can be expected for certain jobs or from certain occupations provide an alternative approach, although it is more commonly available under the training approach because they are often instilled during training. Because most jobs involve an element of judgement and problem-solving in response to shifting job demands and contexts, defining performance simply in terms of either input or output makes little sense. The problem can be illustrated by considering what is involved when a supervisor asks a skilled electrician to change an electric fuse. In simple physical terms, the output is represented by the replacement of the fuse, something many of us can do without any special skill. Nor is the effort involved a terribly useful guide. What the employer is really paying for is neither of these, but rather the application of the electrician's training and judgement to replacing a safety device that has been triggered by a malfunction somewhere. The quality of the electrician's performance is really measured by the safety of the apparatus after the fuse has been changed, in other words, it is dependent on the quality of the diagnostic checks undertaken and of any fault tracing that was necessary. The operation might have stopped at replacing the fuse, or it might have involved repair to a number of faulty circuits. The amount of physical and intellectual effort involved is unknown beforehand. What is known is the standard of safety that should be achieved after the repair. Thus the notion of a performance standard involves the application of skills and knowledge to diagnosis of the problem and the undertaking of appropriate actions. It may therefore involve a variable amount of effort in order to achieve the same standard of performance. In this example, substandard performance becomes apparent when there is a further breakdown or accident, and the skilled person's negligence is revealed. Because a performance standard in this respect is relatively invariant, it is much more suitable for use as a criterion of good performance.

Figure 6.1 illustrates these ideas. The variability of job demands arising from variable contexts is shown by the wavy line at the bottom. The variations in achieved output, because of all the other external factors involved, are shown by the top wavy line. The professional standard is the straight line. In other words, those applying their knowledge and skills in their work agree, or are expected, to provide a variable work input, whatever is needed to achieve the standard of competent performance.

5.2. The efficiency constraint

Satisfying the enforceability constraint shapes the *form* of performance criteria. Their *content* is determined above all by the way the efficiency constraint is resolved: how job demands and worker competencies are aligned. It is therefore critical to the definition of work quality and competent performance. There are two types of standards: organization-specific

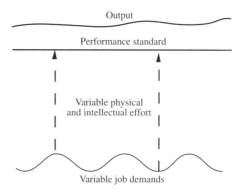

Fig. 6.1. **Job demands, effort and performance**

and occupational or professional ones, associated, respectively, with the production and training approaches. Being simpler to explain, the latter are dealt with first.

One of the strengths of the training approach lies in the wide diffusion of performance standards related to particular professions or occupations. These are usually acquired during training. Scullion and Edwards (1988: 119) describe the craft skills as providing 'norms of high quality workmanship', and a performance standard to which people expect, and are expected, to work. In addition, because they have the same skill, the interchangeability of such workers enables management to develop a practical knowledge of their capabilities, and hence of the occupational performance standard (Zucker, 1991).

A very good example of occupational performance standards at work is given by Maurice *et al.*'s (1986) account of control systems and norms of skilled performance that they found in German firms. The German term '*Leistung*' encapsulates the notion of competence based on training to widely recognized standards. The presence of such performance norms enabled management to delegate a great deal of autonomy to skilled workers as to how they tackled the technical problems arising in their work (p. 113).[13] This was also reflected in patterns of supervision. German supervisors described their work as 'finding solutions to technical problems' rather than hierarchical control (p. 158).[14] The significance of this is brought out by the contrast with French supervisors operating under the production approach. There, management stressed the exercise of hierarchical control, and in a revealing discussion of why job rotation did not lead to higher levels of skill, replied that polyvalent workers could not accede to a higher coefficient because they did not issue orders ('il ne commande pas' p. 124).

Similar observations were made by Jürgens *et al.* (1993), who contrasted the performance norms guiding German skilled automobile workers with those in Japan. At the centre of the German model the authors identified:

the skilled worker and a specific understanding of skilled work as a 'profession'. This understanding includes . . . interest in work, a willingness to accept comprehensive responsibility (also crossing over the borders from one's own task area), and a large degree of self-regulation in carrying out the work. (p. 384)

This, they argue, is based on the vocational training system. The uncoupling of work from the flow of production is a prerequisite for self-regulation with increased responsibility. They contrast the nature of the autonomy of German skilled workers with that of their counterparts in Japanese automobile factories. There too, a central role is given to skilled labour, but it is not uncoupled from production, and the 'ideal typical of the Japanese model is self-regulation under the pressure of the assembly line and the production pace' (p. 385). When looking at the patterns of self-regulation by skilled workers under the two systems, Jürgens *et al.* observe that, in the Japanese car industry, the 'work group is the starting point for an integrated job understanding', and, in contrast to the German model, 'self-regulation is thus not based on skilled worker competence and a professional ethic' (p. 385).

Contrasting 'expert' and 'bureaucratic' authority models, Zucker (1991) analyses the difficulty that bureaucratic organizations have in evaluating the performance of professional experts whom they employ, because they lack the requisite knowledge. To resolve this problem, they often have to rely on other experts:

. . . while monitoring and evaluation of task performance under bureaucratic authority take place within the organisation, generally under direct management control, expert authority relies on assessments by those most capable of making decisions regarding quality: other expert professionals. (Zucker, 1991: 165)

The outside network offers two possibilities. In extreme cases, outside experts may be called upon to assess the performance of other experts. More usually, the organization can learn what standards to expect from the process of employing professionals. Because they work to the same professional standard, professionals are to some extent interchangeable, so the normal process of labour turnover will inform employers of what to expect. However, this is only possible because of the prior existence of such performance standards.

For the production approach, the definition and application of performance standards is more complex because the jobs concerned are usually organization-specific, and lack a common foundation in vocational training. So what alternative options are available to occupational norms? One option might be to focus on the demands of individual jobs, but this is not very robust. Too much idiosyncrasy in jobs leaves management exposed to opportunistic bargaining by employees whose superior job knowledge can be used to their advantage. A common solution to this problem is to establish an agreed language for describing and comparing jobs, namely job evaluation and job classification. Slichter *et al.* (1960) and Jacoby (1985) show how effective this was in creating order out of the old contracting system that had prevailed in US firms in the early part of the century. Although mostly associated in the literature with pay determination, it would be wrong to miss the important contribution of job evaluation and classification to the definition of performance standards. Betters' (1931) study of the role of job classification in creating the conditions for merit rating in the US federal civil service provides an excellent illustration of this point. Once one knows which jobs are comparable, and in what respects they are so, it becomes possible to consider appropriate standards of performance. How much skilled judgement or responsibility can be expected from those doing such and such a job? Establishing categories of jobs also enables comparisons of performance between job holders as a guide to identifying, for example, what is an acceptable standard of diligent performance.

Table 6.1. *Dominant performance criteria dictated by the two contractual constraints*

Enforceability constraint	Efficiency constraint	
	Production: job competence standards	Training: occupational competence standards
Direct/individual accountability	Diligence at demands of individual job (Work post)	Occupational skill standard within own job area (Job territory/tools of the trade)
Indirect/group accountability	Cooperation in tasks/jobs within work group (Competence rank)	Initiative based on professional standard (Qualification rule)

Where jobs are not strongly categorized, there are alternative solutions which focus on codifying worker competencies. One such case was the 'job grade matrix' mentioned in Chapter 2, which displays the range and depth of competencies with which individual employees are credited by their line managers. This has a dual purpose: to inform managers which workers are capable of performing certain kinds of work to a high standard and of instructing junior workers; and to enable workers to compare the capabilities with which they and their colleagues are credited by management and their rank. These provide workers and management with a proxy for the occupational performance norms instilled by training under the training approach.

Taking the two contractual constraints together suggests the dominance of different performance criteria under different combinations of individual versus group accountability, and the training versus the production approaches. These are sketched in Table 6.1. Taking the production approach first, individual accountability is likely to emphasize diligence, as it rules out relational activities, and group accountability is likely to emphasize cooperation. Both are likely to play down the importance of skills. Under the training approach, skill has a special position. With individual accountability, the craft or skill of the individual worker is likely to be stressed, as there is a one-to-one relationship between the job and the skill applied. With more diffuse accountability, there is greater scope for initiative built upon the skill, and so one could expect it to be the leading performance criterion. The leading position of each of these criteria is strengthened when we consider the employer's concern with moral hazard and the scope for employee discretion over performance left by each of the four transaction rules dealt with in the next section.

6. MORAL HAZARD, TRANSACTION RULES AND PERFORMANCE CRITERIA

Generally, employers and employees have different concerns in relation to performance standards. Employers are more concerned about the kind of moral hazard issues raised by the 'principal-agent' approach, and in particular, how they might harness the discretion that employees have in their jobs to their own advantage. Workers, on the other hand, are more likely to want protection against employers' raising performance standards unilaterally, or using their ambiguity to withhold payment or other benefits. Viable performance criteria have to be mutually acceptable: to ensure that employers get the quality of services they have contracted for, and that employees can maintain limits on their employers' demands and ensure that ambiguities about performance standards are not used to deprive them of their due rewards. This section looks first at the reasons why employers would emphasize certain performance criteria given certain transaction rules, as shown in Table 6.1. It then looks at how these can be acceptable to workers because the transaction rules give them adequate defences against opportunism over the application of performance standards. The treatment of employer and employee interests is not symmetrical: whereas employers will give greater emphasis to efficiency criteria, employees are more likely to stress enforceability.

6.1. Employer protections against moral hazard by employees

For employers, one of the key concerns of performance management is to influence the discretion that employees have over the effort and attention they put into their jobs. Such discretion creates scope for moral hazard: employees may exercise it to do as little as possible, or they may go beyond their immediate obligations to their employers. It is in the employers' interest to motivate their employees to operate near the top of the range. This is the critical zone for performance management, and the key to it lies in developing suitable performance criteria that are adapted to the kind of discretion available to employees. Each of the four transaction rules leaves different areas of performance subject to employee discretion, giving rise therefore to different types of potential moral hazard. Thus, one can expect employers to concentrate the focus of performance management on these areas, so, given a particular rule, they will stress the kind of performance criteria that correspond to the key areas of employee discretion that it leaves open. The relative positions of the other criteria under each employment rule are summarized in Appendix 2.

Diligence is likely to be the critical performance criterion under the 'work post' rule. Many areas demanding initiative and cooperation have been limited by job design. Indeed, Holmstrom and Milgrom (1991) argue that clashes between inconsistent performance criteria can be avoided by designing jobs so that they contain only tasks which can be assessed in the same way. Otherwise, they argue, the danger is that employees will concentrate their activity on those that are most easily monitored, especially if pay is tied to measured performance. Reynaud (1992) offers a similar explanation of the focus on quantitative measures under traditional Taylorist systems of work organization: reducing employee discretion to a single dimension simplifies the tasks of monitoring and performance measurement, and thus of pay incentives. Diligence is also something that is easily individualized, and this too favours its dominance in work post systems.

One of the most revealing illustrations of this logic can be found in Maurice *et al.*'s (1986) discussion of polyvalence in a work post system. At first sight, one might expect management to try to resolve problems of variable loads on different posts due to normal absenteeism and varying work demands by encouraging workers to accept flexible work assignments. However, such flexibility is hard to integrate with the logic of work post systems, and under such a system it would be hard to reward given that pay is tied to work posts and not to individuals. Thus, management need cooperation to deal with the unpredictable incidents that occur, but they have no consistent means of rewarding it. Cooperation is valuable, but dependent entirely on goodwill. As the work post system is a rather low-trust one, goodwill remains fragile, and there are few costs to employees from withdrawing it. The solution that French management adopted, therefore, was to create a special category of polyvalent workers, able to occupy a wide range of work posts. Thus diligence prevails over cooperation as a valued dimension of performance because that at least is susceptible to management control. Tying competence to job demands also deprives the work post system of any reference to externally recognized skill standards as a guide to required performance.

In contrast, under the competence rank system, cooperation stands out both as the critical performance criterion, and as the one whose reward is built into the structure of jobs. Without a great deal of worker cooperation, flexible job structures cannot function. Unlike the work post system, cooperation by moving flexibly between work assignments is built into the incentive system, as it is the key to personal skill enlargement and future upgrading. Group accountability makes cooperation among group members critical to overall performance, and moral hazard, for example, in the form of free-riders, or strategic bargaining among group members of the kind observed by Sainsaulieu, would deeply damage the process. It is often suggested, misleadingly, that the long hours of work by Japanese workers show the emphasis on diligence. However, this overlooks the very heavy stress on the quality of cooperation in job rotation and skill development, which, for example, in Best's account of appraisal in a major Japanese steel firm, was accorded more weight than attendance. Indeed, Dore's (1973) own discussion of long hours indicates that the key pressure sustaining them was fear of the impact on one's colleagues if one worked fewer hours. Hence, it reflected as much the dynamics of within-group cooperation as simple diligence.

Moral hazard problems under the 'job territory' and 'tools of the trade' rules arise from the autonomy that skilled workers expect from supervision, and thus the scope to work below the standards of their trade. By stressing the importance and status of the skills in question, the peer group's skill norms are emphasized. By making the skill itself a leading performance criterion, one is placing a burden on the reputation of the trade for quality work. As mentioned earlier, craft skills have been described as providing 'norms of high quality workmanship' to which people expect, and are expected, to work. The autonomy of those with craft skills from direct supervision in their work is something which depends on the continued reputation of their peer group for quality work (Scullion and Edwards, 1988: 119). However, the peer group is essentially one that extends beyond the firm, and the principle of individual accountability has the effect of confining performance within the limits of the individual's skill, and thus to standard operations within its main area of competence.

In contrast, the 'qualification' rule, while espousing the same kind of occupational standards based on vocational training, is able to embrace initiative to a much greater extent. Because accountability is broader, and recognized job boundaries less-sharply defined, there is greater scope for embracing tasks outside one's immediate job. This opens up a much wider range of problem-solving activities, and increases the scope for initiative. Problem-solving activities broaden and deepen skills, but they require initiative. This enables the transformation of skills beyond the scope of initial training into something more flexible and more valuable to employers. Hence, while skill is important, and provides a guide to expected competence standards, the scope for initiative broadens it into something different from the skills under the job territory rules. It becomes the basis for a degree of task flexibility undertaken autonomously of management, and based on skilled workers' judgement. Thus, Maurice *et al.* (1986) and Jürgens *et al.* (1993) note the high level of training of skilled of blue-collar workers in German plants, but also the role of job rotation in developing that skill, their high degree of autonomy and their willingness to work across occupational boundaries. To conclude, for employers, the main types of performance criteria help them to regulate the different elements of employee discretion left open by each of the four transaction rules.

6.2. Employee protections against employer opportunism

For employees, the main concern is that management should not be able to use their dominant role in performance management to jack up work demands unilaterally, or to manipulate performance criteria to justify with-holding rewards. The effects of each of the four rules is illustrated in Table 6.2.

The two task-centred rules provide a good degree of protection against pressures on individual employees to raise their work effort. The discrete nature of job boundaries, combined with the interdependence of jobs, means that firms cannot raise effort demands on individual posts in isolation because that would simply upset the flow of work. Likewise, on cooperation, the two task-centred rules provide employees with a strong fall-back position should they feel that management's demands for cooperation are unreasonable. In essence, they offer workers individualized defences against attempts by management to jack up performance demands unilaterally. Neither of these defences are offered by the two rules that allow more diffuse patterns of accountability, but they do offer some compensating strengths. The more diffuse job boundaries give management greater flexibility than do the two task-centred rules, but this can be withdrawn. Although the more diffuse job boundaries make it easier for management to crank up individual workloads than under the task-centred rules, the lack of a safety net of specific minimum employee obligations leaves management more exposed should cooperation break down. So the risks for management of pushing workers too far are greater under the diffuse job rules.

For cooperation, under both task-centred rules, the stronger accountabil-ity for individual jobs associated with the work post and job territory rules prescribes a minimum level and pattern of cooperation. For the two diffuse rules, cooperation opens up scope for a degree of regulation by the work group itself because of interdependency between jobs. The same work group strength that facilitates cooperation in tasks between workers can also provide collective strength against management should its demands be perceived as excessive.

Skill and initiative relate to the application of knowledge and job com-petencies, and so raise rather different problems of opportunism. A very common bone of contention in worker–management relations revolves around the recognition of skills and initiative, and their possible reward. Should workers be paid according to the skills they bring to the job, some of which may only occasionally contribute to their performance, or should they be paid according to the core demands of their jobs? If performance declines because they are pushed beyond the limits of their competencies, should they be penalized by management for substandard performance?

In the case of occupational skills associated with the training approach, knowledge of the appropriate standard of work is widely diffused among other employers and workers. The guidance offered by such external stan-dards is lacking in the two rules of the production approach. Under the work post rule, this lack tends to push skill and workers' job knowledge into a twilight world in which its recognition is problematic (Dugué, 1994). As jobs are designed according to the organization's own internal demands, skill at particular jobs cannot be related to external qualifications. This leaves job

Table 6.2. *Work quality: a summary of employee defences against opportunism. Means of limiting excessive job demands in performance evaluation under the production and training approaches*

	Production approach		Training approach	
	Work post	Competence rank	Job territory/tools of trade	Qualification rule
Diligence	'Fair day's work', fixity of job boundaries & 'balancing the line' problem		'Fair day's work', fixity of job boundaries & 'balancing the line' problem	
Cooperation	Fall back on detailed job description	Strong work groups for horizontal job cooperation	Fall back on clear job boundaries ('getting quality on the cheap')	Strong work groups for horizontal cooperation inherent in job rotation
Initiative	Fall back on detailed job description	Strong work groups can reduce cooperation in group problem-solving & skill transmission	Limited to boundaries around skill territory	Strong professional groups underpin problem-solving within & across skill areas
Skill	Position in job classification & job evaluation	'Job grade matrix'	Professional norms of skilled performance	'Leistung'

demands as the only readily available criterion, but they raise two difficult problems. First, job demands themselves do not define performance standards, as one still has to agree what is competent performance at a particular job. Secondly, if management wishes to adapt work organization to changing production demands, then job demands will themselves change over time, so they will not provide a stable basis for performance standards. One solution is to place jobs in a classification system which establishes equivalencies between jobs according to the nature of job demands. Classification eases many of the quality of performance problems in individual cases, because workers and management can refer to performance in similarly graded jobs in different parts of the organization.

Under the competence rank rule, classification may also be used as a guide for workers and management as to what levels of performance can be expected, but they lack the reference to work posts. Instead, one has to find a way of classifying worker competencies. Not to do so would have two likely consequences. To rely entirely on the knowledge of performance standards within the work group and its supervisor, with little possibility of external control, would be too heavily dependent on work group dynamics and relations with individual supervisors. Higher management would face potential coalitions between work groups and supervisors against themselves, and possibly also against other work groups. The other likely outcome, in the absence of some form of systematic classification, would be that pure seniority would prevail within work groups over upgrading and assignment to more complex and difficult work. That would weaken incentives for junior workers to develop the necessary skills and to participate fully in job rotation.

One solution to these difficulties is the 'job grade matrix' mentioned earlier. If interpersonal comparisons based on the matrix give line managers a criterion for identifying competent performance by workers in different ranks, they also give workers a guide to accepted performance standards for given recognized job demands or competencies. Thus, each of the four transaction rules helps the parties navigate through a sea of potential opportunism, and this is a powerful reason for their adoption.

7. CONCLUSION: SOCIETAL INFLUENCES ON PERFORMANCE CRITERIA

At the beginning of this chapter, it was proposed that performance management is the innermost area of management prerogative within a firm. So far, the chapter has shown that management's choice of performance criteria is strongly limited by both the inherent difficulties of performance management in an environment of potential opportunism, and that it is shaped by the prevailing transaction rule regulating work assignments. Societal influences impinge on the choice of performance management system in two ways: they are reflected in the prevailing transaction rules themselves; and the robustness of performance criteria is greatly enhanced if similar criteria are widely used by other firms and organizations. The very advantages of conformity bring disadvantages of non-conformity.

At the micro-level, the advantages of conformity are that widely understood performance criteria are more robust and better trusted by workers and their line managers. Using the same kinds of performance standards as other firms also means that one can recruit people familiar with them from the external market, and less effort has to be devoted to socializing new recruits to one's own particular standards. Such factors help to institutionalize performance criteria at this level, and give a first source of societal differentiation.

These micro-level pressures can be reinforced by inter-firm institutions that enhance the stability and predictability of performance standards. When firms' use of them is underwritten by collective agreements or by well-understood conventions, then individual employees know that their employers will normally have to go through certain procedures before changing them. This is more stable than simply relying on the dictates of firms' self-interest, which could change with circumstances. Institutionalization also insulates performance norms from the pressures of turnover among senior managers, something Appelbaum and Batt (1994) argued had destabilized a number of high performance work systems in the US, which was discussed in Chapter 3.

Generally, these processes make performance norms more robust. For example, when many workers are familiar with the patterns of accountability associated with the work post system, it is relatively easy to introduce them into a new workplace. It can also be harder to change them in established 'brownfield sites'. Dugué's (1994) and Clark's (1994) studies of the introduction of high performance work systems against a background of task-centred rules show how workers carried over the old norms into the new systems, and sought to recreate the same protections against employer opportunism.

The occupationally based performance standards, as will be argued in Chapter 8, are another clear example of societal influence on firms' human resource policies from the inter-firm level. The norms are effective because of their widespread recognition, and that depends upon a well-established occupational market. Such markets, it will be shown in Chapter 8, depend strongly on an institutional support. In the case of performance standards within internal labour markets, although firms may develop their own classifications, as was seen in Chapter 4, they often follow the contours of industry classification agreements, as in France, or other conventions, such as the Dictionary of Occupational Titles, which was long influential in the US.

The costs of non-conformity reflect the element of constraint in choice of performance criteria. Firms often have the freedom to develop their own solutions and their own approaches to performance management. Otherwise, experimentation and change would rarely happen. On the other hand, in creating their own performance management systems, firms need to socialize their employees into a new set of performance norms before they can function predictably. One of the interesting problems observed by Marié's studies of immigrant workers in French industry was that they were unaccustomed to the work methods and supervisory styles in French firms and found it hard to relate to them. Thus, one can always cite examples of firms that have chosen to insulate themselves from their societal context and develop their own internal systems of work organization and performance management, such as the IBMs and the Hewlett Packards of this world. Nevertheless, they remain exceptional because of the large investment that they must make in order to do so successfully. On revisiting a number of the large non-union firms of his famous study, Foulkes (1988) found that many of them had been forced to abandon key elements of their former employment systems because they had proved too expensive to operate in the US environment.

APPENDIX 1

Some examples of criteria used in performance appraisal

In its guidance on appraisal-related pay for personnel managers, ACAS (1990) presents two of the most common approaches: appraisal against objectives and performance in the job as a whole. The first was illustrated in the main body of the chapter. The second approach is to focus on the job as a whole, and ACAS provides examples of some common schemes and their criteria. One of these gives a list of ten criteria against which staff performance should be rated. These include: time keeping/attendance, work volume, work quality, job knowledge, relationships with colleagues, communications and problem-solving. Another of them gives: time keeping and attendance, job knowledge, quantity of work, quality of work, relationships with others, communications, problem-solving, safety awareness, acceptance of responsibility and forward planning. In each case, personnel managers are advised to agree objectives with individual staff in advance and then to appraise them against achievement of these.

The British civil service appraisal scheme, up to the early 1990s, when it was broken up into agencies, applied a 'whole job' scheme. The Inland Revenue version, which was very similar to the others, comprised thirteen different criteria on which staff were appraised, as follows.

Standard of work:

(a) quality

(b) quantity

Personal skills:

(c) planning

(d) problem-solving

(e) negotiation (if applicable)

(f) decision making

Management:

(g) of staff (if applicable)

(h) of other resources

Communication:

(i) oral

(j) written

Working relationships:

(k) with colleagues

(l) with the public

Knowledge:

(m) professional and technical knowledge

(Source: Inland Revenue Staff Report Form E1A (C&T), cited in Marsden and Richardson, (1992).)

In a National Health Service Trust Hospital, the following criteria were used for the purposes of individual performance agreements. First, employees had a 'job contribution profile' consisting of:

- occupational skills;
- client care (including patients and colleagues);
- decision-making and problem-solving;
- interpersonal skills;
- leadership; and
- planning and administration.

Appraisal also took account of a number of other factors, notably: absence, disciplinary procedures, additional duties undertaken, and special or outstanding performance. Employees agreed annual performance objectives with their line managers against which they would be assessed later on. The scheme noted that objective setting depended on the amount of discretion that employees had in their jobs, it being greater the more managerial they were, and that for many employees the target might simply have been their job contribution profile.

As with the civil service example, the criteria can be classified fairly easily into the four broad categories of diligence, cooperation, initiative and skill. The scheme's acknowledgement that detailed objectives may not be relevant for many staff bears out the frequent convergence in practice between rating

Table 6.3. *Individual assessment matrix in a Japanese steel firm (Sumitomo Metal Industries)*

Element for assessment		Grade of evaluation				
		a*	a	b	c	c*
Skill	Degree of skill	50	40	30	20	10
	Positive achievement	25	20	15	10	5
	Ability of application	25	20	15	10	5
Attendance	Condition	50	40	30	20	10
Character	Positiveness	25	20	15	10	5
	Cooperation	25	20	15	10	5

Source: Best (1984).

by looking at the job as a whole (its contribution profile) and setting objectives.

A third example comes from the Japanese steel industry (Best, 1984: 21 ff.). The appraisal system there focused on two key performance elements which enabled the workers to earn the 'duty points' needed for progression through the ranking hierarchy.

Stage 1 is the assessment of the individual employee against three elements: Skill, Attendance and Character—with the elements of Skill and Character subdivided as shown. Broadly, the points available are evenly divided between:

- a judgement of the individual capability (i.e. skill—innate and trained—in a flexible, rotational working structure); and
- a judgement of individual personality (compatibility with the required management style, supervisory qualities and organization of working relationships, together with regularity of attendance).

Table 6.3 shows the points awarded for different grades of evaluated performance. A forced distribution is applied with 15% 'a's, 70% 'b's and 15% 'c's. A small percentage also get the starred grades. The scores are totalled to calculate the 'classification of ability' on the basis of which the number of 'duty points' awarded for the year is calculated. More highly ranked workers are awarded a higher number of 'duty points' for a given overall grade. Similar processes apply for white-collar workers.

APPENDIX 2

Transaction Rules and Performance Standards

Table 6.4. *Transaction rules and job performance standards*

Transaction rule	Diligence	Cooperation	Initiative	Competence
Work post	Tightly defined boundaries of jobs imply little gain for mgt by boosting diligence in individual wps. But, dil. an indicator of potential cooperation & acceptance of firm's norms	Essential because of uncertainty of production & rigidity of task assignments to work posts. Coop. v. problematic because it is outside obligations of wp & so mgt depends on workers' goodwill	Limited role because much prescribed by mgt because of way wp designed & narrow skill base limits technical value of initiative	Heterogeneity of jobs (because of prodn approach) implies few common criteria of performance so hard to evaluate, except by such general indicators as seniority which show duration of socialization
Rank	1	2	3	4
Competence rank	High scope for diligence because diffuse job boundaries imply flex. for individuals to expand work roles & long hours as an indicator of commitment, esp. in QC activities	Job rotation & flex. working key to skill, but hard to measure objectively, so critical focus of merit ratings	Hard to monitor outside small group activities, although there is scope for its use	Job heterogeneity means there are few objective criteria for competent performance of individuals because competence heterogeneous. Hence reliance on dil. & coop.
Rank	2	1	4	3
Qualification	Effort not of value in itself because professional work involves assessing work needed in a given context to reach professional standard of performance	As for job territory rule except that absence of rigid job boundaries implies coop. even less problematic because built into job & so covered by prof. standard	Broader than for job territory rule because management can delegate more, thus increasing the scope for initiative	Prof. standard can be monitored because widely shared & jobs homogeneous by design (training approach). Basis for establishing criteria of 'competent performance'
Rank	4	3	1	2
Job territory/tools of the trade	As for qualification rule, but value of diligence additionally limited by strict accountability & job boundaries	Broader sk. than under wp implies coop. less problematic because fewer job boundaries involved	Strict job boundaries limit the scope for initiative to within the job	Prof. standard as above, but confined to strict area of tasks identified by the occupation
Rank	4	3	2	1

Key: wp, work post; dil., diligence; sk., skill; coop, cooperation. The rank of 1 indicates the most important performance criterion for each type of transaction rule. The shaded boxes denote the most important performance criterion for each type of transaction rule.

ENDNOTES

[1] This is referred to as the 'equal compensation principle' by Milgrom and Roberts (1992: 228).

[2] The 'ideal widget' approach might seem attractive because of the widespread practice of automobile and other manufacturers, in their quest to raise quality, of using demonstrations of correctly assembled parts to help assembly staff get the job right (Marsden *et al.*, 1985). However, whatever the value of such demonstrations for didactic purposes, they do not define performance standards.

[3] 'Plus il y a de règles, plus il est possible de se définir une stratégie personnelle en jouant sur leurs imperfections ou sur la lettre même des textes' (Sainsaulieu, 1988: 119).

[4] A recent special report in *Le Monde* ('La notation, casse-tête des fonctionnaires' 29.10.97) on staff appraisals in the French public service revealed that similar problems there were widespread.

[5] Marsden and French show that they conformed to the canons of best practice identified by such organizations as the Institute of Personnel and Development (see Armstrong and Murlis, 1994) and the Arbitration, Conciliation and Advisory Service (ACAS, 1990), and that the two government departments had earned the praise of the government's efficiency watchdog, the National Audit Office, for their innovative use of performance benchmarking (NAO, 1989). The problems encountered by the schemes were not therefore due to lack of careful design and implementation.

[6] Cropanzano and Fulger's (1991) review of experimental and workplace research suggests that when organizations operate procedures that are judged as fair and just by their employees, they are more likely to accept the justice of even adverse appraisals and rewards. Thus, they argue, procedural justice can help overcome problems generated by distributional injustice.

[7] In many respects, these findings echo the problems of suspicion in interpersonal relations with colleagues and with management found by Crozier (1963) and Sainsaulieu (1988) in their studies of French bureaucratic organizations in the 1950s and 1970s.

[8] For the US, Milkovitch and Wigdor (1991: 104) cite evidence that the objective-based approach (MBO) is most widely used for appraisal of managers and professionals.

[9] Both Cole (1979: 233) and before him, Roethlisberger and Dickson (1939: 505) comment on the common prohibition under US work post systems on helping fellow workers.

[10] 'Quand on a une affaire embêtante, par exemple, on ne peut pas la faire, quand on a peur que ça fasse trop de temps, ou on a peur de ne pas comprendre, on essaie de la refiler au voisin. Ben finalement, on arrive toujours à placer l'affaire à quelqu'un d'autre, mais sans forcer la personne, vous voyez, et c'est à charge de revanche' (Sainsaulieu, 1988: 134).

[11] Their argument is that given the sharing rule for partners' income, there is a moral hazard problem that new partners might be tempted to conceal a disposition for working fewer hours than the other partners. Therefore, associates seeking promotion to partner status work very long hours in order to signal their disposition towards hard work. Someone who placed a high value on non-work activities would find such long hours more costly than someone who enjoyed working hard.

[12] This point was made to me in a seminar in May 1998 at the Erasmus University Rotterdam by a senior member of the pay policy team of one of the Dutch employers' associations responsible for negotiating over performance pay and appraisal.

[13] 'le système de travail tendra alors à respecter davantage l'autonomie des travailleurs et à rétribuer plutôt l'efficience liée à leur professionalité que leur adaptation à l'organisation' (Maurice *et al.*, 1986, French edn: 113). The other page references in the paragraph also refer to the French edition.

[14] In contrast, French supervisors in the sample firms would spend 70–80% of their time dealing with non-technical problems. Similar findings of British–German comparisons of supervisory work also highlight the extent to which German supervisors and middle-managers work as 'player-managers' rather than as specialist coordinators (Stewart *et al.*, 1994).

7

Pay and Incentives

1. A THEORY OF PAY AND CLASSIFICATIONS

'For what do employers pay when they hire labour?' This apparently simple question hides a number of tricky assumptions about the nature of employment and the rules governing pay. The most common is that labour use is an incremental process that incurs incremental costs. Such a conception may be appropriate for incremental purchases of certain types of goods, such as in a supermarket, but even when these are repeat purchases, each one is a separate transaction. It might also seem appropriate for many casual labour markets.

A moment's thought about the essential insight of Coase and Simon shows just how misleading this assumption is. The open-ended nature of the employment relationship both in time and in the nature of the duties to be undertaken makes the hiring and reward of labour radically different from buying goods at a supermarket. When firms and workers embark upon an employment relationship, in effect, they exchange a set of mutual obligations. The employee undertakes to be available to work in a way determined by the firm, and the firm incurs a set of obligations relating to rewards and conditions of work. In both cases, the obligations extend over time even though both parties remain theoretically free to terminate the relationship subject to certain conditions. Even in the US, where employment remains nominally 'at will', in practice the great majority of employees are covered by dismissal procedures and the need to show that practices are non-discriminatory, just as they are in Europe and Japan.[1]

This chapter argues that the price of labour should be treated as a rule rather than a number, reflecting its key position in the obligations exchanged by firms and workers in the employment relationship. It then goes on to trace out the effects of the transaction rules on pay rules and pay structures, looking particularly at the relationship between 'rate for the job' and 'rate for the classification' rules and performance incentives, and at the impact of the production and the training approaches in generating respectively 'hierarchical' and 'occupational' pay structures.

1.1 The price of labour is a rule not a number

The supermarket analogy encourages us to think of price as a number, x for a particular item. This is misleading in two respects. First of all, the prices of labour services are rarely a single number. Far more often they are schedules of prices relating to different labour qualities, and varying conditions under which labour services are supplied. Secondly, it is more accurate to think of price as a rule rather than as a quantity. Although fundamental, neither insight is particularly new. Recognition of the first has been built into the revolutionary methodology used by the US Bureau of Labor Statistics to construct its Employment Cost Index (ECI), a version of which is now being adopted in the European Union, and has been considered also for Canada. Recognition of the second, that labour's price is a rule, was fundamental to Dunlop's famous comparative treatise on industrial relations systems (Dunlop, 1958: 14). He identified two types of rule, 'procedural' and 'substantive', the most important example of the latter being the rules determining the rewards of labour, and which he argued were shaped by their institutional, market and technological contexts.

(a) Wages and salaries are schedules of prices, not a single number

One of the most striking features of the 'price' of labour is its sheer complexity. It is not a single price for a piece of work, but rather a complex schedule of prices. Its many different elements may include base pay, individual and collective incentive payments, overtime, monthly and annual bonuses, allowances for different working conditions, pay for time not worked such as vacations and sickness, fringe benefits, pension and social contributions, and so on. Base pay may be a simple rate for the job, or it may be a whole pay scale with annual increments which may be service or performance related. The variety is rich. As a simple illustration, one could take the broad composition of hourly labour costs in the five countries considered here (Figure 7.1).

In all five countries, non-wage and salary costs account for at least a quarter of the price of labour (the Japanese data include sickness and vacation pay in basic salaries). Each of these broad components itself contains a great diversity of systems. For example, basic wages and salaries are determined by a wide variety of incentive schemes ranging from simple time-based pay to individual and collective bonus schemes, and allowances, and also to different rules about pay progression over time.

In public debate, employers especially have often complained that many of the components of labour costs, notably social contributions, are a tax that they have to pay over and above what they pay in wages. Consequently, it might seem wrong to argue that these are a part of the 'reward package' paid to employees. However, the argument is based on a fallacy. Hamermesh and Rees (1993) show that given the low elasticity of supply of most types of

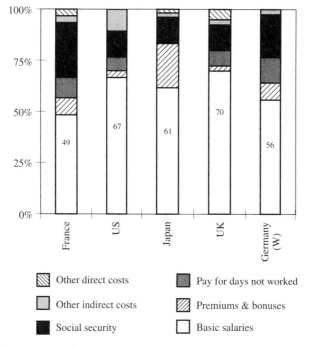

Fig. 7.1. The structure of hourly labour costs 1992/4 (industry and construction)
Source: Eurostat (1995), Labour Cost Survey 1992 (Europe, 1992; Japan, 1991; and US, BLS (1994) Employment Cost Index).

labour, much of the burden of social charges is in fact shifted onto workers. Similarly, Nickell and Bell (1995) use the equalization of unit total labour costs internationally, as opposed to the simple pay element, as evidence that employers' social contributions are shifted onto labour. If the burden were shifted to direct taxation, in the long run employers would have to pay higher wages. It is therefore justified to treat them as a part of employees' total remuneration.

Looking within the wage and salary cost component, a similar degree of complexity can be found. Employees' pay is made up of a wide variety of different types of bonuses and allowances, and different rules for the progression of basic pay and different rules for the payment of hours not worked such as sickness absence and paid holidays. Studies by the CERC (1987) and by Reynaud (1992), discussed later, show how the types of pay system correspond to different types of human resource policies.

(b) Price as a rule

Recognition that labour prices are most commonly schedules of prices rather than single figures leads to a second observation: that prices are rules rather than numbers. The different components of labour cost shown in Figure 7.1, and revealed in the variety of incentive and other payments that make up wages and salaries, serve to highlight the importance of the time dimension in both performance and reward. When payment for job performance is not instantaneous but is spread over many time periods, employers and employees come to rely heavily upon promises that extend over time.

Indeed, the phrase, the employer's 'pension promise', was used to characterize one such obligation in Gustman *et al.*'s review (1994) of current research on pensions in the labour market. It is perhaps the longest term commitment an employer enters into for its employees, but a large number of other benefits are similarly deferred into the future. Paid vacations, sick pay, annual bonuses, incremental pay scales and so on, all represent cost obligations employers build up in exchange for the employee's obligations to provide work as requested.

The promises relate not just to payment for past performance, but also to the calculation of future rewards. Should overtime hours, for example, be paid at an enhanced rate or at the normal hourly rate, or should they be deemed a part of an employee's normal duties? The particular rule applied in this case is but one of the set of rules making up the price of labour services. The promise also relates to some future rewards: for example, when employers offer incremental pay scales that increase annually with either seniority or performance. In this case, the price includes a series of increasing payments that extend over several years. The difference with the spot price in a casual labour market is not that in one case we have a schedule of prices and the other a single number, but rather, the schedule in the casual market is very simple.

A practical illustration: the US and European employment cost index

The conceptual complexity of the 'price of labour' has come to the fore in a very practical context: that of designing a new index to measure short-term changes in labour costs in the EU, inspired by the US Employment Cost Index.[2] With the approach of monetary union, it has become essential for EU member states to be able to detect inflationary tensions in their labour markets and deal with them early on. However, the conventional methods used to measure movements in the price of labour give misleading signals and so can cause governments to respond too late to rising inflation, or to hold the pressure on for too long in the face of slackening labour markets. In both cases, the economic and social cost is high.

The commonest indicators used by national governments have been short-term wage indexes which measure changes in only one component of labour costs, and indexes of labour costs. The latter can be very inaccurate because in fact they measure changes in the volume of firms' expenditures per hour worked. In doing so they combine the effects of both changes in the price of labour and in the amount used. For example, when faced with increased demand, many firms start by using more overtime until they have a better idea of how long the higher demand will last. Because overtime is conventionally paid at a higher hourly rate, employers' expenditure on labour may rise without there having been any change in wage rates. Incremental pay scales, which are extremely common, can also cause conventional labour cost indexes to give a misleading impression. When recruitment increases and labour markets tighten, such indexes may hide inflationary pressures because firms typically hire near the bottom of their pay scales, and when recruitment falls at the start of a recession, they give the impression of continued inflation. In casual or spot labour markets, conventionally measured labour cost and price are very close, but the more complex the nature of the employment relation and its related pay rules, the more the two concepts diverge. The solution to this problem is to identify a change in the price of labour as a change in the schedule of labour prices, and hence in price rules.

The operation of this principle can be illustrated with the treatment of pay for overtime hours, and of service-related increments. When workers are hired, it is already known that a schedule of prices applies: $x per hour for normal hours and $x + a$ for additional weekly or monthly hours, or that pay will increase by a certain amount each year as workers move up their incremental pay scales. In both cases, employers and their employees agree a schedule of prices and not a spot price. Moreover, it is the anticipated effect of the price schedule on costs and on income that will determine the employer's hiring decision, and the employee's job acceptance. Thus, to say that the price increases when the employer decides to use more overtime, or when the employee enters the second year of service is a confusion derived from the idea of price as a number.

The treatment of overtime hours was one of the most difficult points in the European ECI discussions. For some, it seemed counter-intuitive to construct the index by holding overtime hours constant at their level in the base year, yet if the price is seen as a schedule of two pay rates, one for normal and one for overtime hours, then it is clear that there is an increase of price only when the rate for one or both types of hours increases, and not when employers increase their use of more expensive hours. This reasoning seems counter-intuitive because many of us still have the implicit model of the spot labour market at the back of our minds.[3]

Another pre-employment notion that persists in thinking about labour cost is that it should be standardized by reference to physical hours actually worked rather than hours of availability, or 'transaction hours'. This misconception again seems plausible because one thinks of labour being exchanged in certain units, rather than following the logic of Coase and Simon's position that it is an exchange of obligations. It would be more appropriate to take the hours of availability from which cost obligations arise because these are the true focus of the exchange between employers and employees as argued in the earlier chapters.[4] Given that hours probably have to be used in order to standardize price changes across full and part-time employees, the appropriate measure is the number of hours subject to a particular regime of working. For example, for benefits that accrue only on the basis of normal hours, such as paid vacations, the latter would be the appropriate measure of working time. These are the hours that bear the employer's cost obligation. In this case, a reduction in normal weekly hours would raise the hourly price of a given number of days of paid vacation, but an increase in overtime hours would leave it unchanged because the overtime hours do not bring any additional leave entitlement.

1.2 Price and job classifications

A precondition for any kind of competitive labour market is that there should be a minimum degree of categorization of types of labour (Eymard-Duvernay, 1989). Without this employers cannot judge what kinds of work job applicants can undertake, and job seekers cannot compare job offers of different employers, and there can be no 'law of one price'. In firms and labour markets, such categories are provided by job classifications. These set the basic ground rules according to which labour services are to be priced. As argued in Chapter 4, classification systems are holistic in that they apply certain basic principles to define and divide up jobs within an organization or across a labour market. These principles organize the valuation of different kinds of labour because they stress certain criteria for reward at the expense of others and establish contours of equivalence.

A key influence which classifications exert on pay structures stems from the relative weight they give to the different criteria they apply. They may do this either serially, applying first one criterion, and then another, or simultaneously, by weighting each criterion. The first criterion to be applied, or the one given the greatest weight, will have the greatest effect on pay differentials, and so establish the dominant incentive for employees.

In Figure 7.2, jobs are first classified by level or type of skill, and then by responsibility. A third criterion could be another job characteristic, or it could be the length of service or individual performance of the employees occupying them. In this particular example, skill is the dominant classifying criterion, the others being defined within this. In German and British blue-collar classifications, 'Skill A' might well contain recognized craft skills, whereas 'Skill B' could contain semi-skilled occupations. Experienced semi-skilled workers may well earn more than newly qualified craft workers, but the limited amount of overlap follows from the strong position of craft skills in the classification. If, instead of occupation, the dominant criterion were competence rank, as in many Japanese firms, then the amount of overlap would be considerable, as more experienced workers in lower ranks can earn quite a bit more than less-experienced higher-ranking workers. But rank remains the key because workers of the same seniority but higher rank

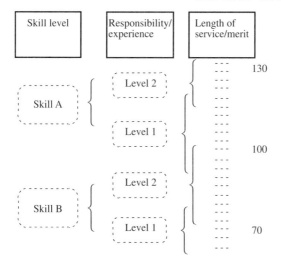

Fig. 7.2. An illustration of how classificatory principles determine pay

will earn more. In the example in Figure 7.2, the same pay outcome could be achieved either by applying the criteria hierarchically or by assigning different weights, as the size of the weights on the initial criterion will determine how far other criteria can enable workers to 'catch up'.

The dominant criterion affects the weight given to subsequent criteria, and also their nature. For example, the 'Parodi system',[5] which held sway in France from the 1940s to the late 1960s, had been strongly influenced by a form of craft organization that was prevalent in the small and medium-sized firms that were still dominant in the late 1930s, when current industry classification systems were first established. The system was primarily a classification of occupations (*métiers*), with semi-skilled production jobs treated as if they were a weak form of craft (Jobert, 1990).

In this system, trades were broadly ranked according to the time taken to learn them. But otherwise, they were mostly discrete categories. By the 1960s, many firms were finding this system unsuitable to factory and office organization because it generated a number of anomalies, notably over the ranking of certain older skills whose skill content had declined, and under-valuing many highly technical and demanding firm-specific jobs.[6] Employers sought the unions' agreement to a revised system based on job evaluation so that jobs could be defined and ranked according to a common set of criteria more in line with the production approach to work organization which by then was widely used. Thus, the 1968 Grenelle agreement set in motion negotiations to revise the system, leading in the metal industry, for example, to the 1975 agreement on four major classification criteria (*critères classants*) which comprised job knowledge, autonomy, responsibility and type of activity (its simplicity and complexity) (Carrière-Ramanoelina and Zarifian, 1985). Employers favoured the new system because it enabled them better to link pay to the kind of work organization systems they were developing, which were more oriented towards their own production systems than the older trade-based classification.

The next three sections explore how different types of price rule, through the action of classification systems and performance management, influence pay structures in the countries in which they predominate. They explore the impact of classifications looking at three questions:

- the role of rate-for-the-job rules in supporting job classifications and controlling opportunism;
- the link between classifications, and pay for performance; and
- the impact of 'hierarchical' and 'occupational' classifications.

2. PRICE AS A RULE AND 'RATE FOR THE JOB'

The convention of there being a 'rate for the job' is one of the deep-rooted principles that bind pay structures to job classifications. There are two main reasons for this. Because labour services are exchanged for pay, there is an element of 'zero sum' within the employment relationship, and hence a need to control potential opportunism. The link also brings an element of predictability without which incentives cannot really work. Each of the four transaction rules indicates a different approach. The work post system offers the purest form of rate-for-the-job rule with the narrow identification of a key rate of pay for a particular job, whereas the competence ranking system offers a more complex relationship combining seniority and recognized performance. A more appropriate, but more cumbersome, term would be 'pay for classification', so the two will be used interchangeably.

2.1 Rate for the job and opportunism

The reason for the development of rate-for-the-job rules stems from the problems of cooperation and opportunism that lie at the heart of the employment relationship. Both Coase and Simon stress the advantages of employment over open-market contracting because it economizes on transaction costs and reduces the incentives for manipulating information to get a short-term bargaining advantage. As shown at the end of Chapter 1, a major reason why employers abandoned the 'drive system' in favour of employment was to stabilize their workforces and reduce the turnover and related continuous bargaining they faced. The employment relationship eliminates neither the difference of economic interest nor the need to negotiate rewards. What it provides is a framework within which problems of co-operation and negotiation can be handled more effectively.

To reduce the volume of negotiation and the scope for opportunistic bargaining over pay one needs a counterpart to the codification of jobs, which helped to rationalize task allocation and work organization. The convention of there being a rate for the job fulfils the same function on the pay side, and at the same time, binds pay relations to the classifications used to define the nature of employees' contribution to their organizations. Rate-for-the-job rules enable employers and employees to deal with three important problems:

- to eliminate spot bargaining;
- to provide objective and robust criteria for rewards, such as job demands or recognized skills, and;
- to provide predictability and ease of enforcement.

Spot bargaining brings a number of dangers and costs outlined earlier, and in particular, it creates an incentive for manipulating information about jobs and workloads. The management problems that Willman analysed in the British automobile, printing and dock industries would not have been so serious had decayed pay systems not fuelled shop floor bargaining (v. Chapter 2). Although workers themselves were often frustrated at the loss of incentive earnings as a result of their colleagues' disputes with management, the system had evolved into one in which almost any variation in work load rapidly became the pretext for renewed negotiation over pay and work assignments. And once a sizeable part of a person's pay depends upon a miscellany of bonuses and other payments gained in previous negotiations or held on a one-off basis, one becomes locked into the system. To hold back from spot negotiations simply means falling behind what one's work colleagues are getting. The idea of a rate for the job greatly simplifies this process, and enables bargaining to be confined to certain key occasions. In Coase's example, the worker agrees to accept management's right to manage within a particular job and the rate of pay attached to that job. If the rate could be continually renegotiated, as Alchian and Demsetz (1972) suggest, then there would be little saving of transaction costs, and as Williamson (1975: 74) argues, the door would be wide open to opportunistic bargaining.

Spot bargaining can also be to workers' disadvantage, especially if the employer controls relevant information on the state of the market. This may also cause workers to prefer invariant rate-for-the-job rules over linking their pay to their company's or their own performance. Although a strong performance link could make variable pay an alternative to job cuts, the difficulty is that employers have a built-in incentive to exaggerate the severity of adverse conditions, for example, to pressurize their employees into accepting a deeper than necessary pay cut. For the employer, the cost of such action is small compared with potential increase in profits. In contrast, the situation is different if the announcement of bad news has to be accompanied by actions, such as lay-offs, which are costly to the employer. Thus, given the general background of potential opportunism surrounding the employment relationship, one can see why workers would often prefer a rate-for-the-job system with occasional lay-offs to one in which pay responds to varying product market conditions. By allowing occasional lay-offs, workers maintain easily enforceable pay rules, and give the employer some discretion to respond to shifting markets, but at a price high enough to discourage opportunistic claims. It is notable that when workers do agree to market-related pay variations, it is usually done either through concession bargaining or through a carefully ring-fenced part of their pay, such as the variable annual bonuses paid by large Japanese firms. In the case of linking pay to their own performance, similar problems arise, especially if the employer controls performance assessment, as was seen in Chapter 6.

Robust criteria for determining pay are critical, just as they are for task allocation rules, and this is something provided by rate-for-the-job rules. Workers need to know what they are being paid for, and their line managers need to be able to justify payments to them. One of the biggest problems under old fashioned payment–by–results systems, and under modern performance-related-pay systems, is that employees often complain that they do not understand how their pay has been determined. This generates the suspicion that management are manipulating the rewards to their own benefit. While this may foster compliance because people feel coerced, it is likely to make workers cynical, and to encourage opportunism on their part when the chance arises. Tying pay to the job or to the classification provides publicly observable criteria for rewards, and so reduces the element of subjective interpretation that creates scope for manipulation. When management have the upper hand it protects workers, and in times of labour shortage it protects management.

Finally, *predictability of outcomes* is improved, and if one follows 'expectancy theory', this implies a stronger relationship between pay and performance than otherwise (Lawler, 1971). Expectancy theory, which remains the most influential psychological theory concerning the link between pay and performance, postulates a looped relationship between the employees' valuation of the rewards, their willingness to exert effort to earn them, that effort generating performance and the performance being translated into the desired reward. Establishing all of these links generates a positive motivation to perform, but cutting any of them causes the relationship to break down. Tying pay to classification has the important advantage of creating predictability so that employees can see under what conditions their exertions are likely to be rewarded. If the link between effort and reward becomes too uncertain, then the pay system functions more like a lottery than a motivational system. As will be seen later, when employers in recent years have sought to strengthen the link between pay and individual employees' performance, it has mostly been within the framework given by classification systems.[7]

Thus, rate-for-the-job rules play a critical part in regulating the employment relationship and controlling opportunism. However, tying pay to job or classification can be very rigid, and we need to consider the forms of flexibility that are introduced for:

- dealing with contingencies;
- dealing with special categories of labour (such as trainees); and
- incentives for marginal increments in performance.

The first two are dealt with in this section (§2.2 and 2.3), and performance in the next (§3).

2.2 Dealing with contingencies: why pay schedules are so complex

Although Williamson's contrast between the employment relationship and 'contingent claims' contracts has been influential, in fact, the former contains many elements of the latter. By building certain contingencies into pay systems, the parties are able to combine the predictability and ease of enforcement of rate-for-the-job rules with a measure of flexibility. Many contingencies to which the employment relationship must respond occur regularly and can be anticipated, although their precise timing is uncertain. Establishing standard rules for dealing with them also helps to avoid the pressure to reopen negotiations any time workloads or other conditions change. Many of the diverse components of labour cost shown in Figure 7.1 correspond to such contingencies. These are of two main kinds: contingencies related to variable demands on workers; and those geared to different time horizons within the relationship. The first provide a degree of flexibility, and the second help to reinforce the relationship over time by stressing obligations that overlap in time.

One of the striking features of pay is the wide range of allowances of different kinds that are included in the final payment. There may be special payments for overtime hours, weekend working, holiday pay, fall-back pay, special compensation for working conditions, bonuses for certain kinds of performance, profit-shares and so on. One way to make sense of many of these elements is that they reflect different contingencies to which employment is subject. For example, when an employer contracts to buy labour services during a normal working week of 40 hours, but finds that in some weeks its demand is considerably higher, overtime working is a common response. In effect, the employee agrees to offer additional hours when needed, but at a higher rate of pay. Weekend working may be another way of dealing with peak loads. Although such working may be voluntary, employees know that if they refuse too often, their employer will seek alternative mechanisms, and then the opportunity for extra work and pay will dry up. In some industries, special allowances are payable for working in especially adverse conditions. These might take employees beyond their intended zone of acceptance of managerial authority, but rather than pay for unlimited availability or risk reopening negotiations, the employer chooses a pay schedule that covers the employees' willingness to work under the conditions that hold most of the time, and adjusts remuneration under special conditions.

Other examples of special contingencies relate to temporary interruptions of supply from employees such as sickness absence and vacations, and in the supply of work, such as downtime, and even short-time working and temporary lay-offs. Obligations vary, as does the ability to fulfil them, and some way of accommodating this has to be found. Thus, rules for sick pay, vacation pay, fall-back and so on are common. With the 'white-collarization' of blue-collar employment in many firms, other ways of dealing with these have been found. For example, with annualized hours in some firms, workers have agreed to give up overtime working and its related payments in favour of a monthly salary, with the agreement to allow the employer to vary weekly hours in response to demand, subject to an annual hours budget.

When certain events occur frequently, it is possible to define the contingencies in a fairly standard and robust way, and to integrate them with rate-for-the-job rules. Indeed, they add considerably to the flexibility of rate-for-the-job rules without detracting from the protections which they offer against opportunism.

Another type of pay rule concerns the reach of employment obligations over time. Many fringe benefits are linked to tenure, for example, the number of weeks paid vacation a year commonly increases with seniority. Many company pension schemes penalize 'early leavers' deliberately because they are intended to foster stability and loyalty among their employees. Many such benefits have different time horizons, from the current year for purchase of company products to retirement. In setting benefits up in this way, firms are creating a set of overlapping bonds with their employees, all of which help to reinforce the basic idea of the employment relation: that employers wish to assure themselves of the availability of labour when they need it, and under predictable cost conditions.

2.3 Dealing with exceptions to 'rate for the job': the example of trainee pay

Rate-for-the-job rules can be adapted to market and productivity constraints if one takes account of their function in restraining potential opportunism, and then seeks to adjust them accordingly. A good example in this respect has been the treatment of special discounts on trainee pay. For transferable skills, Becker (1975) showed that trainees would bear the full cost of training most commonly by accepting a rate of pay below the value of their output during the training period. But this requires that an exception to the rate-for-the-job rules be made.

Although the economic logic of Becker's argument is clear, the institutional preconditions for workers accepting a departure from rate-for-the-job rules are less so (Marsden and Ryan, 1990). In a perfect market with flexible wages, skilled workers have nothing to fear from low-paid trainees so long as the ratio of their employment costs equals that of their marginal products. However, should they diverge, and, notably, if skilled workers manage to bargain up their pay, then employers have an incentive to substitute cheaper trainees at least for some of the more-routine skilled tasks. Especially towards the end of a period of training, trainees are capable of undertaking a large number of skilled tasks, indeed, traditionally, it was by doing so that they paid back their employers for their training costs (Elbaum, 1990). Nevertheless, this convention has often proved difficult to enforce. In the US employers found it hard to enforce the long duration of apprenticeships, and, on the other side, in Britain, unions commonly complained of employers hiring excessive numbers of apprentices.

Controlling the risk of substitution holds the key to gaining workers' acceptance of such cost sharing. Too great a risk of substitution will stimulate opposition from experienced skilled workers to low rates of trainee pay, but at the same time, too high a rate of trainee pay may discourage an employer from providing the necessary training places. Given the difficulty of aligning pay and trainee outputs, the best alternative is some form of institutional regulation of training and of the work to which trainees are put. For young workers training for skilled positions, apprenticeship has offered such an institution. When well-organized, it provides a clear status for young trainees, and clear objectives and standards for their training. This means that other workers can easily identify the kind of work to which they may be put, enabling therefore a more effective monitoring of employers' use of apprentice labour. Even such institutions are not always sufficient, and Ryan (1986) documents the numerous complaints made by skilled unions in Britain during the slack labour markets of the 1930s that apprentices were used as substitutes, and he showed that during the inter-war years, apprentices were employed in greatest numbers where their relative pay was lowest. The difficulty of regulating apprentice use was one factor contributing to the decline of apprenticeship in Britain during the 1960s, and it encouraged unions to allow an upward drift in apprentice pay, which choked off the supply of training places (Marsden and Ryan, 1990). In contrast, much stronger workplace regulation of apprenticeship in Germany has meant that low apprentice pay rates have been no threat to skilled adults, and so they have persisted there.

Under internal labour market (ILM) systems it is much harder to gain exceptions to rate-for-the-job rules for new trainees, and also for young workers. The reason lies in their weak status differentiation. Under such circumstances, adult workers are likely to insist on rate-for-the-job rules, hence the resistance to low youth trainee rates of pay in many EU countries. Japan appears to stand out as a major exception to this argument. Internal labour markets have been great absorbers of young workers, and pay rates rise steeply in the initial years without there being any formal apprenticeship-type institutions (Sako, 1991). However, there the promise of long-term employment protects skilled workers from possible substitution by cheap youth labour. Indeed, having the right balance of new young labour entering the firm helps to offset the rising cost of more senior workers as they are promoted, and so helps to protect their job security. In contrast, in France and the US, although there is also long-term employment, the promise is felt to be less binding on employers.

3. RATE-FOR-THE-JOB CLASSIFICATION AND PAY FOR PERFORMANCE

The other problem area exposed by rate-for-the-job rules is that of motivating individual performance in the job. The 'new economics of personnel' has raised a fundamental issue concerning performance incentives by introducing formally the notion that employees have discretion over the level of performance they provide—something Simon assumed was covered by management prerogative—but it also leaves some fundamental questions unanswered. How is performance to be defined and assessed? This is often assumed to be a technical problem, but, it will be argued, this neglects the contribution of classification systems to defining the performance baseline. Mostly performance-related incentives seek marginal increments in performance from that base line. Hence, it will be argued, the margin is shaped by the classification system.

3.1 Moral hazard and performance pay

In most work environments, workers have some discretion over the quantity and quality of work they provide. This was true even under classic forms of Taylorist work organization. They can meet their performance obligations in a perfunctory way, doing the minimum that they can get away with, or they can work with varying degrees of care and attention. The scope for such discretion is one of the sources for flexibility within the employment relationship, and is a direct consequence of its open-ended nature.

A 'moral hazard' problem arises when employees have some discretion over effort or performance which management are unable to monitor closely. They might also be unwilling to do so because heavy supervision can be demotivating. Management therefore depend upon their staff not taking advantage of the information asymmetry. Principal-agent theories argue that incentive schemes have a special role to play in encouraging the performance patterns desired by management. This section builds on this analysis, but argues that it needs to be taken a step further to consider how the transaction rules shape the definition of performance and determine the scope for employee discretion.[8]

The principal-agent problem with work performance can be explained as shown in Figure 7.3. An employer, the principal, knows that within a certain job, its employees, the agents, can provide either a low or a high level of effort or care in their work. Both parties know that it is difficult to monitor the level of effort. If workers are self-interested and keen to maximize the return on their effort, then the most likely outcome with a simple rate-for-the-job pay system is that they will provide the smallest effort that they can get away with. Management might simply opt to pay the wage corresponding to the lower value of output, but this is not always feasible. For example, the firm may not wish to operate in the low-quality low-price end of the market, and it may not be able to recruit and retain sufficient labour at that wage.

Alternatively, the firm could design an incentive pay system that will reward high effort and penalize low effort, and tie pay to observed output or performance. Both parties know that output is not perfectly correlated with effort. Sometimes, hard work does not produce results because equipment fails, management may be badly organized, staff may lack training and so on. Equally, one may be lazy and lucky. As a result, there is a probability distribution of output associated with each level of effort. In Figure 7.3, an observed level of output 'x' could be achieved with the low effort 'a_1', although it would be more likely with the high effort 'a_2'. Management might therefore take the risk of tying pay to output or to performance because, on average, rewards would follow performance. On the other hand, the employ-

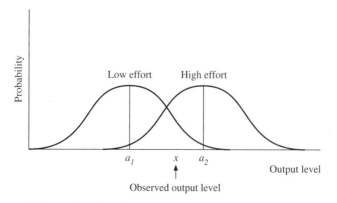

Fig. 7.3. **Moral hazard and performance incentives**

ees themselves might be opposed because of the uncertainty it introduces into their pay, and because the chance element makes it harder to assess whether or not management is operating the scheme fairly.

This analysis captures a number of important features in the development of performance-related pay in recent years. Management has a permanent concern to prevent effort and performance levels from drifting down towards 'a_1', and to push them towards 'a_2'. Often 'a_1' will not represent the minimum effort consistent with keeping one's job but rather some conventional effort norm that management wishes to 'shake up', especially if competitive pressures are rising.

Figure 7.3 also shows the ambiguity of performance measures, and hence one of the fundamental difficulties of linking pay to performance. In most work environments, it is always hard to isolate individual performance with any certainty, and so line managers often find staff appraisal a very difficult process, made all the more so when pay is linked to the outcome. For similar reasons, employees are often reluctant to have more than a small percentage of their pay tied to performance.[9] It is among sales and some higher management where individual performance is more easily identified that individual performance incentives are most widely used. Nevertheless, the desire of senior management to press ahead with performance-related pay stems from a recognition that employees do have discretion over their performance, and that established rate-for-the-job systems deprive them of a potential means of stimulating additional effort.

Beyond this, however, a closer look at the experience with performance pay systems brings out two central concerns of the theory of the employment relationship developed so far: first, there will always be a tension between the desire of management to appraise and reward performance and the need for employee confidence in the fairness with which reward systems operate; and second, performance pay operates primarily at the margin, seeking to encourage marginal increments in performance. The margin can only be defined with reference to the type of work, that is to say, the job classification system. Both factors give rise to a permanent tension between discretionary and determinate forces.

The difficulty that management faces in maintaining the discretionary element of reward is well illustrated by the history of length-of-service pay scales in many organizations. Many such pay scales started life with an important element of management discretion that became eroded over the years. For example, in the British civil service, annual pay increments were never intended to be automatic, yet the Megaw Committee of Inquiry (Megaw, 1982) noted that, by the early 1980s, the existing provisions for withholding pay increments and for giving accelerated ones were rarely, if ever, used. Similar pressures could be seen at work in the US federal civil service merit pay scheme set up in 1962. By 1977, when the President's Reorganization Project reported, it found that 99% of employees were rated as 'Satisfactory' (PMRS, 1991). It is easier to find public sector examples because of greater research access, but there is little reason to believe that such processes are peculiar to it. Indeed, the 'nenko' system of large private Japanese firms, which combines merit with seniority, has also shown a shifting balance between the two principles over time.[10] Management would like discretion to reward good performance, but then finds it hard to implement because of the difficulty of rating employees and the need to be seen by them to be acting fairly. Thus what begins as discretionary pay slowly becomes seniority based.

The other problem is that one cannot define performance in the abstract. When linking pay to staff appraisal, management has to be able to define levels and improvements in performance in terms of the jobs actually undertaken. By talking of 'low' and 'high effort', the analysis of Figure 7.3 ignores this problem. Yet, when we look more closely at the evidence on performance pay, it is mostly 'individualized' only within job categories. In a study of twenty French firms with innovative pay policies, Linhart et al. (1993) noted the large investment made by such firms in defining job categories and performance standards more carefully so that defensible evaluations of employee performance could be made. As one manager whom they interviewed put it: 'individual performance within a job can lead to individual performance pay, but the job itself cannot be individualised' (p. 43).[11] That would lead to the 'coefficient binette', rewarding the 'blue-eyed'. More generally, the spread of performance pay in both France and Britain has been accompanied by a spread of goal setting and appraisal interviews between staff and their line managers, and these depend upon a mixture of judgement and fact on the basis of which both parties can discuss targets and performance, as Landy and Farr predicted. In other words, there needs to be a shared understanding about the range of duties included in the job, and the kind of performance that can be expected.

If performance must be defined in relation to jobs, then how the jobs are defined will also affect the definition of performance, and the marginal variations that may attract performance pay. In the previous chapter, it was argued that because of problems of potential opportunism, performance could only be defined in a limited number of fairly simple and robust ways, not because performance itself was simplistic or crude, but because only simple rules can be enforced economically. There it was argued that each transaction rule would stress different criteria for defining performance and also leave different areas of discretion that would be subject to moral hazard problems.

3.2 Job classification and rewarding performance at the margin

Discretionary performance has to be defined if it is to be rewarded, and its non-provision sanctioned. As shown in Chapter 6, the criteria for assessing it have to be robust and easily understood, and to be consistent with the broad principles underlying the job and pay classification, so the effort and performance levels shown in Figure 7.3 need to be set in the context of different transaction rules. The dominant criteria for assessing marginal performance under each type of rule were the following:

- work post: diligence;
- competence rank: cooperation;
- job territory/tools of the trade: skill; and
- qualification: initiative.

(a) The work post

In many respects, the analysis in Figure 7.3 comes closest to the conditions of the work post system. Management has a strong influence over job design, and adapts it to its own organizational needs. Apart from following the production approach, it also has scope to design jobs in such a way as to minimize conflicts between incompatible performance criteria. Milgrom and Roberts (1992) show that unless two performance criteria are compensated equally, employees will focus their efforts on the one best, or most reliably rewarded (the 'equal compensation principle'). For example, if reward depends upon achieving quantitative output targets because these are easier to measure, it is very likely that quality will be sacrificed in order to achieve them. The solution proposed by Holmstrom and Milgrom (1991) is to separate the two kinds of tasks as far as possible into separate jobs, and appraise them separately and apply different criteria. Thus, in an employment office, one might separate job seekers who can be dealt with routinely from those who are hard to place and therefore require more attention, and give different placement targets to staff dealing with each group. In this way, the logic of the work post system lends itself to classic output measures by job design because the scope for employee discretion is confined to a single dimension of performance (Reynaud, 1992).

Several writers have commented on the decline of traditional Taylorist output measures in French firms (e.g. Reynaud, 1992) and their replacement by other forms. In particular, there has been a powerful expansion of 'individualization', performance-related pay, whereby employees receive individualized pay increases each year instead of the 'same increase for all' that prevailed during earlier years. Individualized pay increases grew in coverage from the middle 1980s to cover by the early 1990s about 60% of employees, who received either wholly individualized increases or a mixture of individualized and general pay increases. After that it stabilized and declined to about 50% in 1994, probably due to the slowing of inflation and the smaller amount available for nominal pay rises (INSEE, 1996). Notable in this development has been the spread of enterprise agreements setting out 'differentiated general increases', and the establishment of formalized performance appraisal procedures, especially in large firms (Ministère du Travail, 1992).

Why should performance-related increases have spread so rapidly and so widely in France? One argument put forward has been that firms could not afford generalized pay increases and so chose to concentrate them on better performers. However, firms in other countries faced similar pressures and did not respond in the same way. More important is that the system of work organization lends itself to performance pay increases. The system of work posts individualizes employees' productive contribution, and, as argued in Chapter 6, the main dimension of performance over which many employees have discretion is that of effort or diligence. This point is underlined by the relatively high percentage of French firms using individualized bonuses and premiums linked to individual effort (CERC, 1987: 103). This is a quantitative notion and so well-suited to performance pay systems. Although firms may have been interested in introducing such practices earlier, it was made possible by the growth of enterprise bargaining once the 1982 Auroux laws had bedded down. Most of the mixed forms of general and merit increases were introduced by enterprise agreements.

(b) Competence rank

The competence rank model has also been closely associated with appraisal-based performance incentives which are combined with seniority-related payments. 'Nenko', we are often reminded, involves a combination of length of service and merit. An illustration of how it works in Sumitomo Metal Industries was given by Best (1984). There employees' monthly remuneration was made up of basic pay, which was primarily determined by length of service, efficiency pay (based on efficiency savings) which was also tenure related, and job and ability pay. The latter were based on the location of an employee's job, and his or her rank. The former reflected work conditions, and the latter, the cumulative benefit of performance appraisal points. The different components are added together to get gross pay. The calculation of bonus went through a similar process. The relative weight of the different elements alters as one moves up the ranks, with length of service playing a diminishing part. Koike makes similar observations.[12]

Progression through the ranking hierarchy provides the performance-related element of pay, and, as shown in Chapter 6, the exercise of relational skills in cooperative working, and the willingness to take on new functions within the group and share knowledge, and to take part in small group problem-solving activities are all assessed in staff appraisals. In his example from Sumitomo, Best shows that individualized performance does not count for nearly as much in the appraisals as being a good member of the work team, and this is what feeds into the pay system.

There is a danger with the dependence of rank on appraisals that supervisors and management abuse their power. Such fears are not absent from the workers in firms using these systems. The 'job grade matrix' (see, Chapter 2 §4) used in many firms shows one method by which employees have sought to exert some control over the appraisal process. In this way, even though the appraisals are subjective, employees can monitor how even-handedly they are being treated, and managers can be made accountable for their judgements. The comparison with individualization in French industry is striking. Different criteria are being used, and above all, the Japanese firms appear to place much less emphasis on individual workers' output and more on their contribution to the effort of their team or work group. This is because the Japanese firms operating the competence rank system are primarily concerned with marginal performance that relates to cooperative work relations rather than assiduity in an individual work post.

(c) Job territory/tools of the trade

The training approach appears to be less amenable to appraisal of individual performance because, as outlined in Chapter 6, occupational or professional standards play an important part in determining performance standards (Zucker, 1991). They could function in two ways: disciplining individual workers to maintain the standards of their trade; and resisting pressure from management to adopt different performance standards. One reason why workers in such occupations are better able to resist management pressures than can those with organization-specific skills is that they know the ins and outs of their skills better than management. Although first-line managers are often themselves trained in the same skill, and play a key role in organizing in-company training, they are often also part of the same occupational community and so have a double loyalty to management and to their trade.

Another feature of occupationally skilled work is that much of it cannot be judged in quantitative terms because the key aspect of performance lies in the application of judgement. In the electrician example discussed in Chapter 6, good performance is defined as making sure the appliance is safe to use after a repair, and the boundary between competent and incompetent work is a very sharp one. A bit less effort or care does not make the equipment a bit less safe: it makes it unsafe. If it is dangerous, the employer may be liable for injury caused to other staff or customers.

The occupational job territory rule with the accompanying idea of exclusive competence over a certain range of tasks also fosters the idea that different jobs are more akin to discrete groupings of tasks rather than a rational and continuous ordering of work along certain principles. Consistent with this argument are the generally greater opposition to individualized performance pay among craft and professional groups, and the lesser opposition among office occupations. This has been the experience in the parts of the public sector surveyed by Marsden and French (1998). There was widespread acceptance of the principle of performance-related pay, except among the professional groups such as nurses, other health professionals and head teachers.

(d) The qualification rule

The qualification rule appears also to be fairly resistant to the idea that variable individual performance should be evaluated and rewarded by management. This is because the occupation itself plays an important part in determining the performance standards, as under the job territory rules. Another reason for this is that there is already a functionally equivalent performance incentive, geared to the qualification rule: what Jürgens *et al.* (1993) called 'wage increase by job design'. This makes initiative one of the key areas of marginal performance (see Chapter 6 above). Across much of German industry, a compromise has been struck between allowing management a good deal of freedom in job design provided they respect two things (Meil, 1992: 22; Sengenberger, 1992: 248). The evaluation and measurement of performance should be under the joint administration of management and works council, and where jobs include tasks that should be performed by workers with recognized skills, then they should be so assigned (Düll, 1986). Heavy works council involvement in performance management helps protect workers against manipulation of standards by management, a protection that is reinforced by the training that works councils give to their own job evaluation experts. Allowing management to group work for jobs, while at the same time maintaining that skilled work goes to those with recognized skills, reinforces the training approach. Too many miscellaneous duties would simply waste the time of expensive labour. At the same time, allowing management to add new tasks that enable jobs to grow provides an incentive for workers to show initiative in expanding their jobs and in developing their skills. If one can show management that one's job can grow, for example, by working out new or better ways of doing things, then there is a powerful reward for taking initiative. Developing one's own skills is also rewarded by acquisition of additional recognized vocational skills, and can lead to promotion. In the public sector, training is formalized into progression through the career groups, thus sending a very positive signal that one raises one's performance by acquiring additional skills that may be applied in one's work (Brandes *et al.*, 1990).

In Germany, implementation of performance pay has progressed much less than in the countries where the other transaction rules predominate. This is despite the interest some leading German employers have expressed in more discretionary pay systems,[13] and that some firms have developed such schemes (Schudlich, 1991). Indeed, the public sector has even developed enabling agreements to this effect, although their implementation has been extremely slow (Tondorf, 1997). In part, this reflects opposition from skilled workers concerned that works councils could lose their strong position in performance management, and in part, the influence of different criteria for identifying marginal performance. Much of the emphasis elsewhere within performance pay and individualized pay schemes has been on increasing work quantity, whereas under the qualification rule it is more important to stimulate initiative.

To conclude, each of the four rules and its classification system play a key role in defining the kinds of marginal performance subject to employee discretion. Although the simple principal-agent analysis of Figure 7.3 captures important quantitative aspects of the problems underlying performance pay, performance is not a purely quantitative concept, and is shaped by the principles of job classification.

4. HIERARCHICAL VERSUS OCCUPATIONAL CLASSIFICATIONS AND PAY STRUCTURES

Apart from their influence on performance criteria, the four transaction rules influence pay structures because each adopts a different leading classification criterion. One of the most important influences lies in the contrast between the production and the training approaches: whether skills are classified according to firm-specific principles or whether they relate to occupational skills. In terms of Figure 7.2, this means that the order of the first two criteria is likely to be reversed. Under the production approach, firm-based experience and responsibility will be the key criteria, whereas under the training approach, they are likely to take second place to occupational qualifications. The order with which these two types of criteria are applied will determine whether firm-based considerations dominate, leading to an overall coherent ranking of pay groups within the organization at the expense of occupational skills, or whether occupational skills be recognized but at the expense of internal hierarchical considerations within the firm. In a word, will a continuous hierarchical pay structure hold between different job grades within the organization, or will there be a discontinuous one due to the pay contours established across labour markets by occupational skills?

Ideally, such propositions would be tested directly by looking at job classification principles and pay across many organizations, but in the absence of such data, one test is to compare pay structures under different transaction rules. Three features of pay structures lend themselves to such a test:

- the impact of hierarchical and occupational principles on the size of pay differentials;
- the degree of overlap of pay levels between blue- and white-collar occupations; and

- the degree to which pay reflects occupational skills or firm-specific factors.

These are examined in the next sections. One final note: much use is made of national-level observations, whereas a more rigorous approach would require detailed analysis of individual data drawing out national differences while holding other factors constant. The comparative study led by Tachibanaki (1998) goes a long way towards this, although differences between data sources and occupational classifications make precise comparisons tentative. On the other hand, Saunders and Marsden (1981) did test a number of national-level patterns in industrial wage structures in Western Europe and found them to hold up at the level of individual sectors.

4.1 Hierarchical and occupational pay structures

The diversity of job and skill classification principles discussed in Chapter 4 means that international comparisons of occupational pay differentials can never be more than approximate, especially when different classification systems are in force. Nevertheless, the resulting patterns of pay inequality are likely to affect incentives and employers' costs, so the question remains an interesting one. The main prediction of the theory developed so far is that, other things being equal, the greatest degree of pay inequality by occupation or job grade is likely to occur under work post systems.

The most important reason for large inequalities under the work post system is connected with the heavy emphasis on individual accountability, and the fact that cooperation among employees is closely organized by management. As a result of individual accountability, many important decisions are the responsibility of single individuals holding certain key posts, and these individuals need to be motivated to perform and possibly sanctioned in the event of serious lapses in performance, on account of the cost of their failures to the organization as a whole. With responsibility concentrated on key posts, it makes sense to concentrate rewards as well.

A common argument against rewarding single individuals is that this inhibits cooperation among work group members. However, in the work post system, such cooperation is strongly organized by management through the design of individual work posts and the allocation of limited decision powers to each one. Thus, the model of work organization itself minimizes the need for horizontal cooperation among colleagues so that the potential loss from individualized rewards is also minimized. Thus, comparing the work post and the competence rank models, the clear expectation is that rewards will be strongly differentiated by job level in the first case, but not in the second.

Turning to the systems using the training approach, again the expectation is that the work post system will lead to greater occupational or job level differentials. This is because occupational skills will generally be broader based than those growing out of work post OJT enabling management to delegate more work-related decisions to skilled workers. This affects both the pay of skilled workers and that of management. By delegating more, workers assume greater responsibility, and management's role is correspondingly less crucial to the effective conduct of work.

For the competence rank model, there are two mutually offsetting effects on occupational differentials. On the one hand, the more limited autonomy of skills under the first system would lead one to expect greater differentials, but on the other, the key importance of cooperation and flexible working would imply smaller differentials between workers in different jobs.

Bearing in mind the severe data limitations, Table 7.1 differentiates the countries in this study into two groups and shows the expected pattern of occupational pay inequalities. The primary focus is on the industrial sectors of the economies, as these were the best documented cases for the predominance of one or other type of transaction rule (see, Chapter 5). For the three European countries, Eurostat has collected earnings data on a common occupational classification, but the same one is not used in either Japan or the US. Hence, the need to infer the scale of occupational differentials from dispersions and data on educational pay differentials shown in the bottom rows of the table.

Some evidence on occupational differentials and dispersions

The surest ground for international comparison lies within the EU, using the European Structure of Earnings of Survey (ESES), although the 1995 ESES results were not yet available at the time of writing, leaving the most recent comparative data at 1978. Selected figures for the industrial sector (industry and construction) are shown in Table 7.2, with the greatest occupational differentials to be found in France, confirming earlier work by Saunders and Marsden (1981) on the 1972 survey. Moreover, the latter authors observed a similar pattern of occupational difference across a number of industries, indicating that this was not the result of differences in industrial mix between the countries. For Britain, 1979 was the start of a long rise in pay

Table 7.1. *Overview of the size of occupational pay differentials by country*

	US	France	Japan	Britain	Germany
Large pay differences in occupational pay	✓	✓	✘	✘→✓	✘
Large pay dispersions	✓	✓	✘	✘→✓	✘
Large educational differentials	✓		✘		

Table 7.2. *Monthly earnings by occupation, 1978 and 1986*

	UK 1979	Germany 1978	France 1978a	France 1978b	Japan 1978	France 1986	Japan 1986
Managers & Prof.							
excl. top mgt	157	172	272	276	167	262	161
Assistants (technicians)	110	126	153	n/a	n/a	n/a	n/a
Supervisors	114	137	149	155	126	151	126
Clerical	87	96	118	n/a	n/a	n/a	n/a
Skilled	108	105	107	n/a	n/a	n/a	n/a
All non-manual	120	142	177	175	122	175	121
Male manual	100	100	100	100	100	100	100

Notes: Full-time average monthly earnings. UK, Germany, France (a) NACE 1–5, in establishments with > 10 employees; France (b) 1978 and 1986, and Japan: manufacturing establishments with > 100 employees, and excluding overtime pay.
Sources: UK, Germany, and France (a), Eurostat ESES (1978); France (b) matched to Japanese data for 1978 and 1986 by Nohara (1995).

dispersions and occupational differentials, carrying it towards the position in France and the US.

Neither Japan nor the US have directly comparable occupational pay data, but other dimensions of earnings support the idea that the US has large occupational differentials and Japan has smaller ones, somewhere in between those of France and Germany. For Japan, Table 7.2 includes Nohara's (1995) comparison of French and Japanese pay structures for 1978 and 1986. His finding of smaller occupational differentials in Japan confirms Koike's (1988) earlier comparison between Japan and selected western-European countries for 1972. Allowing for differences of classification methods, Koike shows that differentials between managerial, supervisory and other white-collar occupations are smaller than those in France, and probably of similar magnitude to those in Germany. Precise comparison was not possible, owing to the much more inclusive definitions of managers and supervisors in the Japanese than in the European data. These results are reflected in the co-efficients on the dummies for managerial and professional occupations estimated by Tachibanaki's group which control for gender, age, tenure, education, industry and firm size. They find large pay relativities for manage-rial and professional groups over production workers in France and Britain as compared with Japan and Germany.[14]

Because the US and Japanese occupational classifications are not easily comparable with those used for the EU countries, we turn to data on pay dispersions (Figure 7.4) in order to see whether the US and Japan lie among the countries with relatively high or relatively low occupational differentials. The same data also provide a check on the classification of the EU countries. The justification for this is that occupation has generally been the largest single source of variation in earnings (CERC, 1988; Tachibanaki, 1998).

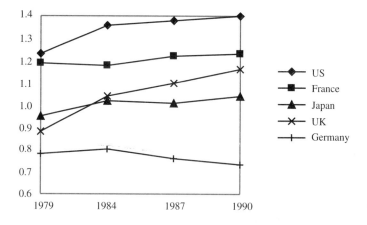

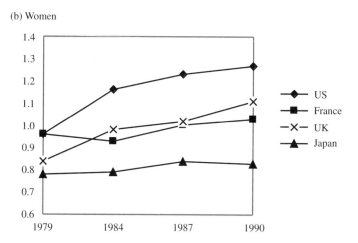

Fig. 7.4. Pay dispersions 1979–90
Based on Katz *et al.* (1995) and Freeman and Katz (1994, 1995). Dispersions measured as the log wage differential between the top decile Q90 and the lowest decile Q10. Hourly earnings used, except for Japan where they are monthly. French data: annual data converted to an hourly basis for 1979–87, updated to 1990.

For the US, there is plenty of evidence that overall pay inequalities are greater in the US than in either Japan or the western-European countries (Figure 7.4). Freeman and Katz (1994) show the US and France to have been very close in 1979, but then pay inequalities took off in the US while remaining rather steady in France. Likewise, the dispersion of pay in the US was considerably greater than in either Japan or Germany. In the UK, also, the pay dispersion increased sharply during the 1980s but still trailed that in the US.

Figure 7.4 compares the ratio of the top to the bottom deciles, but as part of the comparison between the hierarchical and the occupational pay structures hinges on the relationship between management and other staff, it is worth looking also at the ratio of the top decile to median earnings. On this count, France and the US stand out initially as the countries with the greatest management-to-worker inequality, although Britain moves up to join them by 1990. Japan, in contrast, remains stolidly egalitarian (Katz *et al.*, 1993).[15]

For a second fix on occupational differentials in the US and Japan, we turn therefore to differences in pay by level of education. Koike (1988) compares age–earnings patterns for male college graduates and senior and junior high school graduates in the US and Japan for the 1960s, and shows a smaller spread of monthly pay at all ages. Davis (1992) shows that earnings differentials by education level followed a downward trend in Japan from the mid-1960s to the late 1980s, when his series stops, but they increased in the US, their decline in the 1970s being more than reversed by the late 1980s. Taken together, these two pieces of evidence suggest that occupational and job grade differentials are markedly greater in the US than in Japan, and given the Japan–Germany comparison, they are also considerably greater than in Germany and the UK as it was around 1980. Thus, a first conclusion is that work post systems are indeed more likely to be associated with large occupational or job-level pay differentials.

4.2 Pay continuity between the blue- and white-collar hierarchies

A notable contrast between the production and training approaches lies in the degree of continuity within the management hierarchy, and the relationship between blue- and white-collar work. Under the training approach, workers have a strong external point of reference in their occupational skills. In effect, management take their skills as given and organize work accordingly. As a result, management has less direct influence over their work, and in particular, over their manner of working. In contrast, under the production approach, management has more direct influence over work design and organization, especially under work post systems.

This is reflected in the logic of the classification systems, which establish a more continuous hierarchy of jobs within the firm than under the training approach. Particularly revealing are the positions of supervisors and the pay relativity between clerical and skilled blue-collar workers. Two indicators of such continuity or discontinuity in firms' job hierarchies can be found in the level of pay of foremen and supervisors relative to other white-collar job levels, and in the wage differential between skilled blue-collar and clerical staff, summarized in Table 7.3.

Table 7.3. *Production versus the training approaches: continuous versus discontinuous job and pay hierarchies*

	US	France	Japan	Britain	Germany
Supervisor's pay ≤ technicians	✓	✓	✓ [a]	✖	✖
Skilled blue-collar earn > clerical	✖	✖	✖ [a]	✓	✓

[a] Probable position after controlling for strong age effects.

Looking at the European countries, Table 7.2 (see the previous section) shows that, in the late 1970s, in Germany and Britain, skilled industrial blue-collar workers earned more than clerical staff, but the reverse applied in France. This confirms the findings for the early 1970s by Saunders and Marsden (1981: 138). More generally, they found a clear distinction between France, Italy and Belgium on the one hand, which had continuous pay hierarchies from unskilled to senior management, and Britain and Germany, where skilled exceeded clerical pay.[16] Indeed, among men, semi-skilled pay also exceeded clerical pay. Moreover, the plant level studies of Maurice *et al.* (1986) show, at least for France and Germany, that such overlap is not simply the result of differences in statistical classification. Indeed, the authors observed that the pay advantage of white-collar employees in France tended to undermine the occupational identity of blue-collar skilled workers by encouraging upward mobility into white-collar jobs to a degree not found in Germany.

The reason for the different structures can be explained by the logic of occupational skills under which clerical work is deemed unqualified. The critical factor is whether the job requires a recognized vocational qualification. If it does not, no matter how much experience is needed, it will not be recognized. In contrast, where a hierarchical work post logic prevails, as in France, the vocational skills of blue-collar workers are recognized only in so far as they can be fitted into the firm's job hierarchy, with the result that blue-collar skills are less highly valued compared with those of clerical workers.[17]

Turning to the US, a very tentative matching of occupational earnings data from the CPS suggests the influence of the production approach on skilled blue-collar and junior white-collar earnings (Table 7.4). There, 'administrative support' and lower paid sales occupations, which are close to the European definition of 'clerical', earn about the same as skilled production workers.

There are no suitable comparative data for Japan due to the nature of the occupational classification used for earnings statistics and the different approach to job classification used in companies. Nevertheless, it is very likely that there is a good deal of overlap between skilled blue-collar and junior white-collar occupations because of the small size of occupational

Table 7.4. *Skilled blue-collar and supervisory occupations in the US*

US 1994	Men	Women
Supervisors (admin. and precision production, craft and repair)	120 (119)	116 (104)
Technicians	119	117
Admin. support occupations and sales reps (non-retail and non-financial)	96 (84)	94 (93)
Precision production, craft and repair	94	93
Median for all occupations	100	100

Source: BLS, Employment and Earnings; CPS Median weekly earnings, all sectors. Note: figures in parentheses for supervisors exclude admin. supervisors; and for admin. support exclude sales reps.

differentials and the relatively large variation in pay by age and seniority (Genda, 1998: 37).

Thus, while not explaining every aspect of pay structures, the adoption of one or other transaction rule can be shown to influence the structure of rewards for workers in different occupations and at different job levels. First, the work post system is associated with greater occupational or job-grade pay differentials, largely because of the incentive problem. The system concentrates critical decisions on certain key positions, and firms have to be able to attract the right people and provide suitable rewards for performance. A second feature is that the work post system tends to generate a continuous pay hierarchy within the firm from unskilled blue-collar to senior management, whereas the training approach introduces an element of discontinuity. Under the latter, skilled blue-collar workers earn more than clerical employees with only a general education. In terms of vocational skills, the latter count as being less qualified. In the work post system, the same clerical employees are part of the management structure and so classified and paid above skilled blue-collar staff.

The competence ranking system, owing to its emphasis on horizontal cooperation and loosely structured work patterns, has some features of the pay structures associated with the training approach. It shares the narrower occupational pay differentials and more overlap between blue- and white-collar hierarchies, but the underlying reason is different. Life-cycle factors such as age and length of service, which help to stress the individual's position within a group and so promote flexible working, blur the pay relationships based on job grade and function.

4.3 Pay for organizational versus occupational skills

Because of the focus on organization-specific skills, firms using the production approach are more likely to stress and reward length of service than those using the training approach. When skills are developed within the production approach, pay for length of service can reward workers for their increasing level of experience gained within the organization. As learning by doing is often hard to measure, length of service becomes a simple indicator on which both management and employee can agree. Management's risks are usually limited by restricting the number of service increments before further promotion is needed. In contrast, workers with occupational skills are more likely to be interested in enhancing the rewards for their occupational skills than in payments for length of service with their current employer. As Becker (1975) showed, it is hard for firms to fund length of service premiums by tilting tenure-pay profiles because this would mean lowering starting pay to below that offered by their competitors without any corresponding short-term gain for workers. If such premiums are to be funded out of productivity gains from work reorganization, then this could conflict with the training approach, and encounter opposition from skilled workers leery of adapting their skills in a way that would reduce their marketability to other firms.

Thus, under the training approach, one expects to find that job and pay classifications focus on occupational skills and play down length of service, whereas under the production approach, one would expect greater recognition of internal factors, notably length of service, and that external qualifications would be relegated to a secondary position.

Given the evidence for the predominance of the production approach in France, Japan and the US, one would expect length of service to influence pay more strongly there than it would in Germany and Britain, where the training approach holds sway. In the latter two countries, one would expect the presence of strong occupational linkages between pay structures within firms in Germany and Britain. The expected position is shown in Table 7.5, and detailed evidence supporting this was given in Chapter 5 (§2.5).

Table 7.5. *Pay for skills and length of service*

	US	France	Japan	Britain	Germany
Certified skills	✘	✘	✘	✓	✓
Length of service	✓	✓	✓	✘	✘

4.4 Company employment practices and pay systems

A slightly different angle on the effects of ways of managing the employment relationship on pay systems is given by a study of practices in a sample of

French firms (CERC, 1987). This avoids the problems of interpreting data on industries that contain many different kinds of firms, and also sheds useful light on variation of employment models within countries. It also extends the analysis usefully to non-wage benefits.

The CERC identified four types of personnel and performance management:

- bureaucratic;
- organized flexibility;
- unorganized flexibility; and
- craft-type.

The first and last are of greatest interest because one strongly reflects the work-post logic of bureaucratic personnel management and the other, the skill-based logic of craft employment systems which in France hold sway in the construction and repair sectors. The firms conforming to the bureaucratic model, as compared with the craft model, had lower labour turnover, a smaller percentage of blue-collar workers, fewer foreign workers and stronger workplace union presence. They also tended to be large and state- or foreign-owned, whereas the craft firms existed in all size ranges but were primarily privately or family owned. In many respects these firms conformed to Stinchcombe's (1959) characterization of bureaucratic and craft patterns of personnel management. Firms practising 'organized flexibility' were rather similar to the bureaucratic ones, but offered less employment stability and had higher turnover but fewer temporary jobs. Unorganized flexibility was characterized by high turnover, temporary jobs, weak unions and large numbers of women workers.

One of the most interesting differences lies in the use of fringe benefits, widely provided by the 'bureaucratic' firms that offered full coverage of sickness absence, the 'thirteenth month' bonus payment and time-based pay (Table 7.6). The craft system, consistent with the shorter expected duration of jobs, offered the smallest coverage of sickness absence and the fewest annual bonuses. However, adopting the craft system did not imply a crudely individualistic approach to personnel management. Time-based payment was widespread, and, most significantly, there was high use of collective productivity bonuses, in this case mostly site bonuses for completion of projects on time. The scale of such bonuses reflects the strong interdependence between different crafts in construction work and the difficulty of measuring individual performance at all meaningfully.

A final comment is needed in relation to the diffusion of different human resource models, and the 'societal effect'. Just as Stinchcombe's (1959) work illustrated the coexistence of the bureaucratic and craft models within the US, so the CERC study shows the same for France. This further emphasizes the dangers of identifying 'societal' factors, which in this book relate to the scope of distinctive employment systems, with 'national' differences, a theme resumed in the concluding chapter.

Table 7.6. *Pay systems and flexibility management*

	Blue-collar annual pay, FF 1984	Ratio of mgt to blue-collar pay	Full sick pay from first day, % of firms	Individual incentive pay, % of firms	'13th month' paid to blue-collars, % of firms	Collective productivity bonuses, % of firms
Bureaucratic	98,600	2.66	100	7	94	25
Organized flexibility	72,600	3.21	78	33	59	41
Unorganized flexibility	63,700	4.36	55	21	55	17
Craft-type flexibility	68,700	n/a	21	14	38	59[a]

[a] Mostly 'site bonuses' for completion of projects or stages of projects, on time.
Source: CERC (1987: 103).

5. CONCLUSION

Looking at pay within the context of employment systems places the spot-light on the price of labour as a rule rather than a quantity of money. It is in fact a complex schedule of prices relating to different contingencies and different time dimensions of the employment relationship. Competitive pressures are present, but they are transmitted through the job classification systems that organize and structure the supply of different types of labour. Although individual workers can move between jobs and between job classifications, the categories that these classifications establish are essential to the competitive process in two ways.

First, they provide a framework of categories that make it possible for employers and employees to contract. A central argument of this book is that given bounded rationality and partially opposing interests, cooperation between workers and firms is always under threat from opportunistic action by either side. Therefore, stable cooperation demands a framework of rules, an important part of which lies in the systems for defining categories of labour and relating price rules to them.

Secondly, they organize the information necessary for the competitive process to function. Competition demands informed choice, which requires comparison of qualities and prices, which in turn requires a stable structure of information. Simon (1991) made a similar observation in asking why the state commonly took control of large sections of market econ-omies during wartime and national emergencies, whereas the market took over during peacetime. The reason, he suggested, was that in wartime, the grave disruptions to normal supply and demand relations mean that the price mechanism becomes overloaded. Individual agents cannot easily interpret the rapid shifts in prices and make suitable plans. In peacetime, market prices can convey information about the long-term shortages that represent new investment opportunities. Stability is essential for an efficient price mechanism to work. In the same way, job classification systems estab-lish the categories on which the price mechanism can bite. Without them, firms cannot easily compare what different workers offer, and within organizations, it is difficult to compare performance levels. The impact of classifications is to organize the space on which competitive forces work.

What of outcomes? Although the data readily available rule out a quanti-tative analysis of how job categories shape pay levels, the chapter has attempted to bring together indicative evidence on the structure of labour prices and the nature of the pay–performance links under different types of classification system, and to explore the effect of these systems on pay relativities. What it shows is that the different types of classification system define marginal increments in performance in different ways, and that they establish different pay contours between what are essentially the same kinds of work. Thus, the work post system tends to define performance in somewhat quantitative terms, partly because job design can be used to separate activities that require incompatible performance criteria into separate jobs, and partly because the production approach enables the employer to organize a coherent internal pay hierarchy. This gives rise to a more internally homogeneous set of principles dividing up work and determining marginal increments in job performance. Thus, we see not only a spread of individualized performance appraisal and pay, but also the treatment of blue- and white-collar hierarchies as a consistent whole.

In contrast, under the training approach, not only are the job categories more discrete because of the presence of occupational skills that have to maintain similar standards across firms, but there is also greater resistance to allowing management judgement a role in appraising the quality and level of skilled performance. There is a conflict between the professional and occupational performance standards and management's desire to gain a lever on performance at the margin. The influence of skill formation is also reflected in the overlapping occupational hierarchies, as blue-collar occupational skills and even semi-skills are more highly valued than junior white-collar skills.

The impact of the enforceability constraint is also visible in shaping the options open to firms. Pay incentives are able to embrace more subtle performance standards under the competence rank and qualification rules than under the two task-centred ones. In practical terms, the two function-centred rules offer management scope to provide incentives for cooperation and initiative that are much less accessible under the task-centred rules.

ENDNOTES

[1] According to Bridges and Villemez' Chicago study (1994: 61), for about 80% of employees and 65% of plants, management must give a reason for dismissing someone, for 50% of employees this has to be written, and for over 60% of them, the employer must give advance notice or severance pay.

[2] The Employment Cost Index is a Laspeyres index using employment composition in the base year so that changes in the index will not reflect changes in workforce composition, and it follows movements in pay, fringe benefits and employers' social contributions (for an account of the index see Sheifer, 1975, and BLS, 1992: ch. 11). The author had the privilege of working as an advisor to Eurostat on the construction of the European Employment Cost Index and thus of witnessing the discussions among working statisticians from the national institutes who would have the practical task of gathering the data and compiling the index.

[3] Indeed, even Triplett (1983), one of the architects of the US ECI, proposes the 'cost of hiring an incremental unit of labour in current period from both incumbent workers and new hires' as the starting point for defining labour price and price change.

[4] The argument has been developed in more detail in two working papers by Makaronidis (1995) and Marsden (1996). I am grateful to Alex Makaronidis of Eurostat, with whom I discussed many of these ideas at length.

[5] The Parodi system was named after the minister who signed the government regulation (*Arrêté*, 11.4.46) setting up the classification system in 1946.

[6] According to Touraine (1955), the craft logic of discrete skills was already in conflict with the models of work organization that were coming to dominate the French automobile industry by the early 1950s. The Parodi system belonged to the 'craft' system of work organization, whereas the 'technical system' was already becoming increasingly influential.

[7] Recent French research shows that the main exception to this has been in small firms, where relations are in any case much less formalized.

[8] The section also builds on joint work on the economics of performance incentives in the public sector with Sandro Momigliano of the Bank of Italy, see Marsden and Momigliano (1997).

[9] In France, for example, in 1992, around 15% of all private sector employees outside construction received premiums linked to individual performance. On average, these represented about 8% of gross pay, but the median percentage was 4.3%, and only 10% got more than 15.6% of their pay as individual performance pay. Interestingly, this latter percentage was rather similar for all four major occupational groups (INSEE, 1996: 25ff).

[10] I am grateful to M. Miyamoto for drawing my attention to this point.

[11] 'La performance individuelle à l'intérieur de l'exercice d'un métier peut conduire à une individualisation des rémunérations, mais ce qui n'est pas du tout individualisable, c'est le métier' (Linhart *et al.*, 1993: 43).

[12] The useful feature of Best's study is that, being a senior manager from British Steel, he gives a number of detailed illustrations of how the different pay levels are worked out, which are not usually available in academic publications which are mostly rather cryptic on such issues. There remains a problem of representativeness of such studies. I have also had the opportunity to discuss such issues with a number of Japanese trade union officials on training programmes at the LSE who find the picture familiar, although the details of such practices vary between companies.

[13] In 1996, Klaus Murmann, president of the federal German employers association put the case for a reform of collective bargaining, and stressed the need for individual performance related pay, which he presented as inadequately developed in German industry. See *Financial Times* (3.1.96), 'German employers urge big reform of pay bargaining'.

[14] In their study, the coefficient on German managers' pay seems too high in relation both to other sources and to professionals, and is based on only 37 observations. Their figures for managers and professionals in the US seem too low in view of the evidence on dispersions, and may reflect a more inclusive definition of these groups.

[15] The picture is less pronounced for women, but then they are much underrepresented in higher management positions. Blau and Kahn (1996) also highlight the importance of looking separately at both ends of the earnings distribution, particularly because of the importance of effective minimum wage laws and bargaining provisions that can raise the wages of the lowest paid.

[16] In The Netherlands, skilled pay roughly equalled clerical pay.

[17] The pay advantage of clerical over skilled blue-collar workers was confirmed across most industries by data from the 1986 French wage structure survey (Rothbart, 1991).

8

Skills and Labour Market Structure

1. INTRODUCTION

The existence of a stable framework governing work assignments is a key condition for workers and firms to be able to invest in skill development. This chapter argues that by their regulation of job design and job boundaries, the transaction rules provide an essential underpinning to both workplace skill development and the labour market structures that serve to allocate labour. The protection that they provide against opportunism over work assignments, explored in Chapter 2, will be shown to have similar effects supporting skill development, and therefore they shape both the organization of skills and the structure of labour markets. This chapter shows too that the four broad types of transaction rule give rise to four broad types of labour market structure, plus 'secondary' labour markets in which employer monopsony power leaves workers less able to enforce their side of the bargain. However, the transaction rules and labour market structures are also mutually supporting. It will be argued that the first impulse in this relationship comes from the transaction rules, which can be seen as logically prior because, while they are a necessary condition for the stability of the labour skill and market structures, the reverse does not apply. It is also shown that the support to transaction rules provided by labour market structure further institutionalizes them because occupational, and to a lesser extent internal, labour markets depend on strong institutional frameworks. That, in a nutshell, is the main argument of the first part of the chapter. The second part shows how a similar kind of analysis can be applied to the boundary between employment and self-employment, and the growth of 'contingent' employment and the emergence of 'boundaryless' careers. Understanding these provides important clues as to how employment systems are evolving, and why some of the 'new' types of contract represent a less radical break with the past than some commentators suggest.

Before launching into the main argument, it will help to explain a few key terms relating to labour market structure. An 'internal labour market' (ILM) for certain jobs exists when employers regularly fill vacancies for them from among their current employees rather than by external recruitment. Over the years, the definition of ILMs has evolved, and this can be confusing. Kerr (1954) used the term to denote both what have come to be referred to by scholars such as Kalleberg *et al.* (1996) as 'firm' or 'enterprise' internal labour markets (FILMs), characterized by mobility between jobs within the same firm, and craft labour markets, characterized by mobility between firms but within the same occupation. Doeringer and Piore (1971) kept Kerr's definition, but as most of their book is devoted to enterprise internal markets, the term 'ILM' has by many scholars come to be identified with arrangements in individual firms, as for example, by Williamson (1975) and Willman (1986). The other dominant kind of skilled labour market is that of occupational labour markets (OLMs). An occupational market may be defined as relating to persons endowed with a particular skill or qualification, and validated by a diploma or by the opinion of their peer group, and, as will be seen later in this chapter, is usually organized on collective lines.[1] This embraces Kerr's notion of a craft labour market, but whereas Kerr treated the institutional regulation of such markets as one of their defining features, with the implication that the markets for some occupations might be unregulated, in this chapter, it is shown that regulation is a necessary ingredient of their stability. Such are the main types of mass market for skilled blue- and white-collar labour.

For unskilled labour and jobs that require few qualifications there exist also secondary labour markets (SLMs). The much smaller investments in education and training involved have generally led workers and particularly employers to place much less emphasis on employment stability. The skills that differentiate secondary markets from the other two kinds are partly a matter of productive competencies, but also partly one of recognition, as some groups are better able to enforce their rights than others. For example, gender discrimination frequently causes women's skills to be valued less than those of men, as is demonstrated by the number of major 'equal value' cases.

2. EFFECTS OF THE PRODUCTION AND TRAINING APPROACHES ON LABOUR MARKET STRUCTURE

The link between the transaction rules and labour market structure can best be understood by exploring the contribution of stable job structures to investment in skills, and how the transaction rules provide these. By 'job structures' is meant the overall distribution of tasks between jobs. In the case of occupational skills, if we follow Becker's (1975) argument, under conditions of perfect competition, the transferability of such skills between firms means that trainees will have to bear the full cost of such training. Employers would be unwilling to do so because they have no means of ensuring a return on their investment, as the former trainees are free to leave to work elsewhere. However, if trainees, or their families, are to invest heavily in skill acquisition, they need to be sure of a reasonable prospect of suitable jobs. This requires that employers organize work consistently across firms. Like many of his generation, Becker seems to have assumed that use of a common technology would suffice for workplace skills to be transferable. In contrast, the argument of this book is that firms are free to choose their pattern of job design, and that shared technology is not sufficient to generate common patterns of skills and job categories across firms.

In a static world, one might expect that cost-minimizing pressures themselves would lead employers to match their job structures to those of skills being formed. If we assume that workers' investment in training attracts a skill differential, then employers will minimize costs when they align their job demands with the competencies supplied by a particular occupation. If the jobs use only a small number of them, they still have to pay for the 'excess skill'. Equally, if employers' job demands stretch beyond the competencies supplied, they will normally have to pay for any additional training that is needed. Unless such additional training is systematically related to the competencies supplied, it will not enrich workers' skill portfolios on the wider labour market, and it may well detract from the transferability of their occupational skills. Thus, either way, failure to align job demands on the occupation's skills will lead to higher costs for employers.

However, there are many occasions when it might in practice be cheaper for the employer to take such costs. For example, the Finniston Report (1980) on the engineering profession in Britain castigated firms for the widespread practice of assigning their young graduate engineers to what was essentially blue-collar work because of skill shortages. The cost of lost sales was evidently thought greater than that of using more expensive labour for routine tasks. The report recommended establishing a much stronger identity for the engineering profession to ensure the supply of talented new graduate entrants. Clearly then, trainees and their families cannot rely upon cost minimization to ensure an appropriate match of job demands and competencies, and some additional pressure is needed. Otherwise, as Finniston argued, young people will invest in other skills. An occupational market requires some means to ensure that employers follow common patterns of job design and keep to these in their everyday allocation of work. Otherwise, job demands will gradually diverge from the skills supplied and trainees will lose confidence in that particular occupation. How this causes a regression towards internal labour markets will be discussed later on.

What the training approach does is to provide a clear signal to firms and to workers as to the broad principles of job design and hence to the likely structure of job vacancies. This is very explicit with job territory rules, such as the 'tools of the trade', where peer group norms shared by skilled workers and their supervisors underpin the job structures on which their occupational markets depend. As argued in Chapter 2, the rule may well be applied flexibly for much of the time, but everyone knows that it is there, in reserve, should one side cease to play the game. The qualification rule also provides a number of protections over work allocation that also serve to maintain the integrity of the training approach as a basis for investment in skills.

Most of the empirical studies of training costs for occupational skills show that, in practice, employers contribute substantially to the investment, despite the predictions of Becker's theory. Net costs for apprenticeship training are commonly equivalent to one and a half to two years' pay for an adult skilled worker.[2] Such skills and their related occupational markets have the qualities of a public good. A well-stocked occupational market means that employers can expand their work forces readily to meet increased demand, and there are no long lead times that would be required if they had to train their labour from scratch. An occupational market has the additional attraction that workers are willing to bear a substantial part of training costs so that the capital costs are shared. Also, it is often easier for a firm to reduce its skilled work force when the workers have good job opportunities elsewhere. This reduces the need for expensive redundancy programmes and can help the firm cut jobs without devastating workforce morale. Such benefits are considerable, particularly for small and medium-sized firms, but are also important for larger ones as their markets become faster-changing. They are nevertheless public goods in the sense that the very availability of skills made possible by an occupational market creates scope for some employers to cut their own training budgets and rely on the investments made by others. Unless they can be controlled, such opportunities for 'free-riding' make occupational markets unstable.

For internal labour markets too, the processes of skill formation and market organization depend upon predictable job structures, although their nature differs from that of occupational markets. Whereas in Becker's (1975) simple model, the prediction is that employers will bear the full cost of on-the-job training for firm-specific skills, in reality, there is often also a degree of cost-sharing. The firm might wish to offer a wage premium to discourage workers with specific skills from leaving. Even though the latter have no training investment to lose by changing firms, the employer has. To pay for this premium, the employer will wish to encourage the employee to share some of the training costs, possibly in the form of an incremental pay scale, or by linking training to promotion or upgrading. If such on-the-job training depends very much on employee initiative, for example, on a willingness to take risks by assuming more challenging tasks, then it may be necessary to reward them. Once again, stable job structures play an important part in enabling firms and workers to develop skills by on-the-job training and experience. If the reward for employees is upgrading or promotion, or assignment to more interesting work, they need a structure within which they can identify their rewards and judge whether they have been awarded.

The effects of a lack of such structures can be seen in Dugué's (1994) study of attempts to move away from the work post to a more competence-based system of work organization and reward. The employees suspected that their management were unfairly manipulating which competencies they would recognize, and whether they had been achieved. The cross-sectional nature of her study prevents one from judging whether these suspicions led to less employee investment in OJT, but they certainly caused them to express reluctance to do so.

The work post system, in both Doeringer and Piore's (1971) account of American ILMs and Maurice *et al.*'s (1986) account of French ones, provided a stable framework of posts between which employees could move and in terms of which they could plan their internal job moves. This, combined with a strong presumption of seniority even if not formally sanctioned, gave a high degree of predictability. Koike's (1997) account of the job grade matrix (Chapter 2 above), displaying the competencies management recognized different employees as holding, has served a similar function in the internal labour markets of a number of Japanese firms. This enables workers to compare their relative degrees of advancement with the kinds of work to which they are currently assigned. Thus, predictable job structures are an essential underpinning of the process of investment by employees, especially in the processes of vocational and on-the-job training within both occupational and firm internal labour markets.

Turning to labour market structure, the training approach underpins occupational markets, and the production approach, internal labour markets. This is easily seen if we try to imagine the consequences of reversing the relationship. The production approach is incompatible with occupational markets because workers would lack the matching job openings that enable them to apply their occupational skills. Likewise, the training approach is largely incompatible with internal labour markets because it makes skills more transparent to outsiders. Katz and Ziderman (1990), for example, argue that such transparency would make it easier for other firms to poach skilled labour from the firms which train them. Thus, they argue, firms will only pay for transferable training if they can disguise it sufficiently. Likewise, Scoville (1969) argues that firms will use job design in order to discourage mobility by workers to whom they have provided costly transferable skills. In this way, transferable skills are packaged with non-transferable ones, so that firms will avoid training for 'whole roles'. Ryan (1980) provides another illustration in which US shipyards delayed training for the transferable components of welders' skills until later in their training, by which time they would have accumulated a good deal of firm specific knowledge. What all three examples indicate is the difficulty firms face should certain skills in their internal labour markets become too visible to the outside, and in all three cases, the firms avoid combining internal markets with the training approach. If internal training has to be provided off-the-job, then they make sure that it is contained within the broader production approach. Thus, stable internal labour markets are incompatible with the training approach and depend upon adoption of the production approach.

Although the training and production approaches are fundamental to the working of occupational and internal labour markets, transaction rules and market structures are mutually supporting. Occupational markets help to reinforce the training approach and internal labour markets, the production approach. In the first place, the very advantages offered by occupational markets are a strong incentive to employers to adopt the training approach: they enable firms to 'buy into' different occupational markets. Secondly, the presence of an occupational market helps diffuse and homogenize training norms across firms. As argued earlier (Chapter 3), this makes the norms better understood and more robust, thus consolidating the training approach.

Internal labour markets also help to consolidate the production approach. They do so negatively by discouraging workers from developing occupational skills, as these can only be applied after a period of internal mobility within the firm. French cohort studies illustrate the plight of vocationally qualified young workers who have to enter at the bottom and await upgrading into skilled positions several years later (Podevin and Viney, 1991).[3] They also do so positively because, when widely diffused across an economy, their logic becomes incorporated into the job classification systems of individual firms and of industry agreements. As shown in Chapter 4, this helps to reinforce the norms regulating jobs and work allocation in the workplace.

The argument so far indicates that behind the difference between internal and occupational labour markets lies a more fundamental feature of the employment relationship, namely the influence of the production and training approaches that establish the structure and categories of jobs. If internal and occupational markets tend to fall into polar types, then a key factor behind this is the polarization between the two approaches to regulating jobs. Two potential objections need to be dealt with at this stage of the argument. The first is that there might appear to be a degree of circularity: did not Chapter 2 base the distinctness of the two approaches on the instability of the middle ground, and was not this based in part on an argument about labour market structures? The second concerns the treatment of hybrid cases such as the 'occupational internal labour markets' of the kind stressed by Althauser and Kalleberg (1981).

To take the first objection, the instability of intermediate positions between internal and occupational markets certainly contributes to the distinctness of the training and production approaches. This is part of the mutually supporting relationship between labour market structures and transaction rules. There were nevertheless two other important factors which relate directly to the production and training approaches: the different cost considerations underlying them (Chapter 2 §2), and that job norms are less robust when the same kinds of work are covered by two opposing allocation rules within the same organization (Chapter 3 §3).

Turning to the second objection, 'occupational internal labour markets', in many public sector organizations, for example in education and health, it is quite common to move up between recognized occupations, or specialisms within them, while remaining in the same organization. Nurses commonly do this when they upgrade from qualified nurse to midwife, classroom teachers may be promoted to head teacher, and so on. Given the earlier definition of an internal labour market, are these not cases in which employers regularly fill certain vacancies by training and upgrading? There is, however, a crucial difference. Progression occurs between recognized occupations with distinct external mobility openings. Both general nurses and midwives may move between hospitals, whether public or private, on the basis of their qualifications. In effect, they are moving from one occupational market to another with the assistance of their current employer. A similar question arises with internal promotions of apprentice-trained skilled workers in Germany, many of whom move up to 'Meister' after a period of additional, but externally recognized, training (Drexel, 1993).

3. APPROACHES TO ENFORCEABILITY AND FUNCTIONAL FLEXIBILITY

One feature that has been neglected in theories of internal and occupational markets has been that of functional flexibility, that is, the ability to move workers flexibly between tasks of different kinds (see Chapter 1 §1). Doeringer and Piore's model, with its emphasis on job specificity and detailed job classifications, suggests a rather low degree of functional flexibility. In contrast, Aoki's (1988) model of the J-firm, also an internal labour market, suggests the opposite. Likewise, Marsden's (1986, 1990) and Sengenberger's (1987) theories of OLMs, with their emphasis on the need for workers to maintain the transferability of their skills, suggest only limited functional flexibility, yet Soskice (1994) and Streeck (1992) suggest the opposite about Germany. They stress the contribution of occupational apprenticeships to the formation of broad skills, broader than required by their immediate job demands, as the key to German patterns of flexible specialization.

It is hard to resolve these questions solely in relation to the theoretical constructs on which their theories are based. Aoki's J-firm makes little reference to the questions of job specificity that are central to Doeringer and Piore's, and even to Williamson's accounts. Marsden's and Sengenberger's theories likewise stress the importance of skill transferability, and the lack of interest that workers with occupational skills would have in adding firm-specific skills to their own. The latter would undermine transferability and make the workers more dependent on their current employers. Why then do Soskice and Streeck observe a strong interest in continuous training among German skilled workers, and an acceptance of a degree of functional flexibility that would seem to threaten the continued transferability of their occupational skills?

A closer look at this work reveals the combined influence of the two contractual constraints. Job structures associated with ILMs and OLMs differ with respect not only to training considerations but also to their enforceability. The latter provides the key to understanding why some internal labour market and some occupational market patterns give rise to varying degrees of functional flexibility.

The job specificity of Doeringer and Piore's, and Williamson's ILMs reflects the adoption of task-centred rules of job definition. The functional flexibility of Aoki's J-firm can be seen in the adoption of function-centred rules for delimiting workers' obligations and for defining their diffuse jobs. The different ways of satisfying the enforceability constraint also give a different sense to internal mobility and transitions between jobs. Task-centred rules will cause jobs to be organized into discrete work packages, with a designated person responsible for each. Under such conditions, even when jobs are organized into job ladders, each individual job will tend to be only a 'collection of tasks sharing a certain level of technical demands', with no particular logic of skill development (Maurice *et al.*, 1986: 75). As the authors show, under such conditions, job rotation is of limited value to management and of only limited interest to workers. Taking a function-centred approach opens up scope for organizing tasks so that they have a more organic relationship with each other, and there is more room for overlapping jobs and task rotation between workers. In this case, job ladders have a different sense. They are not simply the juxtaposition of a set of work posts into a vertical sequence, but movement is both horizontal and vertical. The horizontal movement develops the breadth of skills, and the vertical movement, increasing levels of technical competence. In some respects, the greater overlap of skills between workers may be less efficient than the work post model, particularly in terms of short-term cost minimization, but there are potential offsetting gains through improved problem-solving by workers, as stressed by Koike (1997).

Thus, the treatment of the enforceability constraint leads to two different models of ILMs. One has rather narrow job ladders and limited possibilities for incremental learning to develop skills, and limited incentives for functional flexibility. The other sacrifices short-run cost minimization in favour of greater scope for using movement between jobs to enhance skill while remaining within the production approach. The latter provides ample incentives for workers to tackle new tasks beyond the confines of their immediate assignments.

The effect of these different systems can be seen in two empirical studies of ILM structure in the US and Japan. One shows that ILMs in the US are characterized by a greater number of job categories and more-detailed job classifications, as one would expect with more narrowly defined jobs (Hanada and McBride, 1986). The other shows that ILM structure in the US

Table 8.1. *Effect of contractual constraints on labour market structure*

Enforceability constraint	Efficiency constraint	
	Product approach	Training approach
Task-centred	'Work post', Taylorist ILMs	Craft/'job territory' OLMs
Function-/procedure-centred	'Functionally flexible' ILMs	'Functionally flexible' OLMs

firms is more closely determined by the production system than is the case in similar Japanese firms. In other words, the influence of complementarities in production on the structure of ILMs is greater in the US than in Japan, reflecting the stronger US emphasis on building ILMs out of individual jobs (Lincoln *et al.*, 1986).

In similar fashion, treating OLM skill categories as based on a specified range of task competencies, identified for example, by the tools needed to carry them out, gives rise to a model of OLM skills in which functional flexibility is restricted. In contrast, defining OLM skills in terms of the function to be carried out and the corpus of knowledge to be applied gives rise to a higher level of functional flexibility.

Thus, the transaction rule typology helps to disentangle one of the major empirical puzzles about the structure of internal and occupational markets. It also gives the key to understanding the different societal experiences with the flexibility of internal and occupational labour markets. The picture is summarized in Table 8.1.

4. INSTITUTIONALIZATION OF TRANSACTION RULES BY OLMS AND ILMS

The institutional structure of labour markets provides the transaction rules with a substantial degree of support, helping both to generalize them across whole occupations and sectors of an economy, and making them more robust because more people are familiar with their operation. It might be thought that such market supports for transaction rules would push the theory of employment systems in a more market-oriented direction. However, the aim of this section is to argue that both internal and particularly occupational markets are in fact institutional phenomena. They are thus because of their critical dependence upon a strong institutional underpinning. For this reason it is legitimate to treat systems of occupational and internal labour markets as contributing to the institutionalization of employment rules. Indeed, they are one of the most important vehicles of this process. The idea that internal labour markets are institutional markets is not particularly controversial, and Doeringer and Piore's view of them as 'administrative units' has wide currency. More controversial is the idea that occupational markets, which gave Alfred Marshall (1920) his paradigm examples of competitive markets for skilled labour, should also be seen as having an institutional nature. We therefore begin with an analysis of the institutional foundations of occupational markets.

4.1 Institutional foundations of occupational markets

A key problem with the skill formation that underlies occupational markets is the need for practical experience that can only be gained on the job: hence the critical role of workplace training. Academic institutions can impart theoretical knowledge, but practical experience is also essential, and it is costly. Trainees require more supervision from experienced staff, they make more mistakes that require rectification and their productivity is generally lower, as there are many tacit skills that have to be learned. As a result, employers inevitably contribute to the cost of training for transferable skills, although there are a variety of mechanisms by which they may be compensated. In Becker's theory, the net cost to employers of training for a transferable skill is zero on account of the trainees' productive contribution and the low trainee pay rate. However, even in his simple model there is a problem of enforcing payments over time. Mostly, the costs of workplace training are high in the early years, when the need for instruction and supervision is greatest and the productive contribution is least. This means that much of the compensation that employers receive comes towards the end of the traineeship, and hence, its duration is a key factor in balancing costs. Given the high early costs, it is unlikely that this could be avoided by a suitable schedule of trainee pay, as the trainee would probably have to pay the employer. The balance of training costs over time raises two kinds of enforcement problem: when trainees bear the full cost; and when employers bear a substantial part.

Enforcement problems when trainees bear the full cost

When trainees bear the full cost of workplace training for transferable skills, two key problems emerge. They need to be offered a reasonable prospect of a return on their investment, and hence need to know that there is a good supply of suitable jobs, as discussed earlier (v. §2); and employers need to know that over the whole traineeship period they can balance their costs. The second problem, that of balancing the employer's outgoings and returns over the training period, places heavy demands on mechanisms for enforcing the duration of traineeships. Elbaum's (1990) study of the decline of apprenticeship in US industry and its survival in Britain in the late nineteenth and early twentieth centuries hinges on the respective failure and success of enforcement mechanisms in the two countries. The critical cause of their demise in the US was the inability of employers to enforce the full training period, and thus to benefit from the trainees' higher productivity in the later years of their apprenticeships. Once they had acquired the essential skills, 'run-away' apprentices could escape their obligations to their employers and set up as craftsmen in a neighbouring state, beyond the jurisdiction of their native state. Often too, lack of cohesion among employers meant that run-aways could also find work quite easily in competitor firms. The survival of apprenticeship in Britain, in contrast, he explains in terms of the British employers' ability to enforce long apprenticeships, a contention supported by the high rates of completion, and documentary evidence of government reports that employers took the contracts seriously and would not engage run-away apprentices. A plentiful supply of skilled labour in Britain, and a shortage in the US, contributed to better enforcement of apprenticeship duration in Britain. Nevertheless, periods of shortage occurred with sufficient frequency in Britain for a potential market for run-aways to emerge there too. What contained the problem in Britain, and led to better enforcement than in the US, were peer group and customary pressures within local business communities and support by national employer organizations such as the EEF[4] (Elbaum, 1990).

4.2 The role of institutions when employers share training costs

The public good nature of occupational markets makes them vulnerable to free-rider problems when employers pay a substantial part of the cost of training for occupational skills. Generally, if the great majority of employers share costs of training for transferable skills, then there is no competitive disadvantage in doing so. A problem arises, however, should the market begin to slide into shortage. This increases the incentives to poach, and as a result, the riskiness of investing in training increases. Then, instead of the price mechanism bringing the market back into equilibrium, a series of forces comes into play which undermines the occupational market itself.[5] Such pressures can be felt in the quantity and quality of training, and in the maintenance of suitable job structures.

A strong institutional structure may counteract a number of these tendencies, giving the OLM greater stability. Both employer and labour organizations play an important part in this, although the nature of their roles differs. Employer organizations help to restrain free-riding on training costs, whereas unions and other employee organizations focus more on maintaining training quality and the training approach to job design.

Quantity and quality of training provided by employers

Maintaining the volume of training is critical to the prosperity of OLMs. Once they enter into shortage, the fear of losing workers one has trained intensifies the incentives either to cut back further on training and to poach, or to internalize skills to reduce their transferability. Thus, the first task of an institutional framework is to ensure an approximate balance between training supply and demand, and hence to keep free-riding to a minimum.

Comparing the recent history of the German and British industrial apprenticeship systems provides some clues as to how institutions support OLMs. During the 1960s and 1970s, both systems faced an urgent need to modernize and to increase the amount of theoretical training received as the sophistication of production methods was increasing. In both countries too, efforts were made to increase the attractiveness of apprenticeships to young people by shortening them, and especially in Britain, raising apprentice pay. So in both countries, the net cost to employers has increased. Yet while the German system expanded where it was already established, and was extended to cover new trades, for example in the steel industry (Drexel, 1980), the British system went into long-term decline, both in absolute terms and as a percentage of the industrial workforce. Moreover, the decline of apprenticeship in Britain did not reflect a corresponding fall in the demand for skilled labour. Throughout most of the period of decline, many employers complained of skill shortages forcing them to curtail their output plans. The decline was indeed one due to a failure of supply of training places to match even a falling demand for skilled labour (Marsden, 1995).

The strength of the institutional framework is most visible in Germany. There, local employer-led chambers of industry and commerce and artisan chambers play a decisive role in managing apprenticeship training. Although the state oversees technical standards and provides off-the-job training in technical schools, examining and day-to-day management are in the hands of the chambers. Additionally, works councils take a keen interest in apprenticeship training within the firm. Membership of the chambers is compulsory, and about 90% of employers in any locality are members. The chambers provide a focus for local employer networks so that peer group pressures can be applied to those not pulling their weight. An illustration of their effectiveness can be seen in the very successful voluntary efforts of German employers to expand apprentice training in order to combat youth unemployment in the 1970s and 1980s. The informal channels within the chambers were strong enough almost to double apprentice numbers in the 1970s, a time when British employers, facing similar cost and product market pressures, were cutting back on training.

Belief in the efficacy of their own informal channels also lay behind the decision by German construction industry employers to maintain their own voluntary system against the threat of state intervention. Streeck (1985) shows how the various employer organizations fought hard to maintain the principle of private regulation, keeping the state out and thereby avoiding such measures as compulsory training levies. Since the employers were seeking to increase apprentice output and considering raising apprentice allowances, it is clear that their motive for keeping the state out was not to reduce costs. Indeed, the levy that they set in their 1976 collective agreement was six times higher than the proposed statutory one.

In the field of training quality, where arguably the scope for free-riding is greater because quality differences are harder to monitor, the same institutions reinforce occupational markets. The chambers reinforce informal peer group pressures by publishing the pass lists for the apprentice exams. These reveal to other employers not only the numbers of apprentices trained in each firm, but even more important, how many of them received sufficient training to pass the exam.[6] Thus, the same device provides a key indicator of both quantity and quality of training provided. Works councils too take a keen interest, in medium and larger firms, in apprenticeship and more generally in further training. This is partly because they have a statutory right to codetermination in this area, but also, skilled workers are well represented and for them their apprenticeship qualification is the key to their economic status. They have therefore both the means and the strongest of incentives to ensure that there is no dilution of quality standards in training. The extent of their influence is illustrated by the agreement in some industries that management should explain their reasons to the works council if they do promote certain workers within a given time after completion of their training (Brossard, 1977).

In Britain, the weak institutional structure has been unable to contain the pressures arising from increased cost and persistent skill shortages. The increased incentives for poaching have made apprenticeship training a less attractive investment for employers who have responded to skill shortages by other methods. Finegold and Soskice (1988) argue that they responded by greater reliance on mechanization and less-skill-intensive production methods, which has also meant a reorientation towards producing less-skill-intensive goods. The case study comparisons of training and products by NIESR[7] provide strong empirical support for their argument in the chosen sectors.

Although the state attempted to shore up the failing occupational markets in the 1960s by setting up industrial training boards which could raise a levy on all employers in their jurisdiction to pay for training, the move was unpopular among employers. As a result of their opposition, the levy was first reduced and then scrapped, along with most of the training boards in the early 1980s. On the whole, employers found the boards bureaucratic and out of touch with their needs, and some resented the strong trade union influence, which helped maintain a focus on apprentice training and certain controls that the unions felt important to the integrity of the training system but which employers had begun to find constraining. Essentially, a key factor that kept the British apprenticeship system going was maintenance of the training approach to work assignments by means of the 'tools of the trade' rule. Sengenberger (1992) captured this essential difference between occupational markets in Britain and Germany thus:

Job design, job assignment and manning levels, as well as the supply of trained labour, which in the Anglo-Saxon countries are firmly in the control of craft unions, are predominantly subject to managerial discretion in Germany. (Sengenberger, 1992: 248)

In effect, British skilled workers could see the eroding market for their skills as a result of the weakness of coordination among British employers. Without the institutional structures keeping German employers within such markets, skilled workers and their unions had little alternative but to insist on more job-focused defences of their labour markets. Thus, rather than defend occupational markets by focusing on training levels, they focused instead on defending job structures, but with the long-run cost of declining efficiency. Hence the growing employer disaffection with apprenticeship.

The mechanisms of such defence need to be explained in more detail. Faced with the threatened erosion of the OLMs that they use, one response for firms that nevertheless require the skills involved is to seek various ways of internalizing their skill requirements. They may use several methods, notably, those discussed earlier which seek to redesign jobs to increase the non-transferable component of their workers' skills and to reduce the skills' transparency to competitor firms. They can also offer incentives tied to seniority. Such moves to tie skilled workers to their firms involve a retreat from the training approach and from the occupational market, and in effect, begin the process of internalization. Generally, given the cost of adopting a whole new job design regime for their current employees, most employers would prefer to approach internalization this way, by incremental steps. Hence, one way in which skilled workers and their unions can defend the integrity of OLMs is by defending the training approach to job design. Not only does their action maintain the job openings for occupational skills, but it also binds employers into providing training for transferable skills even when they face pressures from free-riding. Several writers have argued that employers might still contribute heavily to the cost of transferable skills if the cost of training is less than alternative methods of recruitment. Strong insistence on the training approach has the effect of raising the cost of alternative recruitment methods by closing off incremental adjustments. Stevens (1994) and Dougherty (1987) both argue that the net cost of providing transferable skills needs to be compared with the alternatives, and, developing such a model, Stevens' investment model for apprenticeship training in British engineering explains a considerable part of the decline during the 1970s and 1980s.

The appeal of both authors' models depends on whether one can explain recruitment costs that are equivalent in scale to one or two years' pay of an adult skilled worker. Normally, the standardized nature of the skills and their related work experience itself should help keep the recruitment costs low, but if skill shortages become persistent this ceases to apply. One cost of recruitment which Stevens cites is loss of sales owing to skill shortages. These are greatly reduced if employers can substitute incrementally. If they may only do so for 'whole role' skills, then the cost rises substantially. Considerable reorganization of work is needed, even if agreement to that can be obtained from incumbent workers. Thus, one explanation of such high recruitment costs would be that, when faced with skill shortages, employers are prevented from using incremental substitution.

In this way, one can understand the importance of the 'tools of the trade' rule in defending the position of OLMs in British industry.[8] It was, however, also one of the most likely reasons why employers became increasingly tepid towards apprenticeship, citing its association with restrictive work rules and the difficulties of negotiating change.

Why should employee pay fail to offset employers' costs?

A final question concerns why special low trainee-pay rates should fail to play the role Becker supposed and leave employers paying considerable net costs for investment in transferable skills. As argued in the previous chapter (§2.3), trainee pay is a controversial issue because if set too low it encourages substitution of trainee for skilled labour. If set too high, it fails to compensate employers for providing suitable training places. In the British evidence discussed here, it was so low in the 1920s and 1930s that skilled unions regularly complained of substitution,[9] but by the 1960s, it had swung in the opposite direction.

Normally, in a competitive equilibrium, substitution should not be a problem, as firms will seek to equate the ratio of marginal productivities to that of employment costs of apprentices and skilled workers. However, maintaining that equilibrium can prove difficult. For example, if skilled workers succeed in bargaining up their pay, then employers have an incentive to substitute. In order to defend their position, skilled workers may then seek to do the same for apprentice pay. As a result, employers find themselves paying part of the cost of apprentice training. Another fear could be that as the value of workers' output fluctuates over the business cycle, employers would seek to substitute apprentice labour during recessions, thus adding to the employment uncertainty for skilled workers. Again, they might, as a precaution, seek to bargain up apprentice pay. Ryan (1987) argues this was an important factor behind the rise in apprentice pay in Britain in the 1960s and 1970s.

Similar pressures could have built up in Germany, but a stronger workplace presence in the form of works councils has enabled German skilled workers, who are represented there in force, to keep much tighter control over the work done by young apprentices, as has tighter control over training quality. Both of these reduce the risk of apprentices being used as cheap substitutes, and so reduce the need to protect skilled workers' positions by either apprentice quotas or higher apprentice pay (Marsden and Ryan, 1991).

The problem for OLMs that have no institutional base is that should the trainee pay mechanism break down, there is no automatic self-correcting mechanism. If trainee pay rises are too high, employers bear more of the training cost, and the incentives to free-ride set in. The adjustment to this behaviour does not come through the price mechanism, but by internalization, which undermines the OLM itself.

4.3 ILMs and their institutional supports

There is a strong current running through the literature on internal labour markets suggesting that they are private arrangements confined to the enterprises in which they are established. They are designed unilaterally by management and offered to their employees, who may either accept the whole package or look for a job elsewhere. Such is the dominant view of non-union internal labour markets, although it is not entirely borne out by the experience of large US non-union firms, many of which also offered certain governance structures to provide alternatives to union-organized employee voice (Foulkes, 1980). Kalleberg *et al.* (1996) also highlight the degree to which both unionized and non-union internal labour markets in the US share many of the same features, including formal dispute resolution and other personnel procedures. Thus, at the level of the individual firm, even when ILMs are organized with only limited reference to inter-firm institutions, there remains an important workplace institutional structure assisting the operation of the transaction rules. This reflects the need for workplace institutions to assist enforceability, which was discussed in Chapter 3. Beyond this, the influence of inter-firm institutions can be felt in two ways: in the type of external institutional support; and in relation to the presence of OLMs.

Impact of wider classification systems

With firm internal labour markets, the impact of inter-firm norms is less direct than in the case of occupational markets. There is no equivalent to the pressure of shared occupational training norms shaping job structures. Instead, external norms, and especially those from classification agreements and conventions, generally shape the form rather than the content of job regulation. This reflects the logic of the production approach that task complementarities within the firm should determine individual job contents. But there is still a need to respond to the demands of the enforceability constraint.

As shown earlier (Chapter 4), classification agreements establish ideas such as accountability for individual work posts, broad principles for classifying jobs, the legitimacy of seniority provisions and so on. The most important influences stem from the way job regulation norms are incorporated into the classification systems. For example, classification conventions can reinforce the logic of the work post or the competence rank rules. Classification systems that focus on the attributes of jobs and the demands that they impose on their holders will tend to reinforce the work post system, whereas those which classify by employee qualities, such as their competencies and their status within the work group, will tend to reinforce the more flexible work assignments of the competence rank system.

By classifying jobs and relating them to each other, these systems help to shape the structure of internal labour markets. The norms of French classification agreements help to organize job progression and the accumulation of OJT within many French firms, keeping to the pattern outlined by Maurice *et al.* (1986). One may remember the limited incentives to develop polyvalence and job rotation that stem from the focus on the characteristics of the post rather than the skills of its incumbent (see Chapters 2 and 5). Likewise, the incorporation of the competence rank rule into the classification systems of many Japanese firms provides a strong incentive to patterns of job rotation and skill accumulation. As was seen earlier, the institutional support for inter-firm classification systems was clear for French and German industry, but even where formal agreements are absent, as in the case of Japan, both Koike (1997) and Cole (1989) have shown the importance of coordination among employers, and with unions, in setting the parameters within which broad skills have developed.

In the absence of multi-employer and collectively bargained classification systems, firms are likely to be restricted to variants of the work post rule, and the solutions that they work out to organize their internal labour markets will be constrained by its logic. Although much of the impetus for diffusion will come from its character as an evolutionary stable system, there may still be a degree of institutionalization, albeit weak. Firms' personnel departments keep informed about what other firms do, and consultants spread their views of good practice, all of which help to establish certain norms. Governments too, when designing legislation, take account of the dominant practices within firms, and this too can reinforce certain patterns of ILMs. Thus, if one set of ILM practices emerges as the favoured solution for working with work post systems, it is likely that a process of institutionalization will follow as other actors adapt their own practice to it. In doing so, they affect the attractiveness of alternative models. Thus, even in the absence of inter-firm employer and union organizations, there are a number of other channels through which weakly institutionalized models of ILMs can support the spread of work post-type rules.

What is clear in the case of ILMs is that the degree to which they embody the influence of inter-firm institutions can vary. They are not like OLMs, which are dependent upon a strong institutional support that spans many firms. A private solution is available for individual firms, but at the cost of confinement to the work post rule, unless they are prepared to invest heavily in developing workplace trust. The problems raised by this option are considered in the discussion of high-performance work systems in the concluding chapter.

Relationship with OLMs

A second external institutional influence on the structure of ILMs arises from the attraction of OLMs. As a result of these, firms will mostly choose to hire labour from OLMs if they can, and organize ILMs where this is not feasible. Consequently, the most consistently structured ILMs will generally be found when firms do not have this option, or when OLMs are seen to be failing.

In a study of firms in the Chicago area, Bridges and Villemez (1991, 1994) show that firms developed ILM structures for jobs in which there was no viable external market. They identified the latter, taking national data to compare workers' tenure in their current job with that in their current occupation. Occupations with a viable external market were those in which occupational attachment most exceeded current job attachment.

In Britain, although OLMs have predominated, they have not done so in all occupations, and firms have sometimes developed a dual structure to enable them to draw on OLMs where they can, and use ILMs where they cannot. British coal mining in the 1970s and early 1980s offered a good example of this. Skilled electricians were hired from an occupational market, and face-trained miners were employed on a highly developed internal market. The impact of the two systems was clearly visible in turnover patterns, that of electricians being more sensitive to the state of the external market. In the chemical industry too, a similar dual pattern could be seen in the division between process skills which could not be externally recruited and so were organized on ILM lines, and maintenance skills which drew on local OLMs (Marsden, 1982).

In the British examples, the dual structure has tended to develop where there is a large group of process skills. A more common result has been that use of OLMs for key skilled groups has truncated ILMs for other groups. Eyraud *et al.* (1990) show that, for industry, compared with France, where length of service rose with level of skill, in Britain, there was no such tendency. Unskilled, semi-skilled and skilled tenure patterns were very similar, indicating that such upgrading chances as existed for semi-skilled workers were mostly confined within that grade. In Germany too, semi-skilled workers are likewise excluded from OLMs because they have not the required qualifications and face only restricted upgrading chances. German collective agreements are very strict on just how far workers may be upgraded on the basis of practical experience rather than formal apprenticeship.

In many respects, the widespread use of OLMs for skilled workers means either rudimentary ILMs for the unskilled and semi-skilled, or secondary labour market conditions. With their upward mobility blocked by the lack of apprenticeship qualifications, the semi-skilled have only limited incentives to invest in their current firms, and more important, employers are restricted in the degree to which they can use the semi-skilled as a pool from which more skilled workers may be developed.

To conclude, the structure and operation of ILMs is governed both by workplace insititutions developed within the firm, such as grievance procedures, and often also by powerful inter-firm institutional structures, which consolidate the workings of the transaction rules within the workplace. Prominent among these are the labour market conventions and collective agreements that shape classification rules, and the presence of OLMs. Thus both OLMs and to a lesser extent ILMs can be seen as helping to institutionalize the transaction rules that underpin them.

5. MONOPSONY AND SECONDARY LABOUR MARKETS

Most of the argument in this book assumes that workers have sufficient choice so that one can regard their position as employees as reflecting their own perceptions of their best interests. It assumes that they have the freedom to reject forms of employment that do not protect against opportunism by their employers. There is, however, the important case of monopsony in labour markets, something given renewed impetus by recent research on the economics of the minimum wage by a number of scholars, notably Card and Krueger (1995). Taking account of monopsony in labour markets also offers a way of understanding gender and other forms of discrimination in the constitution of employment relationships.

Although the classic textbook example of labour market monopsony is the increasingly rare case in which a single employer dominates a 'company town', the work of Card and Krueger indicates that it is much more widespread among low-paid employment than has commonly been supposed.[10] Their evidence that increases in the minimum wage from the levels at which they are commonly set have often had little or no effect in reducing employment is most readily explained by employer monopsony. Indeed, this is the path that they favour with their own model of dynamic monopsony. If one considers many of the low-paid groups, this should not be wholly surprising. Many less-skilled married women are restricted in their job choice by the double burden of market and household responsibilities. This often limits them both in the hours of work they can offer and in the distance they can travel to work.

The effect of monopsony in labour markets is to reduce employees' ability to enforce their understanding of their obligations, and so to enable employers to increase them unilaterally. For example, Rubery (1994) observed that many women in secondary market jobs in fact held levels of skill similar to those of men in jobs classified as skilled within internal labour markets, but they were not recognized as such. Employees know the disadvantages they face, so a first implication of the theory of employment systems is that they will prefer job demands to be identified fairly specifically, as these are the simplest to enforce. Employers might ideally like to use their monopsony power to get high levels of functional flexibility, but in view of the low degree of trust likely to prevail, their best bet is do so by means of weakly enforced task-centred job descriptions. These give them more scope to sanction behaviour that they do not want should conflicts arise. Two other considerations will also push secondary labour market employers in this direction. First, should demand increase, then they can use the more specific job descriptions to hold the line against employee pressures for better conditions. Secondly, the higher rates of labour turnover and weaker employee attachment associated with secondary market employment also favour use of more task-centred job descriptions.

The greater job instability and weaker skill recognition in secondary market jobs will both discourage employees from investing in skills, as the returns are too uncertain, and mean that employers have no great interest in training. Hence, the production approach can be expected to prevail. Thus, taking both sets of constraints, one can expect secondary labour markets to be characterized by jobs organized according to the production approach, and based on task-centred rules. In other words, some form of work post rule can be expected to flourish, except that, unlike in more skilled areas of employment, employees will generally have more difficulty in resisting unilateral changes in their job demands by management.

Card and Krueger give a very vivid illustration of how such monopsony can affect job demands to the disadvantage of employees. In effect, firms operating in the low-pay segment can choose whether they pay low wages and experience high turnover, or pay wages that are a little higher and have lower rates of turnover. Because of their monopsony power, many opt for low pay and high turnover on account of the hidden advantages of unfilled vacancies. In most work environments, when firms are short-staffed other colleagues take on at least part of the work of those absent or who have not yet been replaced. The monopsony effect comes about less through pay levels themselves than in the corresponding higher workloads. The lesser ability of such employees to enforce their understanding of their job descriptions means that employers can more easily reassign tasks to cover for absences, and so raise workloads. It was indeed through such a mechanism that Card and Krueger argued that a modest increase in a minimum wage could raise employment: firms would be forced to move to the higher pay–lower turnover situation, and with fewer unfilled vacancies employment levels would rise.

6. EMPLOYMENT AND SELF-EMPLOYMENT

The theoretical model developed in the first chapters made a critical simplifying assumption that workers and firms face a stark choice between two
main forms of relationship: engaging in an open-ended relationship as an
employee subject to management authority; or contracting to provide
specific labour services as self-employed. This idea captures some key
elements of recent developments in labour markets: that employment and
self-employment are two alternative frameworks for supplying labour services. However, the model so far has implied a rather clear-cut division
between employment and other ways of providing labour services. Yet in
recent years, not only has self-employment grown in many countries, but so
too have other forms of what Abraham (1990) described as 'market-
mediated' employment forms such as fixed-term and service contracts,
temping, agency and casual work, and more debatably, part-time employment. These trends all show that the boundary between employee and self-
employed status is broader and greyer than has so far been supposed.

Because of the exaggerated claims made by some authors about the
growth of self, and contingent employment and the impending demise of
the established employment relationship, we have to look first at some of
the statistical evidence on self-employment and other new employment
forms. Often growth rates are cited without reference to the level from
which they start. Once this is done, it is possible to look at interpretations,
and to show the role of the transaction rules in determining the moving
balance between *ex ante* and *ex post* regulation of employers' and employees' mutual obligations.

6.1 Some quantitative evidence on alternatives to the employment relationship

Across OECD countries in 1990, the average rate of self-employment stood at
about one person in eight (OECD, 1992). Among the five countries covered in
this book, the average was about one person in ten (Table 8.2). In many
countries, over the previous two decades there had been renewed growth
after a long period of decline, but across the OECD as a whole, the countries
with an increase in self-employment only just outnumbered those with a
decline. One of the very few countries to experience a major growth in self-
employment was the UK, most of which occurred during the second half of
the 1980s. Thus, whatever the predictions about the impending demise of the
employment relationship, it continues to cover about nine people out of ten
of those gainfully employed.

Behind the overall figures, there are significant underlying changes. Self-
employment growth has concentrated in expanding sectors, suggesting that

Table 8.2. *Distribution of non-agricultural self-employed by occupation 1988/90, and trends 1973–90 (%)*

ISCO major groups	France	Germany	Japan	UK	US
Professional and technical	21.5	23.8	13.2	17.0	17.7
Admin. and managerial	2.6	11.2	0.8	4.2	18.2
Clerical	0.1	2.9	1.2	3.8	3.9
Sales	24.9	26.8	25.3	21.0	20.9
Service	14.6	11.4	13.5	13.0	13.8
Production	36.5	20.8	46.0	40.6	25.6
Total	100	100	100	100	100
All non-agricultural: self-employed as % of civilian employment					
1990	10.3	7.7	11.5	11.6	7.6
1973	11.4	9.1	14.1	7.3	6.7

Note: 1973–90, figures exclude some owner-managers of incorporated businesses except for Germany, and some are excluded in the UK.
Source: OECD (1992: tables 4.1 and 4.A.4).

although employers were not directly substituting self-employment for employment, when they were creating new jobs, these were more likely to be self-employed than in the past. In addition, the fastest growth of the self-employed had been in service industries, and especially financial services, whereas it had tended to stagnate or decline in the mainstream industrial sectors. Thirdly, much of the growth in the self-employed was among those without their own employees, so the self-employed were mostly providing their own labour rather than managing that of others in small firms. Finally, mobility studies reviewed by the OECD (1992) show that the majority who enter self-employment do so voluntarily, and are former employees who later return to employee status, thus giving further evidence of choice between the two forms.

Turning to temporary work and fixed-term contracts, Table 8.3 shows that they have grown in the three European countries, and especially in France between the mid-1980s and mid-1990s. Abraham (1990) reports a similar pattern in the United States. Again, the figures in Table 8.3 help put these employment forms into perspective while at the same time showing there has been an increase in their use. Part-time employment is less obviously 'non-standard' because, in many countries, it is covered by traditional open-ended contracts of unlimited duration. For the UK, Gallie and White (1994) show that over 90% of employees were engaged in permanent employment, and many part-timers were permanent employees (as does Abraham for the US). The remaining 9% divided more or less equally between full-time

Table 8.3. *Non-standard employment forms in Europe 1995*

	% of gainfully employed persons		
	France	Germany	UK
Temporary work	12.3	10.4	7.0
% change on 1983	9.0	0.5	1.5
Self-employment	12.8	9.4	13.0
% change on 1983	−1.2	0.4	2.8
Part-time employment	16.2	16.4	24.5
% change on 1983	6.5	3.8	5.5

Source: Labour Force Survey, Eurostat, cited in Walwei (1997).

Table 8.4. *Temporary workers by occupation and type of temporary work, Great Britain, Spring 1996*

Occupation	Fixed-term contract/task (%)	Agency temping (%)	Casual/ seasonal (%)	All employees (%)
Managerial	8	*	*	15
Professional	32	*	7	11
Associated professional and technical	13	8	4	9
Clerical and secretarial	14	49	13	16
Craft and related	6	*	6	10
Personal and protective services	12	10	24	12
Sales	2	*	13	9
Plant and machine operatives	7	16	10	10
Other	6	6	20	8
All temporary	100	100	100	100
(thousands)	801	201	395	22,020

* denotes that the sample size is too small for a reliable result.
Source: Labour Force Survey, *Labour Market Trends* (Sept. 1997: 351). Analysis relates to employees only (Sly and Stillwell, 1997).

employees on fixed-term contracts of under one year (3%) and 1–3 years (3%), and temporary part-timers (3%).

British evidence for the mid-1990s provides more detailed information on the type of contract by occupation (Table 8.4). What is striking is the predominance of professional qualifications among employees on fixed-term contracts, many of these being employed in public administration, health and education (Sly and Stillwell, 1997). Among agency temps, again what is striking is importance of occupations with recognized vocational training, notably in secretarial and office qualifications, many of these being in the financial sector, but also in public services. Many temps engaged in manufacturing will be in maintenance, again with recognized qualifications. In contrast, the lack of occupational qualifications is most noticeable among casual and seasonal staff, where personal services, sales and unclassified occupations dominate.

Another indicator of potential erosion of the open-ended unlimited duration employment contract is change in job tenures and change in employment stability. These also have been surveyed by the OECD in the early 1990s, and there too the results show only limited changes in employment practices. Job tenures have remained remarkably stable when one considers the amount of restructuring that occurred during the 1980s, and that even in the UK and the US, where job tenures have fallen, that decline has been modest (OECD, 1993). Its survey of job insecurity also concluded that it was employee perceptions of insecurity rather than job instability itself that had increased (OECD, 1997). The perception of reduced security may well influence employees' behaviour, but on the data so far, it is a perception, and could be as much a result of increased uncertainty facing the firms themselves as of any implied change in the employment relationship. Thus, the overall picture is that the data testify to the remarkable resilience of the open-ended employment relationship, but they also show the practical reality of the choice between alternative methods of contracting that underlies the theory developed here.

6.2 Employment systems and market-mediated employment

A useful way of thinking about the boundary between employment as employees and market-mediated forms is in terms of economic transactions that vary as to the mix of obligations that are specified *ex ante* and *ex post*. This is illustrated in Figure 8.1, which shows the varying mix of obligations that are specified *ex ante* and *ex post* as one passes from pure open market contracting to the most diffuse forms of employment relationship. Under perfect competition, contractual relations are usually assumed to be fully specified *ex ante*, enabling workers and firms to compare offers of jobs and services and the associated rewards (position 'A'). The economic value of *ex*

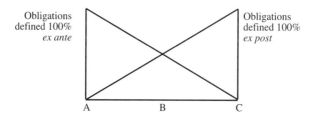

Fig. 8.1. The transition between open-market and employment contracts

post specification, stressed by Coase and by Simon, arises from uncertainty about demand and the difficulty and resulting cost of defining all the relevant information. This is roughly position 'C'. As argued in this book, neither Coase nor Simon gave enough thought to the need for contractual limits on managerial authority, that is, limits on *ex post* definition. As shown, the employment relationship offers a variety of ways of tackling this problem. The combination of the production and the function-centred approaches comes closest to position 'C' in Figure 8.1. Occupational markets fall somewhere to the left of 'C' but to the right of 'B', as they combine an element of *ex ante* definition given by the occupation of reference with varying degrees of *ex post* flexibility. Similarly, if we consider some recent research on contractual relations among firms, such as that of Piore and Sabel (1984) on Italian and French industrial districts, or more recently of Deakin and Wilkinson (1998) on contract law and inter-firm relations, it is clear that *ex post* specification and revision of obligations are also possible among firms. Such relations would be situated a bit to the right of 'A'.

In their wide-ranging field study of outwork, Rubery and Wilkinson (1981: 116) identified the dominant characteristics as being 'that labour can be purchased in discrete and variable amounts, payment is directly related to output, and the labour process is unsupervised'. Thus, self-employment belongs to the left of 'B', but what is also striking both in their study, and in Tables 8.2 and 8.4 above, is the importance of occupational skills to self-employment. Knowledge of what these involve can avoid the need for such extensive *ex ante* definition of tasks to be undertaken, especially where the product cannot be so easily defined. In Simon's example of laying the concrete path, knowledge of the occupation involved makes it possible to give only a broad description of the job to be done, important if there is a big information asymmetry between the small builder and the customer, and for some 'give and take' adjustment afterwards. Rubery and Wilkinson found that outwork could develop for semi-skilled work, particularly if those concerned were former employees of the company, and so shared tacit knowledge of the work process.

Several other market-mediated forms of employment can be thought of as lying in between self-employment and employment. In his study of franchising, Felstead (1991) concluded that in many cases it was a form of 'controlled self-employment' in which the franchiser took a close interest in the work process itself, often specifying it in some detail. The dependence of other forms of market-mediated employment on recognized occupational structures also shows up in the concentration of professional and craft occupations among those on fixed-term contracts, and of secretarial occupations among those engaged as temps (Table 8.4). The one exception is the large number of casual and seasonal workers in personal services and in unidentified occupations. One would expect a finer breakdown of the data to show that these are mostly in secondary labour market jobs.

6.3 Movements between employment forms

Two key factors appear to lie behind the growth in market-mediated forms of employment in advanced industrial countries. The first is the general increase in competition and economic uncertainty facing many firms. This has led them to seek more flexible forms of organization and to cut back on expensive buffers of both inventory and labour. The quantitative side of this can be seen in the recourse to agency employment, which Gorgeu and Mathieu (1998) show explains the rise of agency employment in the French automobile industry: it enables firms using just-in-time production to deal with peaks in production without incurring additional overhead costs.[11] But the qualitative side has also been important with the increased emphasis on coordination through networks, and the resulting restructuring of careers, towards what some have called 'boundaryless careers'. The second factor concerns problems of control over the employment relationship, and in particular, the belief among many employers that it has not delivered the degree of flexibility they expected. Rather than deal exhaustively with all forms and explanations of the shift back towards more market-mediated forms of employment, one example of each of these tendencies is taken: the 'boundaryless career'; and the growth of employee franchising.

(a) 'Boundaryless careers'

One of the factors behind the interest in alternative forms of employment contract has been the decline in bureaucratic employment systems associated with moves towards 'high-performance work systems' and the restructuring of careers within organizations. Osterman (1996) sought to capture the decline in bureaucratic careers in a collection of papers entitled 'broken ladders', and Arthur and Rousseau (1996) used the term 'boundaryless careers' to capture the shift towards new types of lateral career structures between organizations. Although these changes may be only weakly reflected in the aggregate statistics on employment forms and job tenures, they nevertheless represent a direction of change that many organizations are seeking to adopt even though their success rate may fall far short of their aspirations. The nature of these changes can be interpreted as attempts to shift between employment systems, and what is often not recognized is that this involves a transition from one set of contractual constraints to another.

   In many accounts, the villain of the piece is the bureaucratic employment system built around the work post rule. Although its precise form may vary between blue- and white-collar jobs, firms have come to appreciate its limitations overall. This has been in part because market changes often now require swifter structural adaptation than in earlier decades, and in part because of an increased awareness of the flexibility of alternative employment systems practised by large Japanese firms, on the one hand,

and in industrial districts such as Silicon Valley and Hollywood on the other. Several of the contributors to both books recognize the moves made by firms in these directions, although their conflicting requirements are not always fully appreciated.

One of the biggest weaknesses is the failure to recognize the functions fulfilled by the 'bureaucratic' model, that is by the work post system. It is not something dysfunctional imposed by unions nor something adopted by short-sighted managers obsessed with control. The argument of this book has been that it represents a very robust framework for organizing cooperation between workers and management that can withstand fairly low-trust relations. Its great merits are that it restricts opportunism while at the same time allowing management to organize work according to the demands of the production approach.

High-performance work systems as practised within the production approach take one towards functional definitions of jobs and towards greater *ex post* definition of employment obligations. This requires both higher trust and stable employment. The first is required for flexibility, and the second because the production approach gives rise to non-transferable skills. Both impose severe limitations on how far market-mediated employment forms can be developed.

The other direction, analysed very perceptively by Tolbert (1996) and Jones and Walsh (1997), is towards greater market mediation, taking, respectively, Silicon Valley and Hollywood as examples. This is also the path of 'boundaryless careers'. For a viable employment relationship in such an environment, labour mobility requires the training approach and some form of occupational market as well as some means of avoiding the restrictions of the task-centred approach to job definition. The fluidity of relations implied by the project basis of many ventures, if anything, increases the scope for opportunism, and such pressures must be contained if cooperation is to be successful. Workers can lie about their past work experience and their abilities, and firms can lie about the work involved, and both can engage in moral hazard once the other side is committed to the project. In the absence of the guarantees offered by German-style apprenticeship systems and occupational markets, what substitutes are there? In both Hollywood and Silicon Valley, the authors stress the role of the 'occupational' or the 'industrial community' based on personal networks that are structured by occupational or industrial affiliation.

The workings of a project-based form of organization and its substitution for large employing organizations are better documented in the case of Hollywood than for Silicon Valley. Hollywood illustrates many of the problems of such organization: creative work by artists is commercially very important, it is very competitive and the product market is fast moving. Whatever the role of talent, much performance is based upon solid training and experience. The project method of organization superseded the old studios after their dissolution in the 1950s and 1960s, but a solution had to be found to all the problems of opportunism analysed earlier (Paul and Kleingartner, 1994). Creative work generates income that goes beyond simple box office receipts, and its outcomes go beyond the hours 'strutting and fretting upon the stage'. The income accruing from residual obligations, analogous to copyright, and deriving from further use made of the work, for example, from using the film's name in advertisements for other products, is considerable. For the Screen Actors' Guild members in 1988, about 45% of total income came from residuals, compared with 55% from initial compensation. There is often a conflict of interest between creative artists, anxious to avoid overexposure of their work that would tire their public, and the companies keen to earn additional residual income. Other potential conflicts arise between artists and producers, as the former are concerned about how their work is adapted and how this might affect the reputation on which they depend for future work. Scope for opportunism is considerable on both sides.

Essential to the Hollywood case is the functional equivalent of an occupational market. In this case it is underpinned by a strong union organization which administers the all-important 'residual obligations', which are distributed on the basis of film credits. This puts the union at the centre of all the information networks: it must have current addresses in order to distribute residual incomes. Being independent of the producers, it can be better trusted by the artists to keep track of payments and also to follow new sources of residual income as they are discovered by film companies. In the absence of formal qualifications, the information network is a very important vehicle for reputation. Although individual actors may be seen on the screen, the individual contributions of many other creative workers is not so easily identified, and the network provides a channel along which information about good and poor quality competence and performance may be transmitted. With project-based employment, workers do not get continuous employment, but the flow of income from residuals provides some continuity of income between projects.

In Silicon Valley, Saxenian (1996) and other writers stress the critical importance of networks among professionals for work in small hi-tech firms and on projects. But as Tolbert (1996) points out, such networks depend upon the existence of identifiable occupational groups, which echoes Granovetter's (1974) finding that the most effective personal networks for getting jobs depend upon contacts among people in the same occupation. Thus, as Tolbert argues, occupations play a special role in structuring the information flows within 'boundaryless careers'. Although the knowledge in hi-tech activities often progresses much faster than the formal codification of skills associated with established professions, one should not overlook the often important role of major research universities in underpinning labour market networks. Not only are they a source of graduates, but also, as Zucker (1991) argues, the consultancy activities of professors keep them in contact with the wider occupational community in the commercial world, and the university's reputation itself provides a form of quality control, at least in terms of the workers' capabilities if not over their output. Thus, systems of 'boundaryless careers' appear analogous to OLMs in many respects, and although less codified than those of blue-collar crafts and established white-collar professions, they are dependent upon institutional structures to cope with the many problems of opportunism that would otherwise beset them.

(b) Franchising: an example of the breakdown of an employment relationship

One of the commonest forms of self-employment which has been expanding in the service sector in Britain has been franchising (Felstead, 1991). In such cases, franchisees usually operate without close supervision but are required often to follow certain procedures in order to maintain quality. They appropriate the profits of their trade, but only after paying a royalty or a turnover-related payment to the franchiser. Despite buying or leasing the means of production, they are often subject to restriction on their operation. There are certain advantages to both sides: the franchiser can often expand business more rapidly and at a lower capital cost than by setting up a new business, and the franchisee gains autonomy and the opportunity to acquire management and business skills.

More important in the current context is the problem of controlling potential opportunism, and the way this can affect the balance between adopting the employment or the franchise relationship. One particularly revealing study has been the introduction of franchise contracts for doorstep milk delivery staff who had previously worked under an employment contract (O'Connell, 1994).

Milk delivery had always fitted uneasily with the employment relationship owing to the high degree of trust needed and the rather limited skills involved. Trust is needed because of the amounts of money handled, the importance of the dairy's reputation with customers for reliable delivery and accurate billing, and the increasing need to make delivery more profitable by selling other goods as well. Absenteeism was also a problem, owing to unsocial hours and unpleasant weather. Simple incentive contracts had proved difficult to work effectively. Rewarding the number of milk sales in a round implies faster deliveries, whereas collecting money and selling additional services is time-consuming. Because many milk deliverers held second jobs later in the day, they often wanted to finish quickly, and the income from their second job outweighed any bonus that the dairy could offer for developing the customer base and customer relations. With the increased competition from supermarket sales, the established dairies found it increasingly difficult to manage the employment relationship profitably.

Introducing a self-employed franchise system enabled the dairies to shift the monitoring costs, especially on sales, billing and absenteeism onto the franchisee. Under the new system, the franchisee bore the cost of book-keeping and debt collection from customers, and lost income during absence. In return, the franchisee delivered milk and other goods for a fixed margin on sales. According to O'Connell, several problems remained. The dairies were unable to prevent the franchisees from obtaining their own goods for sale from the local cash and carry instead of selling those provided by the dairy. They also found it difficult to get franchisees to expand the customer base. Because the latter carried the financial risk, they were reluctant to take on uncreditworthy customers. The dairies still faced a problem if their franchisees allowed customer debt to build up too much. Overall, the dairies that shifted to self-employed franchising did so because the employment relationship was not working as intended, and in a low-trust environment, mechanisms of bureaucratic control were expensive to operate and not very effective. At the same time, they also discovered, or rediscovered, similar problems of controlling opportunism within the franchise relationship to those found in other studies of outworking, notably around the issue of quality (e.g. Craig *et al.*, 1980, 1982).

7. CONCLUSIONS

At the outset, this chapter sought to show how the four types of transaction rule shape labour market structures, and to show that although they sustain each other, the initial impulse depends on whether firms generally are using the production or the training approaches. As one or other form spreads, so it will favour the expansion of internal or occupational labour markets. Because such markets are themselves institutional forms and sustained by collective action of one kind or another, the support that they provide to the transaction rules is a form of institutionalization. The collective influence is more clearly demonstrable in the case of occupational markets because of their public good characteristics, and their proneness to free-rider pressures when such tendencies are not restrained by forms of collective action. In the case of internal labour markets, employers retain more control over job structures, but, it has been argued, the rules governing them, and in particular the classification rules, owe a great deal to the influence of inter-firm conventions and collective agreements. Thus, employment systems are clearly anchored both in the transaction rules shaping relations within the enterprise and in the labour market structures in which it is embedded. One novel conclusion is a synthetic explanation not just of the emergence of OLM and ILM structures, but also of why they should display greater or lesser degrees of functional flexibility.

The second goal of the chapter has been to show how the rules of employment systems extend to secondary labour markets and to the market-mediated employment forms that have been spreading in recent years. Secondary labour markets differ from ILMs and OLMs primarily in the reduced ability of employees to enforce their understanding of their obligations as employees and to limit management authority. The nature of secondary markets is such that some variant of the work post rule is most likely to prevail. The two function-centred rules are too fragile in the face of likely low-trust relations, and training levels are mostly too low to justify occupational skills.

The growth of market-mediated forms was shown to be one aspect of the shifting boundary between employment and self-employment, and between *ex ante* and *ex post* definitions of employees' obligations. The OECD studies show that the shift away from the employment relationship has been greatly exaggerated, but they also confirm the moveable nature of the boundary between employment, self-employment and other forms of contract, and provide justification for the idea that many firms and workers have real choice in this domain, if not instantaneously at least over time. The examples of new forms in the 'boundaryless' careers and in franchising illustrate that alternative forms of contracting often themselves face difficult problems of opportunism. *Ex ante* definition of an agent's obligations is not easy when much of the relevant expertise takes the form of tacit skills and one's future requirements of different labour services are uncertain. So the employment relationship continues to offer many benefits to employers. The consideration of boundaryless careers and of self-employment also highlighted the role of occupational norms in the definition of duties and standards of performance, just as they do in employment. As Tolbert observed, 'boundaryless' careers depend upon labour market structures. In both the new career structures and the franchising example, the problem in the background lay not so much in the shortcomings of the employment relationship itself as the limitations of the production approach combined with task-centred job definitions. Their great robustness against opportunism no doubt explains their continued popularity and wide diffusion, but their rigidity in the face of swiftly changing market demands has proved an increasing handicap. The irony is that the least institutionally dependent of the employment rules should generate the greatest pressures for more market-mediated relations. This theme is taken further in the next chapter, which is on employment systems and the theory of the firm.

ENDNOTES

[1] The definition is that used in Marsden (1986: 1–2).
[2] Recent German and British sources are analysed in Marsden (1995).
[3] Their study confirmed the findings of an earlier cohort study based on 1970s data by Pohl and Soleilhavoup (1981).

[4] The Engineering Employers' Federation.

[5] This section takes up and extends the argument that occupational markets are unstable in the absence of an institutional support, developed in Marsden (1986: ch. 8).

[6] I am indebted to Ingrid Drexel for this information.

[7] The National Institute for Economic and Social Research. See especially the matched Anglo-German studies of the kitchen furniture and clothing industries by Steedman and Wagner (1987, 1989) which showed the German plants using more skill-intensive methods and producing for the higher-quality end of the market.

[8] Eyraud (1981) also observed the strong concern among British skilled workers with job control issues, often at the expense of higher pay, in comparison with skilled workers in France.

[9] Ryan (1986) shows that in the 1920s, in engineering industries, apprentices were employed in greatest numbers in those regions where apprentice pay was lowest relative to that of adults.

[10] Manning (1996) argues the same for low-paid women's work in Britain.

[11] In 1997, the automobile manufacturers hired about 15% of their staff through agencies, and their suppliers hired up to 50% of their staff in this way.

III

CONCLUSIONS

9

Employment Systems and the Theory of the Firm: Societal Diversity

1. INTRODUCTION

The insights of Coase and Simon have been taken up in this book with the aim of understanding the key principles underlying the employment relationship. Why should firms continue to engage nine out of ten workers as employees across the advanced industrial world, and what does this tell us about the nature of the relationship? As Coase recognized, the employment relationship confers on firms the right to specify the tasks that their employees should undertake 'within certain limits'. Without such limits, few workers would agree to a form of contract that gave their employers these powers, and certainly not the ninety per cent of workers who are employees. This book has sought to understand how those limits are established and regulated. In doing so, it has also sought to explain another aspect of the employment relationship that has emerged from international comparative research: its international diversity. Rather than take an inductive approach, starting from the facts as we know them, it has deliberately taken a deductive approach, and then tried to see how far it explained these facts. There have been two main reasons for this. The first is that a deductive approach places all the key assumptions on the table. If one accepts the assumptions, then one should accept the conclusions if soundly derived. In this case, the assumptions were taken from mainstream theories of economics and sociology, notably 'rational choice theory'. The conclusion is that institutions play a logically central part in the workings of the employment relationship, and that firms are an integral part of their institutional environment. The second reason was to show that the same kind of assumptions could explain why there is such international diversity of employment systems, and relate this to the analysis of the employment relationship.

Some critics of the argument so far might say that there has been a neglect of the obvious empirical presence of the law in labour markets and in the employment decisions of firms, and likewise, for the output of state educational systems. Do these not constrain employers in their dealings with employees and define many of the rights which people have when they are employees? Likewise, do not state educational diplomas shape the categories of labour supplied to firms? As explained in the introduction, this omission was deliberate for reasons of method, evidence and, quite simply, length.

The methodological choice was made because the aim has been to explore how far institutional rules are essential to the working of labour markets, and to see what sort of rules and skill categories would emerge even in the absence of state action. With the retreat of state regulation in many countries under the banner of 'deregulation', and the growth of a large non-union sector in many economies, it has become urgent to rethink some of the basic ideas about the role of institutions in labour markets.

The second reason is that the degree to which legal rules are imposed on labour market actors, 'exogenously', is greatly exaggerated. One may recall Sellier's (1961) comment on the poor enforcement of French industrial relations law, that legislation is like currency. The state's power to impose rules is limited. In a similar vein, the state's power to shape labour skills through state educational systems is also limited. In all five countries in this study, enterprise-based training constitutes a very large component of total national investments in education and training, and this limits the degree to which the state can act independently.[1] For example, the activist French state has sought to impose vocational training schemes on French labour markets, notably to introduce German-style industrial apprenticeships, and on both occasions these have failed. And French unions have sought repeatedly to gain employer recognition for state vocational diplomas in collective agreements, but have been repeatedly rebuffed. The state's more recent success with further training owes much to the way it has been grafted onto existing practices in the firm (Géhin and Méhaut, 1993). To a considerable degree, labour law reflects the wishes of the main interested parties, and is enabling rather than restricting in its nature: a framework to enable them to get on with their business rather than a constraint on their freedom. It is like the 'Highway Code', a set of rules designed to help drivers and pedestrians use the highway system safely and effectively rather than curbing the freedom to drive at high speed. The problem is that the balance of political forces and the organization of interest groups also shapes the law, and taking this into account would go beyond the limits of this book. The same is true of state action through the educational system.

The intention is not to diminish the real importance of both law and educational systems in practice, but rather to see what kinds of institutions would develop out of the free choices of firms and workers, and then to see how far these correspond to such empirical evidence as exists. As was seen in Chapter 5, the international evidence supports the general argument about the types of employment relationship that develop and their diffusion across large areas of industry in different countries, and indicates strong societal differences. The conclusion of this book is that the firm lies at the centre of a complex of labour market institutions. It is an integral part of this complex, and its line management and human resource policies are shaped by these institutions. To see why this is so we need to go back to the theory of the firm discussed at the beginning of Chapter 1.

2. TRANSACTION COSTS, OPPORTUNISM AND KNOWLEDGE

The theory of the firm has witnessed a debate in recent years between those who take their cue from Coase and Williamson and identify the primary cause as transaction costs and the control of opportunism, and those who start from the insights of Penrose, Chandler and Odagiri,[2] seeing the firm as a 'bundle of resources'. Among the most important resources cited are the skills and knowledge of their workers and what Chandler called 'organizational capabilities'. It is the nature of debate to highlight differences, and many authors recognize that it is artificial to treat the opportunism-based and resource-based theories as mutually exclusive (e.g. Conner and Prahalad, 1996; Kogut and Zander, 1996).

The theory of employment systems developed here offers a synthetic view of the two approaches. The restraint of opportunism is necessary for the development of a stable employment relationship, and that is the foundation on which resource-based theories may be built. But also, the appropriate employment rules in a given context have themselves to be learned, so that one might think of them both as a part of the relevant skills and as a basis for other learned organizational routines for cooperation and problem-solving.

The restraint of opportunism is necessary not so much because every individual is seeking to defect in pursuit of short-term self-interest but because we need to be sure that when we cooperate with others, they will reciprocate. Whatever the intrinsic interest of many jobs, employment is primarily an instrumental exchange, and the very conditions that make the *ex post* definition of duties so useful also create a rich bed of potential opportunism. The uncertainty of demand, and the difficulty of analysing and defining tasks that involve a large element of tacit knowledge and skill, which make the relationship so useful, also give rise to major informational asymmetries on both sides. Add to this the economic nature of the exchange and the costs of job changing for employees or of replacing workers with the right skills, and the conditions for opportunism are ripe. If the environment were stable, then a gradual process of 'tit-for-tat' cooperation might develop, but markets are rarely so, and the regularity of unanticipated shocks means that often firms cannot maintain the most sincerely intended commitments to their employees. Good faith is sometimes hard to distinguish from bad faith. Given such problems, why should any party, firm or worker agree to such an open-ended relationship?

The answer has been shown to lie in the way in which the transaction rules provide flexible limits to management authority and to the obligations which employees enter into with their employers. These were shown to restrain potential opportunism both over work assignments and the difficult issue of quality of performance. Without these protections, the employment relationship would not work, and firms would not exist as employing organizations. Hence, control of opportunism is central to the theory of the firm as an employer, but it is also a platform for many other things that firms do. Although it is not possible to do justice to the growing literature on the resource-based and knowledge-based theories of the firm, it is possible to show how far the approach of this book also offers a form of human resource-based theory of the firm. The answer lies in the way the transaction rules influence patterns of organizational learning by establishing some of its basic routines, the way they shape the boundaries of skill flexibility, the control systems they establish and their requirements for trust relations within the enterprise. These are reviewed in the coming sections.

2.1 Organizational learning

Learning is often thought of as an individual process because our first instinct is to think introspectively about our own learning activities. Of course, all learning involves an individual element, but the knowledge generated is often also collective. Learning to drive, for example, is an individual process, yet many of the key routines we are taught have a collective outcome. To enter a roundabout, we learn to give priority to vehicles coming from the right (that is, in Britain, where vehicles drive on the left). This is a simple routine, but it ensures a collective outcome that is also learned, namely, a smooth flow of traffic through the road system. It only works if every driver respects it. Like many such routines, it also economizes on knowledge, as we need to know nothing about the destinations of other drivers, just that they will also respect the same rule and that they expect us to. Such coordination routines, as Nelson and Winter (1982) call them, are an essential component of organizational knowledge. One can therefore regard the adaptation and revision of such routines as a key element of organizational, as opposed to individual, learning.

Part of the learning of such routines consists of discovering when to make exceptions to the rule. In the roundabout example, trying to be 'too polite' and waiving one's priority will usually generate confusion and delay, but there are occasions when it is better to do so. Some are prescribed, as for vehicles on emergency calls, but some are discretionary, such as making way for a truck with an awkward load. In similar fashion, several of the writers cited in this book mention cases in which precise application of the transaction rules is regularly waived in the interests of smooth working, but they remain there as a guide, and to fall back on when in dispute. The application of a rule mechanically has to be learned, but is relatively simple. What is more complex is learning how to be guided by a rule when it is applied flexibly, especially when that same flexibility could be used to erode the rule's integrity.

Beyond simple coordination, employment transaction rules have been shown to exert a strong influence on on-the-job learning and on approaches to problem-solving activities. These, and especially the latter, are key sources of organizational learning. On-the-job learning ensures the reproduction of the stock of organizational knowledge among new recruits and employees moving to new jobs within the organization. It was argued earlier that the job classification systems in which the transaction rules are incorporated are holistic in the sense that they determine the interrelationships and equivalencies among jobs within organizations. These guide members of the organization both on acceptable patterns of job performance, and on what to expect from the holders of other job roles. The performance demands expected from a given job will be strongly influenced by the demands actually met by holders of other jobs similarly classified within the organization.

Problem-solving activities have received a great deal of prominence as organizations have sought to escape the limitations of top-down control systems and as people have become aware of the success of Japanese quality control circles (Cole, 1989). Each of the four transaction rules opens up different possibilities for such activities. They influence organizational learning partly by the way they shape work roles and partly by the incentives that they offer for cooperation. As mentioned on several occasions, the work post rule gives rise to a top-down approach, in contrast with the competence rank rule, which encourages job-level problem-solving. The job territory rule gives rise to broader problem-solving activities than the work post owing to the identification of jobs with occupational skills, but such activities are generally confined within the occupation. In contrast, the qualification rule, by virtue of the weaker correspondence between tasks and jobs allows a more free-ranging approach. Problem-solving activities have a large contextual element in all organizations, some of which may contribute to general experience, but much is also specific to the organization, and thus part of the stock of knowledge that is specific to the organization.

The impact of differences in the methods of organizing collective learning and knowledge associated with the different transaction rules can be illustrated by Lam's (1997) study of collaboration between British and Japanese computer engineers in the case of a joint venture between two major computer firms. It is one of the very rare ethnographic studies in this area. The British engineers were accustomed to a pattern of specialized work roles along the lines of their occupational skills, coupled with managers who acted as specialist coordinators. The Japanese, on the other hand, had broad and overlapping jobs and were supervised by 'player-managers', who combined professional and coordinating work roles. The British engineers sent on placements to the Japanese firm complained that they could not work effectively. They had few written manuals to refer to; work roles were blurred and unclear; and they saw a general state of confusion: 'it's like waiting for revolution' (p. 982) as one young engineer commented. The methods of coordination and problem-solving, clearly influenced by the prevailing societal models, were incompatible even among a group that had undergone broadly similar initial training as graduate engineers. Without judging whether one was more effective than the other, it is clear that there were quite different methods of organizing work roles and distributing knowledge within the two organizations. There was considerable difficulty in translating the results of one method of problem-solving into those of the other in order to enable engineers from the two backgrounds to work together effectively.

Thus, the study of the transaction rules underpinning the employment relationship offers a basis for a theory of the firm in which the different methods of restraining opportunism provide different bases for strategies of organizational learning. It is not that opportunism must be contained before one can begin to build organizational knowledge, but that the same transaction rules provide frameworks for resolving both problems.

3. FLEXIBILITY, PRODUCTIVITY AND SKILLS

The four transaction rules give rise to different organizational models of skills and job flexibility, thus giving greater content to the notion 'resource-based' theories of the firm. Combining the two contractual constraints of efficiency and enforceability leads to four different models of skill formation and job flexibility. The production approach is associated with internal-labour-market-type skills, and the training approach with those of occupational markets. In addition, the approach taken to enforceability has a major influence on the degree of functional flexibility of those skills (see Chapter 8 §3).

In enterprise internal labour markets, classification systems give uniformity and predictability to the rules governing jobs, and establish a language for dealing with skills and work organization. Nevertheless, they leave the employer more freedom to align job contents with its own production considerations than occurs with the training approach. Thus, adoption of the production approach will mostly generate skills that are not transferable between firms, and with that, a premium for employment stability among workers. When the training approach is linked with occupational markets, which is commonly the case, the opportunity of alternative skilled and professional jobs in other firms reduces workers' dependency on their current firm. So a first prediction is that the training approach and OLMs will facilitate acceptance of numerical flexibility among the firms' skilled work-forces as compared with the production approach.

Functional flexibility, on the other hand, is partly determined by the relationship between the tasks comprising individual workers' jobs, and partly by the approach to enforceability. Task-centred rules are more restrictive than those which are function-centred. The work post system faces two limitations. It gives rise to work stations that are discrete sets of tasks shaped by the technical demands of production, but otherwise only accidentally related to each other. In this sense, overlapping and rotating jobs increase the range of tasks which a particular worker can undertake, but do little to advance their level of skill. So the incentive for functional flexibility is weak. The second limitation arises from tying accountability for performance to individual work posts. This also militates against functional flexibility because it blurs the lines of accountability.

When the *production approach* is combined with function-centred rules, as in the competence rank system, then the incentives for functional flexibility can be strong. Learning the skills that come with new task assignments is treated as broadening job competencies, and given the greater autonomy entrusted to work groups, the greater breadth of skill becomes also greater depth, as it enables a more flexible approach to problem-solving activities. Problems rarely arise neatly packaged along the lines of strictly defined work posts, so the greater the range of knowledge individual workers can apply, the more complex the problems with which they can be entrusted.

With the *training approach*, task assignments are aligned with training provision, but one can also expect differences in the degree of functional flexibility depending on whether the task or function-centred rules are in operation. Generally, it is to be expected that functional flexibility will be higher when the function-centred rule is in operation. Compared with the production approach, the incentives for functional flexibility are somewhat weaker. Skilled and professional workers derive their individual bargaining power from the transferability of their skills and too great a departure from these will undermine their core skills from want of practice, and the addition of competencies as needed by their employer will raise the non-transferable component of their skills.

The four rules underpin different models of skill and flexibility. These patterns do not bring any absolute advantages in terms of productivity or general economic performance. Much depends on the circumstances, as a moment's historical reflection will remind us.

The work post system that underpins the 'bureaucratic employment model', like the job territory system, were, in their day, radical social innovations. The strict definition of work posts enabled Ford to run highly complex factories in which workers lacked a common language of communication. In Ford's Highland Park plant, workers spoke over fifty different languages, and many could barely speak English (Womack *et al.*, 1990: 31). In France, the work post system in its manufacturing sector enabled firms to absorb rapidly large numbers of workers, first from the countryside and later from overseas, and so sustain the golden years of French postwar economic expansion. In British shipbuilding, with employment tied to the production of individual ships, the job territory rule gave rise to a very flexible employment system capable of producing high levels of skill, a clear division of labour within individual projects and great flexibility between them. They were perhaps also well-suited to the 'stop-go' macro-economic policies of the 1950s and 1960s.

Although both systems have had a bad press in recent years, the shift of manufacturing activities to less-developed countries is no doubt facilitated by the great robustness of the work post rule. There has been renewed interest in 'neo-craft' patterns of organization, as firms in advanced industrial countries have sought to divest themselves of some of their long-term employment commitments, and interest has grown again in the flexibility of project-based patterns of organization and careers that span several organizations.

The two function-centred rules were in the limelight during the success of the Japanese and German economies in the 1970s and 1980s, especially because of their success in diversified quality production, which many writers associated with the skills and functional flexibility of their workforces. Recent strains have called into question less the value of these systems than their coverage. The function-centred rules are expensive because of the need for mutual commitment between firms and workers, one of the most important gages of good faith that firms can offer being long-term employment. A number of observers have asked whether it is possible to restrict the number of workers accorded such guarantees to those among whom such flexibility is of greatest economic value.[3]

4. THE QUALITY OF TRUST AND COOPERATION WITHIN THE FIRM

Trust has come to be regarded as an important ingredient in the development of cooperative workplace relations, stressed by Human Resource Management specialists as a factor which builds employee commitment. The 'prisoner's dilemma' is often used to justify this as trusting the other party to cooperate and not to 'defect' is regarded as essential to maintaining reciprocity. However, the debate has given too little attention to the contractual basis for trust. Giving greater recognition to this shows how trust relations can be part of the theory of the firm, as the four transaction rules underpin cooperation and trust in different ways. To see how the firm can be a bearer of trust relations it is helpful to look briefly at Fox's (1974) classic statement of the problem, and the shortcomings of his analysis.

The emphasis that Fox (1974) put on workplace trust as going 'beyond contract' signals a contrast that is both unnecessary and misleading. As Fox sets out the theory of low- and high-trust cycles, the latter are fragile and easily sent into the opposite direction. Essentially, he sees managers' distrust of workers' motivation as leading them to set low-discretion work roles, which in turn engender low-trust behaviour by workers and so reinforce management's initial view. The main factors restraining the downward spiral, in his view, were ideology and power: when workers believed that managers had their interests at heart, and when workers had sufficient power to resist low-discretion work roles. At the time he was writing, consensual ideologies were evaporating with the radicalization of industrial conflict, and new technologies were beginning to erode the power of many established skilled groups. The logical conclusion to his analysis could only be pessimistic, as indeed is much of the analysis based on the 'prisoner's dilemma'. It is easy to slide into the low-cooperation cycle and very hard to break out of it. If we follow Fox's argument, then we should expect the degree of workplace cooperation to be rather lower than it appears to be in fact. The reason lies in his misleading contrast between contract and trust, and his identification of contract with close specification of duties.

In this book, the employment contract is a foundation of cooperation, and potentially also of trust relations in the workplace. As has been seen, the employment contract may be associated with detailed specification of duties, as under the work post system, or it may allow a great deal of freedom. Both specific and diffuse obligations are possible, depending on the type of system. Fox's analysis focused primarily on the work post system, but even though it is a relatively low-trust system, the specification of duties cuts both ways. It protects employers from 'shirking' by employees, but it also protects employees from 'intensification' by their employers. Earlier, it was referred to as a 'safety net' which prevents cooperation from dropping to the level at which the employment relationship would no longer be efficient. The two function-centred transaction rules are more heavily dependent on high-trust relations because they lack the safety net provided by the task-centred rules, but they hold out the compensating gains of greater functional flexibility.

Trust relations may develop around all four types of employment rule, although the parameters are different in each case. The safety net protects against opportunistic action, but at the same time, the flexibility that can develop with increased trust is hampered by both the narrower specification of work roles and by the need to maintain the basic integrity of the rules. Because work roles are interdependent, flexibility in one job has a knock-on effect on others, and a narrowly specified system soon loses its coherence if too much flexibility is encouraged. Likewise, the value of employment rules as a safety net is eroded if work roles deviate too far from their original specifications. In all workplaces there is an important element of tacit knowledge and tacit definition of work, and so custom can quickly establish new norms. If the formal job specifications are hardly ever invoked, they lose

Table 9.1. *Effects of the contractual constraints on human resource systems*

	Efficiency constraint	
Enforceability constraint	Production approach	Training approach
Task-centred	• *Work post*: ILMs • OJT and problem-solving limited by narrow jobs • Low functional & low numerical flexibility for core employees • Tight control & individual accountability • Resistant to low-trust relations	• *Job territory*: OLMs • Problem-solving within clearly defined skills • Low functional & high numerical flexibility • Individual accountability • Resistant to low-trust relations
Function-/ procedure-centred	• *Competence rank*: ILMs • OJT enriched by 'unusual' tasks & group problem-solving • High functional & low numerical flexibility for core employees • Group control & accountability • Requires high trust	• *Qualification*: OLMs • Problem-solving within broad skills • Good functional & good numerical flexibility • Occupational autonomy & accountability • Requires high trust

their force, as customary expectations come to define the boundaries of the job as it is done in practice. This is therefore a limiting factor on how far trust can promote flexible working under the two task-oriented systems. The more-detached nature of employment rules from job contents under the function-oriented rules enables trustful cooperation to be taken further, so long as it does not undermine the procedures on which job flexibility rests. In this way, the employment rules, which constitute the base on which the firm is built, enable one to see how different levels of trust relations can be integrated with the theory of the firm.

The influence of the four types of transaction rule on the areas of human resource management just discussed is summarized in Table 9.1. This shows the extent to which the rules that control opportunism, and so make possible the existence of the firm as an employing organization, also constitute a key part of the human resource architecture of the firm and influence the development of its organizational capabilities.

5. THE ROLE OF INTER-FIRM INSTITUTIONS

Treating the firm as a part of its institutional environment is a central feature of the concept of employment systems. The four types of transaction rule represent four types of institutional structure for the employment relationship, but as argued in Chapters 3 and 4, their effectiveness and diffusion are increased by the support of institutions beyond the boundaries of the individual firm.

5.1 The benefits of inter-firm institutions

The most important contributions of wider, inter-firm institutions lie in the way they:

- reinforce the transaction and classification rules within the enterprise, making them more predictable;
- contribute to workplace trust;
- provide the channels for renegotiation; and
- support occupational and, to a lesser degree, internal labour markets.

Predictability comes from two sources: familiarity with the rules and confidence in their enforcement. The former is increased by their incorporation into familiar job and pay classification systems that are used by many firms. These mean that a large number of the actors know the ground rules and what to expect from them. As explained in Chapter 4, classification systems are holistic, proposing certain principles and using these to organize job categories, establishing contours of similarity among, and demarcations between, different jobs. These are also a guide to the expected quality of performance in different jobs within the organization, and so generally help to base the task allocations on rules and criteria with which workers and their managers are familiar.

Confidence in enforcement is also critical, and, as highlighted in the discussion of secondary labour markets, employer monopsony power can make it hard for employees to defend their understanding of the workloads to which they have agreed. However, the problem extends wider because the individual power of all workers fluctuates over the economic cycle and with changing personal circumstances. Collective representation evens out such variations in individual bargaining power and gives workers greater confidence in their ability to enforce the agreed limits on management authority, should this be necessary. Collective organization across firms extends this 'insurance', or risk-spreading, function of bargaining power. The advantages are not all on one side. Stabilizing the employment relationship also protects employers, helping to retain labour and ensure that it is available when needed. For many groups of workers, their employer's individual bargaining power also fluctuates, and a reliance on threats to gain flexibility may work only when there is excess supply. Internal labour market conditions have often been offered by employers to retain their labour (e.g. Taira, 1970; Osterman, 1982), and it will be remembered that a major reason for the decline of the 'drive system' was that it failed to secure an adequate supply of stable labour as markets tightened.

Workplace trust, which enables workers and management to apply job rules more flexibly, can also be increased by the presence of strong representative institutions, as argued in Chapter 3. Strong institutions can validate the information provided by the other party, checking on their continued good faith, and they can restrain their own members from opportunistic action in the interest of maintaining a good long-term bargaining relationship.

Even though the employment relationship is open-ended, there come times when its terms have to be renegotiated. Job structures become obsolete as consumer demand evolves and new production and organizational technologies emerge. Renegotiation is a tricky time. The basic guarantees offered by the transaction rules to both parties are called into question, and there is uncertainty as to how the new rules will function, and possibly even over the good faith concerning the reasons for change (to raise productivity or to weaken the opposition). There is an additional problem of information asymmetry which militates against individual negotiation, namely that while the employer has a view of the whole set of new jobs, employees see only their individual jobs. As a result, there is a strong temptation to resist change because of the uncertain outcome and limited means that individual employees have to control it. Collective negotiation in the firm, as argued in Chapter 3, introduces an important degree of flexibility, and this can be enhanced if negotiators at this level know too that they can call on outside advice and support from the relevant union or employers' organization. Otherwise, the main options for management are to rely on superior power to push change through, with the risk of damaging workplace cooperation over the longer run, or to pay for change. In the latter case, the likely financial cost could well prove higher than with collective representation because of the need to neutralize employee fears.

The final major area concerns especially occupational markets, which, it was argued, are dependent on strong institutions to maintain their stability. When employers bear a significant part of the cost of training for transferable skills, there arises scope for some employers to profit from the training by others by poaching their skilled labour. It was shown, in Chapter 8, that employer organizations particularly can provide a channel for peer group pressures to ensure that all firms engage in a reasonable level of training. Employee organizations can also help close off a number of practices likely to erode occupational markets, notably by monitoring training quality and the maintenance of the training approach.

Notwithstanding these arguments, collective power can be used both positively and negatively. As Freeman and Medoff (1984) warn, there are 'two faces' to unionism, one of which enhances productivity while the other bargains over economic rents. Traditional economic analysis has tended to stress the latter, although recent British evidence indicates that union wage mark-ups tend to follow employers' product market power, so the significance of the 'monopoly' face may be exaggerated (Stewart, 1990; Metcalf, 1993). This of course follows from the standard analysis of the derived demand for labour. If consumers can switch easily to other products or alternative sources of supply, then the power of unions to bargain-up pay will be limited. The same analysis would apply to effort levels. Potentially more serious is the neutralization of the productivity face by adversarial relations, a theme touched on later.[4]

5.2 Consequences of Institutional Weakness

One of the reasons for trying to understand the nature of employment systems by going back to Coase and Simon lay in the growth of the non-union sector in Britain and especially in the United States. If labour institutions are so important, why should so many US firms opt for what Wachter described as 'non-union internal labour markets' (Wachter, 1995), and why should so many studies suggest that non-union workplaces with flexible working practices should outperform other patterns, and especially traditional union and non-union ones (e.g. Ichniowski, 1990). Such studies would seem to show that many US firms are not concerned about their weak institutional environment, and indeed, that they regard it as a benefit.

There are, however, a number of consequences:

- limited and uneven diffusion of high performance workplaces;
- the sustainability of new work systems is reduced in the absence of supporting institutions; and
- a hostile environment impedes the diffusion of high-performance systems, leaving others trapped in the work post system.

(a) Limited and uneven diffusion

Recent US surveys by Lawler *et al.* (1992) of large firms, and by Osterman (1994) of manufacturing plants, show a significant minority of US plants using innovative human resource practices and flexible work organization. However, the same surveys also show that the number of firms practising a full range of high-performance work practices is quite limited. In Lawler's (1992) study, although about one in five Fortune 1000 firms had adopted a range of practices for more than 40% of their employees, the authors noted that only 7% could be described as 'high users' of employee involvement. Similarly, Osterman (1994) found a large number of firms used at least one new practice, but only 5% used all four practices cited in his survey. Such piecemeal adoption of high-performance work practices is all the more noteworthy for the evidence that the best outcomes are obtained when practices are adopted as part of a consistent whole, as Kling (1995) reports in his review for the US Department of Labor. This was also the view of Appelbaum and Batt (1994) in their study of American best practice: why was diffusion limited and uneven given the potential benefits?

Among the innovatory practices, team working is particularly interesting because it, more than most others, characterizes the move from the work post in the direction of the function-oriented systems of job definition. Comparing team working in the US and German automobile industries, and, notably, the flagship NUMMI plant with similar experiments in German auto plants, Turner (1991) observed that the range of task assignments, job cycle times and group decision-making within teams was considerably greater in Germany than the US. In the latter country, the teams were smaller, more hierarchical and more segmented by skill levels. The case studies of team working in the US also indicate narrower jobs and less job-rotation than in Koike's studies of Japan. Although Turner and Auer's (1994) comparisons are mainly based on *unionized* workplaces, they show that within the US there is a great diversity between plants in team design, success rates, and the extent of union influence. Even within GM, the success of its NUMMI plant, as well as that of one or two other schemes, contrasts with failure in a number of other GM plants, such as Van Nuys and Hamtrack. The former could not be made to work and was eventually closed, and in the latter, the team principles were subsequently diluted in management's drive to raise production.

(b) Instability without institutional support

In their wide-ranging review, Appelbaum and Batt (1994) argued that many new work schemes had been unable to sustain early success over time because of changes in management policy resulting from changes in management personnel and in company circumstances. This left employees who had supported new schemes exposed, and generally undermined the mutual trust on which more flexible working practices depend. They argued that union support provides a major organizational asset for introducing reforms because of the greater employee confidence in the outcome. Supporting this conclusion, Eaton and Voos (1992) found unionized plants more likely to accompany new work practices with participation, and non-union ones with profit sharing. Given the greater sharing of management control in participation, this suggests that the more radical schemes occurred in unionized workplaces. Likewise, Kochan and Osterman (1994) argue that recent empirical work of their own and others indicates that the 'active involvement and support of unions increases the sustainability of the innovation process' (Kochan and Osterman, 1994: 105).

In connection with team work, Turner and Auer (1994) concluded that the greater the union involvement, and the more cooperative its stance (the two tend to go together because without the latter there would be little involvement), the more successful and durable are the schemes. The more top-down the approach, the more likely it was that teamwork experiments would be unstable and encounter greater opposition both from within management and from the workforce, as indeed had occurred with quality circles a decade earlier (Hill, 1991).[5]

(c) Inhibiting pressures of a hostile environment

A number of environmental factors have been stressed as potential explanations why the 'American models of high performance'[6] have not achieved wider diffusion, and why so many American firms remain caught within the work post system. It has been argued that high performance firms face problems of 'adverse selection', as the greater employment security they offer attracts less-industrious employees who would be sacked by traditional firms. Their higher skill levels make them rich poaching grounds for other employers; and the long lead times before the investments in new practices bear fruit make the firms very vulnerable to competition from traditionally organized 'cost minimizing firms'. Although none of these arguments has been tested, they are all consistent with the evidence of positive gains from participatory and other flexible working practices,[7] and the low rate of adoption by firms that could potentially benefit from them.

Thus, indirectly, the American non-union sector's experience supports the argument of this book. Firms may opt for the non-union form of ILM because mostly they have versions of the work post system. Of the four transaction rules, this one makes the smallest demands on institutional support, and can function with the lowest levels of workplace trust. The weak institutional environment also appears as one of the obstacles to US firms wishing to break out and to make use of the more functionally flexible employment systems based on function-centred rules. Some firms have managed to avoid the rigidities of work post organization, but generally they have done so by isolating themselves from their labour market environment. For the IBMs and Hewlett Packards of this world, this has involved the considerable expense of establishing their own employee management systems. Arguably, the cost would have been lower had such practices been more widely diffused across the economy, and, of course, they can be afforded only by firms able to pay a significant wage premium.

(d) France: the consequences of institutional weakness

France offers another example of a society in which workplace unionism is weak, this time despite legal support, and where the work post model of organization is very widespread. There, much evidence attests to the

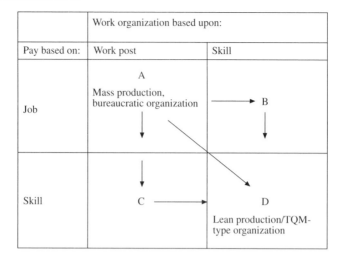

Fig. 9.1. Transition paths from job-based to skill-based work systems
Source: Baraldi *et al.* (1995).

difficulty of breaking away from the work post model, favoured by past union weakness and adversarial relations, and its logic has tended to persist when new work systems have been introduced.

There, the process of change has been made more visible by the 1982 Auroux laws promoting company agreements. As these provide one route out of the constraints of industry level agreements, they offer a window onto how firms are approaching the move to high performance systems. Yet the survey of innovative company agreements on pay systems and work organization by Baraldi *et al.* (1995) found[8] that their number was limited. Even more significant, French firms also found it very hard to break out of the work post system, as French workers lacked workplace representatives with sufficient strength to defend their interests under the new systems. The desire to hang onto the protections of the work post system forced many companies to take indirect strategies, leading to inconsistency between their pay and skill systems. Either they would retain the work post system for jobs and try to promote pay based on employee competencies, or they tried to adopt more flexible jobs while retaining traditional pay principles. In Figure 9.1, this involved either box C or box B, respectively. In both cases, the inconsistencies generated considerable tensions, lack of trust and resistance by employees.

5.3 Function and form of labour institutions

Throughout, this book has been fairly silent on the precise form of labour institutions, stressing their functions rather than their form. Yet, given the dual capacity of unions and other representative bodies for both cooperation and conflict, some structures will be more likely to inspire employer confidence in cooperation. Likewise, institutions able to underpin horizontal coordination across firms are an essential requirement of the training approach.

(a) Cooperative unionism and the function-centred approach

Certain patterns of employee representation are more likely to promote cooperation than others, and so more likely to be found with the function-centred rules. For example, it is possible to have strong representative institutions that are nevertheless structured in such a way as to give considerable powers if used cooperatively, but much less so, if used aggressively, as the author concluded from a comparison of workplace representation in Germany, France and Great Britain (Marsden, 1978). In Germany, the division of powers and mobilizing capacity between unions, works councils and employee board-level representatives has given German workers considerable influence over management and wide powers of codecision-making in many job-related areas. At the same time, it has meant that these powers could not so easily be used aggressively. The confinement of the right to strike to industry-level unions, coupled with the peace obligation on works councils, means that it is difficult to use works council strength to mobilize support for industrial action by the union. Likewise, the focus of unions' strength on industry agreements means it is hard to apply their power directly to individual companies. Board-level representation gives considerable access to company information, which no doubt enables representatives better to interpret management positions, and to assess whether they are able to reciprocate cooperative action by employees, but it cannot be used aggressively.

This division of powers is partly a consequence of the law, but also partly of design by unions and employers. The critical features of both industry-level bargaining and the dominant role of works councils in the workplace are primarily the result of choices by employer and employee organizations. Two examples show this. In the early 1960s, Ford, which had wished to remain outside the metal industry employers' organization, found itself forced by the industrial union and its sister employer organization to fall in with industry bargaining. Facing a successful organizing drive from IG Metall, and the likelihood that it would be forced into direct bargaining with Germany's most powerful union, plus coaxing from the employers, in spring 1963, it decided to sign up with the employers and join the industry bargaining system (Delp et al., 1974). Likewise, in the 1960s and 1970s, the maintenance of the works council as the employer's key negotiating partner in the workplace depended on the determination of both employers and councils to resist growing pressures for shop steward bargaining. At the time, shopfloor power was sweeping away formal representation structures in Britain and Italy. In Germany, neither the unions nor the employers wanted this group of actors to undermine a cooperative institutional balance which had helped deliver Germany's economic miracle. In Japan too, the powers of enterprise unions, as they have grown up since the middle 1950s, are largely conditional on cooperative action. Like their German counterparts, they benefit from considerable information from management, and over the years, they have been able to judge its relevance and reliability (Nakamura, 1997). In both cases, employers came to accept the logic of their work organization, and thus to accept the need for strong, independent, but cooperative employee representatives.

In contrast, employee representation in the other three countries reflects a more adversarial style of representation, and one that is consistent with the task-centred job rules, as these provide cooperation at lower levels of trust than in either Germany or Japan. Given these work systems, employers, and indeed unions, have been less interested in workplace cooperation. In both the US and Britain, it was not until the 1980s that either unions or management showed much interest in employee participation. Unions generally saw it as undermining their bargaining independence, and employers mostly considered it of limited use. The contrast between France and Germany is particularly revealing because of the rough similarity of many representative institutions since the 1950s, and yet their very different style of working (Lorenz, 1995). Whereas German works councils have generally functioned in a cooperative manner, those in France have developed a more confrontational ethos. Gallie (1983) has ascribed this to the polarization between workers and management, and others have stressed the ideological opposition of the communist-led CGT to capitalist management. However, it is also clear that given the work post system, the need for flexible working has been limited. The work post system creates the polarization that Gallie noted because of the division between conception and execution, and that also makes the ideological polarization of management issues appear relevant to workers whatever their general impatience with the political in-fighting between the unions. As was seen in Chapters 2 and 6, job flexibility has little place in the rational plan of the work post system, and because management has no obvious way of rewarding it, it is safer to avoid any need for it. Thus, one can see how the solution to the enforceability constraint can affect the evolution of labour representation as it responds to the needs generated by the employment relationship.

(b) Horizontal coordination and the training approach

The other axis is between the production and the training approaches. A critical factor in the success of the training approach is the capacity for horizontal coordination among the actors. As argued in Chapter 8, in contrast to the production approach, the training approach and the associated occupational markets place a heavy burden on inter-firm coordination over questions of skill development and job design. In essence, they need some

kind of occupational community to underpin these. In Germany, cooperation among employers has played a key role; in Britain, professional and
craft occupational communities have been central; and recent studies of
Silicon Valley (e.g. Tolbert, 1996) and of 'industrial districts' suggest that
similar factors are critical there.

Because much training is provided locally and in the workplace, as is the
monitoring of its quality and of adherence to the training approach, the
institutions supporting occupational structures need to be decentralized.
As argued in Chapter 8, the German chambers have successfully supported
intermediate level vocational training because they have robust signals of
firms' training activity at their disposal, and plenty of opportunity for informal peer group pressures within local business communities to discourage
individual employers from breaking ranks. While these are held in check,
high rates of employer training mean that no firm faces a competitive disadvantage by contributing to the pool of skilled labour available to all local
firms. The strong workplace support for the training system from works
councils dominated by skilled workers also discourages firms from free-
riding. In Britain, Elbaum's (1990) evidence showed that, up to the early
part of the twentieth century, informal networks among local employers
had also been strong, and were certainly strong enough to prevent individual
employers from hiring 'run-away' apprentices—the factor which had proved
so destructive to apprenticeship in the US. The decline of apprenticeship in
Britain from the 1960s illustrates the problems posed when the institutional
framework fails to carry local employers. This threw the burden onto union
action: to let apprentice pay rise in an effort to control substitution of
apprentice for fully-trained labour; and to defend the training approach by
the well-known job demarcation rules. Such factors both raised the overall
cost of training (by raising trainee pay), and increased the rigidity of skilled
work, making apprenticeship increasingly unattractive to employers.

Could the state intervene to reverse an ailing apprenticeship system?
Several factors limit its capacity. The most important is that employer and
employee organizations need to 'own' the system, and take responsibility for
making it work. Heavy state involvement brings the danger that the other
two parties will look to the state for a solution, and try to throw their
responsibility onto the other parties. Cole's (1989) study of the development
of quality control circles into a 'mass movement' across Japanese industry
also illustrates the importance of building employer commitment as opposed
to state intervention (see Ch. 4 §6). Secondly, when enforcement depends
upon action by local employers and employee bodies, there is a stronger
incentive for the parties to act when it is their own system that they are
enforcing than when it 'belongs' to the state. Thirdly, when skills involve tacit
knowledge, and their quality is a practical issue, it is often better that practitioners should settle the difficult issues themselves. For these reasons, the
German construction employers fought hard to keep the state out of administration of their scheme (Streeck, 1985), and, when the British government

sought to standardize job competencies it found itself dragged into defining not just the levels of performance, but also what margins of variation to allow for different local circumstances. What had been intended as simple, practical definitions of skills ended up by requiring complex manuals (Wolf, 1994). The problem is that the state tends to act legalistically, making things explicit, which militates against effective treatment of tacit skill performance norms. One occasion when state action has appeared more hopeful in this area has been in trying to stimulate local employers to build their own training networks based on the government-launched Training and Enterprise Councils (Marsden, 1995). The jury is still out on whether these local employer-led bodies can assume the activities covered by the German chambers and attract the degree of support the latter enjoy. Although it is state action, it is designed to stimulate local organization and initiatives by the key actors themselves, and is focused on developing procedures rather than a top-down national training policy focused purely on outcomes. One of its major weaknesses lies in the dominant role given to employers at the expense of employee representatives.

There are many benefits to a joint and balanced approach by employers and employees. As argued in Chapter 8, a viable occupational market needs the confidence of both employers and employees. This concerns not only levels of investment, but also the spirit with which skilled work is regulated. The impact of one-sided enforcement in Britain was to cause greater rigidity as compared with Germany. This was not just a result of the tools-of-the-trade rule. It stemmed also from the weaknesses of joint institutions, which meant the market's integrity depended upon applying job rules more strictly than otherwise. Only in this way could workers defend the training approach at a time when other aspects of the skill system were being eroded. The less evenly balanced and the more confrontational relations become, the more one is pushed towards the more robust task-centred rules. For the production approach, inter-firm relations play a more limited role, except, as was argued, that externally sanctioned classification rules provide a more robust framework than firm-specific ones.

5.4 Models of corporate governance

Just as unions and employer organizations may be organized for cooperative or for adversarial strategies, so firms' higher management may be geared for different types of personnel policy. In recent years, the merits of 'shareholder' and the employee 'stakeholder' views of capitalist enterprises have been hotly debated,[9] and in particular, the extent to which one or other model better favours long-term investment in human resources and high-performance work systems. On the whole, the argument has been that the incentives of the shareholder model favour tight financial management, whereas those that give greater emphasis to employees as stakeholders favour investments in skills and in cooperative employee management systems. Because human resource investments and their returns are so hard to measure, they tend to be neglected by the main financial indicators except in so far as the investments appear as costs, whereas the returns are not separately identified anywhere. As a result, if human resource investments are to be assessed, it is generally better done when shareholders or lenders are able to monitor performance closely. This implies high costs and a close relationship with the firm, and therefore a concentration of investments in a small number of firms. Thus, efficient stakeholder models will require different patterns of top management from orthodox shareholder models. In particular, they require a combination of large individual share- or debt holdings to enable intensive monitoring, and a rich flow of human resource information that is assisted by employee voice in top management.

There is evidence that a mild form of employee stakeholder capitalism exists in both Germany and Japan in which both shareholder and employee interests are reflected. In contrast, in Britain and the US, and possibly France, shareholder interests are given a freer reign. In a recent study, Prowse (1994) assembled a number of financial and institutional indicators contrasting Germany and Japan, on the one hand, with the US and Britain on the other. On these, Britain and the US differed markedly from Japan and Germany. Compared with the latter pair of countries, firms in Britain and the US made more use of equity finance and were characterized by smaller individual holdings; and when financial institutions held their shares they tended to do so as agents rather than owners. They were also less subject to interlocking share ownership and less likely to have banks or major shareholders on the board; and their management was more exposed to hostile take-overs. In other words, firms in Germany and Japan were more likely to be subject to intensive monitoring by owners and major creditors, whereas US and British firms were subject to simpler monitoring, but their managers were subject to the discipline of losing their jobs in a hostile take-over. In addition, in large German firms, employees have a statutory right to representation on the board, and in many large Japanese companies, intensive communication takes place between management and the enterprise union.

Such a complex issue cannot be dealt with in a few paragraphs, but Prowse's evidence at least suggests that there may be a counterpart in the governance of firms that reflects the choices made at the level of the employment relationship. This raises very important questions of causation: whether corporate governance structures have shaped the choices governing the employment relationship; whether the type of employment relationship has determined the mode of corporate governance selected; or whether there is an interactive relationship between the two. A brief comparison of the way employee interests as stakeholders are institutionalized in Germany as compared with Britain illustrates the complexity of the relationship between the two levels, and suggests a pattern of interactive causation.

Employee voice in and monitoring of top management decisions did not suddenly occur in German firms. Instead, it evolved over a number of decades from the early post-war legislation, with the setting up of supervisory boards of large coal and steel firms with parity employee representation to the 1976 legislation which extended this to all large public companies. A more limited form of board-level representation outside the coal and steel sector had been set up in 1952, and the 1976 law brought this up towards the coal and steel level. Although the law was hotly contested, including an appeal by employers to the Constitutional court, its passage was greatly favoured by the report of a parliamentary commission chaired by a Christian Democrat senator, Kurt Biedenkopf. That report found that the existing system of codetermination had worked well, and according to the law's prescription, in a spirit of 'trustful cooperation' (Biedenkopf, 1970). The involvement of employee representatives in corporate governance had been seen to be working well, and so was extended. Also in the 1970s, in Britain, a government committee of enquiry was set up to look into proposals for employee representation at board level, giving rise to the Bullock Report (1977). Neither employers nor unions were particularly interested in the outcome, nor could the report point to much successful experience in Britain, and it was quickly ignored. Most employers could see little value in either employee or union involvement in board decisions. The unions were concerned that they lacked the organizational skills and personnel to benefit from it, and feared that involvement in management decisions would damage their ability to bargain on their members' behalf. Thus, in both countries, the current practice of employee relations was influential in deciding whether the prevailing systems of corporate governance should be amended to give greater employee voice.

The British–German example suggests two conclusions. The diffusion of the various models of employment relationship will be affected by the ability of corporate governance systems to support the investments in human resources and trust required for the two function-centred rules. In addition, especially in relation to employee stakeholder involvement, the evolution of corporate governance systems will be influenced by the type of employment rules that predominate. The strong shareholder model goes well with the task-centred, and especially the work post, model, whereas the two function-centred rules are likely to favour greater employee involvement on a formal or informal basis. The stakeholder models provide a framework which helps give durability to management commitment to high performance policies, the lack of which, Appelbaum and Batt (1994) argued, had undermined employee involvement and participation in the US.

6. SOCIETAL DIVERSITY OF EMPLOYMENT SYSTEMS

It has become increasingly common to treat national vocational education systems, labour law and industrial relations systems as sources of societal diversity in employment. Behind this lie two implicit assumptions: that the rules emanating from them are in some sense exogenous to, or determined independently of, employment systems; and that the institutions are societal in their span of influence. Several pieces of evidence in this book suggest that the first assumption is mistaken,[10] as is the common, but rather crude, identification of the 'societal' with a 'national-institutional' effect.

The theory of employment systems offers an alternative view of societal diversity in employment, one based on the solutions to the problem of how to regulate managerial authority while at same time providing organizational flexibility. Employment systems are institutional frameworks which enable firms and workers to organize their collaboration while protecting both parties from certain kinds of opportunistic behaviour. They may be considered as institutions at two levels. First, even in sectors from which collective representation is absent, the pressures on firms and workers to conform to the prevailing methods of contracting are very powerful. In this sense, even though each decision by a firm and its workers may be taken individually, there are strong pressures to conformity, and we witness a process of institutionalization of prevailing employment norms. These pressures do not necessarily arise from direct constraints on the parties but, as argued in Chapter 3, from the benefits that stem from using commonly applied rules. It is important that people trust the rules by which they bind themselves. They need to be confident in how they function in different circumstances, and in their ability to restrain common kinds of opportunistic behaviour. The rule then comes to be adopted even though it may not be the one best suited to a particular type of service, because people prefer a rule with which they are familiar and which they trust. The continued strength of the work post system, despite attempts to move to more flexible models, derives from the confidence of firms and workers in how it functions. Introducing more flexible rules brings a considerable degree of risk, especially as they lack the safety net of minimum prescribed performance. This is very much the sense of 'institutionalization' of Powell and DiMaggio (1991). As they diffuse across an economy, the transaction rules are transformed from being techniques for solving the problems of opportunism in employer–employee relations into a social institution. In abstraction from the actions of other firms and workers, the choice might simply be one of choosing the arrangements that optimize results for them. However, as the rule spreads, its effectiveness increases because more people are familiar with it and know the outcomes to expect. Like queuing, people are more likely to queue if they are confident that everyone else will respect the same rule, and they are more confident if they know that the rule is widely used. In this respect, the work post system functions as a set of institutional rules even in the non-union sector. Its power was illustrated by the problems encountered by American employers seeking workplace transformation. The second level of institutionalization concerns the contribution of supporting institutions to the effectiveness of employment rules, as outlined in Chapter 3 and summarized earlier in this chapter. These imply a greater degree of direct constraint on firms and workers to obey certain norms, but they also help consolidate the benefits.

As a result, the employment relationship may be considered a core institution within the firm. Its diversity stems from the choice of transaction rules underpinning it. Their nature is that of social institutions rather than being alternative blue-prints for contracting owing to the pressures for conformity they induce. As stressed earlier, these stem both from the advantages of adopting widely-used norms, and often from the labour institutions supporting them. The institutionalization penetrates deep into the heart of relations within the modern business enterprise, shaping the very nature of managerial authority. This influence is not merely formal, and several chapters have explored the very concrete effects on key areas of firms' human resource and labour policies. These concerned notably job classification, performance management, pay, and skills and labour mobility.

Classification is a holistic activity in which we set out from certain principles and divide up work into different types of jobs. These principles are determined by the four types of transaction rules. The precise job boundaries and one-to-one assignments of the work post system call for one approach to analysing tasks, whereas the diffuse boundaries of the competence rank system imply a different one. For the same basic work, individual tasks may be defined, separated out and assigned differently under the two systems. Likewise, the chapter on performance showed that the logic of employment systems penetrated into the most 'intimate' zones of management prerogative. The same forces of potential opportunism and the rules aimed at dealing with them greatly circumscribed the definition of job performance quality. The definition and measurement of work performance is not just a question of management's deciding what kind of services it wants from its employees, because these have to be defined in a way that both sides feel to be resistant to opportunism. The threat of opportunism chases out subtlety of definition, and the constitutive rules of the employment relationship shape four different approaches to performance criteria. The chapter on pay sought to show that the price of labour is, first and foremost, a rule determining the way rewards will follow employees' performance obligations. That price is multidimensional, in the image of the complexity of labour services and the obligations incurred in their use. With such a conception of pay, it was then shown that the different transaction rules shaped a number of key aspects of pay structures and performance incentives. Again, this has been an area in which Human Resource Management scholars have approached management's reward policies largely in terms of intra-organizational factors. Similarly, the chapter on skills and labour market structures sought to demonstrate the impact of the transaction rules and related institutions on training and mobility opportunities within internal and occupational labour markets. Thus, in four major areas of human resource management, it has been shown that employment systems condition the choices facing managers.

Consequently, an interpretation of the 'societal effect' established empirically by Maurice *et al.* (1986) is that firms in a particular context will manage their human resources in a similar fashion because of the way in which the employment relationship has been institutionalized there. Such institutionalization is not an 'iron cage' because individual firms may still experiment and go outside such norms, but, in general, this is more costly and success is more risky than if the patterns they adopted were widely diffused in their locality. There is an analogy with the efficiency wage theory:[11] firms can break out of the prevailing pattern of employment relations, but they must pay a price. There is also a price if firms seek to opt out at the lower end of the labour market since, as argued in Chapter 8, use of secondary labour markets usually restricts firms to variants of the work post model.

These institutional processes underlie the 'societal effect'. It is 'societal' rather than 'national' because it stems from the influence of employment systems rather than a top-down effect from national governments and their agencies. It is also 'societal' because the empirical outcomes identified in Chapter 5 correspond to widely diffused employment practices in the countries concerned, but this does not imply uniformity within societies. Individual firms may decide, at some expense, to go their own way, and different rules may predominate in different large sectors or for large groups of employees. For example, in many countries, construction and some craft industries apply a variant of the training approach, even though the production approach holds sway in the industrial sector. Likewise, the competence rank model prevails across large parts of Japanese industry, but there too, in some craft sectors and for some licensed occupations there are systems of occupational skills (e.g. Ohkusha *et al.*, 1997). In the US, Silicon Valley and Hollywood have been extensively studied as examples of new occupation-based systems breaking away from the established 'bureaucratic' systems built on the work post. Such exceptions to the dominant norm within a national environment open up the possibility of innovation and change, but there is also a question mark over their longer term stability. Lam (1998), for example, has argued that the Silicon Valley model is dynamic but unstable because of the tension between the tacit firm-based knowledge needed for high rates of innovation and new products, and the high levels of job mobility needed for the rapid diffusion of new ideas. In particular, it lacks the well-structured occupational community that underpins occupational skills where the training approach is more institutionalized, as it is in Germany.

There is a final sense in which one should distance 'societal' from 'national' diversity: societal patterns may span national borders. In practice, this does not occur so often because many of the institutions underpinning employment systems have coincided with national jurisdictions. However, as Piore (1994) has observed, inter-state commerce in the US played a large part in diffusing employment norms from one state to another, the railway companies being particularly important in this because their workforces had to operate across state borders. In the European Union, currently, similar processes are beginning because of the gradual knitting of bonds between firms, employer organizations and unions across national borders within the EU. It was argued earlier that firms could only combine different employment principles by segmenting their workforces. But as firms seek increased interaction among their key staff across national borders, segmentation becomes progressively harder to practise and it becomes an obstacle to flexible organization. Lam's (1997) study of collaboration between Japanese and British computer engineers cited earlier illustrates just how far incompatible organization can be an obstacle to effective working, and it shows the concern of the two firms to resolve this. The gains from access to complementary organizational capabilities and market expertise across the EU give firms a strong incentive to tackle such problems. They have to do so within a fixed menu of types of employment relationship. As a result, the solutions that they develop will lead to the gradual spread of societal norms across national borders. In the long run, their success will also depend upon their being followed by the essential supporting institutions. Within the EU, a number of initiatives are currently preparing the way for this. They include the European social dialogue between unions and employers, the greater contact among employee representatives within multinational firms established by European Works Councils and the greater contacts between regional bodies across national borders. Over the coming decades, such forces are likely to drive an increasing wedge between national jurisdictions and the scope of societal influences.

ENDNOTES

[1] Recent evidence for Britain, Germany and the US is reviewed in Marsden (1995); for France see Géhin and Méhaut (1993), and Japan, see Dore and Sako (1989).

[2] See Penrose (1959), Odagiri (1984) and Chandler (1990).

[3] This point was raised both in the reactions to Moody's downgrading of Japanese firms' credit worthiness and in the *Economist* Magazine's review of the Japanese economy, (see: *Financial Times* (22.11.94) 'Lifetime jobs may hurt company competitiveness'; *Economist* (9.7.94) 'Oriental renaissance: a survey of Japan').

[4] Several recent US studies have highlighted the effect of differences between co-

operative and adversarial union-management relations on productivity and work-place reform, e.g. Cutcher-Gershenfeld (1991) and Belman (1992).

[5] In fact, Hill draws a somewhat different conclusion from the quality circle experience. He agrees that consistent support from top management is essential, but takes the view that it is sufficient, hence his faith in the success of TQM, where quality circles failed.

[6] The term is taken from Appelbaum and Batt (1994).

[7] For a review of the evidence on gains from workplace participation, see Levine and Tyson (1990).

[8] Their number is significant because the 1982 Auroux laws opened the way for widespread company negotiations on such issues. Given the very high coverage of French workers by collective agreements, this channel opens up a means by which firms can legitimate policies that seek to break away from the established work post system. The likelihood is that those firms not using it remain with the work post system incorporated into industry classification agreements.

[9] For a straightforward review, see Parkinson (1996), and Kay and Silberston (1995). Parkinson reviews a number of different potential stakeholders, ranging from shareholders and employees to customers and those affected by environmental pollution. In this chapter attention is confined to employees and shareholders. Arguments for the reform of corporate governance systems to favour long-term investments in human resources are advanced in Appelbaum and Batt (1994) and in Dertouzos, Lester and Solow (1989).

[10] Examples include apprenticeship reform in France and the extension of codetermination in Germany.

[11] See Akerloff and Yellen (1986).

REFERENCES

Abraham, K. (1990) 'Restructuring the employment relationship: the growth of market-mediated work arrangements'. In Abraham, K. and McKersie, R. (eds), *New Developments in the Labor Market: Toward a New Institutional Paradigm*. MIT Press, Cambridge, Mass.

Abraham, K. and Farber, H. (1987) 'Job duration, seniority, and earnings'. *American Economic Review*, 77 (3), June, pp. 278–97.

Abraham, K. G. and Medoff, J. L. (1985) 'Length of service and promotions in union and non-union work groups'. *Industrial and Labor Relations Review*, 38 (3), April, pp. 408–20.

ACAS (1990) *Appraisal Related Pay*. ACAS Advisory Booklet No. 14. HMSO, London.

Akerlof, G. and Yellen, J. (eds) (1986) *Efficiency Wage Models of the Labour Market*. Cambridge University Press, Cambridge.

Alchian, A. and Demsetz, H. (1972) 'Production, information costs, and economic organization'. *American Economic Review*, Dec., pp. 777–95.

Althauser, R. and Kalleberg, A. (1981) 'Firms, occupations and the structure of labor markets: a conceptual analysis'. In Berg, I. (ed.), *Sociological Perspectives on Labor Markets*. Academic Press, New York, Ch. 5, pp. 119–49.

Altmann, N., Köhler, C. and Meil, P. (eds) (1992) *Technology and Work in German Industry*. Routledge, London.

Aoki, M. (1988) *Information, Incentives, and Bargaining in the Japanese Economy*. Cambridge University Press, Cambridge.

Appelbaum, E. and Batt, R. (1994) *The New American Workplace: Transforming Work Systems in the United States*. Cornell University Press, Ithaca, New York.

Armstrong, M. and Murlis, H. (1994) *Reward Management: a Handbook of Remuneration Strategy and Practice*. 3rd edn. Kogan Page, London.

Arthur, M. B. and Rousseau, D. M. (eds) (1996) *The Boundaryless Career: a New Employment Principle for a New Organizational Era*. Oxford University Press, New York.

Ashworth, T. (1980) *Trench Warfare 1914–18: the Live and Let Live System*. Macmillan, London.

Atkinson, J. and Meager, N. (1986) *Changing Working Practices: How Companies Achieve Flexibility to Meet New Needs*. National Economic Development Office, London.

Axelrod, R. (1984) *The Evolution of Cooperation*. Basic Books, New York.

Baraldi, L., Dumasy, J-P. and Troussier, J-F. (1995) 'Accords salariaux innovants et théorie du salaire'. *Économie Appliquée*, 48 (4), pp. 105–37.

Baron, J., Davis-Blake, A. and Bielby, W. (1986a) 'The structure of opportunity: how promotion ladders vary within and among organizations'. *Administrative Science Quarterly*, 31 (2), June, pp. 48–273.

Baron, J., Dobbin, F. and Devereaux Jennings, P. (1986b) 'War and peace: the evolution of modern personnel administration in US industry'. *American Journal of Sociology*, 92 (2), Sept., pp. 350–83.

Barrat, O., Coutrot, T. and Mabile, S. (1996) 'La négociation salariale en France: des marges de manoeuvre réduites au début des années quatre-vingt-dix'. In *Données Sociales 1996*. INSEE, Paris.

Bayet, A. (1996) 'L'éventail des salaires et ses déterminants'. In *Données Sociales 1996*. INSEE, Paris.

Becker, G. S. (1975) *Human Capital: a Theoretical and Empirical Analysis, with Special Reference to Education*. University of Chicago Press, Chicago.

Bees, M., and Swords, M. (eds) (1990) *National Vocational Qualifications and Further Education*. Kogan Page, London.

Belman, D. (1992) 'Unions, the quality of labor relations, and firm performance'. In Mishel, L. and Voos, P. (eds), *Unions and Economic Competitiveness*. M. E. Sharpe, New York, pp. 41–107.

Béret, P. (1992) 'Salaires et marchés internes: quelques évolutions récentes en France'. *Économie Appliquée*, 45(2), pp. 5–22.

Béret, P. and Dupray, A. (1998) 'La formation professionnelle continue: de l'accumulation de compétences à la validation de la performance'. *Formation Emploi*, 63, July–Sept., pp. 61–80.

Berg, P. (1994) 'Strategic adjustments in training: a comparative analysis of the US and German automobile industries'. In Lynch, L. (ed.), *Training and the Private Sector: International Comparisons*. National Bureau of Economic Research, University of Chicago Press, Chicago.

Best, S. H. (1984) *And Now for Something Completely Different: a Report on Personnel Management in Sumitomo Metal Industries, Japan*. British Steel Corporation, London.

Betters, P. (1931) *The Personnel Classification Board: its History, Activities and Organization*. Brookings Institution, Washington.

Biedenkopf, K. (1970) *Mitbestimmung im Unternehmen. Bericht der Sachverständigenkommission zur Auswertung der bisherigen Erfahrungen bei der Mitbestimmung*. Deutscher Bundestag, Bochum.

Bishop, J. (1987) 'The recognition and reward of employee performance'. *Journal of Labor Economics*, 5 (4), Part 2, Oct., pp. 36–56.

Blau, F. and Kahn, L. (1996) 'International differences in male wage inequality: institutions versus market forces'. *Journal of Political Economy*, 104 (4), Aug., pp. 791–837.

BLS (1992) 'Employment Cost Index'. In *Handbook of Methods 1992*, Ch. 8. Bulletin 2414. US Department of Labor, Bureau of Labor Statistics, Washington DC.

BLS (1994) *Employment Cost Indexes and Levels 1975–94*, Bulletin 2447. US Department of Labor, Bureau of Labor Statistics, Washington DC.

Booth, A. (1995) *The Economics of the Trade Union*. Cambridge University Press, Cambridge.

Bosch, G. and Lichte, R. (1982) 'Die Funktionsweise informeller Senioritätsrechte: am

Beispiel einer betrieblichen Fallstudie'. In Dohse, K., Jürgens, U. and Russig, H. (eds). (See ref.)

Bowers, J., Deaton, D. and Turk, J. (1982) *Labour Hoarding in British Industry.* Blackwell, Oxford.

Boyer, R. and Orléan, A. (1995) 'Stabilité de la coopération dans les jeux évolutionnistes stochastiques'. *Revue économique,* 46 (3), May, pp. 797–806.

Brandes, W., Buttler, F. *et al.* (1990) *Der Staat als Arbeitgeber: Daten und Analysen zum Öffentlichen Dienst in der Bundesrepublik.* Campus, Frankfurt.

Bridges, W. and Villemez, W. (1991) 'Employment relations and the labor market: integrating institutional and market perspectives'. *American Sociological Review,* 56, pp. 748–64.

Bridges, W. and Villemez, W. (1994) *The Employment Relationship: Causes and Consequences of Modern Personnel Administration.* Plenum, New York.

Brossard, M. (1977) 'La structure de l'organisation du travail dans l'entreprise et les pouvoirs dans le système de relations industrielles'. Thèse pour le Doctorat de Troisième Cycle, Université d'Aix-Marseille II, Sept.

Brown, C., Nakata, Y., Reich, M. and Ulman, L. (1997) *Work and Pay in the United States and Japan.* Oxford University Press, New York.

Brown, J. (1989) 'Why do wages increase with tenure? On-the-job training and life-cycle wage growth observed within firms'. *American Economic Review,* 79 (5), Dec., pp. 971–91.

Brown, W. E. (1973) *Piecework Bargaining.* Heinemann, London.

Brown, W. (ed.) (1981) *The Changing Contours of British Industrial Relations.* Blackwell, Oxford.

Brown, Wilfred (1962) *Piecework Abandoned: the Effect of Wage Incentive Systems on Managerial Authority.* Heinemann, London.

Büchtemann, C., Schupp, J. and Soloff, D. (1993) 'Übergänge von der Schule in den Beruf: Deutschland und USA im Vergleich'. *Mitteilungen aus der Arbeitsmarkt- und Berufsforschung,* 26 (4).

Bullock, A. (Lord, Chairman) (1977) *Report of the Committee of Inquiry on Industrial Democracy.* Department of Trade, Cmnd 6706. HMSO, London.

Burawoy, M. (1979) *Manufacturing Consent: Changes in the Labor Process under Monopoly Capitalism.* University of Chicago Press, Chicago.

Buttler, F., Franz, W., Schettkat, R. and Soskice, D. (eds) (1995) *Institutional Frameworks and Labour Market Performance: Comparative Views on the US and German Economies.* Routledge, London.

Buttrick, J. (1952) 'The inside contract system'. *Journal of Economic History,* 12 (3), Summer, pp. 205–21.

Campinos-Dubernet, M., Grando, J-M., Möbus, M. and Margirier, G. (eds). (1991) *Europe et Chantiers: le BTP en Europe: Structures Industrielles et Marché du Travail.* Ministère de l'Equipement, du Logement, des Transports et de l'Espace, Paris.

Cannell, M. and Wood, S. (1992) *Incentive Pay: Impact and Evolution.* Institute of Personnel Management/National Economic Development Office, London.

Card, D. and Krueger, A. (1995) *Myth and Measurement: the New Economics of the Minimum Wage.* Princeton University Press, Princeton, New Jersey.

Carrière-Ramanoelina, M. and Zarifian, P. (1985) 'Le technicien d'atelier dans la classification de la métallurgie: de la référence au métier à l'analyse de l'emploi; vers un ouvrier-technicien?' *Formation Emploi,* 9 (1), Jan.–Mar., pp. 11–24.

Carroll, M. (1993) 'Performance-related pay: a comparative study of the Inland

Revenue and a high street bank'. MSc dissertation, Faculty of Technology, UMIST, Manchester, Oct.

Cartter, A. M. (1959) *Theory of Wages and Employment*. Richard D. Irwin, Illinois.

CERC (Centre d'Etude des Revenus et des Coûts) (1987) *Salaires et compléments de rémunération: analyse des pratiques d'entreprises*. Documents du CERC, No. 87, 4ème trimestre, Documentation Française, Paris.

CERC (1988) *La Structure des Salaires dans la Communauté Economique Européenne*. Documentation Française, Paris.

Chandler, A. (1990) *Scale and Scope: the Dynamics of Industrial Capitalism*. Harvard University Press, Cambridge, Mass.

Clark, J. (1994) 'Greenfield sites and the "New Industrial Relations"'. ISVET-IRRU (ed.). *Participation, Involvement and Company Performance in Great Britain*. Franco Angeli, Milan.

Clark, R. and Ogawa, N. (1992) 'Employment tenure and earnings profiles in Japan and the United States: comment'. *American Economic Review*, 82 (1), Mar., pp. 336–45.

Clegg, H. (1972) *The System of Industrial Relations in Great Britain*. Blackwell, Oxford.

Coase, R. H. (1937) 'The nature of the firm'. *Economica*, Nov., pp. 386–405.

Cole, R. E. (1979) *Work, Mobility and Participation: a Comparative Study of American and Japanese industry*. University of California Press, Berkeley.

Cole, R. (1989) *Strategies for Learning: Small-group Activities in American, Japanese and Swedish Industry*. University of California Press, Berkeley.

Cole, R. (1994) 'Different quality paradigms and their implications for organisational learning'. In Aoki, M. and Dore, R. (eds), *The Japanese Firm: the Sources of Competitive Strength*. Oxford University Press, Oxford.

Commons, J. R. (1924) *Legal Foundations of Capitalism*. Macmillan, New York.

Conner, K. R. and Prahalad, C. K. (1996) 'A resource-based theory of the firm: knowledge versus opportunism'. *Organization Science*, 7 (5), Sept.–Oct., pp. 477–501.

Cook, M. (1993) *Personnel Selection and Productivity*. Wiley, New York.

Craig, C., Rubery, J., Tarling, R. and Wilkinson, F. (1980) *Abolition and After: the Cutlery Wages Council*. Department of Employment Research Paper No. 18, Department of Employment, London.

Craig, C., Rubery, J., Tarling, R. and Wilkinson, F. (1982) *Labour Market Structure, Industrial Organisation and Low Pay*. Cambridge University Press, Cambridge.

Cropanzano, R. and Fulger, R. (1991) 'Procedural justice and worker motivation'. In Steers, R. and Porter, L. (eds), *Motivation and Work Behavior*. 5th edn. McGraw-Hill, New York, pp. 131–43.

Crouch, C. (1995) 'Organized interests as resources or as constraint: rival logics of vocational training policy'. In Crouch, C. and Traxler, F. (eds), *Organized Industrial Relations in Europe: What Future*? Avebury, Aldershot.

Crozier, M. (1963) *Le Phénomène Bureaucratique*. Seuil, Paris.

Cutcher-Gershenfeld, J. (1991) 'The impact on economic performance of a transformation in workplace relations'. *Industrial and Labor Relations Review*, 44 (2), Jan., pp. 241–60.

Dasgupta, P. (1988) 'Trust as a commodity'. In Gambetta, D. (ed.), *Trust: Making and Breaking Cooperative Relations*. Blackwell, Oxford.

Davis, L., Canter, R. and Hoffman, J. (1955) 'Current job design criteria'. *Journal of Industrial Engineering*, 16, pp. 1–7.

Davis, L. E. (1971) 'The coming crisis for production management: technology and organisation'. *International Journal of Production Research*, 9, pp. 65–82.

Davis, S. J. (1992) 'Cross-country patterns of change in relative wages'. In *NBER Macroeconomics Annual 1992*. NBER, MIT Press, Cambridge, Mass., pp. 239–91.

Deakin, S. and Wilkinson, F. (1998) 'Contract law and the economics of interorganizational trust'. In Lane, C. and Bachmann, R. (eds), *Trust within and between Organizations: Conceptual Issues and Empirical Applications*. Oxford University Press, Oxford, Ch. 5. pp. 146–72.

DeFreitas, G., Marsden, D. W. and Ryan, P. (1991) 'Youth employment patterns in segmented labor markets in the US and Europe'. *Eastern Economic Journal*, 17 (2), pp. 223–36.

Delp, V., Schmidt, L. and Wohlfahrt, K. (1974) 'Gewerkschaftliche Betriebspolitik bei Ford'. In Jacobi, O., Müller-Jentsch, W. and Schmidt, E. (eds), *Gewerkschaften und Klassenkampf, Kritisches Jahrbuch '74*. Fischer Verlag, Frankfurt. pp. 161–75.

Dertouzos, M., Lester, R. and Solow, R. (1989) *Made in America: Regaining the Productive Edge. The MIT Commission on Industrial Productivity*. MIT Press, Cambridge, Mass.

DiMaggio, P. and Powell, W. (1983) 'The iron cage revisited: institutional isomorphism and collective rationality in organizational fields'. *American Sociological Review*, 48, Apr., pp. 147–60.

Doeringer, P. B. and Piore, M. J. (1971) *Internal Labor Markets and Manpower Analysis*. Heath, Lexington.

Dohse, K., Jürgens, U. and Russig, H. (1982) 'Hire and Fire?' *Senioritätsregelungen in amerikanischen Betrieben*. Campus, Frankfurt.

Dore, R. (1973) *British Factory—Japanese Factory: the Origins of Diversity in Industrial Relations*. George Allen and Unwin, London.

Dore, R. P. and Sako, M. (1989) *How the Japanese Learn to Work*. Routledge, London.

Dougherty, C. (1987) 'The German dual system: a heretical view'. *European Journal of Education*, 22 (2), pp. 195–9.

Drexel, I. (1980) Die Krise der Anlernung im Arbeitsprozess. *Soziale Welt*, 31 (3), pp. 368–95.

Drexel, I. (1993) *Das Ende des Facharbeiteraufstiegs? Neue mittlere Bildungs- und Karrierewege in Deutschland und Frankreich: ein Vergleich*. Campus Velag, Frankfurt.

Dugué, E. (1994) 'La gestion des compétences: les savoirs dévalués, le pouvoir occulté'. *Sociologie du Travail*, 3, pp. 273–92.

Düll, K. (1986) 'The analysis of new forms of work organisation—results of case studies from the Federal Republic of Germany, France and Italy'. In Grootings, P., Gustavsen, B. and Héthy, L. (eds), *New Forms of Work Organisation and their Social and Economic Environment*. Vienna Centre and Institute of Labour Research Budapest, Budapest.

Dunlop, J. T. (1958) *Industrial Relations Systems*. Holt, New York.

Eaton, A. and Voos, P. (1992) 'Unions and contemporary innovations in work organization, compensation and employee participation'. In Mishel, L. and Voos, P. (eds), *Unions and Economic Competitiveness*. M. E. Sharpe, New York.

Elbaum, B. (1990) 'L'évolution de l'apprentissage en Grande-Bretagne et aux États-Unis depuis les XIXème siècle'. *Formation Emploi*, 31, July–Sept., pp. 72–84.

Eldridge, J. E. T. (1968) *Industrial Disputes: Essays in the Sociology of Industrial Relations*. Routledge, London.

Elger, T. (1991) 'Task flexibility and the intensification of labour in UK manufacturing in the 1980s'. In Pollert, A. (ed.), *Farewell to Flexibility*. Blackwell, Oxford.

Eurostat (1972, 1978) *European Structure of Earnings Survey.* Eurostat, Luxembourg.

Eurostat (1995) 'Labour costs in 1992'. *Statistics in Focus, Population and Social Conditions*, 1995, 14. Eurostat, Luxembourg.

Eustache, D. (1996) *Les Nouvelles Politiques de Rémunération des Entreprises et les Réactions des Salariés.* Centre d'Études et de Recherches sur les Qualifications, Étude No. 69. CEREQ, Marseille.

Eymard-Duvernay, F. (1989) 'Conventions de qualité et formes de coordination'. *Revue Économique*, 40 (2), Mar., pp. 329–60.

Eyraud, F. (1978) 'La fin des classifications Parodi'. *Sociologie du Travail*, 20 (3), July–Sept. pp. 259–79.

Eyraud, F. (1981) 'Action syndicale et salaire: une comparaison France/Grande-Bretagne'. Thèse pour le Doctorat ès Sciences Economiques, Université d'Aix-Marseille II.

Eyraud, F. and Rozenblatt, P. (1994) *Les Formes Hiérarchiques: Travail et Salaires dans Neuf Pays Industrialisés.* La Documentation Française, Paris.

Eyraud, F., d'Iribarne, A. and Maurice, M. (1988) 'Des entreprises face aux technologies flexibles: une analyse de la dynamique du changement'. *Sociologie du Travail*, No. 1, 88, pp. 55–77.

Eyraud, F., Jobert, A., Rozenblatt, P. and Tallard, M. (1989) *Les classifications dans l'entreprise: production des hiérarchies professionnelles et salariales.* Document Travail Emploi, Ministère du Travail, de l'Emploi et de la Formation Professionnelle, Paris.

Eyraud, F., Marsden, D. W. and Silvestre, J. J. (1990) 'Internal and occupational labour markets in Britain and France'. *International Labour Review*, 129 (4), pp. 501–17.

Felstead, A. (1991) 'The social organisation of the franchise: a case study of "controlled self-employment"'. *Work, Employment and Society*, 5 (1), Mar., pp. 37–57.

Finegold, D. and Soskice, D. (1988) 'The failure of training in Britain: analysis and prescription'. *Oxford Review of Economic Policy*, 4 (3), pp. 21–53.

Finniston, M. (1980) *Engineering our Future: Report of the Committee of Inquiry into the Engineering Profession*, Cmnd 7794. HMSO, London.

Foulkes, F. (1980) *Personnel Policies of Large Nonunion Companies.* Prentice-Hall, Englewood Cliffs, New Jersey.

Foulkes, F. (1988) 'Employment Security Developments in the Non-union Sector'. *Industrial Relations Research Association Series*, Proceedings of the 41st Annual Meeting, Dec. 28–30. New York, pp. 411–17.

Fox, A. (1974) *Beyond Contract: Work, Power and Trust Relations.* Faber, London.

Freeman, R. and Katz, L. (1994) 'Rising wage inequality: the United States vs. other advanced countries'. In Freeman, R. (ed.), *Working under Different Rules.* NBER/Russell Sage Foundation, New York, Ch. 2, pp. 29–62.

Freeman, R. and Katz, L. (eds) (1995) *Differences and Changes in Wage Structures.* NBER, University of Chicago Press, Chicago.

Freeman, R. B. and Medoff, J. L. (1984) *What Do Unions Do?* Basic Books, New York.

Gallie, D. (1978) *In Search of the New Working Class: Automation and Social Integration within the Capitalist Enterprise.* Cambridge University Press, Cambridge.

Gallie, D. (1983) *Social Inequality and Class Radicalism in France and Britain.* Cambridge University Press, Cambridge.

Gallie, D. and White, M. (1994) 'Employer policies, employee contracts, and labour-market structure'. In Rubery, J. and Wilkinson, F. (eds), *Employer Strategy and the Labour Market.* Oxford University Press, Oxford, Ch. 2.

Géhin, J-P. and Méhaut, P. (1993) *Apprentissage ou Formation Continue? Stratégies Éducatives des Entreprises en Allemagne et en France.* L'Harmattan, Paris.

Genda, Y. (1998) 'Japan: wage differentials, and changes since the 1980s'. In Tachibanaki, T. (ed.), *Wage Differentials: an International Comparison.* Macmillan, Basingstoke.

Gorgeu, A. and Mathieu, R. (1995) *Recrutement et Production au Plus Juste: les Nouvelles Usines d'Équipement Automobile en France.* Dossier No. 7. Centre d'Etudes de l'Emploi, Noisy-le-Grand.

Gospel, H. (1998) 'The revival of apprenticeship training in Britain?' *British Journal of Industrial Relations,* 36 (3), Sept., pp. 435–57.

Granovetter, M. (1974) *Getting a Job: a Study of Contacts and Careers.* Harvard University Press, Cambridge, Mass.

Greenacre, L. (1990) 'Competence and coherence: opportunities for education and industry in the emerging NVQ framework'. In Bees, M. and Swords, M. (eds). (See Ref.)

Gustman, A., Mitchell, O. and Steinmeier, T. (1994) 'The role of pensions in the labor market: a survey of the literature'. *Industrial and Labor Relations Review,* 47 (3), Apr., pp. 417–38.

Hamermesh, D. and Rees, A. (1993) *The Economics of Work and Pay.* 5th edn. Harper Collins, New York.

Hanada, M. and McBride, K. (1986) 'Organizational structures in Japanese and US manufacturing'. *Administrative Science Quarterly,* 31, pp. 334–64.

Hashimoto, M. and Raisian, J. (1985) 'Employment tenure and earnings profiles in Japan and the United States'. *American Economic Review,* 75, (Sept.), pp. 721–35.

Hashimoto, M. and Raisian, J. (1992) 'Employment tenure and earnings profiles in Japan and the United States: reply'. *American Economic Review,* 82, pp. 346–54.

Hays, W. L. (1973) *Statistics for the Social Sciences.* Holt, Rinehart and Winston, London.

Hill, S. (1991) 'Why quality circles failed but total quality management might succeed'. *British Journal of Industrial Relations,* 29 (4), pp. 541–68.

Hofbauer, H. and Nagel, E. (1987) *Mobilität nach Abschluß der betrieblichen Berufsausbildung.* Mitteilungen aus der Institut für Arbeitsmarkt und Berufsforschung 1/87, Nürnberg, pp. 45–73.

Holmstrom, B. and Milgrom, P. (1991) 'Multitask principal-agent analysis: incentive contracts, asset ownership, and job design'. *The Journal of Law, Economics and Organization,* 7, pp. 24–52.

Hunter, J. E. (1983) 'A causal analysis of cognitive ability, job knowledge, job performance and supervisory ratings'. In Landy, F., Zedeck, S. and Cleveland, J. (eds), *Performance Measurement and Theory.* Erlbaum, Hillsdale, New Jersey.

Ichniowski, C. (1990) *Human Resource Management Systems and the Performance of US Manufacturing Businesses.* NBER Working Paper No. 3449, Sept.

INSEE (1996) *L'Évolution des Salaires jusqu'en 1994.* Synthèses, No. 4. Institut National de la Statistique et des Études Économiques, Paris.

d'Iribarne, Ph. (1989) *La Logique de l'Honneur: Gestion des Entreprises et Traditions Nationales.* Seuil, Paris.

Jacobs, E., Orwell, S., Paterson, P. and Weltz, F. (1978) *The Approach to Industrial Change in Britain and Germany.* Anglo-German Foundation, London.

Jacoby, S. M. (1993) 'Pacific ties: industrial relations and employment systems in Japan and the United States since 1900'. In Lichtenstein, N. and Harris, H. (eds), *Industrial*

Democracy in America: the Ambiguous Promise. Cambridge University Press, Cambridge.

Jacoby, S. M. (1985) *Employing Bureaucracy: Managers, Unions, and the Transformation of Work in American Industry, 1900–1945*. Columbia University Press, New York.

Jobert, A. (1990) 'Les grilles de classification professionnelle: quelques repères historiques'. *CFDT Aujourd'hui*, No. 99, Dec., pp. 6–14.

Jobert, A. and Rozenblatt, P. (1985) 'Portée et limite d'un accord de branche sur les classifications'. *Formation Emploi*, 9, Jan.–Mar., pp. 3–10.

Jones, C. and Walsh, K. (1997) 'Boundaryless careers in the US film industry'. *Industrielle Beziehungen*, 4 (1), pp. 58–73.

Junankar, P. N. (ed.) (1987) *From School to Unemployment? The Labour Market for Young People*. Macmillan, London.

Jürgens, U. and Strömel, H-P. (1987) 'The communication structure between management and shop floor: a comparison of a Japanese and a German plant'. In Trevor M. (ed.), *The Internationalization of Japanese Business: European and Japanese Perspectives*. Campus, Frankfurt.

Jürgens, U., Malsch, T. and Dohse, K. (1993) *Breaking from Taylorism: Changing Forms of Work in the Automobile Industry*. Cambridge University Press, Cambridge.

Kalleberg, A., Knoke, D., Marsden, P. and Spaeth, J. (1996) *Organizations in America: Analyzing their Structures and Human Resource Practices*. Sage, Thousand Oaks, California.

Katz, E. and Ziderman, A. (1990) 'Investment in general training: the role of information and labour mobility'. *Economic Journal*, 100 (403), Dec., pp. 1147–58.

Katz, H. C. (1985) *Shifting Gears: Changing Labor Relations in the US Automobile Industry*. MIT Press, Cambridge, Mass.

Katz, L., Loveman, G., and Blanchflower, D. (1995) 'A comparison of changes in the structure of wages in four OECD countries'. In Freeman, R. and Katz, L. (eds), *Differences and Changes in Wage Structures*. NBER, University of Chicago Press, Chicago, pp. 25–65.

Kay, J. and Silberston, A. (1995) 'Corporate governance'. *National Institute Economic Review*, 84, Aug.

Kern, H. and Schumann, M. (1984) *Das Ende der Arbeitsteilung: Rationalisierung in der industriellen Produktion*. C. H. Beck, München.

Kerr, C. (1954) 'The balkanization of labor markets'. In Bakke (ed.), *Labor Mobility and Economic Opportunity*. MIT Press, Cambridge, Mass., pp. 92–110.

King, L., Hunter, J. and Schmidt, F. (1980) 'Halo in a multi-dimensional forced choice performance scale'. *Journal of Applied Psychology*, 65, pp. 507–16.

Kling, J. (1995) High performance work systems and firm performance. *Monthly Labor Review*, May, pp. 29–36.

Knights, D., Willmott, H. and Collinson, D. (eds) (1985) *Job Redesign: Critical Perspectives on the Labour Process*. Gower, Aldershot.

Kochan, T. and Osterman, P. (1994) *The Mutual Gains Enterprise*. Harvard Business School Press, Cambridge, Mass.

Kogut, B. and Zander, U. (1996) 'What do firms do? Coordination, identity, and learning'. *Organization Science*, 7 (5), Sept.–Oct., pp. 502–18.

Koike, K. (1984) 'Skill formation system in the US and Japan'. In Aoki, M. (ed.), *The Economic Analysis of the Japanese Firm*. North Holland, Amsterdam.

Koike, K. (1988) *Understanding Industrial Relations in Modern Japan*. Macmillan, Basingstoke.

Koike, K. (1997) *Human Resource Development*. Japanese Economy & Labor Series, No. 2, Japan Institute of Labour, Tokyo.

Koike, K. and Inoki, T. (eds). (1990) *Skill Formation in Japan and Southeast Asia*. University of Tokyo Press, Tokyo.

Koyo Shokugyo Sogo Kenkyusho (Institute of Employment and Occupation) (1982) *Kigyo nai Rodoryoku no Yuko Katsuyo ni kansuru Jittai Chosa* (A survey on the utilization of the internal work force). Koyo Shokugyo Sogo Kenkyusho.

Lam, A. (1992) *Women and Japanese Management: Discrimination and Reform*. Routledge, London.

Lam, A. (1994) 'The utilisation of human resources: a comparative study of British and Japanese engineers in the electronics industries'. *Human Resource Management Journal*, 4 (3), Spring, pp. 22–40.

Lam, A. (1997) 'Embedded firms, embedded knowledge: problems of collaboration and knowledge transfer in global cooperative ventures'. *Organisation Studies*, 18 (6), pp. 973–96.

Lam, A. (1998) 'Tacit knowledge, organisational learning, and innovation: a societal perspective'. Danish Research Unit for Industrial Dynamics (DRUID), Aalborg University, Working Paper No. 78–12, Aalborg University.

Landers, R., Rebitzer, J. and Taylor, L. (1996) 'Human resources practices and the demographic transformation of professional labour markets'. In Osterman, P. (ed.), *Broken Ladders: Managerial Careers in the New Economy*. Oxford University Press, New York.

Landy, F. and Farr, J. (1983) *The Measurement of Work Performance: Methods, Theory, and Applications*. Academic Press, New York.

Lane, C. and Bachmann, R. (eds) (1998) *Trust Within and Between Organizations: Conceptual Issues and Empirical Applications*. Oxford University Press, Oxford.

Lawler, E. E. III. (1971) *Pay and Organizational Effectiveness: a Psychological View*. McGraw-Hill, New York.

Lawler, E. E. III (1994) 'From job-based to competency-based organizations'. *Journal of Organizational Behavior*, 15 (3), pp. 3–15.

Lawler, E. E. III, Mohrman, S. A. and Ledford, G. E. (1992) *Employee Involvement and Total Quality Management: Practices and Results in Fortune 1000 Companies*. Jossey-Bass, San Francisco.

Layard, R., Mayhew, K. and Owen, G. (eds) (1994) *Britain's Training Deficit*. Avebury, Aldershot.

Lazear, E. (1995) *Personnel Economics*. MIT Press, Cambridge, Mass.

Leighton, P. (1983) *Contractual Arrangements in Selected Industries: a Study of Employment Relationships in Industries with Outwork*. Department of Employment Research Paper No. 39. Department of Employment, London.

Lemmon, E. J. (1965) *Beginning Logic*. Nelson, London.

Leroy-Beaulieu, P. (1896) *Traité Théorique et Pratique d'Économie Politique*. Guillaumin, Paris.

Levine, D. I. and D'Andrea Tyson, L. (1990) 'Participation, productivity, and the firm's environment'. In Blinder, A. S. (ed.), *Paying for Productivity*. Brookings Institution, Washington DC, pp. 183–244.

Lincoln, J. R. and Kalleberg, A. L. (1990) *Culture, Control and Commitment: a Study of*

Work Organization and Work Attitudes in the United States and Japan. Cambridge University Press, Cambridge.

Lincoln, J. R. and Nakata, Y. (1997) 'The transformation of the Japanese employment system: nature, depth, and origins'. *Work and Occupations*, 24 (1), Feb., pp. 33–55.

Lincoln, J., Hanada, M. and McBride, K. (1986) 'Organizational structures in Japanese and US manufacturing'. *Administrative Science Quarterly*, 31, pp. 338–64.

Linhart, D., Rozenblatt P. and Voegele S. (1993) 'Vers une nouvelle rémunération scientifique du travail?' *Travail et Emploi*, No. 57, pp. 30–47.

Littler, C. (1985) 'Taylorism, Fordism and job design'. In Knights, D., Willmott, H and Collinson, D. (eds). (See Ref.)

Lorenz, E. (1995) 'Promoting workplace participation: lessons from Germany and France'. *Industrielle Beziehungen*, 2 (1), pp. 46–63.

Lutz, B. (1975) *Krise des Lohnanreizes: ein empirisch-historischer Beitrag zum Wandel der Formen betrieblicher Herrschaft am Beispiel der deutschen Stahlindustrie.* Europäische Verlagsanstalt, Frankfurt.

Lutz, B. (1976) 'Bildungssystem und Beschäftigungsstruktur in Deutschland und Frankreich: zum Einfluß des Bildungssystems auf die Gestaltung betrieblicher Arbeitskräftestrukturen'. In Mendius H-G., Sengenberger W. *et al.* (eds), *Betrieb-Arbeitsmarkt- Qualifikation 1.* Aspekte Verlag, Frankfurt.

Lynch, L. (1992) 'Private sector training and the earnings of young workers'. *American Economic Review*, 82, Mar., pp. 299–312.

Lynch, L. (ed.) (1994) *Training and the Private Sector: International Comparisons.* National Bureau of Economic Research, University of Chicago Press, Chicago.

MacKay, D. I., Boddy, D., Brack, J., Diack, J. A. and Jones, N. (1971) *Labour Markets under Different Employment Conditions.* George Allen and Unwin, London.

McKersie, R. B and Hunter, L. C. (1973) *Pay, Productivity and Collective Bargaining.* Macmillan, London.

Makaronidis, A. (1995) 'Main Features of the European Employment Cost Index (EECI)'. (E3/95/Sal.07 EN). Eurostat, Luxembourg.

Malcomson, J. (1997) 'Contracts, hold-up, and labor markets'. *Journal of Economic Literature*, 35 (4), Dec., pp. 1916–57.

Manning, A. (1996) 'The Equal Pay Act as an experiment to test theories of the labour market'. *Economica*, 63, pp. 191–212.

Manning, A. (1998) 'Mighty Good Thing: the Returns to Tenure'. *Centre for Economic Performance Discussion Paper, No. 383.* London School of Economics, London. Mar.

Marsden, D. W. (1978) *Industrial Democracy and Industrial Control in West Germany, France and Great Britain.* Research Paper No. 4, Department of Employment, London.

Marsden, D. W. (1982) 'Career structures and training in internal labour markets in Britain and West Germany'. *Manpower Studies*, No. 4, Spring, pp. 10–17.

Marsden, D. W. (1986) *The End of Economic Man? Custom and Competition in Labour Markets.* Wheatsheaf, Brighton.

Marsden, D. W. (1990) 'Institutions and labour mobility: occupational and internal labour markets in Britain, France, Italy and West Germany'. In Brunetta, R. and Dell'Aringa, C. (eds), *Labour Relations and Economic Performance.* Macmillan, London.

Marsden, D. W. (1995) 'A phoenix from the ashes of apprenticeship? Vocational training in Britain'. *International Contributions to Labour Studies* (Supplement to the *Cambrige Journal of Economics*), 5, pp. 87–114.

Marsden, D. W. (1996) 'The European Employment Cost Index: Methodology and Diffusion'. Report for Eurostat, Luxembourg.

Marsden, D. W. and French, S. (1998) *What a Performance: Performance Related Pay in the Public Services.* Centre for Economic Performance Special Report, London School of Economics, London.

Marsden, D. W. and Momigliano, S. (1996) 'L'utilizzo di sistemi di incentivazione nel pubblico impiego: problemi e possibili soluzioni'. *Lavoro et Relazioni Industriale,* No. 4. Oct.–Dec., pp. 35–69.

Marsden, D. W. and Richardson, R. (1992) 'Motivation and Performance Related Pay in the Public Sector: a Case Study of the Inland Revenue'. *Centre for Economic Performance Discussion, Paper No. 75.* London School of Economics, London.

Marsden, D. W. and Richardson, R. (1994) 'Performing for pay? The effects of "merit pay" on motivation in a public service'. *British Journal of Industrial Relations,* 32 (2), June, pp. 243–62.

Marsden, D. W. and Ryan, P. (1990a) 'Institutional aspects of youth employment and training policy in Britain'. *British Journal of Industrial Relations,* 28 (3), Nov., pp. 351–70.

Marsden D. W. and Ryan, P. (1990b) 'Intermediate level vocational training and the structure of labour markets in Western Europe in the 1980s'. In Ferman, L. A., Hoyman M., Cutcher-Gershenfeld, J. and Savoie, E. J. (eds) *New Developments in Worker Training: a Legacy for the 1990s.* Industrial Relations Research Association, Wisconsin, Madison.

Marsden, D. W. and Ryan, P. (1991) 'Institutional aspects of youth employment and training policy: reply'. *British Journal of Industrial Relations,* 29 (3), Sept., pp. 497–505.

Marsden, D. W., Morris, T., Willman, P. and Wood, S. (1985) *The Car Industry: Labour Relations and Industrial Adjustment.* Tavistock, London.

Marshall, A. (1920) *Principles of Economics.* Macmillan, London.

Maurice, M., Sellier, F. and Silvestre, J. J. (1982) *Politique d'Éducation et Organisation Industrielle en France et en Allemagne.* Presses Universitaires de France, Paris.

Maurice, M., Sellier, F. and Silvestre, J. J. (1986) *The Social Foundations of Industrial Power: a Comparison of France and Germany.* MIT Press, Cambridge, Mass. (Translated from *Politique d'Éducation et Organisation Industrielle en France et en Allemagne.* Presses Universitaires de France, Paris, 1982.)

Maurice, M., Mannari, H., Takeoka, Y. and Inoki, T. (1988) *Des Entreprises Françaises et Japonaises face à la Mécatronique: Acteurs et Organisation de la Dynamique Industrielle.* Laboratoire d'Economie et de Sociologie du Travail (CNRS), Aix-en-Provence.

Maynard Smith, J. (1982) *Evolution and the Theory of Games.* Cambridge University Press, Cambridge.

Medoff, J. and Abraham, K. (1980) 'Experience, performance and earnings'. *Quarterly Journal of Economics,* 95, pp. 703–36.

Megaw, J. (Chair) (1982) *Inquiry into Civil Service Pay: Report.* Cmnd 8590. HMSO, London.

Meil, P. (1992) 'A stranger in paradise—an American's perspective on German industrial sociology'. In Altmann, N., Köhler, C. and Meil, P. (eds), *Technology and Work in German Industry.* Routledge, London.

Mendius, H-G., Sengenberger, W. *et al.* (1976) *Betrieb- Arbeitsmarkt- Qualifikation 1.* Aspekte Verlag, Frankfurt.

Merit Systems Protection Board (1988) *Towards Effective Performance Management in the Federal Government*. US Government Printing Office, Washington DC.

Metcalf, D. (1993) 'Industrial relations and economic performance'. *British Journal of Industrial Relations*, 31 (2), June, pp. 255–84.

Milgrom, P. and Roberts, J. (1992) *Economics, Organization and Management*. Prentice-Hall, New Jersey.

Milkovitch, G. T. and Wigdor, A. K. (eds) (1991) *Pay for Performance: Evaluating Performance Appraisal and Merit Pay*. National Academy Press, Washington DC.

Ministère du Travail (1992) *L'Individualisation des Salaires en 1991*. Premières Informations, No. 291, 11 August, Service des études et de la statistique, Ministère du Travail, de l'Emploi et de la Formation Professionnelle, Paris.

Mitani, N. (1998) 'France: internal labour markets and wage structure'. In Tachibanaki, T. (ed.), *Wage Differentials: an International Comparison*. Macmillan, Basingstoke.

Morel, C. (1979) 'Le droit coutumier social dans l'entreprise'. *Droit Social*, No. 7–8, July–Aug., pp. 279–86.

Mottez, B. (1966) *Systèmes de Salaire et Politiques Patronales: Essai sur l'Évolution des Pratiques et des Idéologies Patronales*. Centre National de la Recherche Scientifique, Paris.

Nakamura, K. (1997) 'Worker participation, collective bargaining and joint consultation'. In Sako, M. and Sato, H. (eds). *Japanese Labour and Management in Transition: Diversity, Flexibility and Participation*. Routledge, London.

National Audit Office (1989) *Manpower Planning in the Civil Service*. Cm 398. HMSO, London.

Nelson, R. R. and Winter, S. G. (1982) *An Evolutionary Theory of Economic Change*. Harvard University Press, Cambridge, Mass.

Nickell, S. and Bell, B. (1995) 'The collapse in demand for the unskilled and unemployment across the OECD'. *Oxford Review of Economic Policy*, 11 (1), pp. 40–62.

Nihon Keieisha Dantai Renmei (1975) *Shin-jidai no Nihonteki-keiei—chôsen subeki hôkô to sono shutaisaki, Nihon Keieisha Dantai Renmei, 17 May*. Cited in Yamanouchi and Okazaki-Ward (1997: 205).

Nohara, H. (1995) 'Les Salaires en France et au Japon: comparaison des structures de salaires dans l'industrie manufacturière des deux pays de 1978 à 1986'. *Travail et Emploi*, No. 62, 1/95, pp. 59–71.

North, D. C. (1990) *Institutions, Institutional Change and Economic Performance*. Cambridge University Press, Cambridge.

O'Connell, J. (1994) 'What do franchisers do? Control and commercialisation in milk distribution'. *Work, Employment and Society*, 8 (1), Mar., pp. 23–44.

O'Reilly, J. (1992) 'Where do you draw the line? Functional flexibility, training and skill in Britain and France'. *Work, Employment and Society*, 6 (3), pp. 369–96.

Odagiri, H. (1984) 'The firm as a collection of human resources'. In Wiles, P. and Routh, G. (eds), *Economics in Disarray*. Blackwell, Oxford.

OECD (1992) *Employment Outlook 1992*. OECD, Paris.

OECD (1993) *Employment Outlook 1993*. OECD, Paris.

OECD (1994) *Employment Outlook 1994*. OECD, Paris.

OECD (1997) *Employment Outlook 1997*. OECD, Paris.

Ohkusha, Y., Brunello, G. and Ariga, K. (1997) 'Occupational and internal labor markets in Japan'. *Industrial Relations*, 36 (4), Oct., pp. 446–73.

Ohta, S. and Tachibanaki, T. (1998) 'Job tenure versus age: effects on wages and the implication of consumption for wages'. In Ohashi, I. and Tachibanaki, T. (eds), *Internal Labour Markets, Incentives and Employment*. Macmillan, Basingstoke.

Ohtake, F. (1998) 'The United States'. In Tachibanaki, T. (ed.) *Wage Differentials: an International Comparison*. Macmillan, Basingstoke.

Osterman, P. (1982) 'Employment structures within firms'. *British Journal of Industrial Relations*, 20 (3), Nov., pp. 34961.

Osterman, P. (1988) *Employment Futures: Reorganization, Dislocation, and Public Policy*. Oxford University Press, New York.

Osterman, P. (1994) 'How common is workplace transformation and who adopts it?' *Industrial and Labor Relations Review*, 47 (2), Jan., pp. 173–88.

Osterman, P. (ed.) (1996) *Broken Ladders: Managerial Careers in the New Economy*. Oxford University Press, New York.

Parkinson, J. (1996) 'The Stakeholder Business'. Employment Policy Institute, *Economic Report*, 10 (2), Feb.

Paul, A. and Kleingartner, A. (1994) 'Flexible production and the transformation of industrial relations in the motion picture and television industry'. *Industrial and Labor Relations Review*, 47 (4), July, pp. 663–78.

Penrose, E. (1959) *The Theory of the Growth of the Firm*. Blackwell, Oxford.

Perlman, S. (1928) *A Theory of the Labor Movement*. Augustus Kelley, New York.

Pfeffer, J. and Cohen, Y. (1984) 'Determinants of internal labor markets in organizations'. *Administrative Science Quarterly*, 29, pp. 550–72.

Piore, M. J. (1968) 'The impact of the labor market on the design and selection of productive techniques within the manufacturing plant'. *Quarterly Journal of Economics*, 82 (4), pp. 602–20, Nov.

Piore, M. (1994) 'European labour market integration: an American perspective'. *Social Europe*, Supplement 1/94, European Commission, Brussels, pp. 129–36.

Piore, M. J. and Sabel, C. F. (1984) *The Second Industrial Divide: Possibilities for Prosperity*. Basic Books, New York.

Podevin, G. and Viney, X. (1991) 'Sortir de la catégorie des ouvriers non qualifiés pour les jeunes de niveau V: promotion et/ou reclassement?' *Formation Emploi*, 35, July–Sept., pp. 47–58.

Pohl, R. and Soleilhavoup, J. (1981) 'L'entrée des jeunes et mobilité des moins jeunes'. *Economie et Statistique*, No. 134, June.

Polanyi, M. (1967) *The Tacit Dimension*. Doubleday Anchor, New York.

Pollard, S. (1965) *The Genesis of Modern Management: a Study of the Industrial Revolution in Great Britain*. Edward Arnold, London.

Powell, W. and DiMaggio, P. (eds) (1991) *The New Institutionalism in Organisational Analysis*. University of Chicago Press, Chicago.

PMRS Review Committee (1991) *Advancing Managerial Excellence*. Performance Management and Recognition System Review Committee, US Office of Personnel Management, Washington DC.

Prais, S. J. (1981) 'Vocational Qualifications of the Labour Force in Britain and Germany'. *National Institute Economic Review*, No. 98, pp. 47–59.

Prowse, S. (1994) *Corporate Governance in an International Perspective*. BIS Economic Papers, No. 41. Bank for International Settlements, Basel.

Rees, A. and Shultz, G. (1970) *Workers and Wages in an Urban Labor Market*. University of Chicago Press, Chicago.

Reynaud, B. (1992) *Le Salaire, la Règle et le Marché*. Christian Bourgeois, Paris.

Reynaud, J-D. (1975) *Les Syndicats en France*. Seuil, Paris.

Ribeill, G. (1984) *Les Cheminots*. La Découverte, Paris.

Rivero, J. and Savatier, J. (1970) *Droit du Travail*. Presses Universitaires de France, Paris.

Roethlisberger, F. J. and Dickson, W. J. (1939) *Management and the Worker*. Harvard University Press, Cambridge, Mass.

Rômugyôsei Kenkyûgo (ed.) (1994), cited in Yamanouchi and Okazaki-Ward (1997: 206). Nihonteki keiei no kenshô to sono mirai-ge (Examination of Japanese style management and its future, Part 3), *Rôseijihô*, No. 3158, 15 Apr.

Rotbart, G. (1991) *La structure des salaires en France: la dernière enquête de 1986*. Institut National de la Statistique et des Études Économiques, Emplois Revenus, No. 23, Résultats No. 157, INSEE, Paris.

Rowe, J. W. F. (1928) *Wages in Practice and Theory*. Routledge and Kegan Paul, London.

Roy, D. (1952) 'Quota restriction and goldbricking in a machine shop'. *American Journal of Sociology*, 67 (2), pp. 427–44.

Roy, D. (1955) '"Efficiency" and "the fix": informal intergroup relations in a piecework machine shop'. *American Journal of Sociology*, 60, pp. 255–66.

Rubery, J. (1994) 'Internal and external labour markets: towards an integrated analysis'. In Rubery, J. and Wilkinson, F. (eds), *Employer Strategy and the Labour Market*. Oxford University Press, Oxford, Ch. 1.

Rubery, J. and Wilkinson, F. (1981) 'Outwork and segmented labour markets'. In Wilkinson, F. (ed.), *The Dynamics of Labour Market Segmentation*. Academic Press, London.

Ryan, P. (1980) 'The costs of job training for a transferable skill'. *British Journal of Industrial Relations*, 18 (3), pp. 334–52.

Ryan, P. (1986) 'Apprentices, employment and industrial disputes in engineering in the 1920s'. Paper presented to the Workshop on Child Labour and Apprenticeship, University of Essex, May.

Ryan, P. (1987) *Trade Unionism and the Pay of Young Workers*. Junankar, P. N. (ed.). pp. 119–42. (See Ref.)

Ryan, P. (1994) 'Training quality and trainee exploitation'. In Layard, R., Mayhew, K. and Owen, G. (eds). (See Ref.)

Sainsaulieu, R. (1988) *L'Identité au Travail: les Effets Culturels de l'Organisation*. Presses de la Fondation Nationale des Sciences Politiques, Paris.

Sako, M. (1991) 'Institutional aspects of youth employment and training policy: a comment on Marsden and Ryan'. *British Journal of Industrial Relations*, 29 (3), Sept., pp. 485–90.

Sako, M. (1997) 'Shunto: the role of employer and union coordination at the industry and inter-sectoral levels'. In Sako, M. and Sato, H. (eds), *Japanese Labour and Management in Transition: Diversity, Flexibility, and Participation*. Routledge, London.

Saunders, C. T. and Marsden, D. W. (1981) *Pay Inequalities in the European Community*. Butterworths, London.

Saxenian, A. (1996) 'Beyond boundaries: open labor markets and learning in Silicon Valley'. In Arthur, M. and Rousseau, D. (eds), *The Boundaryless Career*. Oxford University Press, New York.

Schasse, U. and Vatthauer, M. (1990) 'Betriebszugehörigkeitsdauer und Einkommenshöhe: Senioritätsentlohnung oder "Job-Matching"?'. In Gerlach, K. and Hübler, O. (eds), *Betriebszugehörigkeitsdauer und Mobilität-theoretische und empirische*

Analysen, SAMF working paper, 1990–4. Arbeitskreis Sozialwissenschaftliche Arbeitsmarktforschung (SAMF), Paderborn, pp. 95–120.

Schmiede, R. and Schudlich, E. (1976) *Die Entwicklung der Leistungsentlohnung in Deutschland: eine historisch-theoretische Untersuchung zum Verhältnis von Lohn und Leistung unter kapitalistischen Produktionsbedingungen.* Campus Verlag, Frankfurt.

Schudlich, E. (1991) 'Traditionelle Leistungslohnpolitik in der Sackgasse: neue Asätze der tariflichen Leistungspolitik'. *WSI Mitteilungen*, 44 (3), pp. 181–8.

Schudlich, E. (1994) *Von der externen zur internen Arbeitsmarktpolitik: zur arbeits-marktpolitischen Rationalisierung des Produktionsprozesses um die Jahrhundert-wende.* Arbeitspapiere 1994–2. Arbeitskreis Sozialwissenschaftliche Arbeitsmarkt-forschung (SAMF), Gelsenkirchen.

Scoville, J. G. (1969) 'A theory of jobs and training'. *Industrial Relations*, 9 (1), Oct., pp. 36–53.

Scullion, H. and Edwards, P. (1988) 'Craft unionism, job controls and management strategy: "Premier Metals", 1955–1980'. In Terry, M. and Edwards, P. (eds), *Shopfloor Politics and Job Controls: the Post-war Engineering Industry.* Blackwell, Oxford.

Sellier, F. (1961) *Stratégie de la Lutte Sociale: France 1936–1960.* Les Éditions Ouvrières, Paris.

Sellier, F. (1984) *La Confrontation Sociale en France 1936–1981.* Presses Universitaires de France, Paris.

Sengenberger, W. (1987) *Strucktur und Funktionsweise von Arbeitsmärkten: die Bundesrepublik Deutschland im internationalen Vergleich.* Campus Verlag, Frankfurt.

Sengenberger, W. (1992) 'Vocational training, job structures and the labour market: an international perspective'. In Altmann, N., Köhler, C. and Meil, P. (eds), *Technology and Work in German Industry.* Routledge, London.

Sheifer, V. (1975) 'Employment cost index: a measure of change in the "price of labor"'. *Monthly Labor Review*, July, pp. 3–12.

Shirai, T. and Shimada, H. (1978) 'Japan'. In Dunlop, J. and Galenson, W. (eds), *Labor in the Twentieth Century*, Academic Press, New York, pp. 241–322.

Simon, H. A. (1951) 'A formal theory of the employment relationship'. *Econometrica*, 19 (3), July, pp. 293–305.

Simon, H. A. (1991) 'Organizations and Markets'. *Journal of Economic Perspectives*, 5 (2), Spring, pp. 25–44.

Slichter, S. (1919) *The Turnover of Factory Labor.* Appleton, New York.

Slichter, S., Healy, J. and Livernash, E. (1960) *The Impact of Collective Bargaining on Management.* Brookings Institution, Washington DC.

Sly, F. and Stillwell, D. (1997) 'Temporary workers in Great Britain'. *Labour Market Trends*, Sept., pp. 347–54.

Sorge, A. and Warner, M. (1986) *Comparative Factory Organization: an Anglo-German Comparison of Management and Manpower in Manufacturing.* Gower, Aldershot.

Soskice, D. (1994) 'Reconciling markets and institutions: the German apprenticeship system'. In Lynch, L. (ed.), *Training and the Private Sector: International Compar-isons.* National Bureau of Economic Research, University of Chicago Press, Chicago.

Statistisches Bundesamt (1993–4) *Gehalts- und Lohnstrukturerhebung 1990.* Heft 1–3, Löhne und Gehälter, Fachserie 16, Statistisches Bundesamt, Wiesbaden.

Steedman, H. (1998) A decade of skill formation in Britain and Germany. *Journal of Education and Work*, 11 (1), pp. 77–94.

Steedman, H. and Wagner, K. (1987) 'A second look at productivity, machinery and skills in Britain and Germany'. *National Institute Economic Review,* No. 122, Nov., pp. 84–95.

Steedman, H. and Wagner, K. (1989) 'Productivity, machinery and skills: clothing manufacture in Britain and Germany'. *National Institute Economic Review,* No. 128, May, pp. 40–57.

Stewart, M. (1990) 'Union wage differentials, product market influences and the division of rents'. *Economic Journal,* 100 (403), Dec., pp. 1122–37.

Stewart, R., Barsoux, J-L., Kieser, A. and Ganter, H-D. (1994) *Managing in Britain and Germany.* Macmillan, Basingstoke.

Stevens, M. (1994) 'An investment model for the supply of training by employers'. *Economic Journal,* 104 (424), May, pp. 556–70.

Stinchcombe, A. (1959) 'Bureaucratic and craft administration of production: a comparative study'. *Administrative Science Quarterly,* 4 (2), Sept., pp. 168–87.

Stone, K. (1973) 'The origins of job structures in the steel industry'. Edwards, R., Reich, M. and Gordon, D. (eds), *Labor Market Segmentation.* Heath, Lexington, Mass.

Streeck, W. (1985) *Die Reform der beruflichen Bildung in der west-deutschen Bauwirtschaft 1969–82.* Internationales Institut für Management und Verwaltung, Berlin.

Streeck, W. (1992) 'Productive constraints: on the institutional conditions of diversified quality production'. In Streeck, W. (ed.), *Social Institutions and Economic Performance: Studies of Industrial Relations in Advanced Capitalist Countries.* Sage, London.

Supiot, A. (1995) 'Temps de travail: pour une concordance des temps'. *Droit Social,* 12, pp. 947–54.

Taira, K. (1970) *Economic Development and the Labor Market in Japan.* Columbia University Press, New York.

Taylor, J. C. (1979) 'Job design criteria twenty years later'. In Davis, L. and Taylor, J. (eds), *Design of Jobs.* 2nd edn. Goodyear, Santa Monica, California.

Thévenot, L. (1985) 'Les investissements de forme'. In *Conventions Économiques, Cahiers du Centre d'Études de l'Emploi,* No. 29. Presses Universitaires de France, Paris, pp. 21–71.

Tolbert, P. (1996) 'Occupations, organizations, and boundaryless careers'. In Arthur, M. and Rousseau, D. (eds), *The Boundaryless Career: a New Employment Principle for a New Organizational Era.* Oxford University Press, New York, pp. 331–49.

Tomita, Y. (1998) 'Germany'. In Tachibanaki, T. (ed.), *Wage Differentials: an International Comparison.* Macmillan, Basingstoke.

Tondorf, K. (1997) 'Leistungspolitik und Leistungsbezahlungen im öffentlichen Dienst'. *WSI Mitteilungen,* 50 (4), pp. 241–7.

Topel, R. (1991) 'Specific capital, mobility and wages: wages rise with seniority'. *Journal of Political Economy,* 99, pp. 145–76.

Touraine, A. (1955) *L'Évolution du Travail Ouvrier aux Usines Renault.* Centre National de la Recherche Scientifique, Paris.

Touraine, A. (1966) *La Conscience Ouvrière.* Seuil, Paris.

Triplett, J. E. (1983) 'Introduction: an essay on labor cost'. In Triplett, J. E. (ed.), *The Measurement of Labor Cost.* NBER, University of Chicago Press, Chicago.

Turner, H. A. (1952) 'Trade unions, differentials and the levelling of wages'. *The Manchester School,* 20, pp. 227–82.

Turner, L. (1991) *Democracy at Work: Changing World Markets and the Future of Labor Unions.* Cornell University Press, Ithaca.

Turner, L. and Auer, P. (1994) 'A diversity of new work organisation: human-centred, lean, and in-between'. *Industrielle Beziehungen*, 1 (1), pp. 38–60.

Wachter, M. L. (1995) 'Labor law reform: one step forward and two steps back'. *Industrial Relations*, 34 (3), July, pp. 382–401.

Walwei, U. (1997) 'Flexibility of Employment Relationships: Possibilities and Limits'. *IAB Labour Market Research Topics*, No. 22. Institut für Arbeitsmarkt- und Berufsforschung, Nürnberg.

Webb, S. and Webb, B. (1902) *Industrial Democracy.* Longman, London.

Weber, M. (1908) *Zur Psychophysik der industriellen Arbeit.* Max Weber Gesamtausgabe, Band 11, Schriften und Reden 1908–1912 (1995). J. C. B. Mohr (Paul Siebeck), Tübingen.

Whittaker, H. (1993) 'New technology and organisation of work: British and Japanese factories'. In Kogut, B. (ed.), *Country Competitiveness: Technology and the Organizing of Work.* Oxford University Press, New York.

Williamson, O. E. (1975) *Markets and Hierarchies: Analysis and Antitrust Implications.* Free Press, New York.

Willman, P. (1986) *Technological Change, Collective Bargaining and Industrial Efficiency.* Oxford University Press, Oxford.

Wolf, A. (1994) 'Measuring competence: the experience of the UK'. *European Vocational Training Journal*, 1 (94), pp. 29–35.

Womack, J., Jones, D. T. and Roos, D. (1990) *The Machine that Changed the World.* Rawson Associates, New York.

Wyatt (1989) *Performance Management Survey 1989.* The Wyatt Company, Washington DC.

Yamanouchi, T. and Okazaki-Ward, L. (1997) 'Key issues in HRM in Japan'. In Tyson, S. (ed.), *The Practice of Human Resource Strategy.* Pitman, London.

Zucker, L. (1991) 'Markets for bureaucratic authority and control: information quality in professions and services'. *Research in the Sociology of Organizations*, 8, pp. 157–90.

Zweig, F. (1951) *Productivity and Trade Unions.* Blackwell, Oxford.

INDEX